Democracy and Crisis

Wolfgang Merkel • Sascha Kneip
Editors

Democracy and Crisis

Challenges in Turbulent Times

Springer

Editors
Wolfgang Merkel
WZB Berlin Social Science Center
and Humboldt-Universität zu Berlin
Berlin, Germany

Sascha Kneip
WZB Berlin Social Science Center
Berlin, Germany

ISBN 978-3-030-10225-8 ISBN 978-3-319-72559-8 (eBook)
https://doi.org/10.1007/978-3-319-72559-8

Softcover re-print of the Hardcover 1st edition 2018
Translation based on German language edition: *Demokratie und Krise. Zum schwierigen Verhältnis von Theorie und Empirie*, Springer VS, 2015. All Rights Reserved.

Printed on acid-free paper

This Springer imprint is published by Springer Nature
The registered company is Springer International Publishing AG
The registered company address is: Gewerbestrasse 11, 6330 Cham, Switzerland

Contents

List of Contributors

Sonia Alonso Department of Government, Georgetown University in Qatar, Doha, Qatar

Heiko Giebler Department of Democracy and Democratization, WZB Berlin Social Science Center, Berlin, Germany

Lea Heyne NCCR Democracy, University of Zurich, Zürich, Switzerland

Sascha Kneip WZB Berlin Social Science Center, Berlin, Germany

Jürgen Kocka WZB—Berlin Social Science Center, Berlin, Germany

Werner Krause Department of Democracy and Democratization, WZB Berlin Social Science Center, Berlin, Germany

Onawa Promise Lacewell MyPrivateBanking Research, Berlin, Germany

Pola Lehmann Department of Democracy and Democratization, WZB Berlin Social Science Center, Berlin, Germany

Wolfgang Merkel Department of Democracy and Democratization, WZB Berlin Social Science Center, Berlin, Germany

Humboldt-Universität zu Berlin, Berlin, Germany

Nicolas Merz Department of Democracy and Democratization, WZB Berlin Social Science Center, Berlin, Germany

Alexander Petring Party Executive of the Social Democratic Party of Germany (SPD), Berlin, Germany

Sven Regel Department of Democracy and Democratization, WZB Berlin Social Science Center, Berlin, Germany

Rubén Ruiz-Rufino Department of Political Economy, King's College London, London, UK

Sara Schlote Social Democratic Party of Germany (SPD), Berlin, Germany

Marcus Spittler Department of Democracy and Democratization, WZB Berlin Social Science Center, Berlin, Germany

Dag Tanneberg Department of Comparative Politics, University of Potsdam, Potsdam, Germany

Andrea Volkens Department of Democracy and Democratization, WZB Berlin Social Science Center, Berlin, Germany

Aiko Wagner WZB Berlin Social Science Center, Berlin, Germany

Annika Werner Centre for Governance and Public Policy, Griffith University, Brisbane, Australia

Bernhard Weßels Department of Democracy and Democratization, WZB Berlin Social Science Center, Berlin, Germany

Department of Social Sciences, Humboldt-Universität zu Berlin, Berlin, Germany

Chapter 1
Challenge or Crisis of Democracy

Wolfgang Merkel

1.1 Introduction

In political and social science, hardly any other term has been carried to market as often as crisis: crisis of the welfare state, of political parties, and of parliament; performance crisis; governance, structural, rationality, legitimation, integration, and motivation crises; the Euro crisis; crisis in the Middle East; crisis of dictatorships; and, over and over again, crisis of democracy.

As far as this last instance is concerned, there are three major lines of debate: the public debate, the theoretical discourse on democracy, and empirical democracy research. First is the public debate. At least in Europe, it has been dominated by the opinion that many sub-crises, such as the crises of trust in political elites, parties, parliaments, and governments, have condensed into a general crisis of democracy. There is clearly a marked North-South gap in democratic self-description: Denmark is not Greece, the United Kingdom is not Spain, and Switzerland is not Italy. Although far from endorsing the vulgarized discourse of the public media, political theory has from the outset maintained that democracy is inconceivable without crisis. This view goes back to Plato, Aristotle, and Polybios in antiquity (Held 1996, 13ff.; Meier 2004; Keane 2009); it was shared in early modern times by Thomas Hobbes and later by Alexis de Tocqueville, Karl Marx, and Max Weber (see Schmidt 2008). Talk about a crisis of democracy is hence as old as democracy itself. The discussion gained momentum in the early 1970s. Both left and right conducted the debate with vehemence and to some extent with quasi-structural arguments (see Offe 1984). Claus Offe's *Strukturprobleme des kapitalistischen*

W. Merkel (✉)
Department of Democracy and Democratization, WZB Berlin Social Science Center, Berlin, Germany

Humboldt-Universität zu Berlin, Berlin, Germany
e-mail: wolfgang.merkel@wzb.eu

W. Merkel, S. Kneip (eds.), *Democracy and Crisis*,
https://doi.org/10.1007/978-3-319-72559-8_1

Staates (1972), James O'Connor's neo-Marxist theory of the *Fiscal Crisis of the State* (1973), and Jürgen Habermas' influential *Legitimation Crisis* (1975) determined the crisis discourse on democracy and the (late) capitalist state far beyond that decade. The conservative camp did not counter: it backed this analysis. The report to the Trilateral Commission by Crozier et al. (1975) also painted a gloomy picture of an overburdened democracy.

At the optimistic end of the twentieth century, the crisis debate lost a degree of its persuasive power but gained new momentum and a global response immediately after the turn of the millennium in Chantal Mouffe's neo-Schmittian version (2000), in the post-democracy debate (Crouch 2004; Rancière 2006; Wolin 2008), in neo-democratic postulates (von Beyme 2013), and in post-structuralist (Agamben et al. 2011) or pop-Marxist (Žižek 2011) critique. The overwhelming dominance of government and the economy over successively eroding popular sovereignty (Agamben et al. 2011, 4) and the threat to national democratic sovereignty from progressive globalization (Held 1995) were addressed. Majoritarian, genuinely participatory organizations and institutions such as parties and parliaments are said to have lost legitimacy in comparison with governments, courts, expert commissions, and international regimes (Zürn 1998, 233ff., 2011, 618ff.). And the broad discussion among proponents of a strong (Barber 1984), participatory (Warren 2001, 2009), or deliberative democracy (Fishkin 1991; Elster 1998; Dryzek 2000; Goodin 2008) has explicitly or implicitly assumed that current representative democracy is undergoing a crisis of participation (Saward 2010; Alonso et al. 2011).

The message from left to right, from post-Marxists to neoconservatives in political theory, is clear: democracy *as such* is in crisis and primarily its representative institutions. This assessment draws on an implicit logic, frequently with one of two frames of reference: normatively a democratic ideal (usually not specified) or empirically a putative, at any rate bygone golden age of democracy. When this is supposed to have been is mostly left open or is placed by participation theoreticians in the late 1960s or early 1970s, by post-democrats like Colin Crouch (2004) even in the 1950s.[1]

Empirical democracy research has always been more cautious in its statements. It also concedes—and this is the third line of debate—that democracy faces partial challenges and problems. Russell J. Dalton (2008), for instance, notes declining confidence in political authorities and dissatisfaction among democrats, and Susan Pharr and Robert Putnam posit a deterioration in the capabilities of democratic institutions (Pharr and Putnam 2000, 25ff.). However, they do not see a crisis of democracy as a whole. Pippa Norris (1999, 2011) denies even a crisis of trust in democracy and speaks of "trendless fluctuations in system support" (Norris 2011, 241). And if a—relatively harmless—democratic deficit is admitted, it is attributed to a combination of growing expectations among increasingly critical citizens, the influence of negative reporting in the media, and the shortcomings in the

[1]Women, Afro-Americans, and ethnic or sexual minorities are highly unlikely to agree with this.

performance of democratic governments to which precisely the media have drawn attention.

Is the crisis of democracy then an invention of theoreticians, reasoned but aloof from empirical evidence in pursuit of an exaggerated normative democratic ideal? Or has empirical analysis focused too strongly on partial diagnosis, failing to delve beneath the surface of survey data and electoral analysis, and failing to recognize deeper-lying crisis phenomena produced by the cumulative interdependence between each of such phenomena?

The question of a crisis of democracy can be answered neither by theories from empirical research alone nor solely by empirical investigations indifferent to theory. The two strands have to mesh. Particularly important from the outset is to clarify precisely what we mean by democracy and by crisis. Most studies fail to do this, although clarifying the crisis issue must ultimately depend on the substance and contours of these two key concepts.

1.2 Democracy: A Controversial Concept

Democracy is a controversial concept. In the political thought of antiquity, the normative discourse on (the good) democracy was always central. Since the second half of the twentieth century, it has gained a new intensity. The range of democratic theories is almost too vast to cover (see, e.g., Held 1996; Schmidt 2010; Lembcke et al. 2012; Schaal et al. 2014). To gain an overview, the material can be ordered in various ways. Normative democratic theories can be ordered historically/chronologically, ideologically, in procedural or institutional terms, or by author. The result is usually a mixed system that reads like a long catalogue of democracy with adjectives: conservative, liberal, social, pluralist, elitist, decisionist, communitarian, cosmopolitan, republican, deliberative, participative/participatory, feminist, critical, postmodern, or multiculturalist democracy, to mention only the most important.[2] Simplification is called for. In the never-ending competition for the right to define the concept, substance, and limits of democracy, three groups of democratic theory can be identified: the minimalist (electoral) model, the midrange (proceduralist) model, and the maximalist (substantialist) model.

1.2.1 The Minimalist Model

Minimalists like the influential economist and democracy theorist Joseph A. Schumpeter (1883–1950) assume that free, equal, and secret elections are not

---

[2]David Collier and Steven Levitsky (1997) have counted no fewer than 550 different adjectives for democracy.

only the core of democracy but democracy itself. Through elections, according to Schumpeter's market-like democracy model, political entrepreneurs—such as parties—can offer their programmatic wares, which are sought after, inspected, chosen, or rejected by the voters. The offer most in demand secures the contract and thus the right to represent the preferences and interests of the electorate for a time. At intervals, those represented have the opportunity to take their representatives accountable for the past legislative period by reelecting or voting against them depending on how they perform. Minimalists, who like to see themselves as realists, thus deliberately reduce the essence of democracy to "vertical accountability" between the ruled and the rulers (Przeworski 2007, 475).

Schumpeter's "realistic" democratic theory (1942) is the classic among minimalist theories. While minimalists certainly regard human rights or the rule of law as important preconditions for democracy, they do not see them as necessarily inherent elements. The monitoring of government by civil society, let alone direct democratic intervention by the people, is considered incompatible with rationalist-realistic democratic theory. In any case, they are alien to the competitive model of democracy (see also Downs 1957).

Minimalist concepts are unsuitable for analyzing crisis in mature democracies. The competitive selection of government alone does not reveal, or only very late, whether let alone why a democracy is in crisis unless election analysis takes party organization and vitality into account and investigates whether parties substantially represent the interests of voters in parliament and government, what trust citizens have in the core institutions of democracy, how the rule of law protects civil and political rights, and whether elected representatives actually govern rather than big companies, banks, lobbies, or international organizations and regimes. This goes far beyond Schumpeter, even if some, such as O'Donnell (2010),[3] have sought to interpret Schumpeter's democracy model as far less minimalist.

1.2.2 The Midrange Model

Proponents of the midrange democracy concept consider this understanding of democracy to be thin and inadequate. To the uncontested core of democracy, namely, free, general, equal, and fair elections, they add the rule of law and horizontal checks and balances (O'Donnell 1998). They also do not want to see political participation by citizens reduced to elections. Only free elections embedded in guaranteed human, fundamental, and civil rights, the democratically legitimated genesis of norms binding on the whole of society, and the interlocking of and mutual constraints on the executive, legislature, and judiciary make formally democratic elections also effectively democratic (Beetham 1994, 30). With Jürgen

[3] O'Donnell (2010) himself advocates a normatively far more demanding model of democracy, especially by including the rule of law and horizontal checks on power.

Habermas (2001), the proponents of a rule-of-law model of democracy focusing on procedures postulate the intrinsic "equiprimordiality" of civil protection rights and political participation rights. For them, the rule of law is not a marginal condition of democracy but one of its key elements.

In this view of things, political participation is not exhausted by exercise of the franchise. Additional opportunities for participation such as referendums, civil society activities, and public discourses prevent the aggregation and articulation of societal interests from being the preserve of political parties alone (Barber 1984; Fishkin 1991; Dryzek 2000; Warren 2001). A vibrant civil society is to bring the participatory potential of democracy to fruition and protect it from appropriation by a political class out of touch with the real world. This midrange model includes notions of participative democracy that go beyond the rule-of-law containment of democracy to demand the democratization of further societal and economic domains. A strong civil society and deliberative procedures in smaller groups, in communities, or in neighborhoods are seen as contributing to the further democratization of political decision-making (Fishkin 1991; Fung and Wright 2003). Such factors, as well as direct democratic referendums (Merkel and Ritzi 2017), however intensively they may be institutionalized, are compatible with the midrange procedural model of democracy. Its proponents range from liberal pluralists like Norberto Bobbio (1983) to advocates of strong participation like Carole Pateman (1970) and Benjamin Barber (1984) or the theoreticians of democratic deliberation (Fishkin 1991; Dryzek 2000; Habermas 2001; Warren 2001; Offe 2011).

Common to the minimalist and the midrange concepts of democracy is limitation to norms, principles, and procedures underlying the democratic decision-making process. We can call this the internal performance of democratic institutions. For maximalists, however, this procedural limitation to the input dimension and the participative extension of democratic procedures do not suffice.[4] They see the substantive results of political decisions as an essential element in the assessment of democratic regimes. The quality of democracy has to be measured not least against this yardstick.

1.2.3 The Maximalist Model

In defining democracy, maximalists thus include the output dimension as systemic performance. Under this heading, they place collective goods such as internal and external security, economic well-being, welfare-state guarantees, and fairness—however defined—in the distribution of basic goods, income, social security, and life chances. The focus is mainly on avoiding extreme inequalities in the distribution of income, primary goods, and life chances, for only *social democracy*

[4]Their participative and deliberative demands may well fall short of those advanced by Barber, Fishkin, or Dryzek.

safeguards the principle of political equality. This was the position adopted by the Social Democrat Eduard Bernstein, the Weimar constitutional lawyer Hermann Heller (1934), T. H. Marshall (1950) with his idea of "social citizenship," and today by Thomas Meyer (2007) and Stein Ringen (2007). In the Latin American debate on democracy, social justice has always been a key topos. In North American democratic theory, such maximalism is traditionally rejected both normatively and analytically as being too far-reaching.[5] But three decades of continuously growing inequality in the developed OECD countries have brought the issue of socioeconomic distribution back into the focus of democracy theory.

It might be objected that many of these outputs and political outcomes are not necessarily specific to democracy. They could quite as well be provided by dictatorships: consider only economic growth in China and Vietnam, economic and social welfare under the authoritarianism of Singapore, or socioeconomic equality in Cuba. For this reason, it is not unproblematic to include the output dimension in the concept of democracy directly as a defining property. Nevertheless, socioeconomic performance in democracy determines its vulnerability to crisis and its quality. If it is unable to solve key problems and if it does not deliver what the citizens expect, its output legitimacy will decline, and the stability of the system will be at risk. And even if one prefers not to include socioeconomic inequality issues in the definition of democracy, the actual development of democracies, their stability, and quality cannot be understood without this key limiting condition.[6] Growing socioeconomic inequality can be regarded as an early warning sign for a looming crisis of democracy because it endangers key principles of democracy such as equality of opportunity for participation and representation and threatens to erode the faith of citizens in the legitimation of democracy.

The answer to the question of whether democracy is in crisis thus depends strongly on the concept of democracy chosen. Because of their low theoretical/institutional differentiation, minimalist concepts do not have a sensitive enough nose for crises of democracy beyond the ballot box. The more minimalist a concept of democracy is, the more likely any thesis about crisis is to be denied. Maximalist concepts, by contrast, tend to provoke confirmation of a crisis because normative standards are set so high that very few democracies pass the "social test." The confirmation of crisis is built into democratic maximalism. Moreover, it may easily travel through Latin America, but it rather finds scholarly acceptance in the United States.

For different reasons, the minimalist and maximalist concepts alike are hence unsuitable for the empirical analysis of democracy. We have therefore opted for a midrange approach. We consider "embedded democracy" (Merkel 2004) to be the most fruitful concept for such analytical purposes. It does not deny its normative

[5]Unlike in the political philosophy of justice, in which Rawls (1971), Miller (2001), or Sen (2009) always posit social justice as an integral part of democracy to be institutionalized.

[6]Refusal to extend the concept of democracy into the sphere of (social) policy outcomes is thus not a normative rejection but an analytical one.

background, namely, the "equiprimordiality" of civil and political rights, and stresses their protection through the democratic institutions of the rule of law and checks and balances. In their mutual functional and normative interdependence, these elements combine to form an overall system for the purposes of empirical analysis. Such an overall system not only offers a concept of democracy differentiated into partial regimes but, owing to their explicit functional interdependence, allows the trajectory of crises through partial regimes to be mapped out. Foci of infection, transmission, as well as resistance to crisis in particular subareas of democracy can thus be followed. Moreover, even nonsimultaneous developments can be discovered, i.e., positive trends that enhance the quality of democracy and negative trends that weaken it.

1.2.4 Embedded Democracy as a Midrange Concept of Democracy[7]

The concept of "embedded democracy" (see Fig. 1.1) posits that stable rule-of-law democracies are doubly embedded: *internally* in that the partial regimes of democracy secure their existence through functional interlocking and *externally* in that each partial regime is embedded through rings of conditions enabling democracy and is thus protected against both external and internal shocks and destabilization. If external embedding is damaged or underdeveloped, this too can pose challenges within democracy. The notion of embedding pursues a systemic logic, namely, the interdependence of the component parts. Critical changes in one partial regime can infect other partial regimes. To what extent this occurs depends above all on the intensity of the partial crisis and on the functional propinquity and resilience of each partial regime.

The Partial Regimes of Embedded Democracy
Five regimes constitute embedded (rule-of-law) democracy: the democratic electoral regime (A), the regime of political participation rights (B), the partial regime of civil liberties (C), the institutional safeguarding of mutual constraints and horizontal accountability (D), and the guarantee that the effective power to govern (E) of democratically elected representatives is ensured de jure and de facto.

A. Electoral regime A democratic electoral regime requires universal active and passive voting rights and free and fair elections. These are necessary but far from sufficient conditions for democratic governance. In representative democracy, the electoral regime occupies a key position because elections are the most visible expression of popular sovereignty. Those represented elect their representatives for a fixed period. Via this representative nexus, the addressees of norms can also regard themselves as the authors of norms (Kelsen 1925). Because of the open,

[7]On the concept of *embedded democracy*, see Merkel et al. (2003) and Merkel (2004).

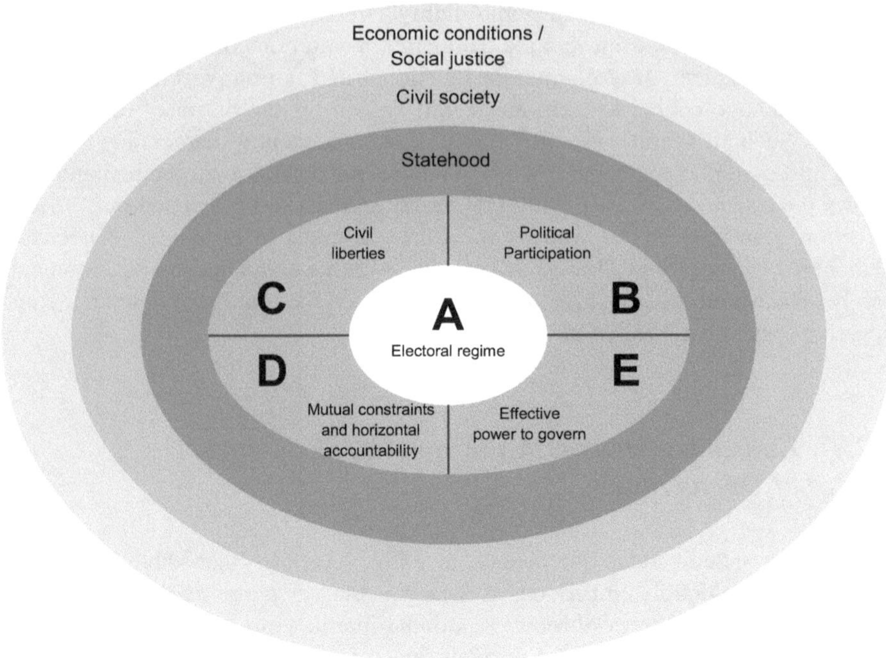

Fig. 1.1 The concept of "embedded democracy." Source: Merkel (2010, 31, modified)

pluralist competition for key governing positions, the electoral regime also constitutes the cardinal difference from dictatorship. This regime is concerned with participation and representation. Apart from the electorate, the most important actors in the regime are political parties and to a lesser extent individual politicians standing for the highest government offices. Elections are principally for parliaments, i.e., legislative assemblies, and under presidential systems, for the head of government, as well. What is at issue is therefore interaction between voters, parties, political elites, and parliaments.

Crisis phenomena If a crisis infects the democratic electoral system, it strikes at the heart of democracy. If rights are curbed and/or the representative function of elections adversely affected, the crisis of democracy is already well advanced. But changes in voting behavior, such as growing abstention, increasing volatility, or persistent de facto discrimination against women, certain ethnic groups, or classes are critical early warning signs that participation and representation do not (or no longer) sufficiently cover the entire demos. What is usually involved in developed democracies is not legal restrictions on free and fair elections, even though changes in electoral district boundaries for party political motives (gerrymandering) can result in similar manipulative distortions of representation. In critical situations in established democracies, we often find serious de facto deterioration of the democratic functions of free elections, provoked by declining voter turnout and factual social selectivity with regard to certain groups and classes.

B. Political participation The political rights of participation, which are the precondition for elections and go beyond them, complete the vertical dimension of democracy. Concretely, they establish the unrestricted validity of the right to freedom of opinion and expression, as well as the right of association, and the right to demonstrate and to petition. Political rights of participation constitute the public arena as an autonomous sphere for political action in which organizational and communicative power unfolds. In this sphere, collective processes of organization, opinion, and will-formation determine and underpin competition for political positions of authority. Here, too, it is about participation and representation, as well as about control. The most important organized actors in this partial regime of established democracies are again political parties. But the domain reaches beyond parties to include social (protest) movements, nongovernmental organizations (NGOs), interest groups, direct democratic forms of participation such as referendums, (deliberative) civic forums, institutional access to the planning of major infrastructure projects, and participatory budgeting. A pluralistic media system without a tendency to biased concentration is the best guarantee for the development of the free exchange of opinion.

Crisis phenomena Changes in parties and in the party system can indicate critical tendencies in the political system. If catch-all parties lose votes, if anti-system and right-wing populist parties gain in strength, if the numerical and ideological configuration of the party system makes a stable government coalition almost impossible, and if parties lose the confidence of the electorate and their own members, mutating into cartels no longer embedded in society, then fundamental organizational pillars of representative democracy begin to totter. Where the lobby system is biased, for instance, toward financially and organizationally strong interests, giving them privileged access to governmental decision-makers, this can also erode the democratic principle of equality.[8]

C. Civil liberties Democratic elections and political participation need to be complemented by civil liberties and individual basic rights. As negative rights against the state, civil liberties limit the claim of the state to exercise power over individuals, thus enlarging the sphere for their free self-determination. Individual civil rights give legal protection to life, liberty, and property; they protect against unjustified detention, torture, surveillance, dataveillance, or unlawful intervention in private life. They curb the urge of the state to expand and control. Apart from this intrinsic value, political rights can be exercised only if civil rights are fully guaranteed. Functionally, civil liberties and rights to political participation cannot be kept separate. They are equiprimordial both normatively and functionally. If the one is weakened, this reduces the efficient functioning of the other; if is it

[8]For lack of space, we shall be concentrating in the studies that follow on parties.

strengthened, it vitalizes the effectiveness of the other. More strongly than in the other partial regimes, individual citizens are direct subjects of civil rights. But individuals need institutions and organizations to safeguard their rights and demands. Courts and civil society associations addressing human and civil rights are the most important institutional and collective actors in this partial regime.

Crisis phenomena If the civil rights of ethnic and religious groups, immigrants, structural minorities, or even of the entire populace are restricted, this worsens the quality of democracy in parts but need not lead to a direct crisis of democracy as a whole. In the long term, however, selective restriction of such rights or effective discrimination undermines the normative foundations of democracy. The same is true when, with the approval of the majority of citizens, government authorities unilaterally cancel the trade-off between internal security and the freedom of opinion and information to the detriment of individual liberties and informational self-determination, as what happened in some Western democracies in the aftermath of 9/11.

D. Mutual constraints and horizontal accountability The fourth partial regime of democracy under the rule of law consists in constitutional rules for the horizontal separation of powers. They are concerned with governmental structures and regulate the legality and monitoring of government action in the sense of the balanced, mutual interdependence and autonomy of legislature, executive, and judiciary. Governments are controlled not only periodically through elections but also continuously through mutually constraining constitutional branches of government. The independence of the judiciary and especially of its judges is of particular importance. The key function of mutual constraints, of checks and balances, is to limit the exercise of power and to ensure permanent reference to the constitution and the law. Especially in times of crisis when the executive often claims special decision-making powers, a functioning separation of powers is of elementary importance for the survival of democracy. The media, too, play a role as an important monitoring force in the form of an extra-constitutional "fourth estate."

Crisis phenomena Crises of democracy are often characterized by a shift in power between the executive and the legislature to the detriment of the latter. This can be a slow, creeping process, but it can also happen fast in the face of economic, foreign, or domestic political crises. If parliaments lose their legislative and control powers, this is a symptom of a crisis whose causes and consequences have to be examined. Constitutional courts as a special part of the judiciary can have an ambivalent effect on democracy. Owing to their relatively poor democratic legitimation, they cannot act in parallel to parliament as a legislature. This would amount to a judicialization of politics incompatible with democracy. But, as the guardian of the constitution, it is their duty to prevent temporary parliamentary majorities from passing unconstitutional legislation (Kneip 2009). This fragile ambivalence must be addressed in analyzing crises in advanced democracies.

E. Effective governance The fifth partial regime, the effective power to govern, determines that the only persons, organizations, and institutions entitled to make decisions binding on society as a whole are those directly legitimated in free elections or indirectly through nomination under constitutional law by constitutional bodies such as the parliament and—with marked reservations—the government. A narrow framework has to be set for such indirect nomination. Governments and parliaments must have the resources and decision-making autonomy to prevent extra-constitutional actors from usurping functionally equivalent governance.

In effective and legitimate governance, too, the constitutional branches of government are the decisive actors. To a limited extent, supranational institutions like the European Union (EU) and international organizations like the World Trade Organization (WTO) or the United Nations can intervene in the governance of individual countries. But the democratic legitimation of the decisions such institutions make, for example, in developing the EU, always needs to be examined. With globalization and the deregulation of financial markets, actors with little or no democratic legitimation such as the International Monetary Fund (IMF), the European Central Bank (ECB), big banks, and hedge funds have been gaining influence.

Crisis phenomena In democracies, neither the military nor powerful companies, banks, or financial funds must be allowed the last word on security, financial, or economic policy. The activities of global institutions such as the IMF and supranational institutions like the ECB must be seen as a problematic limitation of the sovereign prerogatives of parliament and government. This is particularly true for the inadequately democratized EU, above all when it intervenes drastically in the budgetary policy of heavily indebted countries such as Greece, Portugal, Ireland, or Spain. Most particularly in an age of globalization, any crisis analysis must examine the extent to which the democratic sovereignty of the national demos is constrained by international organizations and powers lacking legitimation.

Internal and External Embedding

The partial regimes described can fully develop their impact to the advantage of democracy only if they are mutually embedded. Democracy is thus not understood as a regime all of a piece but as a structure of partial regimes that both complement and limit one another. Each democracy is also embedded in an environment. This environment encompasses democracy, enabling and stabilizing, hampering, or destabilizing it. At issue are the conditions of possibility or impossibility. They improve or worsen the quality of rule-of-law democracies. The most important external embeddings are the socioeconomic context, statehood, civil society, and the international or regional integration of a country in organizations, alliances, and policy regimes, above all in economic, security, and environmental policy. If this external embedding is damaged or underdeveloped, the result is often defective democracy, at best more fragile and vulnerable democracy. Particularly important is the socioeconomic context. At a time when the capitalist economy is ridding itself of much social and democratic embedding, developing increasingly into "disembedded capitalism"[9] (Polanyi 2001[1944], 77), the challenge this variety of capitalism poses for *embedded democracy* needs to be considered.

If one (or more) partial regime of embedded democracy is so badly damaged that the overall logic of democracy is changed, we can no longer speak of a democracy governed by the rule of law. We are then left with a "diminished subtype" (Collier and Levitsky 1997) of democracy. Elsewhere we have called such subtypes "defective democracies" (Merkel 2004, 48). Democracies in crisis are to be distinguished from defective democracies. The latter can be the result of the former. But even in crisis—still to be defined—mature democracies very often do not reach the stage at which a serious disturbance of the functional logic of democracy can be diagnosed. The marked drop in voter turnout in Poland, the extremely low turnout at congressional elections in the United States, the Patriot Act passed under the George W. Bush administration in 2003, the participation in the Austrian government by the right-wing populist FPÖ (1983–1987, 2000–2007), and the fact that for 540 days (2010–2011) Belgium failed to form a government coalition are all signs of crisis in parts of the political system, but they do not mean that democracy in these countries is defective as it is in Indonesia, India, Ecuador, or Ukraine. Even under the reign of Berlusconi, Italy could not without further ado be counted a defective democracy, because effective constitutional control on the part of the judiciary, the president of the republic, and the opposition was considerable. To say a given democracy is in crisis is thus not to describe this democracy as defective.

1.3 Crisis: A Barely Defined Concept

There is no consensus on the conceptualization of democracy; instead there are various ambitious models with differing notions about the type, number, scope, and boundaries of the institutions and procedures involved. However, most concepts can be clearly defined, giving analytical substance to each. The same cannot be said of the crisis concept. Its use in sociology and political science is nothing short of inflationary, but it is nonetheless seldom defined. Particularly the question of when a crisis begins and when it ends remains unresolved. The dividing lines between a normal state of affairs and crisis are not specified; the question whether partial deterioration of democracy (for instance, in participation) can be set off against gains in democracy elsewhere (e.g., in minority rights) is nowhere discussed. What also remains unclear is the basis for comparison that can permit a negative deviation to be diagnosed: is the benchmark an ideal of democracy, however, defined? Is it an average value of actual democracies or a golden age of democracy against which

[9] I take the term *disembedded capitalism* from Karl Polanyi (2001[1944]). In *The Great Transformation*, he describes how in the nineteenth century the economy freed itself from its embedment in society and social relations to obey only its own laws. This process has been repeating itself in a new form since the late 1970s, when neoliberal capitalism increasingly freed itself from the "shackles" of state embeddedness.

the present is measured? Without an explicated frame of reference—whether ideal or normative—the concept of crisis is logically absurd.

Crisis comes from Ancient Greek and originally meant opinion, judgment, or decision. Soon, however, it came to mean uncertainty, alarming situation, escalation, decision, and turning point. "The concept imposed choices between stark alternatives: right or wrong, salvation or damnation, life or death. The medical sense predominated [. . .] almost without interruption until well into modern times" (Koselleck 1972, 617, transl.). From the seventeenth century, it came to be used metaphorically in the fields of politics, economics, and history (ibid.).

Since then, the concept has spread to almost all economic, social, political, and personal domains of societal life. It became ambiguous, a catchword (ibid.). Even economics, so proud of its precision, has no clear and uncontested concept of crisis. It is mostly described as a markedly negative development in economic growth. The cyclical crisis or recession is most clearly defined as two successive quarters of negative economic growth. But other macroeconomic variables such as inflation, employment, capital, and trade flows can also define crises. The threshold of crisis in these fields, however, is mostly not determined. A general economic crisis is defined in neither qualitative nor quantitative terms. There are often differences of opinion on its causes, too, as in the persistent paradigmatic dispute between supply economics and demand theory. In political discourse, the crisis concept has lost all analytical contours and threatens to degenerate into a banal, ubiquitous everyday expression. "The old power of the concept to set unsurpassable, stark, and non-interchangeable alternatives has dissipated in the uncertainty of arbitrary alternatives" (Koselleck 1972, 649, transl.). What Koselleck noted over 40 years ago is more cogent than ever.

Systems theory sees crises as serious cases of disequilibrium. They can be endogenously or exogenously induced (Schmidt 2010, 444). But here, too, no limits are defined. When does disequilibrium begin; when does it end? Moreover, systems theory has nothing to say about the role of actors. But it is the actors involved and their motives, aims, power resources, strategic capabilities, and proclivity for compromise that decide or at least contribute to resolving crises. Systemic disturbances begin with challenges. But a system confronted with challenges is not automatically a system in crisis. Challenges either have first to accumulate considerably or affect the entire central nervous system of the democratic system: parliament, elections, the political community (Jellinek: Staatsvolk), or the state's monopoly of force.

However, the transformation of challenges into system crises is by no means predestined. It depends strongly on how political elites and citizens handle the challenges that arise. As research on political regimes has shown (Burton et al. 1991; Higley and Gunther 1991; Merkel 2010, 91), these elites have a particular role to play. If a crisis occurs, three outcomes are conceivable.

- If challenges cannot be seized by institutional elites as specific opportunities for reform, they will mutate into acute crisis, especially if major extra-parliamentary or anti-system opposition groups, big investors, or the military move against the system with the support of significant sections of the population. In this situation,

democracies can collapse. Italy (1921–1922), Weimar (1932–1933), Greece (1967), and Chile (1973) are typical examples.
- If political decision-makers show little or no willingness to undertake reforms, if the democratic opposition is weak and the population politically apathetic, and if there is no alternative system to democracy in sight, challenges can transform into creeping, latent crisis. Although the loss of democratic quality and legitimation is clearly apparent and erodes the normative substance of democracy, this does not lead to any change in the institutional core of the system.
- If the elites deal productively with challenges, this can produce an innovative wave of reform that adapts key procedures and institutions to the new environment and wins new support from the citizenry. This is the hour of re-legitimation for the political system, which with such input can regain a stable state of equilibrium. Linz and Stepan call such a process "re-equilibration" (Linz and Stepan 1978, 87). If crises do not cause the system to collapse, they can trigger distinctly positive developments. For one thing, they establish "transparency" (Jänicke 1972, 16), a clear perspective on dysfunctionalities in the political system. For another, they can set off learning processes in political elites and institutions, which can lead to innovative reforms and the restabilizing "democratization of democracy" (Offe 2003).

It thus depends strongly on the action or inaction of political elites and their interaction with the citizens whether challenges escalate into crisis. In brief, we can distinguish between two uses of the term crisis:

Crisis I The acute crisis, which is life-threatening for the system, calls for clear action. This is the perspective that Marx, for example, adopts in theorizing on the crisis of capitalism. However, in his economic/determinist variant, there is no way out of the crisis: the internal conditions for capital exploitation inevitably generate a tendency for profits to fall, which, in an intensifying cycle of crises, bringing about the grand crash, the "Kladderadatsch" (Bebel), of the entire capitalist system (Marx 1998[1894]). If we apply this understanding of crisis to the democratic system, crisis can also be seen as the preliminary stage of collapse, i.e., system change toward a hybrid or autocratic regime (Merkel 2010). Although the diluted systems-theoretical/neo-Marxist variant, as in Habermas, no longer posits the collapse of the late capitalist state, including its democratic form, it does foresee a final stage in a sequence of successively intensifying crises (Habermas 1975).[10] If not externally induced, acute crises are an expression of dysfunctionalities within the political system that have accumulated over a longer period. Such systemic disturbances are often accompanied by the growth of radical opposition groups that challenge the system by violent means. Historical instances of such acute crises of democracy are the 3 final years of the Weimar Republic (1930–1933), the period from 1920 to 1922 in Italy, the Second Spanish Republic after 1933, the last 2 years before the colonels' putsch in Greece (1965–1967), and Allende's Chile (1970–1973). Greece

[10]Claus Offe (1972, 102ff.) is more cautious when it comes to the possible collapse of democracy.

is the only country in Western Europe and the world of Anglo-Saxon democracies in which after 1945 an acute crisis of democracy has led to the collapse of the regime and for a limited period to a (military) dictatorship. The outcome of acute crises is extremely ambivalent. It may bring the collapse of the system or structural reforms that enable equilibrium to be reestablished. As we have seen, how such a crisis ends will depend strongly on the action of and interaction between elites and the populace.

Crisis II With the waning of neo-Marxism, the link between crisis and collapse has almost completely disappeared, at least as far as the mature democracies of the old OECD world are concerned. It has been replaced by the notion of latent crisis. Latent means at least two things. First is that the crisis drags on and that the end cannot be conceptualized. Compared with the clear-cut Marxist concept of crisis, this notion is theoretically less precise. Second, it implies that crisis leads to deterioration in the quality of democracy and that its essence is eroded from within (Crouch 2004, 22). Although formal institutions continue to exist, the notion of democratically legitimated government by the people under the rule of law fades away to leave only "zero forms of democracy" (Offe 2003, 138). However, Claus Offe, for one, does take account of possible positive outcomes of the crisis that can lead above all to the "democratization of democracy" (Offe 2003; also 2011) through the establishment of deliberative and discursive elements.

There may be links between a latent and an acute crisis, but not necessarily. In the case of endogenously induced crises, it is highly unlikely that an acute crisis can occur without being preceded by a latent process that contributes considerably to its outbreak. On the other hand, a latent crisis will not necessarily lead to an acute crisis.

For mature democracies in which the collapse of the system is not to be expected, the latter concept of crisis needs to be defined more precisely. Indeterminate as it is, it must be theoretically honed if it is to be used for comparative empirical research on democracy. As many of the following conditions as possible have to be met to make the concept analytically productive:

- Explication of the *standard* against which the current diagnosis is to be measured
- Identification of the *causes* that trigger a crisis of democracy
- Diagnosis of the relevant *symptoms of crisis*
- Mapping of *crisis trajectories*
- Criteria for diagnosing the *beginning* and the *end* of a crisis

1.4 Causes, Symptoms, and Trajectories of Crises

Challenges to democracy are to be distinguished from the causes of a democracy in crisis. Challenges develop into causes only if they are recognized and addressed by the citizens and public opinion as important and if the procedures, institutions, organizations, and persons put in place by the overall democratic system prove unable to deal with them to the satisfaction of the demos, elites, and the general public. For Claus Offe (1972) and Jürgen Habermas (1975), it was the cyclical crises of capitalism that the "politico-administrative system" was (and still is) unable to process adequately. To this extent, the crisis of capitalism as a political challenge almost necessarily becomes a crisis of the state and of its democratic form.

Whereas, 40 years on, Habermas no longer sees this as an insoluble conflict, Wolfgang Streeck (2014) returns to the baseline of the argument. He interprets "[...] the crisis history of late capitalism since the 1970s [...] as an unfolding of the old fundamental tension between capitalism and democracy—a gradual process that broke up the forced marriage arranged between the two after the Second World War" (Streeck 2014, 4). According to Streeck, the challenge to democracy lies in the progressive immunization of the economy against "mass democracy" (ibid.). It withdraws the most important areas of decision-making from the democratically elected representatives and reduces democracy to a "façade democracy" (Streeck 2014, 177). Colin Crouch (2004) had argued along similar lines. He sees the democratic moment for the democracies of Western Europe and North America as long past. Globalization, deregulation, and the loss of collective organizational capacity in society have eroded democracy from within. The formal procedures and institutions of democracy continue to exist, but increasingly they are merely a formal game bereft of democratic substance (ibid., 22). The specific form of neoliberal, globalized capitalism is driving established democracies into post-democracy. Claus Offe (2011) similarly sees economic globalization (in the absence of international regulatory regimes), the cultural hegemony of anti-state economic paradigms, and the fiscal starvation of national democracies as the prime causes of the current crisis narrative of democracy (ibid., 475). The challenge to democracy comes from without, from the economy, and from the specific form of spatially and socially embedded capitalism. From a democratic theory viewpoint, it can be summed up in the question: Who actually rules? Democratically legitimated institutions or global firms, international financial markets, central banks, or lobbies? What Crouch, Offe, and Streeck draw attention to and what economists such as Stiglitz (2012), Krugman (2012), and Piketty (2014) and political scientists such as Hacker and Pierson (2010) have recently underlined is the rapid development of socioeconomic inequality in the OECD world into one of the greatest challenges facing democracy. This raises urgent questions about democracy. Does socioeconomic inequality translate into political inequality? Who is still participating? What interests are being represented? Are representative democracies becoming "two-thirds democracies" in which the lower classes are largely marginalized politically?

Conservatives consider that it is not capitalism but an overburdened state that is behind possible crises of democracy. For them it is not the economy that puts too great a strain on the democratic state; this strain comes from the democratic mechanisms themselves. The report *Crisis of Democracy: Report on the Governability of Democracy to the Trilateral Commission* by Crozier et al.

(1975) begins with the question: "Is political democracy, as it exists today, a viable form of government?" (Crozier et al. 1975, 2). The answer in brief is that, owing to the rapid increase in societal complexity, the proliferation of wide-ranging private interests, the erosion of traditional values, and especially the growing demands of the citizens, democratic governments are progressively losing the ability to articulate the common good or effectively implement it politically. Excessive demands are being made of democratic governments, and they are losing their governmental capabilities.

For conservatives this challenge comes not, as it does for the left, from outside (capitalism): it is primarily endogenous. Progressive political participation in conjunction with unraveling interests in society, they claim, lead to inflationary demands on the part of citizens, not least in the economic field and in social welfare. Parties are driven to outbid one another, and governments face ever-growing public expectations, which they can only inadequately satisfy. At the worst, these excessive demands can make a democracy ungovernable. The result is a loss of public confidence in political authority. An issue well established in conservatism, but in recent decades increasingly taken up in at election time by the populist right, is immigration. Ethnic heterogeneity ("foreign infiltration/Überfremdung") is claimed to be destroying any sense of belonging in the political community. Mutual trust and solidarity, the leaven of functioning communities, are believed to be crumbling. Democracy is said to be losing its socially competent demos.

It is astonishing that holistic crisis theories about the crisis of democracy pay hardly any attention to the core institutions and principle actors of representative democracy. Their implicit assumption is that they have become increasingly anachronistic and impotent in the face of economic and social challenges. This is particularly the case for political parties. Scarcely any notice is taken of political party research, while this research devotes little space to general theories of crisis. Nevertheless, party research can contribute important findings to general research into crises (see, e.g., Katz and Mair 1994; Dalton and Wattenberg 2000; Mair et al. 2004; Mair 2006). Peter Mair (2006) goes farthest in this regard, positing that competition between parties is eroding and that they are departing from their representative functions in society because they have primarily become an appendix of the state.

The terrorist attacks in the United States on 11 September 2001 and the subsequent reaction (or overreaction) by some countries have once again made the relationship between collective security and individual liberties into a challenge for democracy. The vital question for democratic theory is: To what extent can democracies permit personal human rights to be restricted, even if elected representatives or large sections of the demos regard this as a suitable means for guaranteeing more collective security?

Theories of crisis list numerous challenges to democracy. In this book, we shall be addressing the following:

- Socioeconomic inequality as a challenge to the democratic principle of equality in participation and representation

- The alleged decline of catch-all parties and statist parties' loss of their roots in society
- The challenge deregulated (financial) capitalism poses for the democratic primacy of state action
- Globalization as a challenge to national, democratic governance
- The alleged tension between collective security and individual freedom

Four of these categories of challenge are external to the core of democratic institutions (the exception is the decline of [catch-all] parties). But they affect and change these institutions. Every analysis of crisis must pay particular attention to this causal link. Transforming exogenous challenges into internal structural changes in participation, representation, and governance could have two consequences. The first, compatible with democracy, is the productive processing of challenges by adapting existing institutions to changed environments or replacing them by new, more appropriate institutions. Challenges then become the engine of democratic reform and thus an endogenous mechanism for stabilizing democracy. A second possible consequence could be that challenges cannot be productively processed. The substance of democratic procedures and institutions would then suffer damage. Consider, for example, the loss of party roots in society (Mair 2006), the increasing social selectivity of political participation, or the growing dominance of the executive over the legislature. The making of important political decisions shifts from the sphere of democratic politics to the world of business, markets, and supranational regimes. Figure 1.2 shows external challenges and examples for potential threats to the normative basis in the partial regimes of democracy.

The concept of democracy (embedded democracy) and that of crisis (crisis II: eroding and undermining crisis), as well as the essential challenges (five categories) having been defined, we bring them together in examining the following questions:

- Where and how do external challenges translate into critical changes in the normative and institutional arrangements of democracy?
- What symptoms of crisis are to be observed and in which partial regimes of democracy?
- In what areas are crisis phenomena particularly pronounced?
- Are there compensatory developments in any partial regimes of democracy that reinforce democracy rather than contribute to crises?
- How can empirically substantial answers to the crisis question be provided?

These are the questions that guide the investigations and conclusions of the volume.

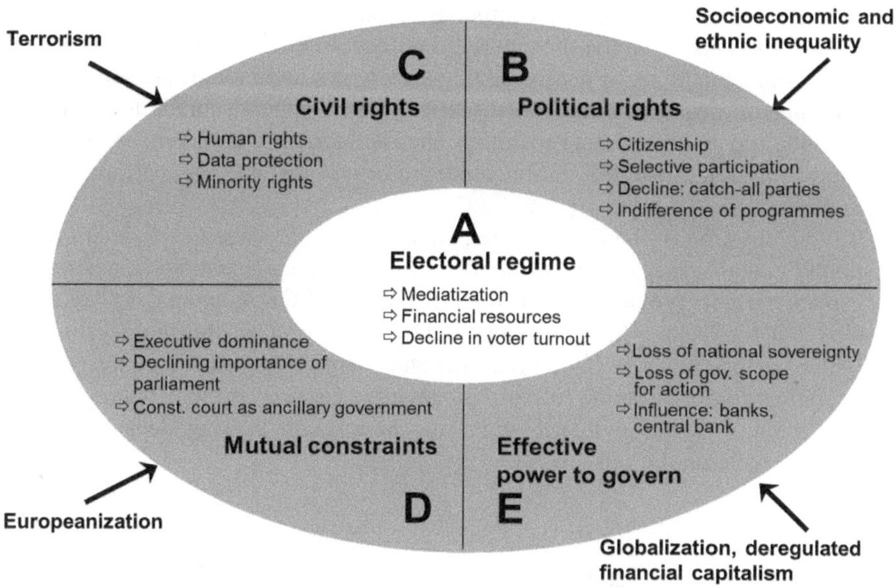

Fig. 1.2 External and internal challenges to democracy. Source: Authors own figure

1.5 Analytical Strategies

We now introduce three strategies for our empirical analysis of crises in democratic systems. None of these strategies are unproblematic, and each leaves blind spots in the analysis. But in combination, they present a promising overall strategy that supplies us with a cautious answer to the question of democracy in crisis.

1.5.1 Strategy 1: Democracy Indices (Objective Assessment)

If we wish to examine whether democracy as a whole is in crisis, we can turn to democracy indices that attempt to capture the democratic quality of political regimes on the basis of expert assessments (*Freedom House*, *Polity*) or of objective indicators (*Democracy Barometer*). Where quality indices cover a significant period of time and reveal downward trends in the quality of democracy, which, given sufficiently differentiation, can be generalized, we can speak of a creeping crisis of democracy.

For the 50 best democracies, Freedom House and Polity show only a minimal variance over the past decade. They are therefore not suitable for examining crisis in mature democracies and could indeed deny the existence of any crisis. The Democracy Barometer (democracybarometer.org) instead has developed an index (100 indicators) highly sensitive to variance in the 30 best democracies. It shows aggregated values for the entire democratic system. But the subindices used also permit conclusions about the three core principles (freedom, equality, control) and the nine "core functions of democracy," namely, participation, transparency, representation, rule of law, individual liberties, public sphere, competition, mutual constraints, and governmental capability. The Democracy Barometer can thus show development trends for the entire democratic systems and for partial regimes since 1990.

But the question of the threshold remains: From what stage in the deterioration of quality in democracy can we speak of crisis? Can such a threshold be determined in general terms? Would it apply for all mature OECD democracies alike, for Greece and for Denmark, for Germany and for Italy? Can threshold values for individual democracies be higher than for others simply because they have a long democratic tradition, a stable rule-of-law governance, or a strong economy? If this is so—as much of the evidence suggests—how much bearing does what such indices say have on the crisis issue?

1.5.2 Strategy 2: Surveys (Subjective Assessment)

One can distrust the opinions of experts and ask the demos, the populace at large. Ultimately it is the citizenry that indicates through "exit, voice, and loyalty" (Hirschman 1970) whether democracy is in crisis. A crisis of democracy would exist (only) if it were to be perceived as a crisis by the majority of the population. This requires no actual theory of democracy, at best theoretical backup from plausible questions like: "Are there political regimes you could prefer as an alternative to democracy?"; "Do you have trust in the government, the parties, the political elites, the courts, central banks, etc.?" As with Max Weber's belief in legitimacy (Legitimitätsglauben), what is at issue is the faith of the citizenry in democracy.

But how far do such surveys get us? Do they describe only the surface to the exclusion of subsurface changes in institutions and procedures they cannot capture? To what extent can they identify internal shifts: for instance, whether public confidence in the core institutions of representative democracy ("majoritarian institutions") such as parties, parliaments, and governments is rising or falling and whether people place more trust in "non-majoritarian institutions" such as the police, the rule of law, the judiciary, and central banks, as is sometimes claimed (see Zürn et al. 2012; Zürn and Ecker-Ehrhardt 2013)? If this is the case, does the legitimacy axis within democratic systems then shift to such a degree that this has to be regarded as a crisis of democracy?

But these are not all the questions raised by survey data. What if only a minority still has confidence in parties as such, but a large majority votes for precisely the parties they allegedly mistrust? What if "objective" indicators developed by democracy experts show a positive trend while general social surveys show a negative one? These are questions we shall be going into in Chap. 2. Such a holistic view can be instructive, but it remains on the surface and permits no causal analysis of the origins, development, and consequences of crisis symptoms. This is the job of partial analyses. They therefore constitute the real focus of this book.

1.5.3 Strategy 3: Partial Analyses

Making do with partial analyses of the key dimensions and the five partial regimes of democracy offers at least two advantages. First, they allow more differentiated insight into certain aspects of democracy. Specific causes, symptoms, crisis trajectories, and improvements within a particular field of democracy can be identified and, by comparing partial analyses, any non-simultaneity between developments, both positive and negative, within mature democracies can be pinpointed. Second, an overall review of single analyses provides an empirically backed understanding of the whole. The partial analyses presented could have been systematically structured in terms of the five partial regimes of *embedded democracy*. But, since these partial regimes are closely interdependent, we have opted to group them under three headings. We examine the challenges to democracy and their possible transformation into crisis phenomena in the following three dimensions: *participation* (partial regimes A and B), *representation* (B), and *governance* (C, D, and E). This covers all five regimes while avoiding any unnecessary breakdown of particularly close functional contexts. The lead questions in the three dimensions are: Who participates? Who is represented? Who governs?

Participation

In his study on "Political Inequality in Voting," *Bernhard Weßels* investigates whether individual political knowledge affects the quality of voting. He asks whether voters with greater political knowledge are better able to ascertain their own political preferences and find the best party to represent and politically implement them. If this is the case, and if less political knowledge can be attributed to a lack of education and membership of a lower social stratum, democracy would, at least in this regard, be unable effectively to guarantee application of the democratic principle of political equality in political participation. There would be a class bias to democracy.

Over and beyond such "stratified" participation, criticism of the state of current representative democracies often addresses political parties and their programs. Doubts are frequently expressed about whether they offer sufficiently clear programmatic alternatives to accommodate the range of preferences in society. A common view proffered—both in intellectual circles[11] and down at the pub—is that such alternatives are no longer discernible. In their ideological and

[11]Chantal Mouffe: "Der Unterschied zwischen Mitte-links und Mitte-rechts ist wie die Auswahl zwischen Coca-Cola und Pepsi-Cola." (taz 1 February 2014, transl.). www.taz.de/Politologin-ueber-die-Krise-der-Demokratie/!132080/. Accessed: 15 August 2017.

programmatic positions, the parties, as it is claimed, have become interchangeable. Whomever you vote for, you always vote for the same program. *Andrea Volkens* and *Nicolas Merz* take a close look at this widespread but empirically shaky thesis on the basis of 2103 election programs of 279 parties in 371 elections between 1951 and 2011.

Right-wing populist parties have emerged in almost all party systems of Eastern and Western Europe during the last three decades. They intend to present a clear alternative to the political "establishment." Their electoral success is often considered as a sign of crisis of democracy. Whether these new alternatives are beneficial or harmful for democracies is, however, far from clear. *Marcus Spittler* investigates whether right-wing populist parties pose a threat to democracy or whether they are a necessary corrective that provides for a proper functioning of modern democracy. With this in mind, he takes a closer look at how the presence of right-wing populists affects the partial regimes of democracy, such as participation and representation, the rule of law, and the public sphere. In doing so, particular attention is payed to the question whether it makes a difference for the quality of democracy if right-wing populist parties are in government or in opposition.

Representation

In democracy, equal opportunities for participation are doubtless a value in themselves. But what is especially important in representative democracy is how the various interests are represented in the legislative institution—parliament—and accordingly transformed into actual politics and policy. *Pola Lehmann*, *Sven Regel*, and *Sara Schlote* therefore go into the widespread suspicion that the lower classes, the "bottom third" of society, are worse represented than the higher strata. Not "descriptive representation" is at issue, i.e., whether the lower strata of society are adequately represented in parliament. They are not and never have been. The study is concerned rather with "substantial representation," i.e., whether the interests, more precisely the preferences of the lower classes, are systematically worse represented than those of the "top third." If this is the case, it would be a clear violation of the principle of political equality. The three authors investigate this by comparing the programmatic positions of members of parliament and their voters. For this purpose, they draw on MP surveys and post-electoral studies for eight European countries between 2006 and 2011.

In modern democracies, political parties are the link between voters, parliaments, and governments. But democracy and party researchers advance the more or less undisputed thesis that parties are in crisis. They claim that things were different in the first three decades after the war. Parties with a large membership are said to have successfully mobilized voters; large class, mass, or catch-all parties had covered the entire spectrum of citizen interests, had offered programmatic alternatives, and had formed stable governments. Since then, more precisely since the mid-1970s, things are said to have gone downhill. Party ties have loosened, catch-all parties have dominated the political landscape, and party cartels have prevented effective competition. The election and party researchers *Heiko Giebler*, *Onawa Promise Lacewell*, *Sven Regel*, and *Annika Werner* examine whether catch-all parties have indeed won the day and whether the representation of interests has become arbitrary and governments more unstable. For this purpose, they have developed an empirically informed typology of "big parties," investigating in 15 Western European democracies over five decades (1960–2010) whether the three major party types (mass party, programmatic party, catch-all party) have performed the three key functions of voter mobilization, interest representation, and government formation worse after 2000 than in the preceding decades.

Alexander Petring looks at the responsiveness of parties. Under the heading "Parties, Hear the Signals,"[12] he asks about the extent to which voter attitudes toward social inequality issues have changed over the past three decades and how party programs have responded to this shift in attitude—the question of whether parties are responsive in their reaction to a key problem of contemporary democracies, namely, growing social inequality, is by no means a trivial one for democratic theory. Although the data situation is difficult, especially as regards long-term changes in people's attitudes toward inequality issues, Petring has managed to compile a representative sample of 14 countries for the period 1987–2009 and on this basis to examine the programmatic reactions of parties.

Rubén Ruiz-Rufino and *Sonia Alonso* address the question whether the citizens in the Eurozone crisis countries like Greece, Portugal, Spain, Ireland, and Italy find themselves in a nightmare of "democracy without choice." Choice is usually considered a core element of democratic governance and electoral competition. Elections are only meaningful if the results make any difference according to policy change. If neither citizens nor governments are able to choose between different policy options, democratic elections become a hollow exercise, and democracy is indeed in crisis. Ruiz-Rufino and Alonso investigate in their contribution whether the bailout decisions of the so-called Troika (IMF, European Commission, European Central Bank) transformed the prior beliefs of citizens about the policy autonomy of their national governments and what this potential transformation means for the crisis of democratic governance in the respective countries. One core question is: Did the conditions imposed by the Troika break the legitimation chain of elections, parliamentary representation, and national government? Although the citizens of the crisis countries continue to vote, do they still have a choice when it comes to key budgetary, social, and wage policy? Have the crisis countries arrived at the point where Crouch and Streeck see many countries landing in the future, namely, in the post-democratic state of "façade democracy?"

Governance

In representative democracy, participation and representation are (essentially) not ends in themselves. Their purpose is to open up procedural opportunities for pursuing the different interests in society in practical politics on a fair basis, opportunities for people and institutions who have been given a democratic and constitutional mandate to do so by the citizens. Fifty years after Robert Dahl asked

[12]An allusion to the first line of the *Internationale* in the German translation.

"Who governs?" the question has taken a new turn in an age of globalization, Europeanization, deregulation, and privatization. The question is no longer only whether the economic and cognitive resources of broad sections of the population suffice to control the government (Dahl 1961, 3) but rather whether financial markets, hedge funds, big banks, global companies, supranational policy regimes, and European institutions have become so powerful that important financial, economic, and employment policies are increasingly escaping the control of democratically elected governments. But most crisis theoreticians agree precisely in this question: globalization, deregulation, and the withdrawal of the state from important policy areas have given other actors with little or no legitimation scope for deciding on the lives and chances of citizens and entire societies, scope that democratic principles do not place within their remit.

Lea Heyne thus asks whether globalization has a negative or positive influence on the quality of democracy. Her study is based on 20 democracies that the Zurich/ Berlin *Democracy Barometer* (DB) (as well as *Freedom House* and *Polity*) has identified as the best in the world. Globalization is covered by the Zurich KOF index. In accordance with this index, Heyne distinguishes three dimensions of globalization: economic, social, and political. Correlating the KOF and DB data, Heyne examines the effects of globalization on democracy as a whole and on its structural principles: freedom, equality, and control.

Wolfgang Merkel addresses a fundamental question that had moved crisis theory as long ago as the early 1970s: Are democracy and capitalism compatible? Do the fundamental principles of the economic and political order contradict or complement one another? But the discussion does not remain at the level of these principles. Distinguishing between varieties of democracy and varieties of capitalism can give greater precision to the compatibility question: What forms of capitalism are compatible or incompatible with which forms of democracy? Merkel's analysis focuses particularly on the impacts that disembedded capitalism has had over the past three decades in embedded democracies.

Aiko Wagner and *Sascha Kneip* devote their chapter to a democratic paradox: Should governments pursue the principle of responsiveness even if in doing so they limit liberal basic and civil rights? Where is the dividing line between responsive reaction to voter wishes and the due protection of individual liberties? How is a balance to be achieved between the not always compatible representation of the collective need for protection and the safeguarding of individual liberties? Setting out from the theoretical discussion on a trade-off between collective security and individual liberties, the two authors examine to what extent and where new surveillance tools have been created and individual rights of citizens, suspects, or convicted persons restricted in the interest of collective security. For a selection of 22 countries, they investigate the extent to which the level of terrorist threats, the rootedness of liberal civil rights, strong constitutional courts, federal structures, and a pluralistic media landscape have influenced this trade-off one way or the other.

The next chapter follows on from the analysis of the balance between security and liberty. It proceeds on the almost uncontested assumption that human rights, especially the right to physical integrity, are the basis for civilized governance. In most democracies, the core human rights are therefore protected by perpetuity clauses or in other ways safeguarded from intervention by majority decision. They are not at the disposition of the sovereign majority will. But in the practice of government, do established democracies abide by this precept even when challenged by massive, for instance, terrorist violence? *Dag Tanneberg* goes into this question with a study of the 30 best democracies in the world (Democracy Barometer) since the 1990s. The aim is to discover what variance there is among democracies with regard to violation of the right to physical integrity and what factors prevent the executive from violating human rights or drive them to do so. Among the independent variables considered are the extent of the threat, vertical accountability to the voter, the strength of rule-of-law institutions, and compliance with mutual constraints. In brief, the author comes to the surprising conclusion that with only four exceptions, all of the democracies under study have violated the most fundamental of all human rights, with South Africa and the United States leading the way.

The alleged judicialization of politics is a standard reproach about the way existing democracies actually function. How, in short, do constitutional courts act when the external boundaries of national sovereignty have become increasingly porous and the internal boundaries between state and citizens have to be constantly readjusted? *Sascha Kneip* is concerned above all with the internal boundaries, especially those between the legislature and the constitutional judiciary, as well as with the dividing line between the state and the citizenry. And do constitutional courts induce crises of democracy or, on the contrary, prevent them? To begin with, Kneip discusses when and to what extent the action of constitutional courts can be a curse or a blessing for democracy. He goes on to examine the empirical validity of the claim, often made most notably in Germany, that constitutional courts are increasingly encroaching on the preserve of the legislature. In conclusion, he reunites theoretical/normative and empirical aspects and discusses what influence constitutional court action has on the quality of established democracies.

The studies collected in this volume show a number of peculiarities. They are not the outcome of any workshop. They are the result of both long and intensive discussions in the Research Unit *Democracy and Democratization* at the WZB Berlin Social Science Center. All the authors are or were members of this research unit while the book was coming into being. The only guest author is Rubén Ruiz-Rufino, who, together with Sonia Alonso, expanded her previous chapter in the German edition of this book. Common to all the studies is the concept of *embedded democracy*. This avoids the arbitrariness attached to treatments of crisis that do not spell out their normative and analytical concept of democracy. Many of the studies take a quantitative approach based on comparative sets of data. Mostly the sample to be studied comprised (old) OECD countries or the best 30 democracies. The periods under study were all after 1945. They vary, depending on the data situation, from 20 to 60 years. A few have preferred to adopt a qualitative approach. They complement the quantitative studies and provide special insight into selected cases.

The book finishes with an overall view of democracy on the basis of the more detailed partial analyses. It is an attempt by a group of empirical democracy researchers to find an informed, empirically well-founded and thus differentiated answer over and beyond anecdotal evidence to the question that has often been affirmed even before it has be put let alone thoroughly examined: Is democracy in crisis?

References

Agamben, G., Badiou, A., Bensaïd, D., Brown, W., Nancy, J.-L., Rancière, J., Ross, K., & Žižek, S. (Eds.). (2011). *Democracy in What State?* New York, NY: Columbia University Press.
Alonso, S., Keane, J., & Merkel, W. (Eds.). (2011). *The future of representative democracy*. Cambridge: Cambridge University Press.
Barber, B. R. (1984). *Strong democracy. Participatory politics for a new age*. Berkeley, CA: University of California Press.
Beetham, D. (Ed.). (1994). *Defining and measuring democracy*. Beverly Hills, CA & London: Sage.
Bobbio, N. (1983). Democraczia. In N. Bobbio, N. Matteucci, & G. Pasquino (Eds.), *Dizionario die Politica* (pp. 308–318). Turin: UTET.
Burton, M. G., Gunther, R., & Higley, J. (1991). Introduction: Elite transformations and democratic regimes. In J. Higley & R. Gunther (Eds.), *Elites and democratic consolidation in Latin America and Southern Europe* (pp. 1–38). Cambridge: Cambridge University Press.
Collier, D., & Levitsky, S. (1997). Democracy with adjectives: Conceptual innovation in comparative research. *World Politics, 49*(3), 430–451.
Crouch, C. (2004). *Post-democracy*. Cambridge: Polity Press.
Crozier, M. J., Huntington, S. P., & Watanuki, J. (1975). *The crisis of democracy. Report on the Governability of Democracies to the Trilateral Commission*. New York, NY: New York University Press.
Dahl, R. A. (1961). *Who governs?* New Haven, CT: Yale University Press.
Dalton, R. J. (2008). *Citizen politics: Public opinion and political parties in advanced industrial democracies* (5th ed.). Washington, DC: CQ Press.
Dalton, R. J., & Wattenberg, M. P. (2000). *Parties without Partisans: Political change in advanced industrial democracies*. Oxford: Oxford University Press.
Downs, A. (1957). *An economic theory of democracy*. New York, NY: Harper & Row.
Dryzek, J. (2000). *Deliberative democracy and beyond*. Oxford: Oxford University Press.
Elster, J. (Ed.). (1998). *Deliberative democracy*. Cambridge: Cambridge University Press.
Fishkin, J. S. (1991). *Democracy and deliberation. New directions for democratic reform*. New Haven, CT: Yale University Press.
Fung, A., & Wright, E. O. (2003). *Deepening democracy: Institutional innovations in empowered participatory governance*. New York, NY: Verso Press.
Goodin, R. E. (2008). *Innovating democracy: Democratic theory and practice after the deliberative turn*. Oxford: Oxford University Press.
Habermas, J. (1975). *Legitimation crisis*. Boston, MA: Beacon Press.
Habermas, J. (2001). *Between facts and norms. Contributions to a discourse theory of law and democracy*. Cambridge, MA: The MIT Press.
Hacker, J. S., & Pierson, P. (2010). *Winter-take-all politics: How Washington made the rich richer—and turned its back on the middle class*. New York, NY: Simon & Schuster.
Held, D. (1995). *Democracy and the global order: From the Modern State to Cosmopolitan Governance*. Cambridge: Polity Press.

Held, D. (1996). *Models of democracy*. Oxford: Polity Press & Blackwell Publishers.

Heller, H. (1934). *Staatslehre*. Leiden: Brill.

Higley, J., & Gunther, R. (Eds.). (1991). *Elites and democratic consolidation in Latin America and Southern Europe*. Cambridge: Cambridge University Press.

Hirschman, A. O. (1970). Exit, voice and loyalty. In *Responses to decline in firms, organizations and states*. Cambridge, MA: Harvard University Press.

Jänicke, M. (1972). Krisenbegriff und Krisenforschung. In M. Jänicke (Ed.), *Herrschaft und Krise* (pp. 10–26). Opladen: UTB-Westdeutscher Verlag.

Katz, R. S., & Mair, P. (1994). *How parties organize. Change and adaptation in party organization in western democracies*. Beverly Hills, CA & London: Sage.

Keane, J. (2009). *The life and death of democracy*. New York, NY: Simon & Schuster.

Kelsen, H. (1925). *Allgemeine Staatslehre. Enzyklopädie der Rechts- und Staatswissenschaften* (Vol. 23). Berlin: Springer-Verlag.

Kneip, S. (2009). *Verfassungsgerichte als demokratische Akteure. Der Beitrag des Bundesverfassungsgerichts zur Qualität der bundesdeutschen Demokratie*. Baden-Baden: Nomos.

Koselleck, R. (1972). Krise. In O. Brunner, W. Conze, & R. Koselleck (Eds.), *Geschichtliche Grundbegriffe. Historisches Lexikon zur politisch-sozialen Sprache in Deutschland* (Vol. 1, pp. 641–649). Stuttgart: Klett-Cotta.

Krugman, P. (2012). *End this depression now*. New York, NY: Norton & Company.

Lembcke, O. W., Ritzi, C., & Schaal, G. S. (Eds.). (2012). *Zeitgenössische Demokratietheorie, Normative Demokratietheorien* (Vol. 1). Wiesbaden: Springer VS.

Linz, J. J., & Stepan, A. (1978). *The breakdown of democratic regimes*. Baltimore, MD: Johns Hopkins University Press.

Mair, P. (2006). *Ruling the void?* The Hollowing of Western Democracy. *New Left Review, 42*, 25–51.

Mair, P., Müller, W. C., & Plasser, F. (Eds.). (2004). *Political parties and electoral change: Party responses to electoral markets*. Beverly Hills, CA & London: Sage.

Marshall, T. H. (1950). *Citizenship and social class: And other essays*. Cambridge: Cambridge University Press.

Marx, K. (1998[1894]). *Capital, Vol. 3, MECW Vol. 37*. London: Lawrence & Wishart.

Meier, C. (2004). *Athen. Ein Neubeginn der Weltgeschichte*. München: Siedler Verlag.

Merkel, W. (2004). Embedded and defective democracies. In A. Croissant, & W. Merkel (Eds.), Special issue of democratization: Consolidated or defective democracy? Problems of regime change, 11(5), 33–58.

Merkel, W. (2010). *Systemtransformation. Eine Einführung in die Theorie und Empirie der Transformationsforschung* (2nd, rev. & exp ed.). Wiesbaden: VS Verlag für Sozialwissenschaften.

Merkel, W., & Ritzi, C. (Eds.). (2017). *Die Legitimität direkter Demokratie. Wie demokratisch sind Volksabstimmungen?* Wiesbaden: Springer VS.

Merkel, W., Puhle, H.-J., Croissant, A., Eicher, C., & Thiery, P. (2003). *Defekte Demokratie* (Vol. 1: Theorie). Opladen: Leske + Budrich.

Meyer, T. (2007). *Theory of social democracy*. Cambridge: Polity.

Miller, D. (2001). *Principles of social justice*. Cambridge, MA: Harvard University Press

Mouffe, C. (2000). *The democratic paradox*. London: Verso.

Norris, P. (1999). *Critical Citizens. Global support for democratic governance*. Oxford: Oxford University Press.

Norris, P. (2011). *Democratic deficit: Critical citizens revisited*. Cambridge: Cambridge University Press.

O'Connor, J. (1973). *The fiscal crisis of the state*. New York, NY: St. Martin's Press.

O'Donnell, G. (1998). Horizontal accountability in new democracies. *Journal of Democracy, 9*(3), 112–126.

O'Donnell, G. (2010). *Democracy, agency and the state: Theory with comparative intent*. Oxford: Oxford University Press.
Offe, C. (1972). *Strukturprobleme des kapitalistischen Staates: Aufsätze zur Politischen Soziologie*. Suhrkamp: Frankfurt am Main.
Offe, C. (1984). "Ungovernability:" The renaissance of conservative theories of crises. In J. Kean (Ed.), *Contradiction of the welfare state* (pp. 65–87). Cambridge, MA: The MIT Press.
Offe, C. (2003). *Die Demokratisierung der Demokratie. Diagnosen und Reformvorschläge*. Campus: Frankfurt am Main.
Offe, C. (2011). Crisis and innovation of liberal democracy: Can deliberation be institutionalised? *Czech Sociological Review, 47*(3), 447–473.
Pateman, C. (1970). *Participation and democratic theory*. Cambridge: Cambridge University Press.
Pharr, S. J., & Putnam, R. D. (Eds.). (2000). *Disaffected democracies? What's troubling the trilateral countries?* Princeton, NJ: Princeton University Press.
Piketty, T. (2014). *Capital in the twenty-first century*. Cambridge, MA: Harvard University Press.
Polanyi, K. (2001[1944]). *The great transformation: The political and economic origins of our time*. Boston: Beacon Press, 2nd ed.
Przeworski, A. (2007). Capitalism, democracy, science. In G. L. Munck & R. Snyder (Eds.), *Passion, craft and method in comparative politics* (pp. 456–503). Baltimore, MD: Johns Hopkins University Press.
Rancière, J. (2006). *Hatred of democracy*. London: Verso.
Rawls, J. (1971). *A theory of justice*. Cambridge, MA: Harvard University Press.
Ringen, S. (2007). *What is democracy for? On freedom and moral government*. Princeton, NJ: Princeton University Press.
Saward, M. (2010). *The representative claim*. Oxford: Oxford University Press.
Schaal, G. S., Lemke, M., & Ritzi, C. (Eds.). (2014). *Die Ökonomisierung der Politik in Deutschland: Eine vergleichende Politikfeldanalyse*. Wiesbaden: Springer Fachmedien.
Schmidt, M. G. (2008). *Demokratietheorien. Eine Einführung* (4th Rev. & exp ed.). Wiesbaden: VS Verlag für Sozialwissenschaften.
Schmidt, M. G. (2010). *Wörterbuch der Politik* (3rd ed.). Stuttgart: Kröner.
Schumpeter, J. A. (1942). *Capitalism, socialism, and democracy*. New York, NY: Harper & Brothers.
Sen, A. (2009). *The idea of justice*. Cambridge, MA: Harvard University Press.
Stiglitz, J. E. (2012). *The prize of inequality. How today's divided society endanger our future*. New York, NY: W.W. Norton.
Streeck, W. (2014). *Buying time: The delayed crisis of democratic capitalism*. London: Verso.
von Beyme, K. (2013). *Von der Postdemokratie zur Neodemokratie*. Wiesbaden: Springer.
Warren, M. E. (2001). *Democracy and association*. Princeton, NJ: Princeton University Press.
Warren, M. E. (2009). Citizen participation and democratic deficits: Considerations from the perspective of democratic theory. In J. DeBardeleben & J. Pammett (Eds.), *Activating the citizen: Dilemmas of participation in Europe and Canada* (pp. 17–40). New York, NY: Palgrave MacMillan.
Wolin, S. (2008). *Democracy incorporated: Managed democracy and the specter of inverted totalitarianism*. Princeton, NJ: Princeton University Press.
Žižek, S. (2011). From democracy to divine violence. In G. Agamben, A. Badiou, D. Bensaïd, W. Brown, J.-L. Nancy, J. Rancière, K. Ross, & S. Žižek (Eds.), *Democracy in What State* (pp. 100–120). New York, NY: Columbia University Press.
Zürn, M. (1998). *Regieren jenseits des Nationalstaats*. Suhrkamp: Frankfurt am Main.
Zürn, M. (2011). Perspektiven des demokratischen Regierens und die Rolle der Politikwissenschaft im 21. Jahrhundert. *Politische Vierteljahresschrift: Zeitschrift der Deutschen Vereinigung für politische Wissenschaft, 52*(4), 603–635.
Zürn, M., & Ecker-Ehrhardt, M. (Eds.). (2013). *Die Politisierung der Weltpolitik. Umkämpfte internationale Institutionen*. Berlin: Suhrkamp.
Zürn, M., Nollkaemper, A., & Peerenboom, R. (Eds.). (2012). *Rule of law dynamics. In an era of international and transnational governance*. Cambridge: Cambridge University Press.

Part I
Participation

Chapter 2
Crisis of Democracy? Views of Experts and Citizens

Werner Krause and Wolfgang Merkel

This first chapter offers an answer to the question whether democracy is in crisis from two perspectives: that of empirical researchers and that of citizens, in other words, from the standpoint of the demos itself. This opposes "objective" (expert) assessment of the state of given democracies to "subjective" appraisal. To begin with we consider how both experts and citizens view the question as a whole. At issue is therefore whether democracy as an actually existing, overall system is in crisis, and whether the quality of developed democracies has deteriorated in recent decades, pointing to a creeping crisis. After considering this holistic perspective, we turn to partial perspectives. We ask how the different dimensions, partial regimes, institutions, and organizations of democracy are seen by experts and citizens. Are nonsimultaneous developments in evidence that allow particular areas to be judged better or worse today than a few decades ago? Are the axes of legitimation shifting within the overall system of democracy, or is everything staying the way it was?

W. Krause (✉)
Department of Democracy and Democratization, WZB Berlin Social Science Center, Berlin, Germany
e-mail: werner.krause@wzb.eu

W. Merkel
Department of Democracy and Democratization, WZB Berlin Social Science Center, Berlin, Germany

Humboldt-Universität zu Berlin, Berlin, Germany
e-mail: wolfgang.merkel@wzb.eu

W. Merkel, S. Kneip (eds.), *Democracy and Crisis*,
https://doi.org/10.1007/978-3-319-72559-8_2

2.1 Experts: Democracy Indices

In political science there are a number of indices that appraise the quality of democracy. Although seemingly addressing the same subject matter, namely, the democratic substance of political systems, they differ in their reference concept of democracy, in the focus of their dimensions, the selection and number of indicators, their mode of aggregation, their country sample, and their time horizon. The more countries an index examines and the farther back its time series reach, the more popular it is in statistical comparative democracy research, which needs large numbers of cases to establish correlations, calculate regressions, and identify trends. This is not the place to either present or criticize these democracy indices (see, e.g., Lauth 2004; Müller and Pickel 2007; Schmidt 2008; Bühlmann et al. 2012). But the most important among them should nevertheless be mentioned.

Polity's *Political Regime Characteristics* (data from 1800 to the present day) and the Freedom House index *Freedom in the World* (since 1973) look at nearly all countries in the world and provide the data sets most frequently used in comparative democracy research. For our purposes, however, they are of no use, because they show practically no variance over the last four decades for the established democracies of the OECD world. The exemplary Scandinavian democracies are thus given the same quality scores as the United States under George W. Bush or Berlusconi's Italy. Lines of development in the best democracies are identical. The message of Polity IV and Freedom House is clear: there have been no essential changes in the quality of the 30 best democracies, let alone any crisis of democracy. The perceived high quality of these democracies apparently does not change if measured against both global and rough scale of democracy covering 200 countries from North Korea to Denmark. The Bertelsmann Transformation Index (BTI), which covers 131 countries, deliberately excludes the mature democracies of the OECD world because it perceives no fundamental transformations there. The Sustainable Governance Indicators (SGI) Index, also from the Bertelsmann Foundation, which concentrates on the OECD world, is still too young: its time series go back only to 2009. These indices can accordingly provide no answer to the question of whether the quality of established democracies in the OECD world has changed for better or worse in recent decades.

A quality index that was developed explicitly for the OECD countries is the Democracy Barometer (democracybarometer.org; Bühlmann et al. 2012). It goes back to 1990, assesses the 30 best democracies in the world on the basis of 100 indicators, and is highly sensitive to differences in quality within this exclusive circle of established democracies. If the thesis of the decline of democracies is correct, at least a general tendency for quality to decline should be detectable despite all the differences between countries. Figure 2.1 shows that this is not the case. On a scale up to a theoretical maximum of 100,[1] the base value in 1990 was

[1]On measurement scaling, see the codebook of the DB: democracybarometer.com. Theoretically a country reaches an overall score of 100 only if for all 100 indicators it exhibits the highest quality

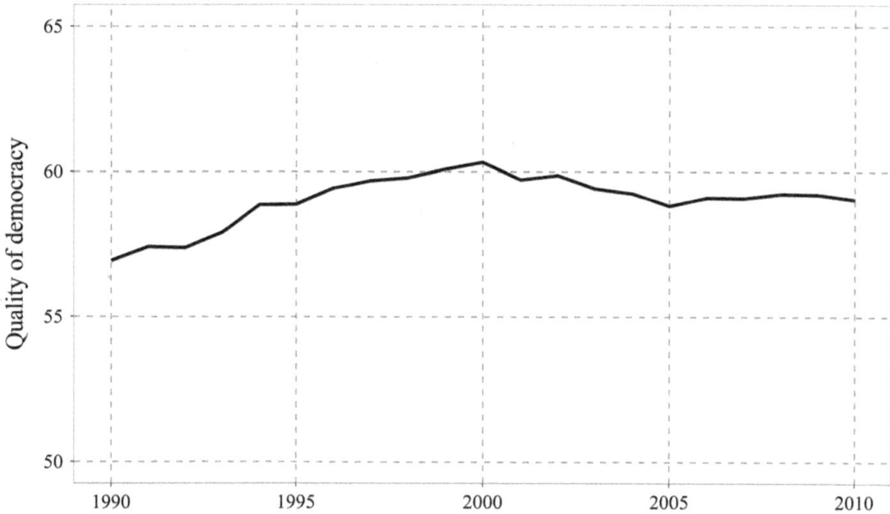

Fig. 2.1 Development of the quality of democracy in the 30 best democracies, 1990–2010. Note: Annual averages for the 30 best democracies of the Democracy Barometer (Australia, Belgium, Costa Rica, Denmark, Germany, Finland, France, United Kingdom, Iceland, Ireland, Italy, Japan, Canada, Luxembourg, Malta, Netherlands, New Zealand, Norway, Austria, Poland, Portugal, Sweden, Switzerland, Slovenia, Spain, South Africa, Czech Republic, Hungary, United States, Cyprus). Source: Bochsler et al. (2014)

just under 57 points, rising in 2010 after a slight curve to a moderately higher score of 59 for 2010. It is clear that the Democracy Barometer is unable to evidence any decline in quality on average for the 30 best democracies. This statement clearly diverges from theoretical assumptions, for example, in the post-democracy debate, that democracy is in sustained decline.

However, the averages conceal considerable variance between countries, for example, between Denmark and France (see Fig. 2.2). Over the 20 years under review, France always came in the last third of the best 30 democracies, whereas Denmark has always been among the best five. Moreover, a look at Italy and the United States shows that certain countries had to accept a deterioration in the quality of democracy over the 20-year period. Such deterioration coincided in these two countries essentially with the terms of office of Silvio Berlusconi and George W. Bush. That there is a causal connection is not a very daring conclusion; it is supported with regard to certain aspects of democracy by Chaps. 12 and 13.

Moving down the aggregation ladder of the overall index to the second level, the three fundamental principles of democracy freedom, equality, and control, there were discernible differences in their realization on the average in the 30 best democracies, but no principle scored worse in 2010 than in 1990 (see Fig. 2.3).

---

of all 30 countries. In reality, Denmark showed the highest democratic quality in 2010, reaching a total score of almost 74.

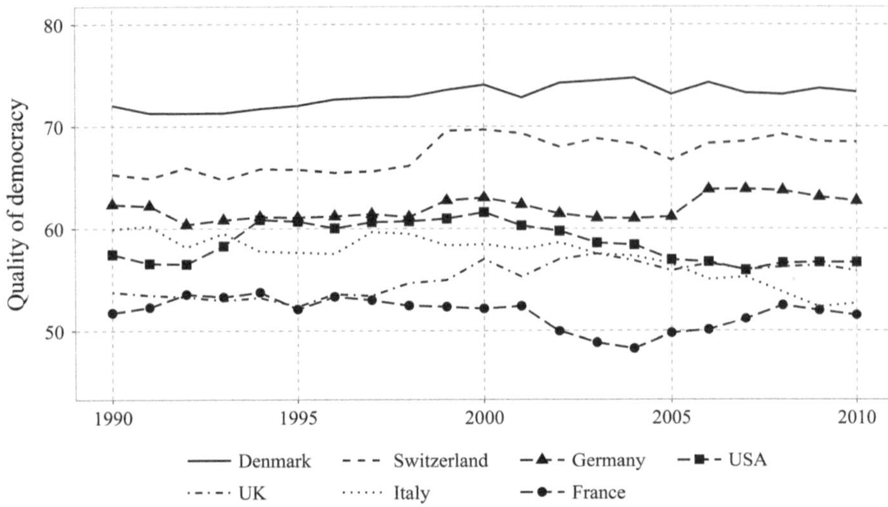

Fig. 2.2 Development of the quality of democracy compared, 1990–2010. Source: Bochsler et al. (2014)

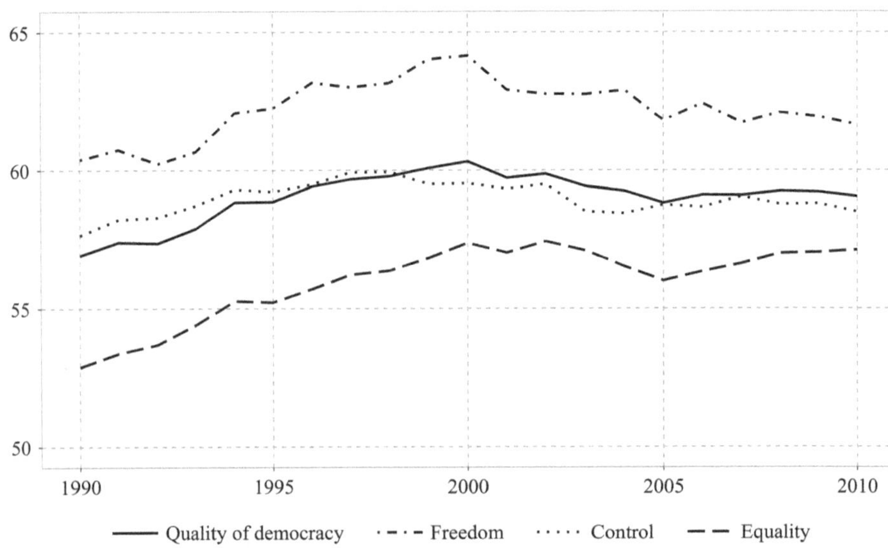

Fig. 2.3 The development of the quality of democracy and the three principles of the Democracy Barometer, 1990–2010. Note: Annual averages for the 30 best democracies of the Democracy Barometer. Source: Bochsler et al. (2014)

The contrary was the case. All showed slight improvement. The principle of freedom was best implemented in these democracies; control was largely at the mean level of overall quality, whereas the greatest difficulty over the period under review was in implementing the principle of political equality. The partial analyses in this volume examine and seek to explain in particular the hypothesis of the special difficulties of democracy with political equality.

In the Democracy Barometer, the principle freedom is subdivided into three functions. Over the period under review, there were moderate changes in these three functions. Despite the accentuation and guarantee of individual liberties, and despite the security laws in the United States and the United Kingdom after 9/11, there has on average been a slight rise in quality for the 30 best democracies over the 20 years from 1990 to 2010. This is to be attributed first to ratification of international conventions against torture and the violation of physical integrity and to a decline in civil disorder and homicide, improved rights in the freedom of movement, the protection of property, and the safeguarding of the freedom of religion (see democracybarometer.org).

The rule of law function, which includes equality before the law, effective independence of the judiciary, judicial professionalism, and confidence in the justice system, showed slight losses. The reasons lie in worse subcomponent scores for the independence of the judiciary and in decreasing trust in the national legal system. The public sphere function, which measures not only freedom of opinion and association but also the range of media on offer, the neutrality of the press, and effective organization in political NGOs and economic interest groups, remains at a low level. The scores for a pluralistic range of media fell slightly, and the degrees of organization in the various societal associations and NGOs who lend a public voice to societal interests have fallen. Of the three functions subsumed under control, the quality of horizontal checks on power and pluralistic political competition has increased minimally. Above all, there was a decline in the quality of the effective capabilities of democratically elected governments: the independence of central banks grew, the effective implementation of government decisions declined, and government stability decreased slightly. On balance, developments were thus mixed with respect to the democratic control principle: positive and negative developments more or less balanced one another out.

Of the three principles of democracy, political equality was the one worst implemented over the past two decades. Since the studies in this volume repeatedly show that political equality is significantly worse for lower income brackets and has also increased in the last two or three decades, it is worth taking a closer look at the principle of equality and disaggregating it further into its constituent functions. Thus in Fig. 2.4, the equality principle is subdivided into three functions through which it is implemented. Overall, transparency has improved with regard to the decisions and activities of the institutions of representative democracy. The public sphere monitors the income and behavior of political elites better than in past decades. The quality of representation has improved, which is almost exclusively attributable to the better "descriptive" representation of women. However, the substantial representation of interests has a class bias, which gains in descriptive representation cannot neutralize (see Chap. 6).[2] There is therefore a decline only in

[2]Chapter 6 shows clearly that substantial representation of the interests of the "lower third" of society is significantly worse than that of the upper third.

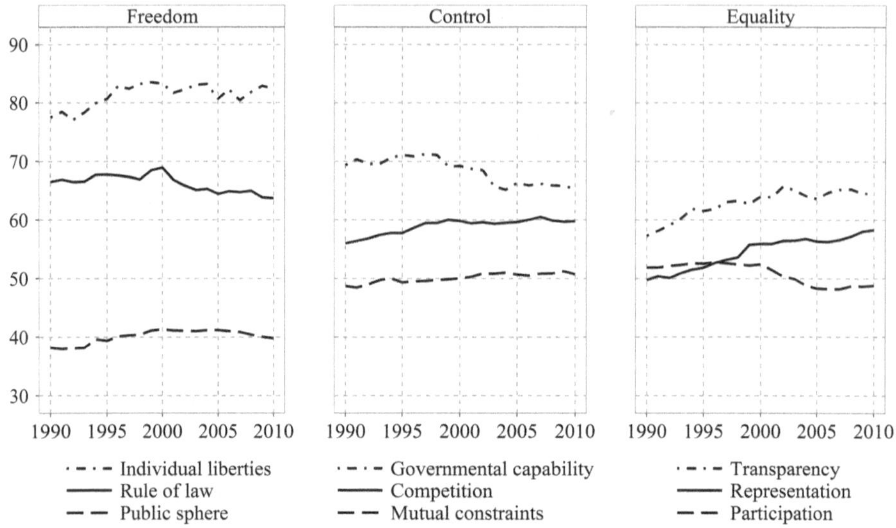

Fig. 2.4 The nine functions of the Democracy Barometer compared, 1990–2010. Note: Annual averages for the 30 best democracies of the Democracy Barometer. Source: Bochsler et al. (2014)

the extent and quality of participation. And this is due above all to the socioeconomically induced self-exclusion of the lower classes from participation.

Comparing participation in the various countries shows not only a general downward trend but also considerable differences. As in the past, Sweden, like most Scandinavian countries, did well above average, whereas the United States was unable to improve its traditionally bad score on participation.[3] The second English-speaking country, the United Kingdom, is slowly approaching the bad scores of the United States; but Germany, too, exhibited marked losses in the quality of political participation, owing not least to the decline in voter turnout and the increase in the social selectivity of conventional political participation (see Fig. 2.5).

On balance, it can be said that the Democracy Barometer indicators that researchers have developed, although showing internal differences in quality and significant variations between countries, do not point to an overall loss in the quality of democracy "per se." With all due caution, this can be described as the *objective dimension* of assessment by neutral experts of the quality of democracies. In what follows this will be complemented by and contrasted with the *subjective dimension*.

[3]For the function participation, the following subcomponents are measured: non-selectivity of electoral participation, non-selectivity of alternative participation, participation rights, effective institutionalized participation, effective noninstitutionalized participation, and rules facilitating participation. On the indicators that measure these subcomponents, see democracybarometer.org, Codebook.

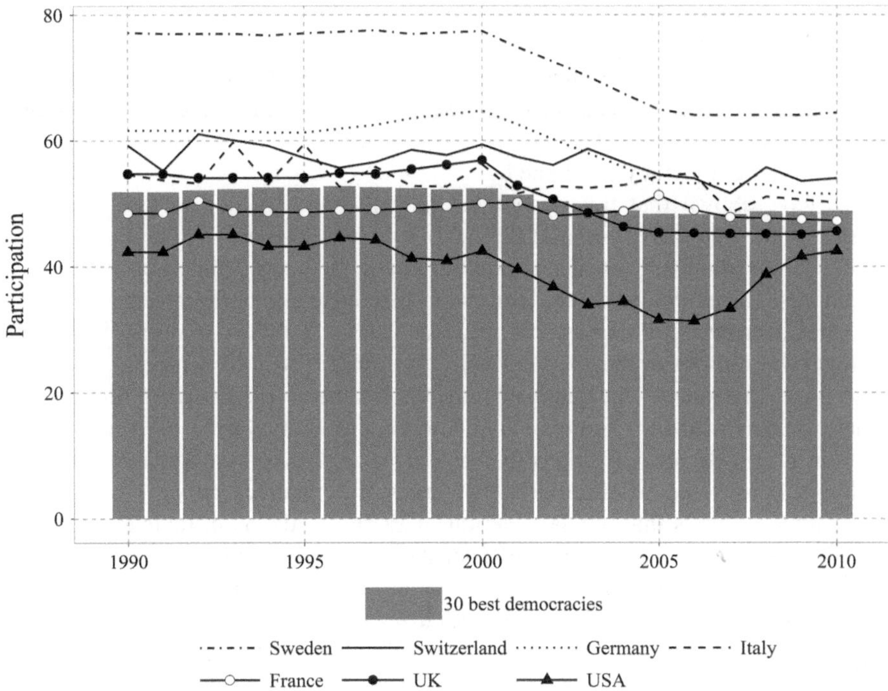

Fig. 2.5 Development of the function "participation" compared, 1990–2010. Note: Gray bars: Annual averages for the 30 best democracies of the Democracy Barometer. Source: Bochsler et al. (2014)

From this perspective, citizens' subjective evaluation of their democracy is examined in depth. Does the demos judge differently from the experts?

2.2 Citizens: Survey Data

In a democracy, it is the citizens, the demos, that decide in the last instance on the legitimacy and stability of a democracy. They decide not only about the "objective" institutions and procedures laid down in the constitution but also about the normative "recognition-worthiness" of a democracy. It is rather the citizens' subjective "belief in legitimacy" (Max Weber), their belief that "their" democratic system is legitimate, fair, and worth supporting that strengthens or weakens democracy. In operationally developing Max Weber's 'belief-in-legitimacy' concept, David Easton (1965) describes it as the support that every political system needs to survive and reproduce in conservational equilibrium. Easton distinguishes analytically between the normative diffuse support of the system itself and the utilitarian-specific support directed toward the efficiency of the system. In the eyes of the citizen, however, the two perspectives merge far more strongly than their analytical separation suggests. The greater the general support of citizens is, the more stable a democratic order will be (Klingemann et al. 2006, p. 3). Modifying the hypothesis of Klingemann et al., we can therefore argue that the stronger the citizens' acceptance of a democratic system is, the higher will be the subjectively perceived quality of the democracy concerned.

We have shown that this cannot be the only way to look at things first by consulting the "objective" appraisal by experts while recognizing that the majority of the demos may very well endorse autocratic or semi-democratic norms and procedures, for example, when democratic discourses or parliamentary deliberations are sacrificed to speedy executive decisions or when minority rights are restricted for reasons of the "popular will." We shall leave this democratic paradox aside for the moment. Our question from the perspective adopted in this book is rather whether citizens' approval of democracy and its various institutions has fallen in recent decades. If this is the case, it would be at least one important fact lending support to assertions about "the" crisis of democracy per se.

Figure 2.6 shows that the satisfaction of EC/EU citizens in their totality with their democracies has not decreased over the past four decades. According to the Eurobarometer, approval was exactly as great in 2013 as in 1973 (see gray bars, which show the average approval rate of citizens of all member states). This is all the more remarkable when one considers that since 2004 the new Eastern European democracies have been worked into the calculation, where the approval rate after 2004 was on average lower than in the old member states of Western Europe. Since the rate of satisfaction peaked in 2002, there has been a visible, albeit moderate decline in aggregated satisfaction figures, which can largely be attributed to the eastward enlargement of the EU. However, in Western Europe, too, satisfaction rates have fallen since 2007. Nevertheless, the overall development of EU citizens' satisfaction with their democracies provides no evidence to support any of the current theories, notably the post-democracy thesis, about a crisis of democracy. The perception patterns of European *demoi* quite clearly differ from those of post-democracy theoreticians.

Figure 2.7 shows again that, despite small losses after 2007, the figures for Western Europe were discernibly higher than those for the 1980s and 1990s. Citizens of established democracies were quite obviously more satisfied with the way their democracies worked than citizens of the new Eastern European democracies. This is hardly likely to be because there was a greater number of critical citizens in Eastern Europe but rather because a stable democratic culture had not developed in most of the new democracies there (Merkel 2010) and the quality of these democracies was also often less high than in Western Europe (democracybarometer.org).

Figure 2.8 shows that satisfaction with democracy varied strongly from member state to member state and over time. The satisfaction of Danish citizens increased markedly. This reflects the good Democracy Barometer figures for Denmark, although "subjective" satisfaction increased much more strongly than the "objective" quality index in the DB (see Fig. 2.2). Satisfaction with democracy among

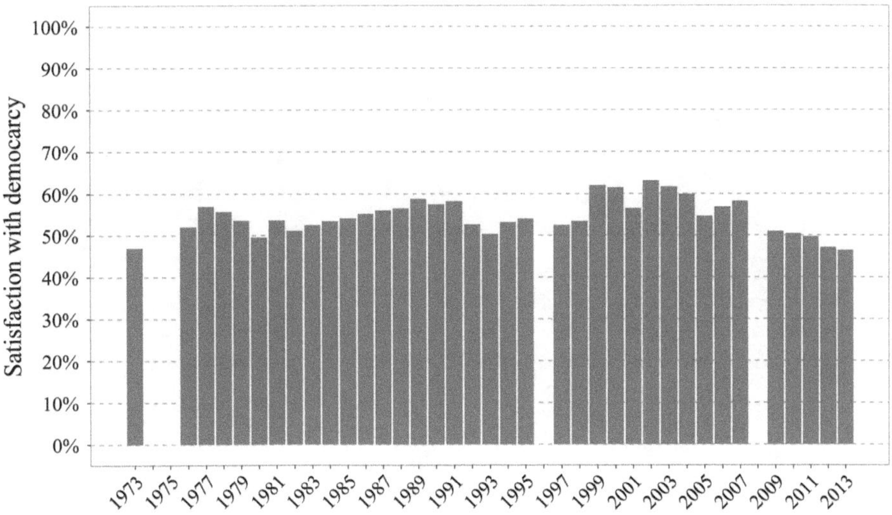

Fig. 2.6 Satisfaction with democracy in the European Union, 1973–2013. Note: Annual averages for member states of the EC/EU in accordance with their historical composition. Indicator: "On the whole, are you very satisfied, fairly satisfied, not very satisfied, or not at all satisfied with the way democracy works in [country]?" Percentages of "very satisfied" and "fairly satisfied" are shown. Source: Schmitt and Scholz (2005), Eurobarometer 2002–2013

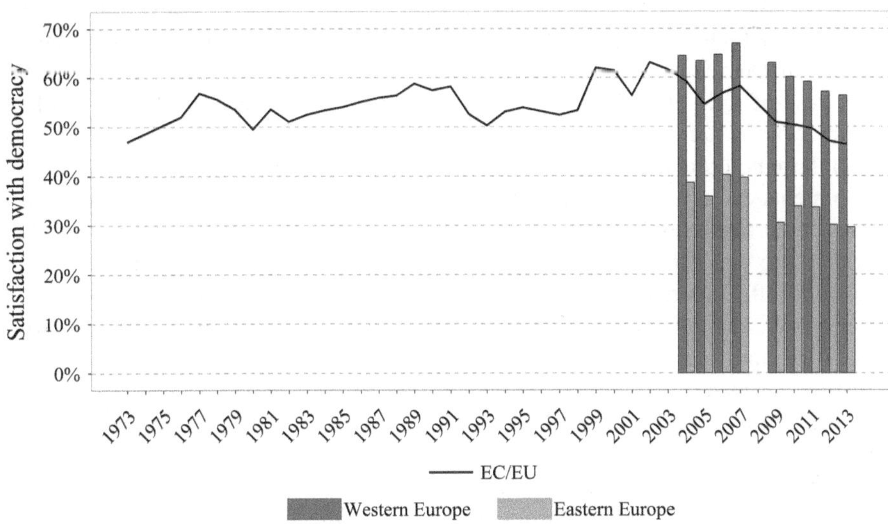

Fig. 2.7 Satisfaction with democracy in the European Union: Western and Eastern Europe compared, 1973–2013. Note: Annual averages for member states of the EC/EU in accordance with their historical composition. Source: Schmitt and Scholz (2005), Eurobarometer 2002–2013

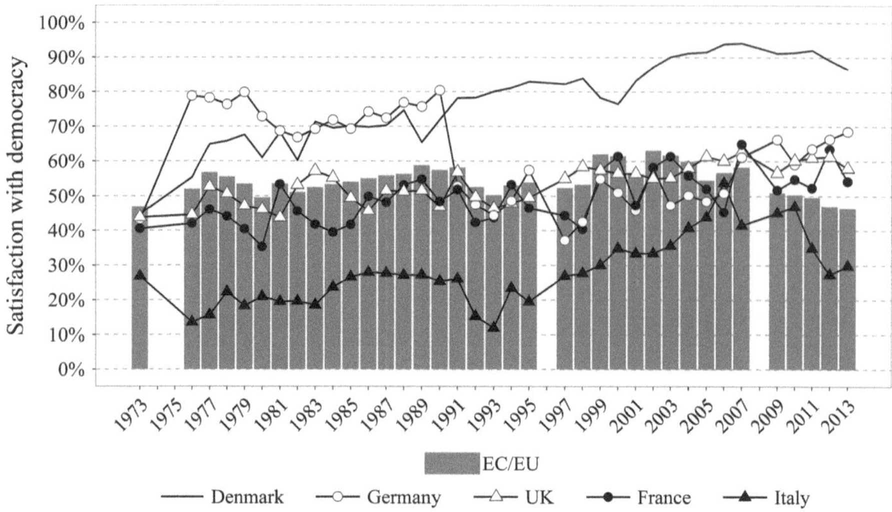

Fig. 2.8 Satisfaction with democracy compared, 1973–2013. Note: Annual averages for member states of the EC/EU in accordance with their historical composition. Source: Schmitt and Scholz (2005), Eurobarometer 2002–2013

Germans fell dramatically upon reunification, but from 2003 rose continually to well above the EU average. Although, as expected, satisfaction rates in individual countries fluctuated much more strongly, they do not point to a trend running contrary to Democracy Barometer quality figures. Things are strikingly different in the case of Italy. The Democracy Barometer quality indicators show a marked deterioration in Italian democracy from the second half of the 1990 to 2010. This period largely coincides with the phase in which three successive Berlusconi governments decisively shaped politics and how politics handled democratic institutions and procedures. But Italians' satisfaction with their democracy developed in precisely the opposite direction. It increased continuously and significantly from 1994 to 2010. Expert appraisal and citizen assessment thus pointed in opposing directions. It was only when the scandals and trials concerning Berlusconi, as well as national and international criticism, began to multiply that satisfaction ratings markedly dropped once again. Over the past 10 (8) years, citizens in France and the United Kingdom have expressed above average satisfaction with their democracy, whereas the Democracy Barometer gives them scores well below the average. Apart from such interesting divergence between "objective" and "subjective" evaluations of democracy in particular countries, the main message is clear: on average the Eurobarometer surveys of the past four decades lend no support to any assumption of crisis in the established European democracies. Citizens do not see their democracy in crisis.

The correlation of the satisfaction with democracy (Eurobarometer) with the quality of democracy (Democracy Barometer) reveals a considerable positive correlation (Pearson's $r = 0.81, p = 0.00$). The subjective (satisfaction) and the objective (quality)

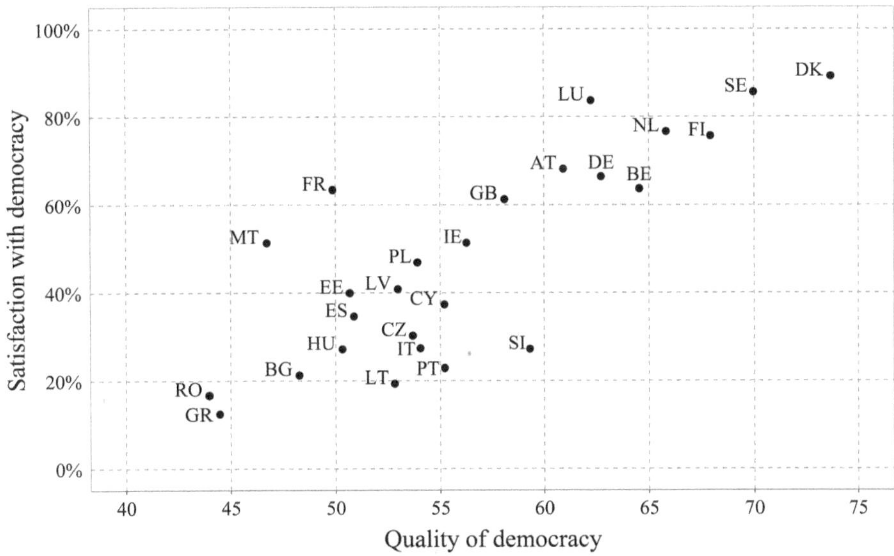

Fig. 2.9 Satisfaction with democracy and the quality of democracy in the European Union (EU-27), 2012. Note: Democracy Barometer data for Slovakia is missing. Source: Bochsler et al. (2014); Eurobarometer 2012

dimensions of the democracies of the European Union are closely positively correlated (2012). Thus, expert ratings and the assessment by the demos coincide. This positive correlation remains—although slightly weakened—if the whole period between 1990 and 2012 for all EU countries is considered (Pearson's $r = 0.76$, $p = 0.00$). Consequently, the quality of democracy corresponds to the citizens' satisfaction: if the former is high, the latter is high as well and vice versa. In this context, France can be considered a moderate outlier since the satisfaction with democracy within the *Grande Nation* ranks considerably higher than expert judgment might suggest (see Fig. 2.9).

The holistic perspective is instructive, but it does not suffice to show shifts in citizens' satisfaction with and trust in individual institutions. Thus one of the claims about crisis posits that even if general approval of democracy as a system is not declining, the level of trust is shifting within the institutional system of representative democracy (see, e.g., Zürn 2011). Trust in the "majoritarian" core institutions such as parties, parliaments, and governments is declining, while trust in "non-majoritarian" institutions such as the military, police, and judiciary is increasing. And such a trend is indeed apparent. Over the period for which solid and comparable Eurobarometer survey data are available, trust in parliaments and governments declined continuously. From an average level of 50%, trust in the two key representative institutions both fell to 30%. Trust in "the" parties remained at the extremely low level of 20%.[4] By contrast, the "non-majoritarian" institutions of the

[4]It should, however, be pointed out that these ratings turn out quite differently if respondents are asked instead about their subjective appreciation of representation. Asked whether they felt

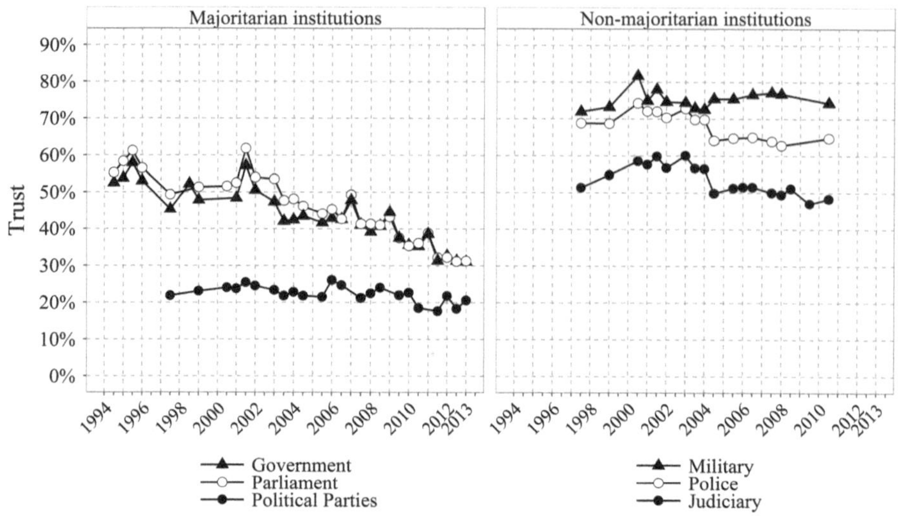

Fig. 2.10 Trust in national state institutions in the European Union, 1994–2013/1997–2011. Note: Semiannual averages for member states of the EC/EU in accordance with their historical composition. Indicator: "For each of the following institutions, please tell me if you tend to trust it or tend not to trust it." Source: Eurobarometer 1994–2013

state enjoyed high and stable trust. "Non-majoritarian" institutions are institutions whose personnel are not chosen by citizens and which perform governmental administrative functions but not democratic representative functions. This is a paradox of democracy: the institutions whose members can be elected by citizens are little trusted by the electorate; by contrast, the institutions in which office holders are not subject to the democratic will of citizens enjoy their confidence. A shift in preferences seems to be taking place in the minds of citizens: expertise, unpolitical administration, and rapid decision hierarchies are valued over voice, pluralistic competition, parliamentary deliberation, and the limited capability of governments to solve problems. If this supposition is correct—and the data suggest that it is—we must conclude that the value system of citizens is undergoing creeping de-democratization. Participation and representation are being left by the wayside and are little appreciated. What is preferred are politically neutral, hierarchically organized institutions in which expertise and efficiency are assumed to reign in the place of "partisan bickering" (see Fig. 2.10).

There are limits to how instructive surveys can be. A great deal depends on formulation, context, and the point in time. If the data alone, without complementary indicators or theoretical background, are treated as the chief evidence for certain trends and tendencies, they can lead to one-sided conclusions. In our specific

themselves to be well represented by at least one national party, more than half the respondent citizens of EU countries gave an affirmative answer (The Comparative Study of Electoral Systems 2013).

case, it is therefore advisable to compare the falling or low survey ratings for parties, parliaments, and governments with voter turnout. Solicited attitudes are thus confronted by the actual political action of citizens. At least for those citizens who no longer have any confidence in the three representative institutions, the rational conclusion would be to abstain from voting. Falling voter turnout would be the result, even if not every voter thinks and acts rationally.

2.3 Voter Turnout

In fact, average voter turnout in Western Europe fell continuously between 1975 and 2010, from 84% to around 75%. This growing abstentionism is to be understood as a general phenomenon occurring in almost all countries. However, at the beginning of the twenty-first century, the trend weakened, so that, although the lowest average rate of participation in Western Europe was recorded for 2010, the figure had fallen only minimally from that for 2002 (−0.4%). In Eastern Europe, the rate of participation fell more strongly. The "founding elections" in the early 1990s had been accompanied by great expectations for democracy. About 80% of Eastern European citizens went to the polls. This figure was just above the Western European average for the same period. Just under 20 years later, only 58% of voters in Eastern Europe exercised their right to vote. In two decades, voter turnout in Eastern Europe fell by 22 percentage points. This is indeed dramatic; it expresses disappointment, indifference, and political apathy, especially since the lack of conventional political participation was counterbalanced even less than in the West by unconventional forms. Differences in the development curves of voter turnout, like the differences in quality between countries in Democracy Barometer surveys and measurements, show that caution is called for when talking about a crisis of democracy per se (see Fig. 2.11).

If we consider the countries with the highest and lowest voter turnout in Europe, we find dramatic differences. Whereas in Malta, turnout over the last four decades was over 90% (1975–2010), in Poland it has since 1990 mostly been well under the 50% mark. The highest voter turnout in a large European country without compulsory voting was recorded in Sweden with an average of 86.5% between 1975 and 2010.[5] The low turnout of voters in Switzerland is a special case, since the political system includes a differentiated referendum system and because the importance of general elections is limited; participation by all major parties in government is provided for from the outset in Swiss consensus democracy. The fall in voter turnout in Eastern Europe is dramatic. Even in the best Eastern European "performer," Slovakia, voter turnout fell from over 95% (1990) to below 60% (2011). The decline in turnout for elections to the European Parliament is also cause for

[5]Voter turnout ranking for the period 1975–2010 is Malta 95.6%, Belgium 92.5%, Luxembourg 89.0%, Iceland 87.0%, Sweden 86.5%, and Denmark 86.0%.

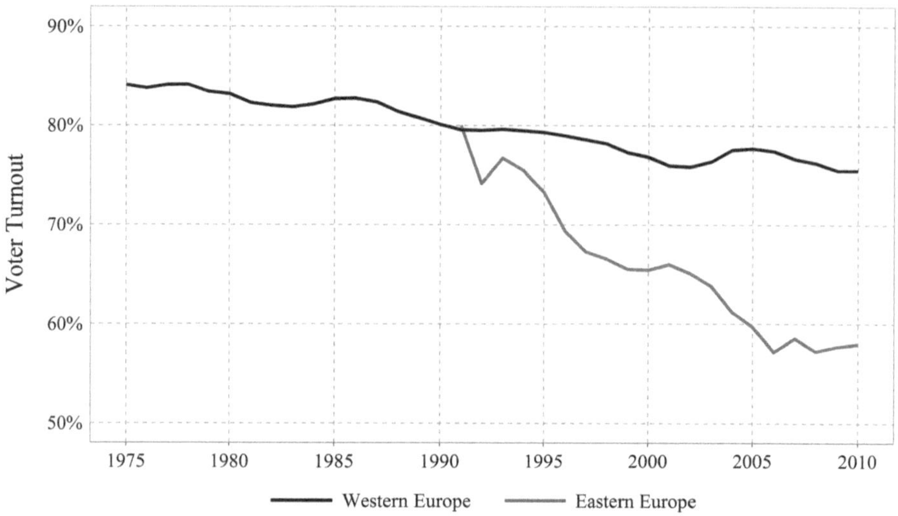

Fig. 2.11 Development of voter turnout in Western and Eastern Europe, 1975/1991–2010. Note: Annual averages, EU-28 + Iceland, Norway, and Switzerland. Only data on national lower houses of parliament were taken into account. Source: WZB (2014)

concern, pointing above all to the meager and decreasing democratic legitimation of this institution. Turnout for these elections is now below the lowest in all national democracies in Europe. This is a serious warning against overoptimism about the real possibilities for democratizing political spaces beyond the nation state.

In terms of the criteria of descriptive representation, women continue to be underrepresented in the parliaments of established democracies. On the other hand, the history of female representation in democratic parliaments can also be interpreted as a success story. It has increased from year to year, and there are no evident reasons why this trend should be interrupted in the future. To this extent, established democracies were doubtless in better condition in 2013 than in the decades before the turn of the millennium when post-democracy is claimed to have arrived.[6] This is first evidence in this book that, depending on the field and the country concerned, the quality of democracy improved or deteriorated. Differences between countries are again made clear in Fig. 2.12, if we compare Sweden, the country with the highest rate of female representation, and Japan, which had the smallest proportion of female members of parliament. In Sweden the figure was just below 50% and in Japan less than 10% in 2013 (see Fig. 2.13).

The statistics presented in this intermediate chapter are deliberately kept at a descriptive level. However, they have been calculated systematically for a broad sample of countries over an extensive time series but differ from the anecdotal and

[6]As the individual studies in this volume show, post-democracy is not to be dismissed in toto; what cannot pass, however, is the empirically untenable claim that democracy per se has its best times behind it.

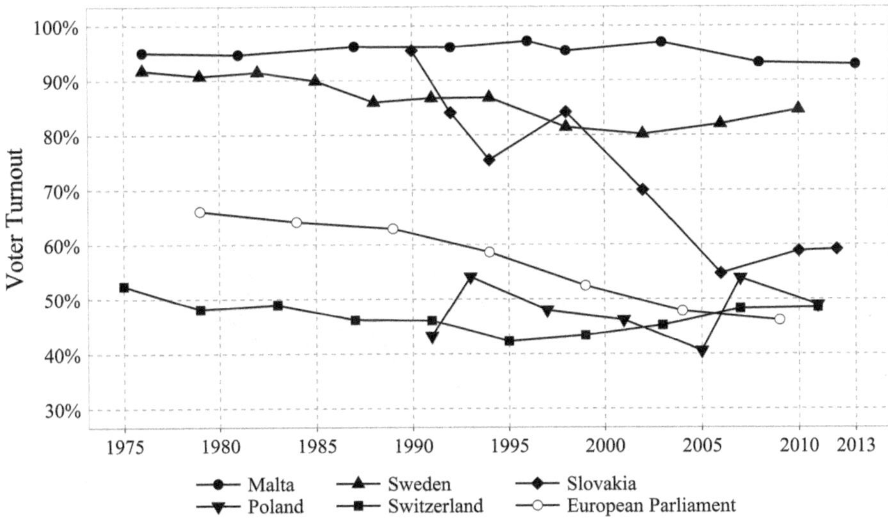

Fig. 2.12 Development of voter turnout in Europe compared, 1975/1990–2013. Note: Included are the countries with the highest and lowest average voter turnout in Western and Eastern Europe. On average, Sweden has the highest voter turnout in Western Europe if European microstates and countries with compulsory voting are excluded. Also shown is the voter turnout in elections to the European Parliament. Source: WZB (2014), European Parliament (2009)

singular data of the sort sometimes used in the theoretical crisis literature as "empirical" confirmation of the crisis thesis. At the highest level of aggregation, the objective measurements of the Democracy Barometer and the subjective survey responses do not point to any "crisis" of established democracies. Below this level, however, the subtrends described can be discerned, which point to a decline in participation, an increase in social selection in political participation, and waning trust in the core institutions of representative democracy. Constants of democracy appear to be changing, the causes of which need to be investigated in greater depth than summary quality indices and surveys allow. The present book is devoted to such analyses.

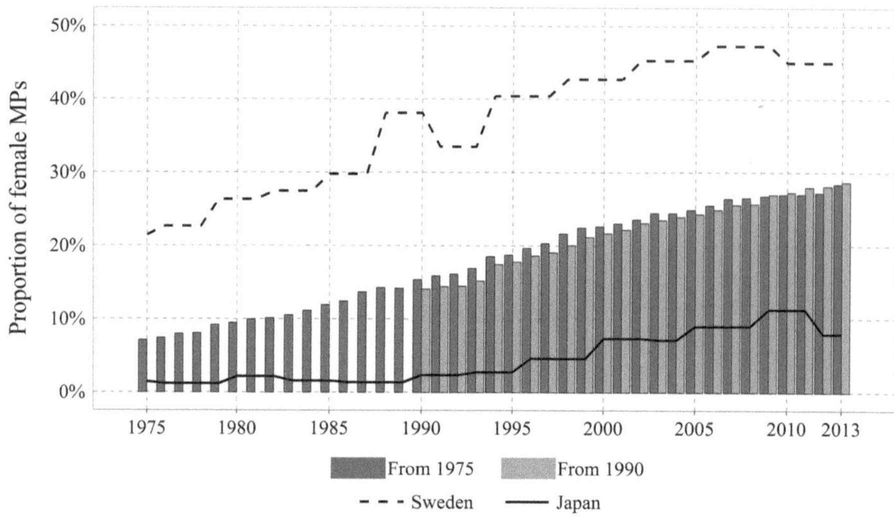

Fig. 2.13 Average proportion of female members in national parliaments, 1975/1990–2013. Note: Annual averages. Owing to the lack of data, the long time series (from 1975) contains only a limited sample of the 30 best democracies (Australia, Belgium, Denmark, Germany, Finland, France, United Kingdom, Ireland, Italy, Japan, Canada, Malta, Netherlands, New Zealand, Norway, Austria, Sweden, Switzerland, United States, Cyprus). The time series from 1990 takes account of all the 30 best democracies of the Democracy Barometer. Only data on national lower houses of parliament were taken into account. Also shown are countries that during the period under review had on average the highest and lowest percentages of female members of parliament. Source: IPU Parline Database (2014)

References

Bochsler, D., Merkel, W., Bousbah, K., Bühlmann, M., Giebler, H., Hanni, M., Heyne, L., Müller, L., Ruth, S., & Wessels, B. (2014). *Democracy barometer. Codebook for blueprint dataset version 4*. Aarau: Zentrum für Demokratie.

Bühlmann, M., Merkel, W., Müller, L., & Weßels, B. (2012). The democracy barometer. A new instrument to measure the quality of democracy and its potential for comparative research. *European Political Science, 11*, 519–536. https://doi.org/10.1057/eps.2011.46.

Easton, D. (1965). *A systems analysis of political life*. Chicago: Phoenix.

European Parliament. (2009). *The European Parliament*. Accessed May 23, 2014, from http://www.europarl.europa.eu/aboutparliament/en/000cdcd9d4/Turnout-%281979-2009%29.html

Eurobarometer. (2013). European Community Studies 3 (1973)—Eurobarometer 79.3 (2013), TNS Opinion & Social, Brussels [Producer]; GESIS Data Archive: ZA0628-ZA5689.

IPU Parline Database. (2014). *Parline database*. Accessed May 23, 2014, from http://www.ipu.org/parline/parlinesearch.asp

Klingemann, H.-D., Fuchs, D., Fuchs, S., & Zielonka, J. (2006). Support for democracy and autocracy in Central and Eastern Europe. In H.-D. Klingemann, D. Fuchs, & J. Zielonka (Eds.), *Democracy and political culture in Eastern Europe* (pp. 1–22). London: Routledge.

Lauth, H.-J. (2004). *Demokratie und Demokratiemessung. Eine konzeptionelle Grundlegung für den interkulturellen Vergleich*. Wiesbaden: Verlag für Sozialwissenschaften.

Müller, T., & Pickel, S. (2007). Wie lässt sich Demokratie am besten messen? Zur Konzeptqualität von Demokratie-Indizes. *Politische Vierteljahresschrift: Zeitschrift der Deutschen Vereinigung für politische Wissenschaft, 48*(3), 511–539.

Schmidt, M. (2008). *Demokratietheorien. Eine Einführung*. Wiesbaden: Verlag für Sozialwissenschaften.

Schmitt, H., & Scholz, E. (2005). *The Mannheim Eurobarometer Trend File, 1970–2002*. Prepared by Zentralarchiv für Empirische Sozialforschung. ICPSR04357-v1. Mannheim, Germany: Mannheimer Zentrum für Europäische Sozialforschung and Zentrum für Umfragen, Methoden und Analysen [producers], 2005. Cologne, Germany: Zentralarchiv für Empirische Sozialforschung/Ann Arbor, MI: Inter-university Consortium for Political and Social Research [distributors], 2005-12-06. https://doi.org/10.3886/ICPSR04357.v1

The Comparative Study of Electoral Systems. (2013). CSES Module 3 Full Release [dataset]. March 27, 2013 version. https://doi.org/10.7804/cses.module3.2013-03-27. Accessed March 27, 2013, from www.cses.org

WZB. (2014). *Database "elections, parties, governments", research unit "democracy and democratization"*. Berlin: WZB Berlin Social Science Center. Accessed March 30, 2014.

Zürn, M. (2011). Perspektiven des demokratischen Regierens und die Rolle der Politikwissenschaft im 21. Jahrhundert. *Politische Vierteljahresschrift: Zeitschrift der Deutschen Vereinigung für politische Wissenschaft, 52*(4), 603–635.

Chapter 3
Political Inequality in Voting

Bernhard Weßels

3.1 Introduction

Voting is said to be the simplest form of political participation. In fact, participation rates in elections are higher than in other forms of political participation. This is due particularly to low levels of time commitment, information, and resources. The mass media provide the necessary information in an easily accessible form; the walk to the polling place is in most cases short. Turnout is accordingly much less socially selective in terms of socioeconomic resources and social status. Compared to other forms of participation, voting is considered "easy." However, the research literature also notes that choosing is not nearly as simple as it seems at first glance. Dalton and Wattenberg therefore gave their contribution to Finifter's *The State of the Discipline* the programmatic title *The Not So Simple Act of Voting* (Dalton and Wattenberg 1993). Subsequent studies have empirically investigated voting errors in electronic voting or voting in referendums and have shown that the act of voting is not as simple as is commonly assumed (Brouard and Tiberj 2006; Herrnson et al. 2008).

Voting, like any other decision, is by no means easy. The act of voting is not without preconditions, because voters have to make a reasoned choice. Therefore, even voting, considered relatively simple compared to other forms of political engagement, demands a certain investment in information gathering and time (Popkin et al. 1976). The resulting general hypothesis of this chapter is that there is inequality in voting, easily overlooked if only turnout and the turnout rates are considered.

B. Weßels (✉)
Department of Democracy and Democratization, WZB Berlin Social Science Center, Berlin, Germany

Department of Social Sciences, Humboldt-Universität zu Berlin, Berlin, Germany
e-mail: bernhard.wessels@wzb.eu

W. Merkel, S. Kneip (eds.), *Democracy and Crisis*,
https://doi.org/10.1007/978-3-319-72559-8_3

Talking about the inequality of voting therefore implies more than looking at differences in turnout. Participation in elections only makes sense for citizens and thus for representative democracy if citizens want to make a choice. Making a choice is demanding and under certain circumstances challenging. To investigate inequality in voting must therefore also address the question of possible inequalities in the preconditions for making a voting decision.

The focus of this chapter is accordingly on the preconditions for voting, how they are distributed across different social groups of voters, and what implications result from disparities in motivation and the quality of the choice itself. The assumption is that political inequality does not start with the translation of socioeconomic inequalities into participation rates but already with the preconditions for participation. This is also true for the (not so simple) act of voting.

Contrary to the popular view of the process, voting does not begin with going to the polling station and end with the electoral decision. Mackenzie and Rokkan described the path to electoral participation as like the process of getting married: "It may be said that electoral procedure is functionally analogous to procedure in a marriage ceremony: 'Do you take this man (or woman) to be your lawfully wedded husband (or wife)?' 'I do.' The point in time at which 'I do' is said is not psychologically a moment of choice or decision—that came earlier; it is the point at which an individual preference becomes a social commitment" (Mackenzie and Rokkan 1968, p. 5). The process of voting thus begins with the determination of a voting intention, a decision that is then converted into a vote in the booth. My analysis thus starts earlier, namely, with the socially induced inequality in the calculus of the voter.

There has been little empirical research on this aspect of political inequality in elections. Our empirical knowledge on the quality of voting choice is surprisingly sparse, although electoral research is advanced enough on political participation, political involvement, and political knowledge to allow tenable hypotheses to be advanced on inequality in the preconditions of political participation. Besides the research gap, a second reason for the importance of this issue is normative in nature. Democracy rests and is based on the assumption and normative claim of political equality. This claim addresses all aspects of political participation by citizens and thus also how voters come to their political decisions. If the quality of their decision depends on the socioeconomic resources available to individuals, this would violate the principle of political equality. This would require a political system to develop democracy in a way that enables citizens to participate in the elections on an equal footing.

The next section develops an analytical framework for examining inequality in voting on the basis of prior research on political inequality, followed by conceptual consideration of the preconditions for voting in section three. The fourth section operationalizes voter knowledge as a core precondition for voting and specifies the hypotheses. This is followed by analysis of the distribution of voter knowledge and the extent of socially induced inequality in the distribution of political knowledge. The sixth section examines whether the degree of socioeconomic inequality in society at large reinforces political inequality in voting by looking at differences in income distribution across countries as a determinant of individual-level political inequality. The chapter ends with conclusions about the consequences for democracy. The data used are post-election surveys of the *Comparative Study of Electoral Systems* (CSES, www.cses.org), module 3. This data set covers 41 countries and 50 elections with a total of more than 80,000 individuals (see Appendix 2).

3.2 Determinants of Inequality in Political Participation

Political inequality is a key topic in participation research, which is not surprising given that democracy is based on the sovereignty of the people and majority decisions on the basis of the political equality of citizens (Ranney and Kendall 1969). Robert A. Dahl (1997, p. 96) defined five criteria for democracy: effective participation, voting equality, enlightened understanding, control of the agenda, and inclusion.

For the question of equal preconditions for voting, the criteria of electoral equality and enlightened political understanding are of immediate relevance. Among other things, enlightened understanding has to do with the cognitive prerequisites for participation; voting equality implies that citizens are neither formally nor materially unequal. Dahl defines enlightened understanding as follows: "Each citizen has adequate and equal opportunity for discovering which of the possible choices on the matter to be decided would best serve the goals, values, or interests of the citizen, of others, and of the collectivity" (ibid., p. 97). Elections and effective participation are closely related, and both are subject to the principle of political equality: "Each member of the community must have the same chance as his fellows to participate in its total decision-making process" (Ranney and Kendall 1969, p. 49). It is certainly not too heroic an assumption that democracies diverge to varying degrees from this ideal; and the greater the deviation is, the lower will be the quality of democratic voting.

From the outset, participation research has had an eye on the social stratification of political participation. The classic study *Participation in America* by Verba and Nie shows for American society in the late 1960s that the more difficult a type of participation is or the more it requires from citizens, the more disproportionately high will be the participation rates of the better educated and wealthy citizens (Verba and Nie 1972, p. 95–101). This finding is not specific to the USA but a general phenomenon. The comparative follow-up study by Verba, Nie, and Kim confirmed the American result with similar findings for seven countries (Verba et al. 1978). The two political action studies of the late 1970s and the late 1980s confirmed the findings for an even larger number of countries (Barnes et al. 1979; Jennings and van Deth 1989). After more than twenty years, in 1995, Verba, Schlozman, and Brady showed that, despite the "participatory revolution," social change, and educational expansion, the early findings on the USA could still claim the same validity today.

Inequality in participation has consequences for political representation. Several studies show it is not only that the more affluent and better educated citizens participate more but also that there is greater congruence between their political orientations and those of political elites, i.e., their representatives, than there is between these elites and the less well-off. Higher participation leads to higher visibility of demands—as opposed to non-articulation—and thus to higher congruence between represented and representatives, producing higher responsiveness to the better-off (Verba and Nie 1972; Klingemann 1985). It is hardly controversial in research on political participation that social inequality translates into political inequality, with the consequence that not only participation rates differ but also the chances of being represented.

3.3 Preconditions for Voting

Why is the act of voting not so easy? Why can we speak of a "not so simple act of voting" (Dalton and Wattenberg 1993)? The preconditions for arriving at a voting choice are easily identified. They lie, however, not only in the hands of the voter. Thomassen (1994) rightly points out that parties must first present voters with distinguishable offers. Only then can voters meet the preconditions. Voters must have political preferences; they need to know the positions of political parties; they must compare their own objectives with those of parties and choose the one with which there is the greatest agreement (Pierce 1999, p. 9). These preconditions are not only essential for deliberative behavior when voting but also the minimal conditions under which a representative democracy—the responsible-party model—can work in accordance with the concept of democratic decision making.

These three aspects, the political offer of parties, the preconditions for voting, and the responsible-party model, all require voters to be informed. Collecting information involves effort and costs, so-called information costs (Popkin et al. 1976). Gathering information mainly costs time; processing information requires cognitive skills.

Political information ranges from such simple things as to know where the polling station is or the date of an election to complex matters like accurate knowledge of political institutions, processes, political parties, and candidates. The costs of obtaining and processing information that leads to a voting preference all come prior to voting. These aspects can thus also be seen as opportunity costs in the sense that citizens may regard other matters as more worthy of attention or urgent than voting or preparing to do so.

Information costs, let alone opportunity costs, are unequally distributed among citizens. The underlying argument is simple: costs are relative to the resources an individual has. In this sense, resources are assets and tools. One asset is the stock of information already available. An important tool is the ability to process new or additional information effectively. The crux of what it costs to vote is that the fewer assets and tools an individual has, the higher his or her information and opportunity costs will be. Higher costs reduce the probability that the necessary information will be collected. Because resources in terms of assets and tools are unequally distributed, information and opportunity costs are also unevenly distributed. The preconditions for voting are thus also unequally distributed.

What are the relevant resources? The usual suspects are education, income, and political knowledge. Political knowledge may also depend on the first two factors. The standard socioeconomic model of participation (SES) determines participation in terms of social position defined by profession, income, and education level (Verba and Nie 1972, Appendix 3). However, Verba, Nie, and Kim emphasized in 1978 that the SES model does not provide an explanation but only describes the phenomenon (Verba et al. 1978). They therefore modified their theoretical framework in their studies of the 1990s. They introduced the factors of the SES model from the perspective of a resource model. The most recent major study from this school speaks explicitly of a resource model of political participation (Brady et al. 1995; Verba et al. 1995). It is argued that the SES model lends itself perfectly to predicting the likelihood of political participation but not to explaining it, because the mechanisms operating between social status and political activity are not specified: "A resource-centered explanation of political activity, then, enhances the SES model by providing an interpretation of the way this model works" (Verba et al. 1995, p. 282). The authors define a concept of civic skills, including organizational skills among others. But income and education remain the key variables in the concept, complemented by the time-budget factor. The affinity of this approach with an investment model of rational action is obvious.

Education is human capital, income economic capital. Both can be invested directly or indirectly in political behavior. Human capital is a universal cognitive resource and can also be a tool. Economic capital can be viewed as universal, too, since it affects the time budget, very probably education and information, and certainly the motivation for political participation. Citizens with higher incomes have a greater "stake in the system," as Wolfinger and Rosenstone (1980) argue, and are therefore more motivated to participate.

Although these considerations relate to political participation, it is probably not unreasonable to assume that they also apply to political involvement, which goes beyond participation. Involvement includes assessing policy issues and searching for and processing information. Building on the findings of the latest participation research, a well-founded assumption is therefore that the conditions applicable to participation also apply to the preconditions for voting.[1] Returning to the prerequisites of voting and the functioning of representative democracy, the process underlying voting can best be described by the flow from preferences to evaluation to voting choice. Figure 3.1 illustrates the process of voting from the perspective of its preconditions.

[1]However, the intensity of preconditions varies across modes of participation. The more demanding a particular mode of participation is, the more preconditions have to be met.

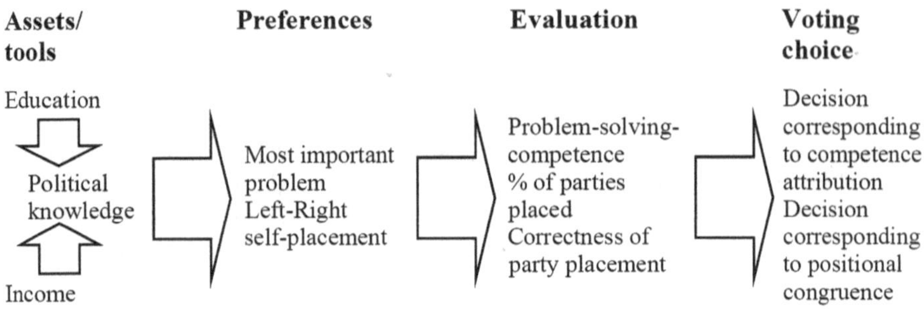

Fig. 3.1 Preferences, evaluations, and decisions. Source: Author's own figure

In the process of voting, evaluation depends on preferences. Without a benchmark, i.e., preferences, it is impossible to evaluate political offers. Whether voting decisions should be consistent with the result of evaluation could be considered a purely normative matter. However, in the context of the mandating process in party democracy and the idea of reasonable choices, consistency between evaluation and decision is a functional requirement. In this sense voting choice should depend on evaluation.

3.4 Individual Voter Knowledge and Its Distribution: Hypotheses and Operationalization

The preceding section has made clear why we can speak of a not so simple act of voting. If a voting decision is to be reasonable, voters require knowledge. Even such a seemingly simple matter as one's own preferences—what issues are important for me, where do I stand politically—can be answered only if certain preconditions are met. If I wish to express my preferences in the act of voting, I need to know what the political offer is in the light of my preferences in order to make a sensible choice. Altogether, knowledge of one's own preferences and the positions of parties and the ability to relate the two can be defined as the voter knowledge necessary to make a reasoned choice. Behind this may but does not necessarily have to be rational choice in the sense of selfish utility maximization. The substance of preferences does not matter. It is, however, important for choice behavior that any preference and any knowledge about political offers—objectively right or wrong—are cognitively related through evaluation, allowing a conclusion to be drawn for one's own decision. The voter must thus have knowledge to make a decision in voting.

3.4.1 Operationalization of Assets and Tools

Assets include income and education. Income is measured by income quintiles in a given country at a given time. Thus, not absolute income but relative income is used to compare income inequality across countries. Education is measured in terms of five categories that permit at least a ranking by data level (for international comparison: up to primary, secondary, post-secondary, university, university degree).

General political knowledge can be treated as an indicator of the tools available to the individual for assessing policy and politics. Political knowledge is measured on the basis of three questions differing in their degree of difficulty. The degree of difficulty is defined in terms of the proportion of respondents who gave a correct answer. Differences in difficulty are taken into account by weighting the correct response by the level of difficulty. The degree of difficulty is the ratio of correct answers to the simplest question to the second most difficult and the most difficult. If the simplest question is answered correctly by 80% of respondents, the next hardest by 60%, and the most difficult by 40%, a correct answer to the simplest question is given a weight of 1, the second most difficult a weight of $80/60 = 1.33$, and the most difficult a weight of $80/40 = 2$. The sum of the weighted values is the score for political knowledge, in our example 4.33.

3.4.2 Operationalization of Preferences

As a measure of political preferences, CSES 3 data provides two variables: what respondents regard as the most important problem facing the country (socio-tropic problem perception) and subjective left-right self-placement.

3.4.3 Operationalization of Evaluation

The evaluative aspect is concerned with whether the respondent names a party or candidate who can solve the most important problem and by estimation of the position of political parties on the left-right dimension. Identification of a party or candidate with the greatest competence to solve the most important problem is a binary variable (yes/no) for the respective party. Evaluation resulting from self and party positioning on the left-right scale is the distance between the respondent and the party (proximity).

As far as measuring voter knowledge on the basis of left-right party placement is concerned, it should be remembered that the number of parties to be assessed differs from country to country. In general, up to six parties can be positioned, but there are party systems with only two relevant parties. Because the measure is to provide information on how complete knowledge is about a given system, the number of parties positioned by a respondent is calculated as a percentage of possible placements in a country (party placement in %). Another variable evaluating voting knowledge addresses the correctness of party placement. It is calculated as the sum of absolute differences between placement by a respondent and the mean for all respondents, standardized by the number of parties placed (correctness of party placement).

3.4.4 Operationalization of the Voting Decision

With regard to electoral choice, the question is the degree to which choice is consistent with evaluation. As we have seen, two measures are available for evaluation: the identification of a party or candidate competent to solve the most important problem and the distance between respondent and party on the left-right dimension. In order to obtain a measure of proximity, the distance is subtracted from the most proximate value, 10.

The variables of voter knowledge (preferences, evaluation, decision) show significant variations. Political knowledge, the scale resulting from values weighted by difficulty, shows a minimum of 0 (no correct answer) to 4.77 (three correct answers) with a mean of 1.99. In identifying the most important problem, 81% of respondents name one. Seventy-nine percent of respondents place themselves on the left-right scale.

Evaluations vary considerably, too. On average, 62% identify a party or a candidate able to solve the most important problem facing the country. Seventy-six percent place parties on the left-right scale. The correctness of party placement ranges from 0.11 to 8 and on average 1.78 scale points on an 11-point scale.

For voting choice, proximity to the party voted for is on average 8.65 of a maximum of 10 and a minimum of 0. For voting in accordance with the evaluation of competence, the mean is 0.62, the minimum 0 and maximum 1 (see Table 3.1).

In sum, the measures for voting knowledge all show high variance, indicating significant differences among respondents. In other words, voting knowledge is unevenly distributed. If it is true that the unequal distribution of resources not only translates into different rates of participation but also into differences in voter knowledge, this has consequences. The ability to develop one's own preferences, to compare one's own preferences with the political offer, and the quality of voting—the fit between evaluation and choice—would differ depending on individual resources. The consequence would be a different degree of reasoned voting depending on resources. Table 3.2 summarizes the respective hypothesis.

Table 3.1 Key figures for voter knowledge

	Mean	Minimum	Maximum
Knowledge, preferences			
Political knowledge	1.99	0.00	4.77
Naming problem	0.81	0.00	1.00
Left-right self-placement	0.79	0.00	1.00
Evaluation			
Naming competent party	0.62	0.00	1.00
Left-right party placement	0.76	0.00	1.00
Correctness of party placement	1.78	0.11	7.79
Choice			
Proximity to party voted for	8.65	0.00	10.00
Competent party voted for	1.00	0.00	2.00

Note: Own calculations, *Comparative Study of Electoral Systems* (CSES) data. On countries and elections, see Appendix

Table 3.2 Hypotheses on resources and voter knowledge

	Assets	Tool	Hypothesis
Education	General knowledge	Capacity to gather information	Higher level of education leads to greater voter knowledge
Political information	Level of information	Evaluation and selection of information	Better information leads to greater voter knowledge regardless of education level
Income	Time budget, general resource indicator		Higher income leads to greater voter knowledge
Voter knowledge			Greater voter knowledge leads to better voting choice

3.5 Unequal Distribution of Voting Knowledge

If voter knowledge is not only different but systematically different because of inequalities in education, income, and political knowledge, the result is political inequality. To determine the extent of inequality, reference points have to be defined. For education, the reference is the group of respondents with low education (primary education); the comparison group are those with higher education (university degree). For income, the reference is the group with low income defined as the lowest income quintile. The comparison group are those with high income defined by the highest quintile. The difference defines the range in voter knowledge between respondents with lower and higher education and lower and higher income, respectively. On average, citizens deviate from the mean of lower groups positively and from the mean of higher groups negatively. The degree to which deviations occur defines the range of socially induced inequality in voter knowledge.

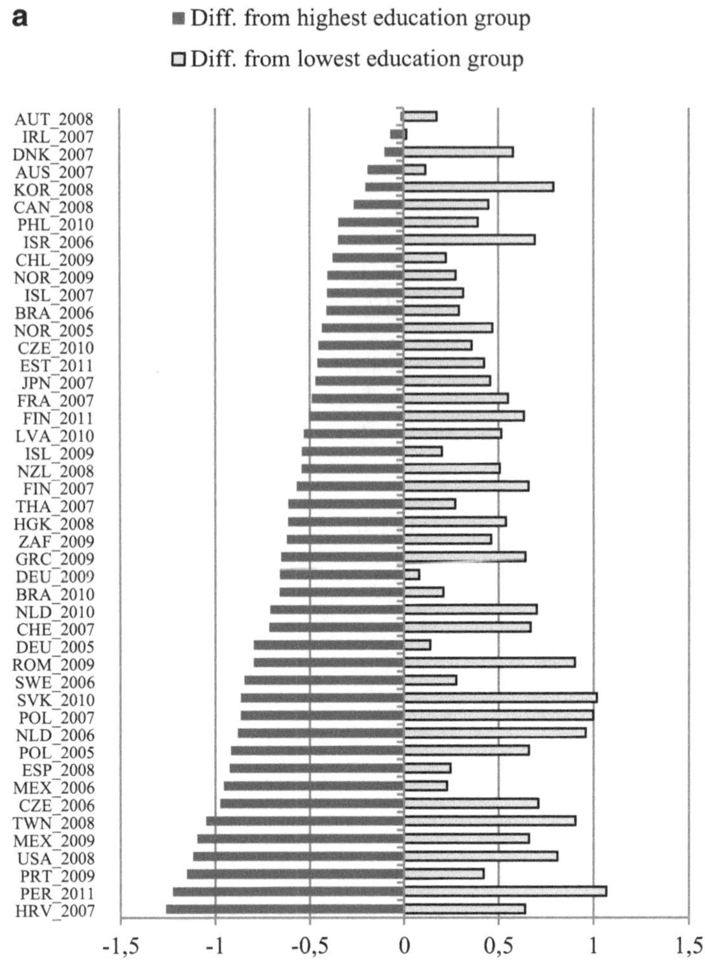

Fig. 3.2 (**a**) Inequality in the distribution of political knowledge measured by the population mean in relation to low and high educational groups. (**b**) Inequality in the distribution of political knowledge measured by the population mean in relation to low- and high-income groups. Note: Mean difference in the population to give comparison group, own calculations

Not only individuals differ in voter knowledge. The extent of inequality in voter knowledge between social groups also varies strongly from country to country. Taking political knowledge as an example, Fig. 3.2a and b show the ranges for this component of voter knowledge. The general message of the figure is that there is a vast range of inequality in voter knowledge for all aspects, i.e., also for evaluation and choice.

The length of the bars of a country indicates two things. If the bar for the difference to higher education or income group is longer than the bar for the difference to low groups, the mean of society or its center of gravity is closer to the low groups. If the bar is longer for the comparison to the low educational and

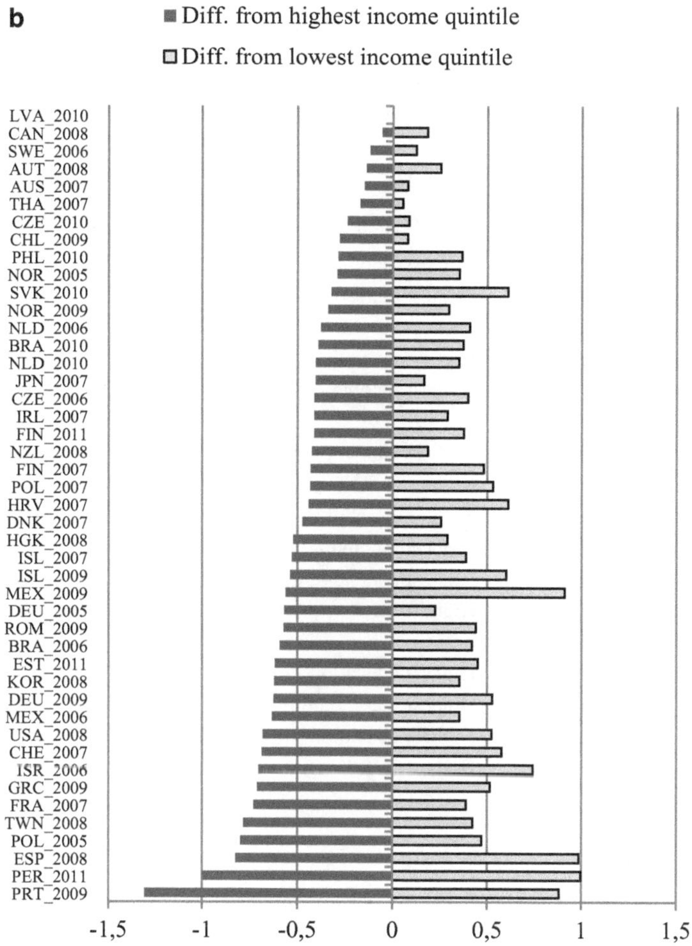

Fig. 3.2 (continued)

income groups than the higher groups, the average citizen is closer to high educational and income groups. Comparison between income groups does not imply any judgment about the relative wealth of a society compared to another society because the income measure is not absolute but relative.

Furthermore, the comparison between the bars for education and income show that the two social characteristics do not produce the same inequality in voter knowledge. The ranking of countries—sorted by inequality due to education in Fig. 3.2a and by inequality due to income in Fig. 3.2b—differs strongly. A different social inequality thus produces different political inequality.

The range of inequality in political knowledge shows high variation. In terms of education and income effects, Portugal and Peru both show strong inequality in political knowledge. The USA shows significant inequality effects, as well.

Table 3.3 Inequality in voter knowledge between social groups with the highest education and income groups as reference

Group under study	Education	Low	Low	High	High
	Income	Low	High	Low	High
	Comparison group	Difference of group under study to comparison group			
Knowledge and preferences					
Political knowledge	Highest education group	-1.30	-0.78	-0.28	0.15
	Highest income quintile	-1.12	-0.55	-0.11	0.31
Problem named	Highest education group	-0.14	-0.04	-0.02	0.02
	Highest income quintile	-0.14	-0.03	-0.01	0.02
Left-right self-placement	Highest education group	-0.19	-0.07	-0.03	0.02
	Highest income quintile	-0.17	-0.05	-0.02	0.03
Evaluation					
Competent party named	Highest education group	-0.13	-0.05	-0.04	0.03
	Highest income quintile	-0.14	-0.05	-0.04	0.02
Left-right party placement	Highest education group	-0.22	-0.11	-0.03	0.02
	Highest income quintile	-0.19	-0.08	-0.01	0.04
Correctness of party placement	Highest education group	0.04	-0.07	-0.32	-0.40
	Highest income quintile	0.07	-0.14	-0.22	-0.35
Choice					
Proximity to party voted for	Highest education group	-0.33	-0.11	-0.08	-0.02
	Highest income quintile	-0.31	-0.10	-0.02	0.01
Competent party voted for	Highest education group	-0.12	-0.09	-0.06	0.01
	Highest income quintile	-0.13	-0.09	-0.09	0.00

Note: Own calculations, *Comparative Study of Electoral Systems* (CSES) data. On countries and elections, see Appendix

In other countries such as Sweden, which has the weakest inequality effects of income, but shows quite strong inequality in political knowledge due to education, the effects of education and income are quite different. For both aspects Germany ranks in midfield. However, the distance of the average citizen to high education and income groups is particularly pronounced. German society as a whole is thus closer to the less privileged.

In what follows, differences produced by the combination of income and education will be investigated because the problematic point of socially induced inequality is that those sections of the population that are strong in resources have an advantage or privilege. The lowest education group will be compared with the highest and the lowest income group with the highest in combination. The combinations for comparison are education low-income high, education high-income low, both low, and both high. Table 3.3 shows the results, which generally correspond to expectations.

Results in line with the hypotheses would always show a large difference in voter knowledge between low education and low income compared to high education and high income and a smaller difference in mixed combinations like low education-high income or vice versa. Table 3.3 shows that this is indeed the case for all aspects: knowledge and preferences, evaluations, and decision. For correct party placement, the values are reversed because the scale for measuring correctness has high values if not correct and low if correct.

Table 3.3 clearly shows that there are significant differences between the least privileged segments of a society (low education and low income) and privileged education and income groups. For the less privileged, the score on political knowledge is 1.3 points lower than that for the highest education group. In terms of scale position, the difference in knowledge is thus some 30% in favor of the better educated. The difference is a little lower for income groups. Identification of the most important problem facing the country is about 14 percentage points lower in groups with low education and income as compared to groups with high education or income, and for left-right self-positioning the difference is 19, respectively, 17 percentage points. There are similar differences for evaluation. About 14% fewer citizens in the low education and income group identify a competent party compared to citizens with high education or income. The proportion of left-right party placement produces even bigger differences. The accuracy of party placement is about half a scale point on a ten-point scale lower for low education and income groups. Since the mean of the scale is 1.78, half a point can be regarded as a considerable difference. Finally, on the question of the degree to which voters opt for the most proximate and/or the most competent party, results again show considerable inequalities. Proximity to the elected party is a third of a scale point lower, and the proportion of voting for the party regarded as most competent is about 12 percentage points lower in the socially less privileged groups of society.

These results indicate that socially induced political inequality takes effect not only in turnout and preferences but also in voter choice because preferences are translated into choice less effectively and correctly in less privileged social groups.

3.6 Income Inequalities of Societies and the Inequality of Voting

The results presented so far point to socially induced political inequality. They show that political inequality interferes much earlier with individuals' capacity for political action than with voter turnout. Furthermore, results are very much in line with what research on inequality in political participation has to say. Is this a challenge to democracy that cannot be met? Do we have to accept these patterns of socially induced political inequality and thus accept the permanent violation of a core norm of democracy, namely, political equality?

Differences between countries in inequality between the less privileged and the most highly privileged members of society show that the degree of political inequality varies considerably. There are countries with rather small differences in voting knowledge between social groups and countries with huge differences.

Obviously, there are social, economic, and cultural contexts that are either conducive or detrimental to the translation of social into political inequality.

One possible explanation could lie in inequality and how it is perceived by citizens. Schattschneider in *The Semi-Sovereign People*, published in 1960, proposed an interesting hypothesis. He argues that the more the rich citizens of a society use their money to dominate the agenda and the subject matter of political debate, the more they push poorer population groups out of the political process. The assumed mechanism is that, due to the dominance of the better-off in the political discourse, the concerns of the poor are displaced so that participation in elections becomes meaningless for them.

He posits that this aspect—the increasing meaninglessness of elections for the less privileged—explains the low turnout in these groups (Schattschneider 1960, p. 102–106). This hypothesis can be applied here to the preconditions for voting. If elections become meaningless to the less privileged because they will not be heard anyway, they cannot be expected to invest in gathering and processing information, evaluating it, and taking it as a basis for political decisions. The underlying process rather suggests a vicious cycle progressively widening the gap between the less privileged and the privileged. With every vote less from the less privileged and with every less well-informed choice, the probability that their interests will be represented diminishes. This process reinforces itself with every election.

These considerations suggest that higher income inequality produces higher inequality in voter knowledge. Conversely, lower income inequality produces less inequality in voter knowledge. A developed welfare state that limits economic inequality would contribute to reducing political inequality. If we accept Schattschneider's hypothesis, this implies that the difference between lower and higher education or income groups in voter knowledge would be smaller in more egalitarian societies. The chain from social inequality to political inequality would at least to some extent be broken. Schattschneider's hypothesis could be rephrased as follows: the higher economic inequality in a society is, the larger is the difference in voter knowledge between low and high education and income groups.

A strategy adopted by Frederick Solt to investigate whether income inequality reduces voter turnout (Solt 2010) can be used to test this hypothesis. He estimates the individual probability of turnout with regression models and then looks at the relationship between predicted voter turnout and economic inequality. This strategy can also be applied to the various aspects of voter knowledge. Regression analysis allows the effect of a particular social characteristic on voting knowledge to be determined under the control of all other characteristics. Furthermore, the method allows controlling for country differences and the correction of clustered errors.

Because the aim is to determine the differences in the effect of social characteristics between contexts, i.e., the degree of income inequality in a society, the difference in voting knowledge between the lowest education or income group and the highest education or income group is the dependent variable (see Table 3.4). The dependent variables are thus those presented in Fig. 3.2a and 3.2b.

Table 3.4 Differences in voter knowledge, comparison of voter groups

Variables	Regression equation
Dependent variable	Difference voter knowledge to highest education/income group = $\alpha+$
Individual variables	β 1 education + β 2 income+
Macro variables	β 3 GDP per capita PPP + β 4 Gini(income) +
Interaction	β 5 income*Gini(income) + e

Note: Regression takes account of clusters (countries)

Regressions were performed for all elements of voting knowledge for each of the social contrast groups. There are eight aspects of voting knowledge and two contrast groups, which gives a total of 16 regressions.

The resulting estimated values for differences in voting knowledge are shown for countries starting with a Gini coefficient—the overall measure of income inequality in a society—below 25, in steps of five up to the countries with a Gini of 49, and those with a Gini of 50 and higher (see Appendix 3).

If the hypothesis is correct that inequality in voter knowledge is higher in countries with high economic inequality, the estimates for the distance of voter knowledge for educational and income groups should increase with the Gini. The expectation is that the relation between income inequality and socially induced political inequality will be approximately linear.

Figure 3.3 shows the values for inequality in voting knowledge across categories of income inequalities in society. Results correspond closely to expectations.

The lines represent the differences in voting knowledge between respondents and the highest education group and highest income group, respectively. It is not a comparison between contrast groups, i.e., lowest to highest, but effectively the mean of respondents including the higher educated or higher income group to the higher groups. Thus, it is a conservative test of inequality. Contrast group differences would be much larger.

Inequality does not increase linearly for every element of voting knowledge. The tendency, however, is clear: in societies with higher economic inequality, socially induced political inequality is higher, the effect of social differentiation on political inequality stronger. Thus, a reasonable conclusion is that political inequality is not inevitable, but can be addressed by political means. If a welfare state policy with an egalitarian orientation were to reduce income differences, it would probably have a negative effect on socially induced political inequality, i.e., lower it. Redistribution is thus one of the options open to politics. A second option not regarded as likely or feasible by many economists is to fence markets in such a way that economic inequalities simply do not rise to the level they have reached.

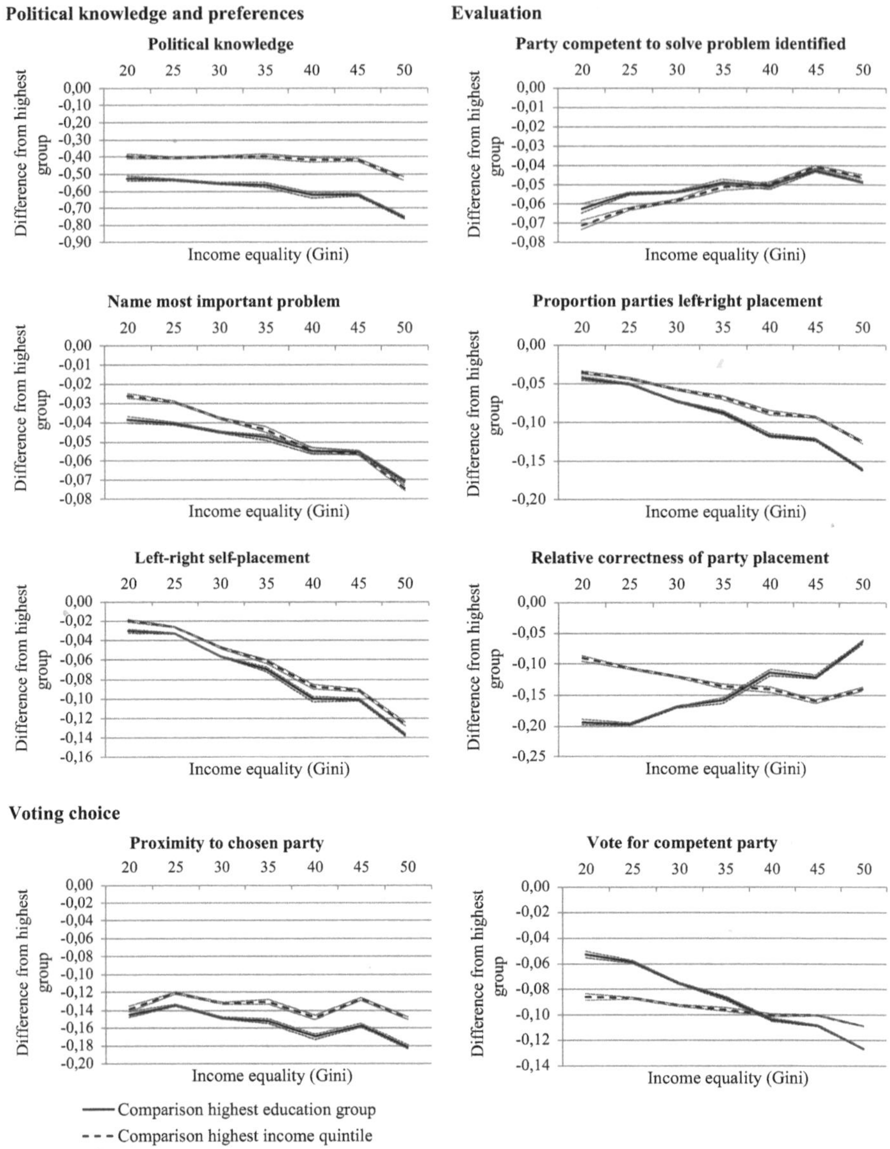

Fig. 3.3 Degree of political inequality in voter knowledge and economic inequality of societies. Source: Own calculations

3.7 Conclusions

Starting with the findings of political participation research on political inequality, the question has been raised whether political inequality does not begin even before participation in elections. More concretely, the issue addressed by this chapter is whether inequality does not start already with the preconditions for voting. The question is of relevance for participation research in general and for participation in elections in particular, because voting is regarded as the easiest mode of participation characterized by the lowest degree of political inequality. At the same time, it is the most important mode of participation in liberal democracies. If inequality occurs in this mode, it is safe to assume that it will be even higher in other modes of participation.

A theoretical framework of the preconditions for voting has been defined with voter knowledge as the core concept. The elements of voter knowledge define the voting process in terms of political knowledge, preferences, evaluation, and (quality of) choice. Empirical results support the hypothesis that already the preconditions for voting are characterized by socially induced political inequality. This finding is a challenge to democracy for two reasons. First, political inequality violates the core norm of democracy, political equality. Second, results suggest that the norm of political equality cannot be guaranteed by securing formal equality. Equality must also be guaranteed in the social and cognitive preconditions for political participation.

The importance of the problem arises from the fact that political inequality can produce a vicious circle harmful to democracy because inclusion of the less privileged may be progressively reduced. Lower turnout by less privileged social groups reduces the translation of existing preferences into election results. This commonplace of participation research is complemented by insight into another mechanism reducing the optimal translation of preferences into election results. Voter knowledge, including the sincere and accurate translation of preferences into voter choice, is unequally distributed across social groups. If such social phenomena translate into political action—or inaction—as Schattschneider's hypothesis suggests, the vicious cycle will become established: the less privileged do not participate in elections because elections become meaningless as they cannot find their preferences reflected in the election result which does not translate into political representation of their preferences. The lower the turnout and the less accurately preferences are translated into voter choices, the worse this will get. It is thus evident that socially induced political inequality poses a problem for democracy.

This situation raises the question of whether political inequality in voter knowledge in socially highly differentiated societies is inevitable. However, the results show clearly that there is not an inevitable level of socially induced political inequality. It varies considerably from country to country; and it varies not randomly but systematically with the degree of income inequality in society at large. Income inequality is accessible to political intervention. Welfare state measures are able to reduce it. In this sense, democracy itself can create the conditions demanded for democracy if it wishes to comply with its central norm of political equality. This will probably never be completely realized. However, the empirical results presented here show that margins matter. Even in highly modern market economies like Denmark, Sweden, or Norway income inequality is comparatively low, with the result that the translation of social differences between low and high education or low and high income into inequality in voter knowledge is very small. By contrast, countries with high income inequality like the USA, Mexico, or Chile show very large differences in voter knowledge between education and income groups. Thus, if democracy takes its own principles seriously, it has the means to produce the preconditions for attaining compliance with democratic principles.

Appendixes

Appendix 1 Wording of Questions

1. *Preferences*

   Most important problem:
   Q2a. What do you think is the most important political problem facing [COUNTRY] today?
   Q2b. What do you think is the second most important political problem facing [COUNTRY] today?
   Left-right self-placement:
   Q13. Where would you place yourself on this scale?
   00. LEFT 10. RIGHT

2. *Evaluation*

   Problem-solving competence:
   Q3a. Thinking of the most important political problem facing [COUNTRY]: which [party/presidential candidate] do you think is best in dealing with it?
   Q3b. And the second most important political problem facing [COUNTRY]: which [party/presidential candidate] do you think is best in dealing with it?
   Left-right placement of parties:
   Q11a-i. In politics people sometimes talk of left and right. Where would you place [PARTY A] on a scale from 0 to 10 where 0 means the left and 10 means the right?
   Using the same scale, where would you place [PARTY B]?
   Where would you place [PARTY C]?
   Where would you place [PARTY D]?
   Where would you place [PARTY E]?
   Where would you place [PARTY F]?
   00. LEFT 10. RIGHT

Appendix 2

Used CSES III Post-Election Studies Comparative Study of Electoral Systems, www.cses.org

Countries and years		
AUS_2007	HGK_2008	POL_2007
AUT_2008	HRV_2007	PRT_2009
BLR_2008	IRL_2007	ROM_2009
BRA_2006	ISL_2007	SVK_2010
BRA_2010	ISL_2009	SVN_2008
CAN_2008	ISR_2006	SWE_2006
CHE_2007	JPN_2007	THA_2007
CHL_2009	KOR_2008	TUR_2011
CZE_2006	LVA_2010	TWN_2008
CZE_2010	MEX_2006	URY_2009
DEU_2005	MEX_2009	USA_2008
DEU_2009	NLD_2006	ZAF_2009
DNK_2007	NLD_2010	
ESP_2008	NOR_2005	
EST_2011	NOR_2009	
FIN_2007	NZL_2008	
FIN_2011	PER_2011	
FRA_2007	PHL_2010	
GRC_2009	POL_2005	

Total of post-election surveys:	50
Total number of respondents	80.163
Average number of respondents per study	1.603
Number of respondents (minimum)	815
Number of respondents (maximum)	4.495

Number of studies per year		
Years	N	%
2005	3	6
2006	6	12
2007	11	22
2008	10	20
2009	10	20
2010	6	12
2011	4	8
	50	100

Appendix 3

Table 3.5 Countries by Gini groups

Gini	Countries
Up to 24.9	DNK_2007, SVN_2008, SWE_2006
Up to 29.9	AUT_2008, CHE_2007, CZE_2006, DEU_2005, DEU_2009, FIN_2007, FIN_2011, ISL_2007, ISL_2009, NOR_2005, NOR_2009
Up to 34.9	AUS_2007, CAN_2008, CZE_2010, ESP_2008, EST_2011, FRA_2007, GRC_2009, HRV_2007, IRL_2007, NLD_2006, NLD_2010, POL_2005, POL_2007, ROM_2009, TWN_2008
Up to 39.9	ISR_2006, JPN_2007, LVA_2010, NZL_2008, PRT_2009 Up to 44.9 KOR_2008, PHL_2010, TUR_2011
Up to 49.9	BLR_2008, MEX_2009, PER_2011, URY_2009, USA_2008
Higher	BRA_2006, BRA_2010, CHL_2009, HGK_2008, MEX_2006, THA_2007, ZAF_2009

Source: Distribution of Family Income, *The World Factbook*. https://www.cia.gov/library/publications/the-world-factbook/fields/2172.html. Accessed 04.02.2014

References

Barnes, S. H., Allerbeck, K. R., Farah, B. G., Heunks, F. J., Inglehart, R. F., Jennings, M. K., Klingemann, H.-D., Marsh, A., & Rosenmayr, L. (1979). *Political action: Mass participation in five western democracies*. Beverly Hills, CA & London: Sage.

Brady, H. E., Verba, S., & Lehman Schlozman, K. (1995). Beyond SES: A resource model of political participation. *The American Political Science Review, 89*(2), 271–294.

Brouard, S., & Tiberj, V. (2006). The French referendum: The not so simple act of saying nay. *PS: Political Science and Politics, 39*(2), 261–268.

Dahl, R. A. (1997). *Toward democracy: A journey. Reflections: 1940–1997* (Vol. Vol. 1). Berkeley: Institute of Governmental Studies Press.

Dalton, R. J., & Wattenberg, M. P. (1993). The not so simple act of voting. In A. W. Finifter (Ed.), *Political science. The state of the discipline II* (pp. 193–218). Washington, DC: American Political Science Association.

Herrnson, P. S., Niemi, R. G., Hanmer, M. J., Bederson, B. B., Conrad, F. G., & Traugott, M. W. (2008). *Voting technology: The not-so-simple act of casting a ballot*. Washington, DC: The Brookings Institution.

Jennings, M. K., & van Deth, J. W. (1989). *Continuities in political action*. Berlin and New York: Walter de Gruyter.

Klingemann, H.-D. (1985). *Formen, Bestimmungsgründe und Konsequenzen politischer Beteiligung*. Berlin: Freie Universität, Universitätsdruck.

Mackenzie, W. J. M., & Rokkan, S. (1968). Elections. In D. L. Sills (Ed.), *International encyclopedia of the social sciences* (pp. 1–21). New York: Macmillan.

Pierce, R. (1999). Mass-Elite issue linkages and the responsible party model. In W. E. Miller, R. Pierce, J. Thomassen, R. Herrera, S. Holmberg, P. Esaisson, & B. Weßels (Eds.), *Policy representation in western democracies* (pp. 9–32). Oxford: Oxford University Press.

Popkin, S., Gorman, J. W., Phillips, C., & Smith, J. A. (1976). What have you done for me lately? Toward an investment theory of voting. *The American Political Science Review, 70*(3), 779–805.
Ranney, A., & Kendall, W. (1969). Basic principles for a model of democracy. In C. F. Cnudde & D. E. Neubauer (Eds.), *Empirical democratic theory* (pp. 41–63). Chicago: Markham.
Schattschneider, E. E. (1960). *The semi-sovereign people. A realist's view of democracy in America*. New York, NY: Holt.
Solt, F. (2010). Does economic inequality depress electoral participation? Testing the Schattschneider hypothesis. *Political Behavior, 32*, 285–301.
Thomassen, J. (1994). Models of political representation: Failing democracy or failing models? In K. Jennings & T. E. Mann (Eds.), *Elections at home and abroad. Essays in honor of Warren E. Miller* (pp. 237–265). Ann Arbor, MI: University of Michigan Press.
Verba, S., & Nie, N. H. (1972). *Participation in America*. New York, NY: Harper & Row.
Verba, S., Nie, N. H., & Kim, J.-O. (1978). *Participation and political equality*. Cambridge: Cambridge University Press.
Verba, S., Lehman Schlozman, K., & Brady, H. E. (1995). *Voice and equality. Civic voluntarism in American politics*. Cambridge, MA: Harvard University Press.
Wolfinger, R. E., & Rosenstone, S. J. (1980). *Who votes?* New Haven, CT: Yale University Press.

Chapter 4
Are Programmatic Alternatives Disappearing? The Quality of Election Manifestos in 21 OECD Countries Since the 1950s

Andrea Volkens and Nicolas Merz

4.1 Introduction

In all modern democracies, political parties are attributed a key role in aggregating and articulating voter preferences (Webb et al. 2002) and in translating voter interests into political decisions (Pierce 1999; Kitschelt 2000; Montero and Gunther 2002; Lawson and Poguntke 2004). In this chain of delegation, party election manifestos are particularly important (Merz and Regel 2013). Only if citizens are offered programs in keeping with their varying political preferences can their interests be represented in parliament and, with corresponding majorities, pursued by governments. And only if the programmatic offer is clearly and visibly formulated can citizens identify the one that fits their preferences. On the supply side of democratic elections, the success of the representative process therefore relies on party programs offering clear alternatives.

In the eyes of many, parties are playing this key role less and less effectively. Falling numbers of party members and core voters and diminishing identification with parties are regarded as symptoms of a crisis in interest aggregation and representation (Dalton et al. 1984; Franklin et al. 1992; Daalder 2002; Dalton 2002; Mair et al. 2004; Thomassen 2005). In the media and among the public, the view prevails that parties are becoming less and less different from one another. In the 1960s, political scientists asserted that cleavage-based parties were turning into indistinguishable catch-all parties (Kirchheimer 1966; critical: Chap. 7) and in the 1990s that they were becoming cartel parties colluding to gain and stay in power, so that their election manifestos no longer differed from one another (Katz and Mair 1995). Rational choice theories predict that the positions of parties will converge if

A. Volkens · N. Merz (✉)
Department of Democracy and Democratization, WZB Berlin Social Science Center, Berlin, Germany
e-mail: andrea.volkens@wzb.eu; nicolas.merz@wzb.eu

W. Merkel, S. Kneip (eds.), *Democracy and Crisis*,
https://doi.org/10.1007/978-3-319-72559-8_4

they compete for voters in the center of the political spectrum to maximize their share of the vote. The trouble with these popular views is that they are based on only anecdotal evidence. In this chapter we investigate whether these theses are empirically tenable by examining the extent to which parties present themselves to the electorate in election manifestos that set substantive priorities and offer alternatives that are visible to the citizens and clearly formulated.

To this end, we elaborate a multidimensional concept of the quality of party programs, and leaning on Bartolini's concept of the "decidability" of the programmatic offer (Bartolini 1999, 2000), we identify four aspects of quality: the differentiation of positions, their visibility and clarity, and the heterogeneity of priorities (Franzmann 2008). On the basis of quantitative content analysis of party election manifestos (Budge et al. 1987, 2001; Klingemann et al. 2006; Volkens et al. 2013) in conjunction with election statistics from the database of the WZB Research Unit "Democracy and Democratization," we were able to analyze comparatively the development of the quality of 2103 manifestos of 279 different parties for 371 elections in 21 OECD countries between 1951 and 2011.

Given this long-term perspective, we take into account that the policy space is not static but can shift over time from the spread of a social welfare-state consensus to the deregulation of the economic and financial systems, from traditional notions of society to multicultural conceptions, and from stress on national sovereignty to Europeanization and internationalization. Especially after 1970, the interplay between long-term processes could have led to a reduction in alternatives in economic, social, and foreign policy, while in the sociocultural field with stable traditional core, programmatic offerings could have broadened with green-alternative parties. Unlike previous analyses of party programs, we therefore do not look at their development on the single, abstract left/right dimension but compare the four quality aspects on three concrete conflict dimensions: socioeconomic, sociocultural, and center-periphery.

In the empirical part of our study, we first explain how programmatic offerings are measured and quality aspects of election manifestos operationalized along the three conflict dimensions. Before examining whether and to what extent the quality of party programs in 21 OECD countries has deteriorated on average over six decades, we consider—with the aid of graphic representations—whether programs still address fundamental conflicts and whether the programmatic space has on average changed or shrunk in the countries under study.

We go on to analyze differences in quality between types of democracy. The quality of programs in two-party systems could be worse than in proportional systems, less adequate in consensus than in competitive democracies, and less acceptable in defective than in stable democracies. In conclusion, we interpret the results of our assessment of the quality of election manifestos in the light of whether there is a supply-side crisis of democratic elections.

4.2 Democratic Norm, Party Competition, and Programmatic Offerings

The “responsible party” model (RPM) (Dalton 1985, 1996; Eulau 1987; Thomassen 1991, 1994, 1999; Schmitt and Thomassen 1999; Schmitt 2001; Rohrschneider and Whitefield 2007; Mair 2008) sets out the basic functional conditions for successful representation by political parties. The baseline is parties that offer voters programmatic alternatives so that they can choose not only between persons but also between policies.

Contrary to the democratic norm of programmatic alternatives, theories of party competition posit that parties pursue strategies that lead to a convergence of their programs, because they have good reason to obscure their positions. Parties are seen as competing for votes by taking a position on issues and setting priorities with regard to these issues. Early theories of party competition assumed that parties offered different solutions for one and the same problem (Downs 1957). In these spatial models, policy alternatives were understood as points along a dimension between the two poles of extreme positions. The difference between two parties could then simply be stated in terms of the distance between them.

According to this spatial understanding of party competition, parties have two basic strategies to choose from. First, they can change their position on a policy dimension to gain more votes. An entire branch of party research is now concerned with shifts in position, their reasons, and consequences (Adams 2012). Particularly in two-party systems, rational choice theory posits that the programmatic positions of parties converge because they adapt them to fit the preferences of voters in the center of the political spectrum in order to maximize votes. In societies with stable basic conflict lines, by contrast, parties offer the corresponding programmatic alternatives because in a state of equilibrium no party can increase its share of the vote by changing its program (Downs 1957).

But, second, parties can obscure their position by either adopting none on a given issue or taking up inconsistent standpoints on very similar issues. Such concealment strategies make it difficult for citizens to deduce the position of a party on a new issue from their knowledge about the position the party took up in the past on similar issues. Parties adopt opportune, obscure, and inconsistent positions for a number of reasons (Rovny 2012), for example, if the wings of a party cannot reach agreement or if their constituencies are divided.

These two strategies of spatial party competition provided the frame of reference for Bartolini’s concept of the decidability of parties’ programmatic offerings (Pappi 2000). Bartolini (1999, 2000) proposed decidability as one of four dimensions of party competition, together with the contestability of positions, the electoral vulnerability of established parties, and the availability of new parties. He asked two questions about party programs: “Parties offer programs [...]. The question is, however, how important is the type and quality of the programmatic offer for electoral competition? Which aspects of the political offer are necessary to guarantee, improve, maximize or otherwise substantiate electoral competition?”

(Bartolini 2000, 33). He explained the importance of the decidability of programmatic offerings in terms of the rejection of the oversimplified application of economic competition theories to the objective realities of political competition between parties. Cooperation between parties and "behind the scenes" agreements could result in a lack of programmatic alternatives.

For Bartolini, the decidability of the programmatic offer is crucially important because its absence adversely affects the functional capability of the other three dimensions of competition. He defines decidability in terms of three aspects on which he does into no detail: "The level of policy or issue position differentiation among parties, and the visibility and clarity of these differences for the voter, are what I call here 'decidability'" (ibid.).

Following Sartori (1976), the differentiation of controversial issues has mostly been treated as polarization between alternative party positions. Despite the problems this can cause for coalition governments (Warwick 1998), it is easier for citizens to decide between two parties if their programs differ greatly. The more alternatives programs offer, the more likely every citizen is to find an offer that fits in with his ideas.

Studies of programmatic differentiation have generally assumed that the distance between parties corresponds to the degree of visibility and clarity of their positions. In contrast to this simplistic assumption, we follow Bartolini in arguing that clarity—which we define as the consistent positioning of the program on related issues—and visibility, defined as the possibility for the voter to learn to know the various positions of parties standing for election, are two further aspects of programs that contribute to the decidability of the offer.

The visibility of the programmatic offer depends on many factors. In the first place, the resources deployed by the party, such as the number of manifestos printed and the electoral campaign input of party members and elites, play a role (Brunsbach et al. 2011, 2012). For this reason, the visibility of programmatic offerings can diminish if fewer and fewer members take an active part in the election campaign for the party. On the other hand, the content of programs is transmitted principally by the mass media (Maurer 2009). What topics and positions the media opt for can hardly be influenced by parties, because reporting in the print and electronic media is generally governed by the selection rules of the media (Maurer 2007). However, the partiality of the press in many OECD countries is still judged to be very strong (Dalton et al. 2011).

But these signs of a decline in the visibility of party programs over time are countered by certain indications to the contrary. Technological developments have produced new ways to publicize party positions, for instance, the electronic election campaign (Römmele 2012) and voting advice applications such as Wahl-O-Mat (Marschall 2011). Moreover, analysis of advertising in the mass media shows that party advertising tends to stress the differences between parties, thus making it easier for voters to differentiate between them (Keil 2003, 2004).

Basically, however, it can be assumed that big parties not only have greater financial clout and human resources but that their positions also attract greater attention in the media than those of small parties (Marcinkowski 1998). For a number of reasons, visible alternatives may differ less strongly than the alternatives represented in parliament. Thus, the big social democratic and Christian democratic or conservative parties are said to be particularly strongly affected by the transformation of cleavage-based parties into indistinguishable catch-all parties (Kirchheimer 1966) and to compete for votes in the political center (for a critical treatment, see Chap. 7).

Changes in government have hardly any consequences for policy if there is hardly any difference between the programs of the big governing parties. Research on budgets (Klingemann et al. 1994) and on individual election promises (Mansergh and Thomson 2007) clearly shows that program implementation can be decisively influenced by the big parties in coalition governments because they generally provide the head of government and most ministers. Therefore, the visibility of programmatic alternatives between the two big parties in a party system is especially important for the voter.

The fact that parties compete not only with alternative positions but also with different priorities also speaks against a purely spatial understanding of party competition: "Parties therefore do not compete by arguing directly with each other, but by trying to render their own areas of concern most prominent" (Budge and Farlie 1983, 23). According to this salience theory, parties set differing priorities in their programs, their campaigns, their parliamentary decisions, and their governmental action. However, parties have two contradictory motives in establishing priorities. On the one hand, they seek to emphasize topics where they enjoy an advantage over other parties because they are considered to be particularly competent in the given field. For example, left-wing parties often stress social justice issues because the voters credit them with the ability to solve problems in this area. By focusing on particular issues, parties then seek to direct voters' attention to problems from which they hope to gain an advantage (Iyengar and Kinder 1987; Druckman 2004). On the other hand, parties also have to react to actual events and the strategies of other parties. They are therefore obliged to address issues on which they are not (yet) considered to be competent but which are on the public agenda (Green-Pedersen and Mortensen 2010). This limits differentiation in their priority setting.

Such differentiation is addressed by the concept of programmatic heterogeneity developed by Franzmann (2008). For Western European countries, Franzmann is able to show that programmatic differentiation differs with regard to positions and priorities in both level and course. According to positional competition theory, we can expect less positional differentiation if parties are competing for voters in the political center. Salience theory suggests that party competition limits the differentiation of priorities.

If all parties cooperate, both positions and priorities can converge. This could be particularly true in concordance democracies (Lehmbruch 1992; Lijphart 1999), where political decisions are sought with the consensus of all political actors. Furthermore, defective democracies are to be distinguished from stable democracies. All competition theories are based on stable patterns (Eckstein 1968) of interaction in party systems (Sartori 1976) which can be found only in embedded democracies.

4.3 Changes in Programmatic Offerings on Three Conflict Dimensions

Investigating changes in parties' programmatic offerings in the course of long-term societal, political, and economic developments requires longitudinal data on party programs. Of all the methodological approaches for measuring party positions (Benoit and Laver 2006; Volkens 2007), only the classical quantitative analysis of election manifestos (Budge et al. 2001; Klingemann et al. 2006; Volkens et al. 2013) and the data set of the MARPOR project (Manifesto Research on Political Representation, DFG GZ VO 1000/2-2, https://manifesto-project.wzb.eu/) based on it provide such long time series.

4.3.1 Data and Operationalization of Party Positions

The MARPOR project divides each election manifesto into so-called statements. A trained coder assigns each statement to one of 56 categories. These categories cover a range of political goals such as development of the welfare state, improvement of environmental protection, and more market regulation. The data set shows how often each of these 56 goals is mentioned in each of the election manifestos under study. It includes 3679 election manifestos of 923 parties with at least one seat in 55 parliaments since 1945 or the date when democratic elections first took place (Volkens et al. 2013).

We limit our analysis to the 21 OECD countries that have held democratic elections since 1951 (Australia, Belgium, Canada, Denmark, Germany, Finland, France, the United Kingdom, Ireland, Iceland, Italy, Japan, Luxembourg, New Zealand, Netherlands, Norway, Austria, Sweden, Switzerland, Turkey,[1] and the United States). The MARPOR project analyzes the programs of parties that have won at least one seat in parliament. We assume that parties that have failed to enter parliament have failed to present a program that is relevant for the further representative process.

Studies on changes in the quality of party programs have limited themselves either to detailed analysis of single parties or to the international comparison of left-right positions of important parties. The assumption behind the left-right dimension

[1]With one exception, parliamentary elections were held in Turkey every three to 4 years between 1950 and 2011. The longest interruption of the regular election cycle between 1977 and 1983 due to military intervention lasted just under 5 years.

is that the positions of parties on various issues correlate with a single latent dimension. On the basis of open questions to voters, it has been shown that left and right are categories that are understood in similar terms in different countries and thus provide universal anchor points in communication with parties (Fuchs and Klingemann 1995). Left-right gives voters a heuristic scheme for comparing their own preferences against those of parties. And the positions of parties as perceived by voters do in fact largely correspond to those actually set out in election manifestos (van der Brug 1999).

On the left-right dimension, changes in programmatic polarization between left- and right-wing parties in Western European countries were regularly determined. Contrary to all crisis theories, the findings give little cause to fear that the programmatic offer is deficient. The positions of parties tend rather to follow a cyclical pattern, since periods of convergence are followed by periods of divergence and vice versa (Volkens and Klingemann 2002; Volkens 2003). Measured against the span separating the extreme left from the extreme right in parliament (Laver and Budge 1992), parties have hardly converged at all.

The objection to one-dimensional models, however, is that not only the importance of the left-right dimension (Green-Pedersen 2007) but also the differences between parties on this dimension have diminished (Albright 2010). New conflicts, in particular, can reduce the importance of the left-right dimension. Eurosceptic parties, for example, are to be found on the left and on the right side of the political spectrum, which shows that this conflict has little in common with the traditional understanding of left/right. Moreover, the ranking of parties on numerous issues does not always coincide with the general left-right axis. On economic matters in Germany, for instance, the FDP is well to the right, whereas on societal issues it is the CDU/CSU (Pappi and Shikano 2004). Taking only one dimension into account disregards such differences. What is more, the left-right dimension can be said to display a certain asymmetry, because the positions of left parties on issues are more consistent than those of right parties (Cochrane 2011).

4.3.2 Operationalization of Three Conflict Dimensions

Calculating party positions on the basis of MARPOR data is now a standard procedure in comparative party research. Numerous suggestions have been made (Kim and Fording 2002; Franzmann and Kaiser 2006; Elff 2013; Volkens et al. 2013; König et al. 2013). The common method is to estimate the left-right positions of a party by summing the frequencies of *left* categories and subtracting the total from the frequency of *right* categories (Laver and Budge 1992). This method can be used to calculate left-right positions but also for the pros and cons of single issues or, as in this section, for a selection of contrary categories on specific conflict dimensions.

There is, however, no consensus among party researchers on the number of relevant conflict dimensions nor on the composition of the political issues covered by a conflict dimension. Basically, a distinction is made between deductive and inductive approaches (Benoit and Laver 2006, 2012). Deductive approaches set out from theory, identifying dimensions and issues on the basis of various theoretical considerations; inductive methods usually use statistical methods such as factor analysis to bring together the many individual political issues empirically to form policy dimensions. Whereas deductive methods operate with a limited number of dimensions of policy competition (one to three) (Heath et al. 1994; Shikano and Pappi 2004; Ansalobehere et al. 2008; Bornschier 2010; Stoll 2010; Bakker et al. 2012; Kriesi et al. 2012; Evans and de Graaf 2013), inductive methods produce a large number of dimensions, namely, ten or more (Laver and Budge 1992; Lijphart 1999; Benoit and Laver 2006).

On the basis of the many preliminary studies on dimensionality and the importance of certain dimensions and conflict lines, we have opted for a deductive approach in determining conflict dimensions. We thus take account of the multidimensionality of most party systems. In many comparative studies, three conflict lines are mentioned over and over again either on their own or in combination (Warwick 2002; Bakker et al. 2012; Rovny and Edwards 2012; De Vries and Marks 2012): socioeconomic, sociocultural, and center-periphery.

The *socioeconomic conflict dimension* describes the traditional conflict between labor and capital (Lipset and Rokkan 1967). As shown in Table 4.1 for the individual categories of the data set, this dimension includes disputes on issues such as how strongly government should intervene in the economy, disputes between employers and trade unions, and differences on budgetary policy and economic growth.

The *sociocultural conflict dimension* covers issues of social coexistence. This dimension is to be found in the literature under many names and in wide-ranging forms. Predominant is the so-called new policy agenda (Hooghe et al. 2002), represented by green parties, a consequence of the shift from material to post-material values. The extreme poles of the sociocultural dimension are progressive-libertarian policy and conservative-authoritarian policy.

The third conflict dimension covers issues concerning the role of the nation-state. With the formation of nation-states, this conflict line is developed between old regional and new centralized decision-making authorities and is therefore referred to as the *center-periphery conflict* (Lipset and Rokkan 1967). Europeanization and internationalization have increased the number of issues concerning the transfer of sovereignty rights to international organizations, protectionist economic policy, and cultural nationalism. This conflict line is increasingly apparent in Europe in countries with Eurosceptic parties (De Vries and Hobolt 2012).

On each dimension we identify five issues that can be operationalized with the MARPOR category scheme. For these issues, we calculate a priority and a position for each party at each election. We measure the priority by means of the salience value by summing the relative frequencies of categories relating to the issue. For the welfare-state issue, for example, this would be addition of the relative frequencies of categories 505 (welfare state: negative) and 504 (welfare state: positive).

Table 4.1 Conflict dimensions and codes in the MARPOR data collection

Socioeconomic conflict dimensions		
	Pro market	Pro state
Role of the state	401 Free market: positive 402 Incentives for entrepreneurial activity	403 Market regulation: positive 404 Economic planning 412 Controlled economy 413 Nationalization: positive
Welfare state	505 Welfare state: negative	504 Welfare state: positive
Trade unions	702 Labor/trade unions: negative	701 Labor/trade unions: negative
Financial policy	414 Economic orthodoxy	409 Keynesian demand management
Growth	410 Economic growth	416 Anti-growth economy
Sociocultural conflict dimension		
	Conservative	Progressive
Multiculturalism	608 Multiculturalism: negative	607 Multiculturalism: positive 705 Minorities
Environment	411 Infrastructure development	501 Environmental protection
Peace	104 Development of the military	105 Disarmament 106 Peace
Progressive-alternative moral values	605 Traditional moral values: positive	604 Traditional moral values: negative
Civil rights	605 Law and order policy	202 Democracy
Center-periphery conflict dimension		
	Strengthening of the nation-state	Weakening of the nation-state
European integration	110 European integration: negative	108 European integration: positive
Protectionism	406 Protectionism: positive	407 Protectionism: negative
Multilateral cooperation	109 Internationalism: negative	107 Internationalism: positive
Nationalism	601 Nationalism: positive	602 Nationalism: negative
Centralization	302 Centralization	301 Decentralization

We calculate the position of a party on an issue by subtracting the percentages in the right-hand column from those in the left-hand column *and* by dividing them by the sum of the two relative frequencies (salience) (Laver and Garry 2000; Kim and Fording 2002). These so-called ratio-scaled position values are not influenced by the share of statements on single issues and dimensions in the program and are thus independent of salience. Since with respect to programmatic offerings we distinguish analytically between positions (differentiation, its visibility and clarity) and priorities (heterogeneity), it is necessary to implement this distinction in operationalization, too. We calculate aggregated party positions on the three conflict dimensions as the mean value of the five issue positions in a program weighted by the salience of each issue.

4.3.3 The Importance of the Three Conflict Dimensions

"In societies with strong conflict lines, parties are monopolistic suppliers of policy in their submarkets [. . .]" (Pappi 2000, 93), which seek only to mobilize their own clientele (Sani and Sartori 1983). However, political, societal, and economic changes raise the question of whether and to what extent parties still address fundamental conflicts at all. Former milieus, particularly marked in the Netherlands with a system of pillarization into social democratic, conservative, Catholic, and Protestant sub-societies with their own associations, customs, and parties, have dissolved and—according to Lijphart (1989) only since the late 1980s in the Netherlands—have been replaced by pluralization and party competition. For all modern societies, Evans notes a "blurring of social boundaries through processes of social and economic change" (Evans 2010, 635).

Researchers agree that the size of societal groups associated with particular parties, so-called cleavage groups, has diminished. However, whether and to what extent we can speak of a general de-alignment, a decrease in the binding force of (remaining) class membership and religious affiliation, remains an open question (Brooks et al. 2006; Evans 2010). A very recent study on the link between class membership, religious affiliation, and choice of party shows that clear programmatic alternatives can contribute to strengthening these societal cleavages, thus demonstrating the importance of the design of programmatic offers for democratic elections (Evans and de Graaf 2013).

In order to establish the importance of conflicts in party programs, we first look at the number of statements devoted to areas of conflict. This importance is calculated as the sum of the relative frequencies of all goals of a dimension weighted in terms of the strength of parties for the average of all relevant parties in 21 parliaments between 1951 and 2011 (see Fig. 4.1).

Of the three fields of conflict, socioeconomic goals take up the greatest space in election manifestos, namely, 25% of mentions. Like most studies on the left-right dimension in Western Europe, we find a slight decline in socioeconomic conflicts in the late 1960s and between 1980 and 1990. Between 1970 and 1980 and since the mid-1990s, parties tended more strongly to set themselves socioeconomic goals, so that the importance of socioeconomic conflicts at the end of the time series was almost as great as at the beginning of the 1950s. Socioeconomic conflicts can therefore not be said to have decreased in importance on average in all 21 OECD countries.

With 15% of mentions, sociocultural conflicts take second place on average of all party programs. This figure grew almost continuously to reach the level of socioeconomic topics in the early 1990s. Although green parties had contributed since the 1980s to the spread of the "new policy" agenda, they benefited from the time of their foundation from the growing importance of this policy field.

With an average 10% of mentions, center-periphery conflicts are addressed less frequently than the two other types of conflict. Despite internationalization and Europeanization, issues in this field have not gained in importance over time.

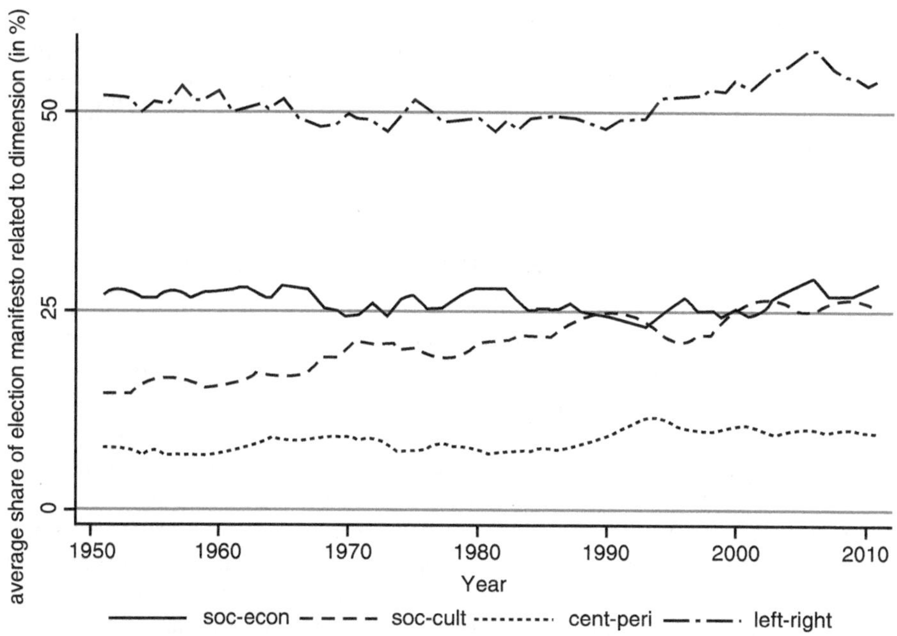

Fig. 4.1 The importance of three conflict dimensions and the left-right dimension (in 21 OECD countries). Source: Own presentation on the basis of Volkens et al. (2013)

Today, as 60 years ago, party manifestos for national elections are predominantly concerned with national issues.

Regardless of this finding, socioeconomic issues have attracted lasting attention, and sociocultural issues have even increased in importance. Given these differences in development, correlation between the three dimensions is only weak (socioeconomic-sociocultural: Pearson's r 0.28) to very weak (sociocultural-center-periphery, 0.15; socioeconomic-center-periphery, 0.06). Our theoretical conflict dimensions are accordingly autonomous dimensions of competition. On the other hand, we find a relatively strong link (Pearson's r 0.78) between the left-right and socioeconomic dimensions. We can infer from this strong correlation that the left-right dimension is determined above all by socioeconomic issues. Correlation between the left-right dimension and the other two dimensions is much weaker: 0.49 for the sociocultural dimension and 0.22 for the center-periphery dimension. These two conflict dimensions are thus largely independent of a general left-right dimension. Consideration of the programmatic offer on these three conflict dimensions is therefore useful because they are both empirically and theoretically independent and because they describe far more than a general left-right dimension.

After the turn of the millennium, as in the postwar decades, half of all statements in the average election manifesto in OECD countries were concerned with right or left positions. In this regard, we also find no loss of importance for the left-right dimension.

Over time, the importance of the left-right dimension—50% of all statements—equals the summed average of the three conflict dimensions we have identified. With the growing importance of sociocultural conflicts, however, the number of these statements since the 1970s increasingly surpassed the number of left-right statements.

4.3.4 Changes in Location in the Programmatic Space

Like Bartolini, Albright (2010) is concerned with programmatic alternatives and the clarity of these positions as "indication how easy it is for voters to identify where parties are located" (Albright 2010, 712). But unlike Bartolini, Albright addresses not the visibility of positions but stresses the importance of the center of gravity of programmatic offers, operationalized as the mean of party positions on one of the policy dimensions weighted by party strength. In this instance, similarly differentiated, clear, visible, and heterogeneous programmatic offerings can differ: electorates are confronted by different programmatic alternatives if the political space, for example, in welfare states, shifts to the left and in libertarian states to the right. If all parties in welfare states provide only more or less markedly welfare-state offers, the preferences of liberal voters are neglected, whereas libertarian democracies can disregard welfare-state voter preferences with more or less libertarian offers.

With the programmatic center of gravity, we also take into account that the policy space is not static but can shift in the course of time because established parties can change their positions, parties can die, and new parties can come into existence. If established and new parties in a party system shift their positions in the same direction, this decisively changes the content of policy alternatives while the distances between parties can remain the same. Such changes in the center of gravity on the socioeconomic and center-periphery dimensions indicate "the end of the ideological age" as early as the beginning of the 1960s: "Today, these ideologies are exhausted" (Bell 1962, 402).

These both apodictic and premature diagnoses at the beginning the 1960s were followed only two decades later by globalization and Europeanization processes (see Chap. 10) and economic and financial crises (see Chap. 11), which could have shifted the center of gravity of socioeconomic offerings in a different direction. International capital markets, economic interdependencies, and international organizations could have induced parties initially to deregulate and open markets, only to call for more government intervention when the problems and risks of this policy become apparent. Figure 4.2 shows changes in the center of gravity on all three conflict dimensions between 1951 and 2011 on average for all 21 OECD countries.

As diagnosed by Bell (1962), the socioeconomic location shifted from 1950 onward in favor of intervention in the economic system and extension of the welfare state, shown in Fig. 4.2 by the shift to the left. Between 1970 and 1995, this trend reversed, as expected. In this period, the average socioeconomic policy

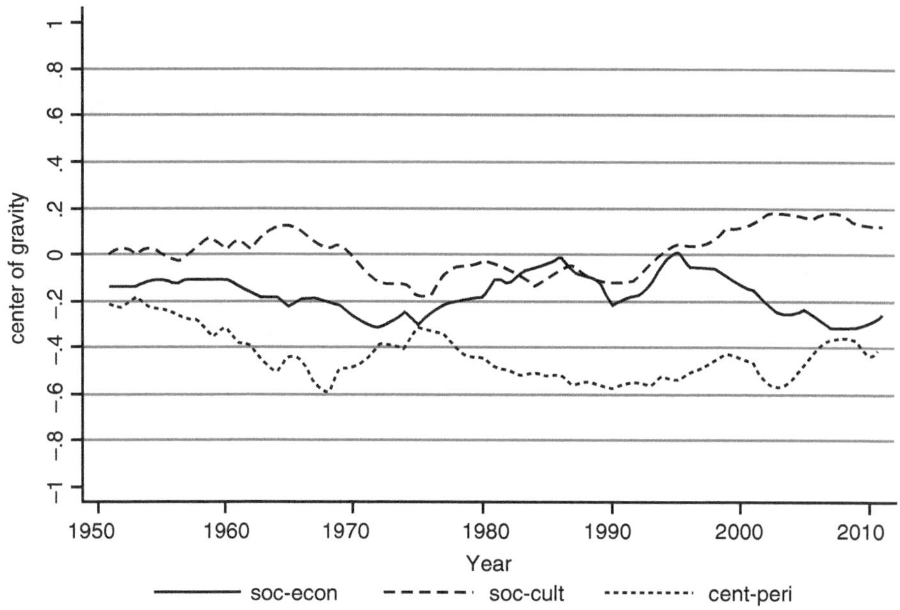

Fig. 4.2 Location of policy offerings on three conflict dimensions (in 21 OECD countries). Note: Socioeconomic conflict dimension: −1 = pro state, +1 = pro market. Sociocultural conflict dimension: −1 = progressive, +1 = conservative. Center-periphery conflict dimension: −1 = contra nation-state, +1 = pro nation-state. Source: Own presentation on the basis of Volkens et al. (2013)

offering in the 21 OECD countries was increasingly dominated by free market positions, and parties were less and less in favor of further expanding welfare-state measures. After 1995, however, the trend reversed for socioeconomic issues. Albright (2010) analyzes the programmatic offer of party families in Western Europe and, between 1980 and 2000, finds a strong swing to the right by social democrats, who in the 1990s had in some cases adopted a *third way* policy in government (Merkel et al. 2008). The loss of votes and government power has clearly induced these parties to put more stress on economic regulation and welfare-state measures in their socioeconomic policy.

Under the impact of societal modernization and value change (Inglehart 1977; Inglehart and Welzel 2005), the sociocultural dimension is said to have shifted from traditional to more strongly progressive-liberal from the end of the 1970s. However, the mean figures for the 21 OECD countries shown in Fig. 4.2 contradict this. Programmatic changes in a progressive-liberal direction had already set in in 1960 but persisted only until the late 1980s. Since then, the sociocultural offer has again become increasingly traditional, although the sociocultural conflict dimension includes all issues—such as the environment, peace, and equality—addressed by the new social movements of the 1970s and 1980s and institutionalized in green-alternative parties. We can only speculate about the reasons for this surprising result. In multiparty systems, the rise of green-alternative parties seems to have induced their political opponents to stress traditional positions more than before. Moreover, green parties have not managed to establish themselves everywhere. In systems without new progressive-liberal parties, established parties were not forced to take new competitors into account. What is more, in some countries, new far-right parties with traditional leanings reinforced this trend. For whatever reasons, sociocultural policy offerings in the OECD countries are surprisingly traditional.

Globalization and Europeanization processes extend old national conflicts between the national center and regional periphery to include new conflicts between the decision-making centers at the European and international levels and nation-states as the new periphery. As expected, consensus on decentralization became widespread in party programs between 1950 and 1970 and on internationalization from the end of the 1970s onward. However, this trend reversed in the late 1990s. In the new millennium, new Eurosceptic parties have attracted attention. Since then the center of gravity shifted back to national sovereignty.

4.4 Quality Aspects of Parties' Programmatic Offers

The concept of programmatic center of gravity differs essentially from the concept of programmatic quality. Whereas gravity measures the parties' programmatic location on a policy-defined dimension between substantive poles of alternative policies, the quality aspects of a program vary between the poles of greater or lesser quality.

4.4.1 Operationalization of Four Quality Aspects

We identify four aspects of quality in party programs: differentiation, visibility, clarity, and heterogeneity. These aspects of the programmatic offer are calculated for a single election and separately for each conflict dimension and then updated for the years until the next election with the same value. All values are different aggregations of party positions on the given conflict dimension.

The differentiation of positions describes how broad policy offerings are. We operationalize it in terms of the range of the policy offer (see Table 4.2). We determine the distance between the two parties that occupy the extreme positions.

The visibility of position differentiation expresses the extent to which these differences are visible to voters. The statistic developed for this purpose does not cover the entire breadth of the offer but takes only the differences between the two strongest parties into account. We argue that differences are particularly visible where the two biggest parties have differing programs. In multiparty systems, too, the strongest parties generally provide the head of government and most ministers

Table 4.2 Operationalization of aspects of party program offerings

Aspect	Estimation	Scale (theoretical min and max)
Differentiation	Distance between the position of the party most to the left and that most to the right rescaled to 0 to 1	0: No difference 1: Extremely big differences
Visibility	The distance between the position of the biggest and second biggest party rescaled to 0 to 1	0: No difference 1: Extremely big differences
Clarity	The squared distances between issue positions and general position on the conflict dimension for each party are calculated. These distances (weighted by the share of issue salience in the salience of all conflict dimension issues) are then summed. On the basis of these specific party and conflict dimension values, values can then be estimated at the election level by calculating the mean weighted by party strength (share of vote)	0: Very inconsistent position 1: Fully consistent position
Heterogeneity	The average variance of party issue priorities in an election on a conflict dimension divided by the squared number of parties (see Franzmann 2008)	0: All parties have the same priorities >0: Parties have no common priorities (the greater, the more different)
Location	The average position on a conflict dimension (weighted by votes) of all parties in an election	−1: Left pole of the party system +1: Right pole of the party system

and thus dominate government policy. Whereas the differentiation of positions and priorities between parliamentary parties reflects the span of the interests represented in parliament, differentiation between the two big parties measures the possible alternatives in government action.

To measure programmatic clarity, for every program, we first estimate the position between pro and contra for each issue of the given conflict dimension. We measure how consistent the issue positions of a party are on each of the three dimensions (see Table 4.2).

Heterogeneity registers how much party priorities differ. To measure this we estimate the variance of salience for each issue of the conflict dimension across all parties in an election. We then calculate the mean of the variances across all issues of the conflict dimension. We divide this number by the root of the number of parties to correct for the size of the party system (see Franzmann 2008).

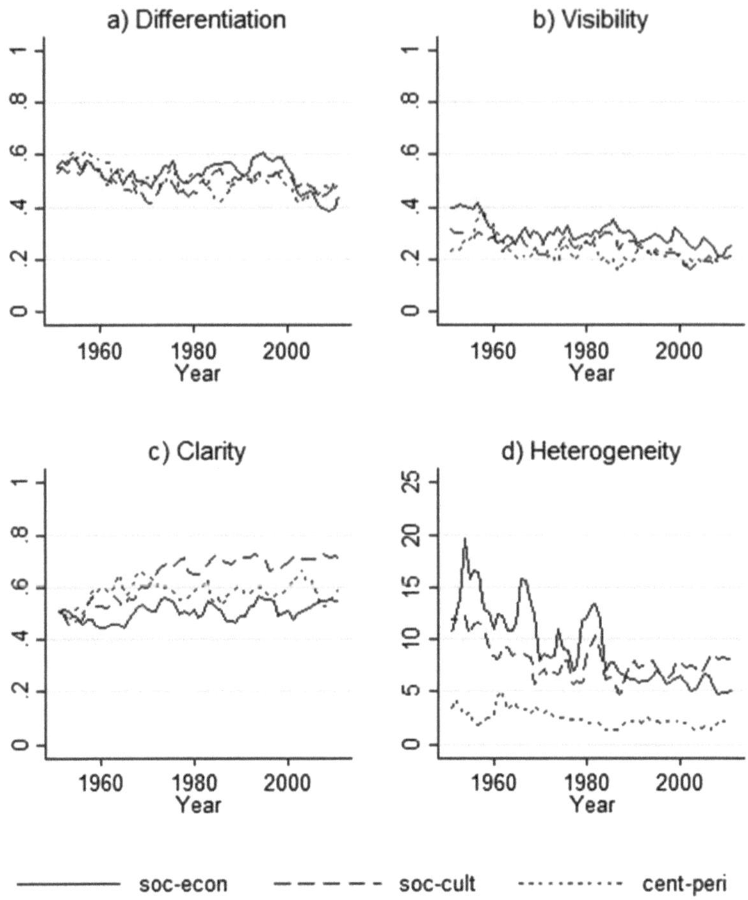

Fig. 4.3 Four quality aspects on three conflict dimensions. Note: (**a**, **b**, **c**) 0 = bad offer, 1 = good offer. (**d**) The higher the value, the better the quality (open-ended scale). Source: Own presentation on the basis of Volkens et al. (2013)

4.4.2 Changes in the Quality of Party Programs, 1950–2011

Our analysis focuses on trends in the development of party programs. The literature on crises in parties and democracy would lead us to expect negative effects on the differentiation, visibility, and clarity of the socioeconomic and center-periphery offer and positive effects on the differentiation and clarity of the sociocultural policy offering. A mere glance at Fig. 4.3 on the development of these quality aspects on the conflict dimensions shows that, on average for 21 OECD countries, these expectations are met only to a limited extent.

With regard to differentiation, we find a cyclical development on all three conflict dimensions. To begin with, the positions of parties converged.

Between 1950 and 1970, their positions converged on all three conflict dimensions in keeping with Bell's de-ideologization diagnosis. But in 1970, this consensus between parties failed. For the differentiation of socioeconomic positions, we find that between 1970 and 2000, differences between programs increased with the spread of neoliberal positions. At the turn of the millennium, a further cycle of socioeconomic dedifferentiation set in because neoliberal positions were adopted less frequently.

In long-term comparison, however, both differentiation and its visibility tended to remain stable rather than to deteriorate or improve. But if differentiation is compared with the visibility of this differentiation, there is a strikingly big difference between the values recorded at all points in time. This difference is indicative of discrepancies between program alternatives represented in parliament and those implemented by government action.

As expected, the clarity of sociocultural offerings developed correspondingly well. Contrary to our hypotheses, however, clarity did not deteriorate on the two other dimensions; instead, it tended to increase. At any rate, we find no evidence of growing obfuscation tactics due to a spread of cartel strategies.

For the heterogeneity of priorities, we had expected limited differentiation of programs due to party competition and responsiveness to real problems. We find such limited differentiation in only two regards. The differentiation of sociocultural priorities and in particular the differentiation of priorities for the distribution of power between center and periphery were weak and stable throughout the period under study.

Contrary to our expectations, however, the heterogeneity of socioeconomic priorities declined considerably. It seems that, with the dissolution of milieus, parties increasingly address the same voters and valence issues such as the reduction of unemployment or corruption that find the consent of all voters (Stokes 1963). At least more recent programs thus score badly on heterogeneity.

Despite all the differences between the topics addressed by a program, it must convey an overall impression to voters if they are to decide for or against the party concerned. We have therefore aggregated the three conflict areas in terms of the space devoted to these topics in the manifestos. The resulting programmatic package shows, first, divergent developments and, second, emphasizes the great stability in the key quality aspects.

On average for the conflict topics, improvement in position clarity is more apparent than deterioration of priority heterogeneity (see Fig. 4.4). Whereas the differentiation of alternatives improved minimally between all parties in parliament in the course of time, differentiation between the two big parties continued to be almost nonexistent. The positions stated in the party manifestos of the big parties are thus very similar. At no point in time did voters have a choice between big parties with crucially divergent positions.

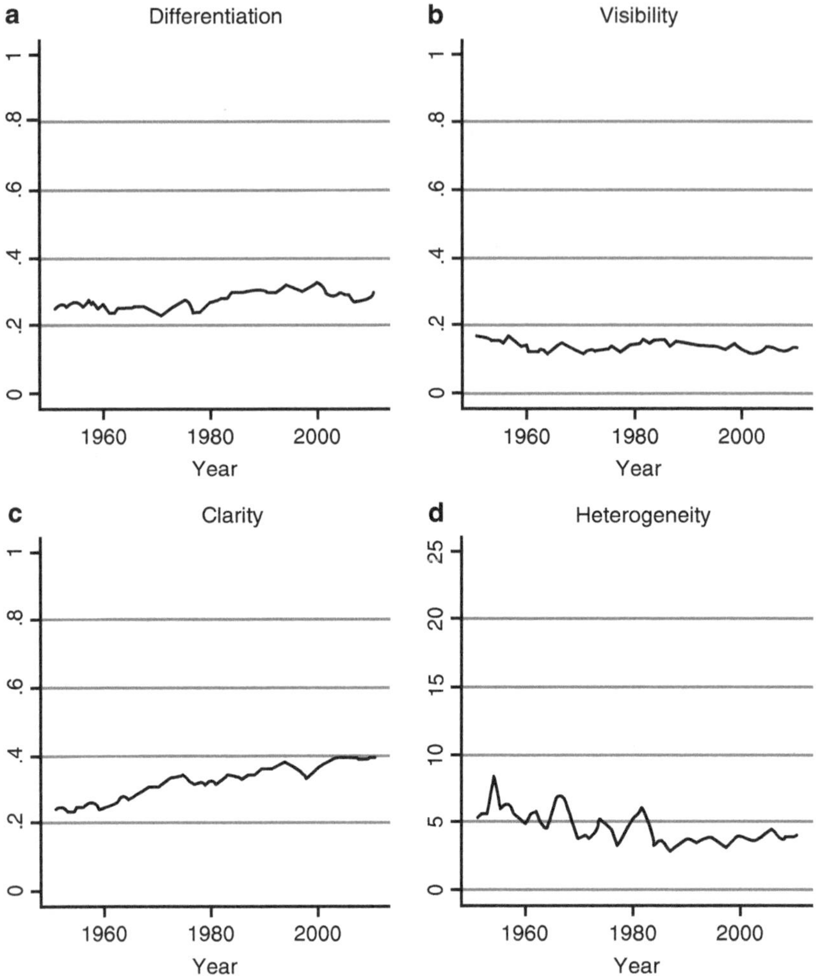

Fig. 4.4 Aggregated quality aspects of the programmatic offer. Note: (**a**, **b**, **c**) 0 = bad offer, 1 = good offer. (**d**) The higher the value, the better the quality (open-ended scale). Source: Own presentation on the basis of Volkens et al. (2013)

4.5 Differences in Quality Between Groups of Countries

So far we have been looking at the development of quality on average for 21 established democracies. However, we suspect that these average values hide differences between three groups of countries. We tested the hypotheses developed in the theoretical section on the basis of the difference in the mean values for three types of democracy shown in Table 4.3 in comparison with the mean value for the 11 democracies that do not fall into any of these three groups.

Table 4.3 Quality aspects by type of democracy

	Differentiation	Visibility	Clarity	Heterogeneity
Majoritarian democracies	0.20	0.15	0.35	4.90
Concordance democracies	0.31	0.14	0.37	4.50
Defective democracy (Turkey)	0.16	0.10	0.25	1.71
Control group	0.33	0.16	0.35	4.49

Source: Own presentation on the basis of Volkens et al. (2013)

In keeping with spatial competition theory, we expect deterioration of the programmatic offer above all in two-party systems regarding the differentiation of positions (Downs 1957). In these countries, a majoritarian electoral system means that two big parties alternate in forming the government. Such countries include the United States as a pure two-party system, as well as the United Kingdom, New Zealand until the switch from majoritarian to proportional voting in 1996, and Australia. Although three parties take part in government in Australia, two, the National Party and the Liberal Party, are in permanent coalition and, like the CDU/CSU in Germany, do not compete in most constituencies. In fact, the differentiation of positions in majoritarian democracies is lower than in consensus democracies, but the quality of visibility, clarity, and heterogeneity does not differ from the comparative group.

If all parties in a party system pursue cartel strategies and cooperate "behind the scenes," they could be expected to have converged programmatically in multiparty systems, as well. This could, secondly, be the case particularly for consensus democracies (Lehmbruch 1992; Lijphart 1999), in which as many political actors as possible are involved (Belgium, Luxembourg, Netherlands, Austria, Switzerland), and should be especially true for the visibility of differentiation between the two big parties, because the social democratic and Christian democratic or conservative parties are said to have been particularly strongly affected by transformation into indistinguishable catch-all parties (Kirchheimer 1966). Contrary to these hypotheses, the quality of the programmatic offer in consensus democracies does not differ from that in other stable democracies. The quality values shown in Table 4.3 are almost identical. The score for visibility (0.14) differs little from that for the comparative group (0.16).

Finally, defective democracies can be expected to differ from stable democracies because stable competitive structures, such as those underlying party development theories, exist only in stable embedded democracies. Most of the (old) OECD countries are such stable democracies. One exception is Turkey, where military intervention, new constitutions, and party prohibitions have frequently interrupted the democratic continuity of party competition. Mainly because of the discontinuities in the party system, we suspect quality to be poor in all aspects. This hypothesis is fully confirmed. In every regard, the quality of Turkish party manifestos is poorer than those in all other types of democracy. Particularly striking is the poor quality in the differentiation of positions and priorities. As a result, defects in program quality accumulate in Turkey, perpetuated because conflicts are not politicized by the parties.

4.6 Summary

In representative democracies, parties have to compete regularly for votes. They woo voters with manifestos and can win a mandate to implement their programmatic positions in parliament and government (Budge 1993). The quality of their programs is therefore especially important from a democracy theory point of view for the aggregation, articulation, and implementation of voter preferences. We have therefore investigated whether party programs offer voters what they need to make a choice that corresponds with their interests. We have identified four aspects of the quality of programmatic offers—the differentiation of positions, their visibility and clarity, and the heterogeneity of priorities—and three dimensions of conflict—socioeconomic, sociocultural, and the center-periphery.

Within the interpretative framework of embedded democracy and its functional conditions, the programmatic "supply side" of an electoral regime is deemed to be in crisis if all aspects of quality are adversely affected to a crucial degree. Contrary to the assertion that parties no longer differ in their programs, our investigation of the quality of election manifestos in 21 countries between 1951 and 2011 has produced little evidence of deteriorating programmatic quality. There is no indication that the importance of fundamental conflicts has diminished in party programs. The importance of sociocultural conflicts has, on the contrary, even increased, and even for the more abstract left-right dimension, they take up an almost stable 50% of the average party manifesto. What has changed is the location of the offer. Particularly for socioeconomic policy offerings, we have identified three cycles: the spread of a welfare-state consensus between 1950 and 1970, the spread of neoliberal notions between 1970 and the end of the 1990s, and a return to more market regulation and welfare state after the turn of the millennium. Above all the socioeconomic heterogeneity of programs has deteriorated. The voter can now discern hardly any priority setting on socioeconomic matters. By contrast, the clarity of positions has improved, so that deterioration of one aspect has been balanced out by improvement in another.

With regard to different types of democracy, too, we find no indication of a general crisis on the supply side of democratic elections. We suspected that majoritarian systems offer citizens fewer differences in socioeconomic positions than proportional systems. But these two types of democracy do not differ in any of the other three quality aspects. The quality of consensus democracies is on a level with competitive democracies. Only in the defective democracy, Turkey has shortcomings accumulated as expected.

References

Adams, J. (2012). Causes and electoral consequences of party policy shifts in multi-party elections: Theoretical results and empirical evidence. *Annual Review of Political Science, 15*(1), 401–419.

Albright, J. J. (2010). The multidimensional nature of party competition. *Party Politics, 16*(6), 699–719.

Ansalobehere, S., Rodden, J., & Snyder, J. M. (2008). The strength of issues: Using multiple measures to gauge preference stability, ideological constraint, and issue voting. *American Political Science Review, 102*(2), 215–232.

Bakker, R., Jolly, S., & Polk, J. (2012). Complexity in the European party space: Exploring dimensionality with experts. *European Union Politics, 13*(2), 219–245.

Bartolini, S. (1999). Collusion, competition and democracy: Part I. *Journal of Theoretical Politics, 11*(4), 435–470.

Bartolini, S. (2000). Collusion, competition and democracy: Part II. *Journal of Theoretical Politics, 12*(1), 33–65.

Bell, D. (1962). *The end of ideology*. New York, NY: Free Press.

Benoit, K., & Laver, M. (2006). *Party policy in modern democracies*. New York, NY: Routledge.

Benoit, K., & Laver, M. (2012). The dimensionality of the policy space: Epistemological and methodological considerations. *European Union Politics, 13*(2), 194–218.

Bornschier, S. (2010). The new cultural divide and the two-dimensional political space in Western Europe. *West European Politics, 10*(3), 419–444.

Brooks, C., Niewbeerta, P., & Manza, J. (2006). Cleavage-based voting behaviour in cross-national perspective: Evidence from six post-war democracies. *Comparative Political Studies, 28*(4), 88–128.

Brunsbach, S., John, S., Volkens, A., & Werner, A. (2011). Wahlprogramme im Vergleich. In J. Tenscher (Ed.), *Superwahljahr 2009. Vergleichende Analysen aus Anlass der Wahlen zum Deutschen Bundestag und zum Europäischen Parlament* (pp. 41–64). Wiesbaden: VS Verlag für Sozialwissenschaften.

Brunsbach, S., John, S., & Werner, A. (2012). The supply side of second order elections: Comparing German national and European election manifestos. *German Politics, 21*(1), 91–115.

Budge, I. (1993). Parties, programs and policies: A comparative and theoretical perspective. *The American Review of Politics, 14*, 695–716.

Budge, I., & Farlie, D. (1983). *Explaining and predicting elections: Issue effects and party strategies in twenty-three democracies*. London: Allen & Unwin.

Budge, I., Klingemann, H.-D., Volkens, A., Bara, J., Tanenbaum, E., Fording, R. C., Hearl, D. J., Kim, H. M., McDonald, M., & Mendez, S. (2001). *Mapping policy preferences. Estimates for parties, electors, and governments 1945–1998*. Oxford: Oxford University Press.

Budge, I., Robertson, D., & Hearl, D. (Eds.). (1987). *Ideology, strategy and party change. Spatial analysis of post-war election programmes in 19 democracies*. Cambridge: Cambridge University Press.

Cochrane, C. (2011). The asymmetrical structure of left/right disagreement. Left-wing coherence and right-wing fragmentation in comparative party policy. *Party Politics, 19*(1), 104–121.

Daalder, H. (2002). Parties: Denied, dismissed, or redundant? A critique. In R. Gunther, J. R. Montero, & J. J. Linz (Eds.), *Political parties. Old concepts and new challenges* (pp. 39–57). Oxford: Oxford University Press.

Dalton, R. J. (1985). Political parties and political representation: Party supporters and party elites in nine nations. *Comparative Political Studies, 18*(3), 267–299.

Dalton, R. J. (1996). *Citizen politics. Public opinion and political parties in advanced industrial democracies* (2nd ed.). Chatham, NJ: Chatham House Publishers.

Dalton, R. J. (2002). *Parties without partisans: Political change in advanced industrial democracies*. Oxford: Oxford University Press.

Dalton, R. J., Farrell, D. M., & McAllister, I. (2011). *Political parties and democratic linkage. How parties organize democracy*. Oxford: Oxford University Press.

Dalton, R. J., Flanagan, S. C., & Beck, P. A. (1984). Political forces and partisan change. In R. J. Dalton, S. C. Flanagan, & P. A. Beck (Eds.), *Electoral change in advanced industrial democracies* (pp. 452–476). Princeton, NJ: Princeton University Press.

De Vries, C., & Hobolt, S. B. (2012). When dimensions collide: The electoral success of issue entrepreneurs. *European Union Politics, 13*(2), 246–268.

De Vries, C., & Marks, G. (2012). The struggle over dimensionality: A note on theory and empirics. *European Union Politics, 13*(2), 185–193.

Downs, A. (1957). *An economic theory of democracy*. New York, NY: Harper & Row.

Druckman, J. N. (2004). Political preference formation: Competition, deliberation, and the (Ir) relevance of framing effects. *American Political Science Review, 98*(4), 671–686.

Eckstein, H. (1968). Party systems. In D. L. Sills (Ed.), *International encyclopedia of the social sciences 17* (pp. 436–453). New York, NY: McMillan and Free Press.

Elff, M. (2013). A dynamic state-space model of coded political texts. *Political Analysis, 21*(2), 217–232.

Eulau, H. (1987). The congruence model revisited. *Legislative Studies Quarterly, 12*(2), 171–214.

Evans, G. (2010). Models, measures and mechanisms: An agenda for progress in cleavage research. *West European Politics, 33*(3), 634–647.

Evans, G., & de Graaf, D. (2013). *Political choice matters: Explaining the strength of class and religious cleavages in cross-national perspective*. Oxford: Oxford University Press.

Franklin, M. N., Mackie, T. T., & Valen, H. (Eds.). (1992). *Electoral change. Responses to evolving social and attitudinal structures in western countries*. Cambridge: Cambridge University Press.

Franzmann, S. (2008). *Programmatische Heterogenität und ideologische Polarisierung in den europäischen Parteiensystemen*, contribution to the Joint Session of the Deutschen Vereinigung für Politische Wissenschaft (DVPW), the Österreichischen Gesellschaft für Politikwissenschaft (ÖGPW), and the Schweizerischen Vereinigung für Politische Wissenschaft (SVPW) "Die Verfassung der Demokratien," 21–23 November 2008, University Osnabrück.

Franzmann, S., & Kaiser, A. (2006). Locating political parties in policy space. A reanalysis of party manifesto data. *Party Politics, 12*(2), 163–188.

Fuchs, D., & Klingemann, H.-D. (1995). Citizens and the state: A changing relationship? In H.-D. Klingemann & D. Fuchs (Eds.), *Citizens and the state* (pp. 1–23). Oxford: Oxford University Press.

Green-Pedersen, C. (2007). The growing importance of issue competition: The changing nature of party competition in Western Europe. *Political Studies, 55*(3), 607–628.

Green-Pedersen, C., & Mortensen, P. B. (2010). Who sets the agenda and who responds to it in the Danish parliament? A new model of issue competition and agenda-setting. *European Journal of Political Research, 49*(2), 257–281.

Heath, A., Evans, G., & Martin, J. (1994). The measurement of Core beliefs and values: The development of balanced socialist/laissez-faire and libertarian/authoritarian scales. *British Journal of Political Science, 24*(1), 115–132.

Hooghe, L., Marks, G., & Wilson, C. J. (2002). Does left/right structure party positions on European integration? *Comparative Political Studies, 35*(8), 965–989.

Inglehart, R. F. (1977). *The silent revolution: Changing values and political styles among western publics*. Princeton, NJ: Princeton University Press.

Inglehart, R. F., & Welzel, C. (2005). *Modernization, cultural change and democracy*. New York, NY: Cambridge University Press.

Iyengar, S., & Kinder, D. R. (1987). *News that matters: Agenda-setting and priming in a television age*. Chicago, IL: University of Chicago Press.

Katz, R. S., & Mair, P. (1995). Changing models of party organization and party democracy. *Party Politics, 1*(1), 5–28.

Keil, S. I. (2003). *Wahlkampfkommunikation in Wahlanzeigen und Wahlprogrammen*. Frankfurt am Main: Peter Lang.

Keil, S. I. (2004). Parteiprogrammatik in Wahlkampfanzeigen und Wahlprogrammen 1957-2002: Und es gibt ihn doch—den (kleinen) Unterschied. In F. Brettschneider, J. van Deth, & E. Roller (Eds.), *Die Bundestagswahl 2002. Analysen der Wahlergebnisse und des Wahlkampfes* (pp. 353–388). Wiesbaden: VS Verlag für Sozialwissenschaften.

Kim, H. M., & Fording, R. C. (2002). Government partisanship in western democracies, 1945–1998. *European Journal of Political Research, 41*(2), 187–206.

Kirchheimer, O. (1966). The transformation of the Western European party systems. In J. LaPalombara & M. Weiner (Eds.), *Political parties and political development* (pp. 117–200). Princeton, NJ: Princeton University Press.

Kitschelt, H. (2000). Linkages between citizens and politicians in democratic polities. *Comparative Political Studies, 33*(6/7), 845–879.

Klingemann, H.-D., Hofferbert, R. I., Budge, I., Keman, H., Pétry, F., Bergman, T., & Strom, K. (1994). *Parties, policies, and democracy*. Boulder, CO: Westview Press.

Klingemann, H.-D., Volkens, A., Bara, J., Budge, I., & McDonald, M. (2006). *Mapping policy preference II: Estimates for parties, electors and governments in Eastern Europe, the European Union and the OECD, 1990–2003*. Oxford: Oxford University Press.

König, T., Marbach, M., & Osnabrügge, M. (2013). Estimating party positions across countries and time—a dynamic latent variable model for manifesto data. *Political Analysis, 21*(4), 468–491.

Kriesi, H., Grande, E., Dolezal, M., Helbling, M., Höglinger, D., Hutter, S., & Wüst, B. (2012). *Political conflict in Western Europe*. Cambridge: Cambridge University Press.

Laver, M., & Budge, I. (Eds.). (1992). *Party policy and government coalitions*. New York, NY: St. Martin's Press.

Laver, M., & Garry, J. (2000). Estimating policy positions from political texts. *American Journal of Political Science, 44*(3), 619–634.

Lawson, K., & Poguntke, T. (Eds.). (2004). *How political parties respond. Interest aggregation revisited*. London: Routledge.

Lehmbruch, G. (1992). Konkordanzdemokratie. In M. G. Schmidt (Ed.), *Lexikon der Politik, Die westlichen Länder* (Vol. 3, pp. 206–211). München: C.H. Beck.

Lijphart, A. (1989). From the politics of accommodation to adversarial politics in the Netherlands: A reassessment. *West European Politics, 12*(1), 139–153.

Lijphart, A. (1999). *Patterns of democracy: Government forms and performance of twenty-seven democracies*. New Haven, CT: Yale University Press.

Lipset, M. S., & Rokkan, S. (1967). Cleavage structures, party systems, and voter alignments. An introduction. In S. M. Lipset & S. Rokkan (Eds.), *Party systems and voter alignments. Cross-national perspectives* (pp. 1–64). New York, NY: The Free Press.

Mair, P. (2008). The challenge to party government. *West European Politics, 31*, 211–234.

Mair, P., Müller, W., & Plasser, F. (Eds.). (2004). *Political parties and electoral change. Party responses to electoral markets*. Beverly Hills, CA: Sage.

Mansergh, L., & Thomson, R. (2007). Election pledges, party competition, and policymaking. *Comparative Politics, 39*(3), 311–329.

Marcinkowski, F. (1998). Massenmedien und Politikinhalte. Empirische Fallstudie auf einem unterbelichteten Forschungsfeld. *Duisburger Materialien zur Politik- und Verwaltungswissenschaft* 19.

Marschall, S. (2011). Nutzer und Nutzen—Der Wahl-O-Mat zur Bundestagswahl 2009. In E. J. Schweitzer & S. Albrecht (Eds.), *Das Internet im Wahlkampf* (pp. 136–153). Wiesbaden: VS Verlag für Sozialwissenschaften.

Maurer, M. (2007). Fakten oder Floskeln? Die Inhalte der Wahlprogramme im Bundestagswahlkampf 2005 in der Tagespresse. *Publizistik, 52*(2), 174–190.

Maurer, M. (2009). Wissensvermittlung in der Mediendemokratie: Wie Medien und politische Akteure die Inhalte von Wahlprogrammen kommunizieren. In F. Marcinkowski & B. Pfetsch (Eds.), *Politik in der Mediendemokratie* (pp. 151–173). Wiesbaden: VS Verlag für Sozialwissenschaften.

Merkel, W., Petring, A., Henkes, C., & Egle, C. (2008). *Social democracy in power. The capacity to reform*. London: Routledge.

Merz, N., & Regel, S. (2013). Die Programmatik der Parteien. In O. Niedermayer (Ed.), *Handbuch Parteienforschung* (pp. 212–238). Wiesbaden: Springer VS.

Montero, J. R., & Gunther, R. (2002). Introduction: Reviewing and assessing parties. In R. Gunther, J. R. Montero, & J. J. Linz (Eds.), *Political parties. Old concepts and new challenges* (pp. 1–38). Oxford: Oxford University Press.

Pappi, F. U. (2000). Zur Theorie des Parteienwettbewerbs. In M. Klein, W. Jagodzinski, E. Mochmann, & D. Ohr (Eds.), *50 Jahre Empirische Wahlforschung in Deutschland. Entwicklung, Befunde, Perspektiven, Daten* (pp. 86–105). Wiesbaden: Westdeutscher Verlag.

Pappi, F. U., & Shikano, S. (2004). *Ideologische Signale in den Wahlprogrammen der deutschen Bundestagsparteien 1980 bis 2002*. Mannheim: MZES Mannheimer Zentrum für Europäische Sozialforschung.

Pierce, R. (1999). Mass-elite linkages and the responsible party model of representation. In W. E. Miller, R. Pierce, J. J. A. Thomassen, R. Herrera, S. Holmberg, P. Esaiasson, & B. Weßels (Eds.), *Policy representation in western democracies* (pp. 9–32). Oxford: Oxford University Press.

Rohrschneider, R., & Whitefield, S. (2007). Representation in new democracies: Party stances on European integration in post-communist Eastern Europe. *Journal of Politics, 69*(4), 1133–1146.

Römmele, A. (2012). Electronic campaigning. In N. Kersting (Ed.), *Electronic democracy. State of the art and future perspectives* (pp. 103–124). Opladen: Leske + Budrich.

Rovny, J. (2012). Who emphasizes and who blurs? Party strategies in multidimensional competition. *European Union Politics, 13*(2), 269–292.

Rovny, J., & Edwards, E. E. (2012). Struggle over dimensionality. Party competition in western and Eastern Europe. *East European Politics & Societies, 26*(1), 56–74.

Sani, G., & Sartori, G. (1983). Polarization, fragmentation, and competition in western democracies. In H. Daalder & P. Mair (Eds.), *Western European party systems. Continuity and change* (pp. 307–340). Beverly Hills, CA: Sage.

Sartori, G. (1976). *Parties and party systems. A framework for analysis*. New York, NY: Cambridge University Press.

Schmitt, H. (2001). Politische Repräsentation in Europa. *Eine empirische Studie zur Interessenvermittlung durch allgemeine Wahlen*. Frankfurt am Main: Campus.

Schmitt, H., & Thomassen, J. J. A. (Eds.). (1999). *Political representation and legitimacy in the European Union*. Oxford: Oxford University Press.

Shikano, S., & Pappi, F. U. (2004). *The positions of parties in ideological and policy space: The perception of German voters of their party system*. Mannheim: MZES Mannheimer Zentrum für Europäische Sozialforschung.

Stokes, D. E. (1963). Spatial models of party competition. *American Political Science Review, 57*, 368–377.

Stoll, H. (2010). Elite-level conflict salience and dimensionality in Western Europe: Concepts and empirical findings. *West European Politics, 10*(3), 445–473.

Thomassen, J. J. A. (1991). Empirical research into political representation. A critical reappraisal. In H.-D. Klingemann, R. Stöss, & B. Weßels (Eds.), *Politische Klasse und politische Institutionen. Probleme und Perspektiven der Elitenforschung. Dietrich Herzog zum 60. Geburtstag* (pp. 259–274). Opladen: Westdeutscher Verlag.

Thomassen, J. J. A. (1994). Empirical research into political representation: Failing democracy or failing models. In M. K. Jennings & T. E. Mann (Eds.), *Elections at home and abroad: Essays in honor of Warren E. Miller* (pp. 237–264). Ann Arbor: University of Michigan Press.

Thomassen, J. J. A. (1999). Political communication between political elites and mass public. The role of belief systems. In W. E. Miller, R. Pierce, J. J. A. Thomassen, R. Herrera, S. Holmberg, P. Esaiasson, & B. Weßels (Eds.), *Policy representation in western democracies* (pp. 33–58). Oxford: Oxford University Press.

Thomassen, J. J. A. (Ed.). (2005). *The European voter. A comparative study of modern democracies*. Oxford: Oxford University Press.

van der Brug, W. (1999). Voters' perceptions and party dynamics. *Party Politics, 5*(2), 147–169.

Volkens, A. (2003). Parteiendemokratie in Europa: Die Frage des Politikangebots. In H.-D. Klingemann, E. Roller, A. Volkens, B. Weßels, & J. Alber (Eds.), *Entwicklung und Perspektiven der Demokratie in Ost und West*. Final colloquium of the research unit institutions and social change with an introduction by Jürgen Kocka (pp. 23–28). Berlin: WZB Berlin Social Science Center.

Volkens, A. (2007). Strengths and weaknesses of approaches to measuring policy positions of parties. *Electoral Studies, Special Symposium: Comparing Measures of Party Positioning: Expert, Manifesto, and Survey Data, 26*, 108–120.

Volkens, A., Bara, J., Budge, I., McDonald, M., & Klingemann, H.-D. (Eds.). (2013). *Mapping policy preferences from texts III. Statistical solutions for manifesto analysts*. Oxford: Oxford University Press.

Volkens, A., & Klingemann, H.-D. (2002). Parties, ideologies, and issues. Stability and change in fifteen European party systems 1945–1998. In K. R. Luther & F. Müller-Rommel (Eds.), *Political parties in the new Europe. Political and analytical challenges* (pp. 143–167). Oxford: Oxford University Press.

Volkens, A., Lehmann, P., Merz, N., Regel, S., & Werner, A. Lacewell O. P., & Schultze H. (2013). *The manifesto data collection. Manifesto project (MRG/CMP/MARPOR)*. Version 2013. Berlin: WZB—Berlin Social Science Center.

Warwick, P. V. (1998). Policy distance and parliamentary government. *Legislative Studies Quarterly, 23*(3), 319–345.

Warwick, P. V. (2002). Towards a common dimensionality in West European policy spaces. *Party Politics, 8*(1), 101–122.

Webb, P., Farrell, D. M., & Holliday, I. (Eds.). (2002). *Political parties in advanced industrial democracies*. Oxford: Oxford University Press.

Chapter 5
Are Right-Wing Populist Parties a Threat to Democracy?

Marcus Spittler

5.1 Introduction

The latest election to the European Parliament in 2014 not only yielded a record-low turnout rate; much more concerning for the EU integration project was that the number of Europeans casting their vote for Eurosceptic parties was higher than ever (Treib 2014). While Euroscepticism is not a singular feature of the political right, the majority of Eurosceptic parties consist of right-wing populist parties (RWPs). Since the late 1980s and especially in the last decade, these parties have been able to firmly establish themselves in their respective countries' party systems. Despite a modest average vote share of 9% in Western Europe and 15% in Eastern Europe in 2016, RWPs have become large parties, if not the largest parties in some countries. In contrast to earlier expectations, RWPs neither turned out to be only a short-lived phenomenon nor softened their populist rhetoric after entering into government in some countries. As the case of the Freedom Party of Austria (FPÖ) illustrates, RWPs may come unprepared into office, fail there, and still enjoy great popularity only a few years later (Heinisch and Hauser 2016). There is further evidence that over the years RWPs have expanded their anti-elitist rhetoric and have not adjusted to their mainstream competitors (Akkerman et al. 2016, 46).

The electoral growth of RWPs simultaneously increased their access to political power. RWPs have acted as formal and informal supporters of minority governments, been accepted by mainstream parties as coalition partners, and even exercised leadership of government in an increasing number of countries (Akkerman and de Lange 2012; Mudde 2013). Figure 5.1 shows the government involvements of RWPs in Europe between 1990 and 2014. Out of 290 cabinets, which lasted longer than

M. Spittler (✉)
Department of Democracy and Democratization, WZB Berlin Social Science Center, Berlin, Germany
e-mail: marcus.spittler@wzb.eu

W. Merkel, S. Kneip (eds.), *Democracy and Crisis*,
https://doi.org/10.1007/978-3-319-72559-8_5

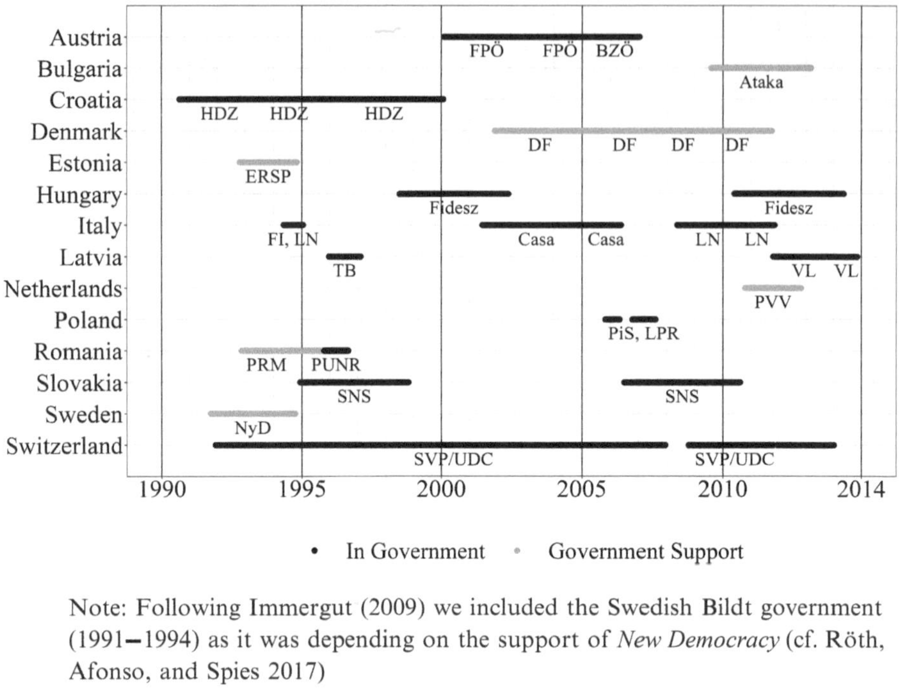

Fig. 5.1 Right-wing populist parties in government, 1990–2014. Source: WZB, author's own figure

6 months, RWPs have been attached in some form to 54 cabinets, including 15 cases where they have been the leading party (namely, in Croatia, Hungary, Italy, Poland, and Switzerland). Most commonly, RWPs have been in formal coalitions with mainstream conservative parties (as junior partners in Austria, Latvia, Romania, Slovakia), but in other cases they have refrained from holding office and only agreed to support minority governments (Denmark, the Netherlands).

Various terms have been used in the literature to describe the uneasy relationship between populism and democracy. *Friend or foe*, *threat and corrective*, or *cure and malaise* are only a few examples. While the theoretical debate on whether populism is a "dangerous threat to democracy" (Abts and Rummens 2007, 470; also Müller 2016) or the purest form of democracy (Tännsjö 1992; Mouffe 2000, 2005; Laclau 2005a, b) is still ongoing, empirical research highlights negative and damaging effects of RWPs on contemporary democratic systems. Studies conclude that RWPs regularly pursue policies which target liberal values such as the rule of law, minority rights, or the freedom of the press and have, therefore, damaging effects on liberal democracy in particular (Albertazzi and Mueller 2013; Batory 2016; Fomina and Kucharczyk 2016). Others even suggest "rethink[ing] the uniqueness of historical accounts in which authoritarian regimes (may) originate by democratic means" (Markowski 2016, 11). Huber and Schimpf (2016) have, to the author's knowledge, conducted the first and, to date, only comparative, *large*-n study investigating the impact of RWPs on the quality of democracy. They, too, observe a negative influence of RWPs on democratic quality under the condition that RWPs are in government, but do not find any significant effect when RWPs are only part of the opposition. In contrast, the theoretician Chantal Mouffe (2005) even argues that strong populist parties in opposition may contribute to a positive repoliticization of "post-political" societies.

In this chapter, we seek to build on the results presented by Huber and Schimpf (2016) by taking a closer look not only at the overall quality of democracy but also at its specific functions. In line with Mudde and Rovira Kaltwasser (2017), we assert that RWPs may have both a negative and a positive impact depending on the context and the inclusion of RPWs into the political system. Adhering to the overarching framework of this edited volume, this chapter seeks, therefore, to contribute toward answering the questions: Do right-wing populist parties pose a threat to the quality of democracy and do their successes, therefore, constitute a crisis of democracy?

The chapter proceeds as follows. In the theory section, we discuss, along with an outline of a general theoretical framework, how we expect the relationship between populism and democracy to look like and formulate hypotheses on this basis. The third section describes the research design, the data used, and the operationalization of key variables. Section 5.4 puts these assumptions to an empirical test. First, we will give descriptive evidence on how populist parties manage to occupy an underrepresented space of electoral competition, while in the subsequent part the effect of right-wing populist parties on the quality of democracy will be presented. The conclusion discusses whether these findings indicate a threat to democracy that may potentially trigger a serious crisis.

5.2 Theory

5.2.1 A Concept of Right-Wing Populism

Before we can study populism's relationship to democracy, we need to clarify what is meant by both terms. Populism, in particular, was considered for a long time to be a "notoriously vague term" (Canovan 1999), as its application varied from being a strategy of political communication (Weyland 2001), a syndrome of a lack of democracy, a movement, or a full ideology (MacRea and Gellner 1969; Albertazzi and McDonnell 2008). Attempts to formulate a general theory were quite unsuccessful since populists neither pursue a shared political style nor choose a unifying form of organization (Rooduijn et al. 2014). Today, the definition of populism and its relation to democracy are far from reaching a scholarly consensus.

Adherents of a "liberal approach" (Rovira Kaltwasser 2012, 186) see populism as a "pathology" or an "excess" and mainly as a sign of democratic malfunction. Taggart, in his attempt to define an ideal type of populism, included populism's hostility toward representative politics as part of a common core (Taggart 2000, 2002). Aspects of democracy under threat from populism in this perspective are the principles of majority rule, the rule of law, and individual liberties. In contrast, a "radical approach" has regarded populism, first and foremost, as a positive and inherent *part of* democracy (Canovan 1999). Laclau and Mouffe (1985), Mouffe (2005) see populism as a discursive practice and a logic of constructing the political and stress populism's ontologically constitutive and potentially beneficial function of aggregating different "democratic demands" and ultimately the reoccupation of the realm of public contestation by a popular subject. Noteworthy for our study of right-wing populist parties is that this radical approach does not pay much attention to the content of the aggregated demands; what unites both the radical and the liberal approaches is that they valuate ex ante the relationship between populism and democracy (Rovira Kaltwasser 2012). But as we want to assess both negative and positive effects of populism on democracy, we need a more parsimonious definition.

Rovira Kaltwasser (2012) convincingly argues that the most promising approach to describing the relationship between populism and democracy is to use a minimal definition of populism, which is less normative and does not presuppose a specific conception of democracy. Such a minimal definition is proposed by Mudde (2004), which today a wide range of scholars is increasingly agreeing on.[1] According to Mudde, "*populism [is a thin-centred] ideology that considers society to be ultimately separated into two homogeneous and antagonistic groups, 'the pure people' versus 'the corrupt elite', and which argues that politics should be an expression of the* volonté générale *(general will) of the people*" (Mudde 2004, 543, italics in the original).

Accordingly, populists present themselves as the self-declared representatives of "the people," whose popular sovereignty has been abused by the elite, and seek to reassert this sovereignty. Populism is thin-centered insofar as "the people" and "the elite" represent *empty signifiers* that need to be filled with meaning (Rovira Kaltwasser 2011). "The elite" regularly includes the established parties, mass media, constitutional courts, intellectuals, and the upper class, while "the people" is constructed via recourse to an idealized conception of the political community and a retrospectively imagined "heartland" (Taggart 2002). However, which parts of society are included in "the people" depends much more on the ideological direction of the populist party. Hence, the basic assumption of populism is reduced to the elite-people relationship, which is portrayed as antagonistic and morally charged (Panizza 2005). This "inherent incompleteness" (Taggart 2004, 275) makes it necessary for populism to be linked to a certain core ideology.

Today the predominant form of populist parties in Europe is ideologically of the political right, while in recent years left-wing populist parties (*Syriza*, *Podemos*) have also been electorally successful. Right-wing populist parties are usually described as nativist, since they combine either ethnic or civic nationalism with xenophobia. In the view of RWPs, the ideal of cultural and ethnic homogeneity is under threat by outsider groups such as immigrants, particularly Muslims. These non-native groups are considered to be incompatible with the cultural values of the

[1]For a recent argument to the contrary, see Aslanidis (2016).

majority, thus rendering their inclusion or integration impossible. Further, RWPs pursue a law-and-order strategy against the alleged criminal behavior of these outsider groups. While for most RWPs socioeconomic issues are secondary (Inglehart and Norris 2016), they most often pursue a welfare chauvinist strategy, as they want to restrict any welfare-state benefits to the native population (Golder 2016).

RWPs are therefore mainly *exclusionary* populist as they seek to exclude certain groups from social benefits and political rights (Mudde and Rovira Kaltwasser 2013). Hence, in addition to "the elite," non-native groups make up a second group for right-wing populists' construction of an external enemy. Some authors have even argued that contemporary RWPs should be considered primarily exclusionary and only secondarily populist (Wodak 2015). Stavrakakis et al. (2017, 433) assert on the basis of a discourse analysis of the French *National Front* and the Dutch *Party for Freedom* (PVV) that populism is "clearly not the core discursive/ideological feature on the basis of which one can understand the specificity of their profile." Huber and Schimpf (2016) have also suggested analyzing populism only in conjunction with the core ideology of these parties. For our analysis, this means that the effect of RWPs on democracy might be predominantly caused by their right-wing core ideology and, therefore, the results cannot necessarily be generalized for other populist parties.

Nevertheless, right-wing extremist parties can be distinguished from right-wing populist parties insofar as populists challenge democracy from within (Abts and Rummens 2007). While RWPs might at best be semi-loyal parties to democracy, as they are at odds with certain aspects of liberal democracy, they are not directly anti-constitutional (Betz 1994). Extremists and populists also differ strongly in their line of argumentation and their semi-loyalty or disloyalty to the democratic system. While right-wing extremists stress the necessity for a leadership that guides and leads in the sense of a "Führerstaat" (Stavrakakis and Katsambekis 2014), populist parties, in contrast, oppose some elements of multicultural liberal democracy and claim solely to be the "true" representatives of the people (Mudde and Rovira Kaltwasser 2017).

5.2.2 Populism's Theoretical Relationship to the Quality of Democracy

The term democracy is defined here according to the concept of *embedded democracy* (Merkel 2004; see also Chap. 1). This is a midrange model of democracy, as it adds to the minimal criterion of free and fair elections further principles such as civil liberties, horizontal accountability, and the actual power to govern. Hence, we investigate here the impact of populism on a specific form of *liberal* democracy.

Mudde (2013) identifies in his review article only a limited impact of populist radical right parties on democracy up to that point while also noting that the empirical literature on the topic is comparatively small. As stated in the introduction of this chapter, most efforts to demonstrate the effect of populism on democracy have been theoretical (Pedahzur and Weinberg 2001; Mény and Surel 2002; Abts and Rummens 2007; Rovira Kaltwasser 2012) or are the result of case studies (e.g., Lewandowsky 2012; Batory 2016), of which some are comparative (Decker 2006; Albertazzi and Mueller 2013; Otjes and Louwerse 2015). Quantitative accounts of the effect of populism on democracy have been given by Huber and Schimpf (2015, 2016) for Latin America and Europe.[2]

The impact of RWPs has been studied most thoroughly in relation to the public policy field of immigration and integration, though the results are rather ambiguous and inconsistent (Mudde 2013). Possible indirect effects of RWPs, so-called contagion effects on mainstream parties, have been a subject of interest of various scholars, who assert that the electoral success of RWPs puts pressure on mainstream parties (Schain 2006; Van Spanje 2010; de Lange 2012; Bolin et al. 2014). These parties are then forced to adjust to the new RWP competitor and to harden their immigration policy positions accordingly. While other scholars have doubted such a contagion effect and have regarded it as overestimated (Alonso and Claro da Fonseca 2012; Akkerman 2012, 2015; Mudde 2013; Rooduijn et al. 2014), indirect effects on democratic quality make up one possible influence we need to take into account.

RWPs' indirect effect on democracy was expressed by Arditi in the metaphor of populists showing up like a "drunken guest at a dinner party" (Arditi 2005, 90; see also Huber and Schimpf 2016). As they are not bound to well-established conventions, RWPs can circumvent mediating institutions and appeal to what Canovan (1999) has called the "redemptive" face of democracy. In this sense, RWPs can bring up issues, which would have been ignored otherwise, and express them in a tone unsuspected by mainstream parties—and may thus increase electoral participation. As explained further below, there is in fact evidence that populist parties stimulate democracies, especially in terms of participation and turnout.[3]

Nevertheless, the indirect effect of RWPs is by no means primarily positive. RWPs can be harmful for democracies as their populist discourse potentially undermines the rights of minorities and respect for the rule of law, thus poisoning the social climate. Further, RWPs might apply only a vote-seeking instead of an office-seeking strategy. Accordingly, they are able to maximize support for their issues and raise expectations for their parties but do not undertake any efforts to transform them into policies. For the Netherlands, Akkerman et al. suggest that the PVV might have even provoked other parties to establish a *cordon sanitaire* around the party, as Geert Wilders was unwilling to be involved in a government coalition (Akkerman 2016, 158; for Austria, see Albertazzi and Mueller 2013).

---

[2]For the effect of populist radical right parties on socioeconomic issues, see Röth et al. (2017).

[3]Moreover, European populists invariably portray themselves as the only "true democrats" (Canovan 2004). In their view, they are the only saviors of democracy against political and economic elites, whom they accuse of betraying "the people" (Albertazzi and Mueller 2013, 345).

Rather than influencing policy outputs as policy-makers themselves, RWPs outside of government can act as agenda-setters and influence other political actors, the media, and ultimately the voters in a manner potentially harmful for liberal democracy (Akkerman 2012, 514). Taking up the notion of a possible indirect effect and right-wing contagion, we assume here that RWPs can already impact on democratic quality or its partial regimes (see introduction) by the time they become electorally relevant. We further expect this indirect effect to be stronger as the "electoral power" of RWPs increases (Mudde and Rovira Kaltwasser 2017, 79), as parties gain with electoral successes more attention from the public, the media, and their competitors.

As the discussion of RWPs' indirect effect on democratic quality has shown, there are good reasons to assume either a positive or negative effect of RWPs outside government. On the one hand, they may enhance participation and representation, but, on the other, they can also reduce the quality of the public sphere. Hence, for RWPs' indirect effect on the quality of democracy, we formulate a two-tailed, nondirectional hypothesis:

Hypothesis 1a Right-wing populist parties exert an indirect effect on democratic quality, which increases with their electoral power.

Once elected into government, RWPs can directly affect policy outputs. Case studies point out that RWPs in office especially target checks and balances and constitutional courts and also adopt new laws to limit media influence. Like other RWPs, the Polish *Law and Justice* party (PiS) and the Hungarian *Fidesz* have pursued an agenda of anti-immigration and anti-judiciary policies, which seem to regularly clash with liberal democracy (Fomina and Kucharczyk 2016; Batory 2016). Nevertheless, in most cases, RWPs need to take into account the policy positions of their coalition partners. Regarding the policy output of RWPs in Western Europe, Akkerman (2012, 511) concludes that it "deviates significantly from center-left and center cabinets, but does not differ much from that of center-right cabinets." Hence, one can argue that populist parties in government are under pressure to tone down their radicalness at the expense of their populist core. Due to this "inherent structural weakness," some authors have put the long-term success of populist parties in government into question (Mény and Surel 2002; Heinisch 2003).

In fact, most RWPs in government have responded to this threat by pursuing a double strategy of acting as an opposition in government, with "one foot in, one foot out" (Albertazzi et al. 2011, 484). While they push for anti-migration policies, populist parties in government have discovered various ways to continuously tap into political discontent. The *Swiss People's Party* (SVP) is a case in point of a party deeply rooted in the political system of its country and still very effective in retaining an antiestablishment profile (Mazzoleni 2016). As much of the populist appeal rests on the invocation of the "other" (Rovira Kaltwasser and Taggart 2016, 205), populists in power have shifted their criticisms of the elite toward attacks on opposition parties, courts and judges, journalists and intellectuals, and those institutions that allegedly or actually block their agenda. The current right-wing populist governments in Poland and Hungary are cases in point.

Furthermore, observers of RWPs' behavior in office emphasize that RWPs often act amateurish and are not prepared for working in government (Heinisch 2003). They regularly face difficulties in transitioning from opposition into government. Looking at right-wing populists' turnover rates of ministers in Austria and the Netherlands, Akkerman and de Lange (2012) assert that most FPÖ and LPF ministers ended up resigning due to incompetence.

Therefore, in concurrence with Huber and Schimpf (2016), we assume that RWPs in government impact the quality of democracy predominantly negatively. We expect this effect when RWPs are minor or major coalition partners or form a majority government themselves. Further, we expect this effect to be distinct when RWPs have the leadership over a government. Thus, on the basis of the preceding discussion, we assume the following effects of RWPs on democratic quality:

Hypothesis 1b Right-wing populist parties in government, particularly when exercising government leadership, exert a negative effect on democratic quality.

5.2.3 Representation

If RWPs have an effect on the quality of democracy as stated in the hypotheses above, we should consequently be able to detect RWPs' effect on particular functions of democracy. In this section, we have selected five democratic functions, which we expect to be particularly at odds with the policy agenda and rhetoric of RWPs.

One key feature of populist parties is their repeated recourse to the will of "the people." The main positive effect of RWPs might be their aspiration to give voice to those groups of people which do not feel adequately represented (Mudde and Rovira Kaltwasser 2012, 209). According to Mouffe, such a demand for representation is to be expected and, indeed, justified in principle, as the neoliberal "consensus at the centre" (Mouffe and Wagner 2013, 93) has led to a crisis of representation, which renders the voices of democratic citizens unheard. Populists' conception of democracy is further characterized by their demand to strengthen plebiscitary measures, such as referendums (Mudde 2007, 151). Therefore, we assume that if RWPs exert a positive effect on representation, it should be visible for substantive representation, which includes structural possibilities for the inclusion of preferences and provisions to express oneself by means of direct-democratic instruments.

RWPs are expected to be harmful for the representation of minority groups, such as migrants, Muslims, or in some cases homosexuals. This is not only due to the nativist core ideology of RWPs. Various authors have stressed populism's "radical interpretation of majority rule" (Mudde and Rovira Kaltwasser 2013, 164) and its inherent anti-pluralism, which aims for the exclusion of outsider groups (Golder 2016; Müller 2016). For representation, we therefore assume the following:

Hypothesis 2a Right-wing populist parties exert a positive effect on substantive representation by including preferences of the unrepresented.

Hypothesis 2b Right-wing populist parties exert a negative effect on the representation of minority groups.

5.2.4 Relationship to Selected Functions of Democracy

A further implication of RWPs' sweeping invocation of popular sovereignty is that they do not acknowledge constitutional constraints and other regulations which limit the power of the majority. RWPs "speak and behave as if democracy meant the power of the people and only the power of the people" (Mény and Surel 2002, 9) and do not acknowledge that the power of the majority has to be limited in order to protect individual liberty rights. Further, populist reasoning is based on the imaginary of a closed, collective identity, a fiction which neglects and ultimately suppresses individual differences (Abts and Rummens 2007, 416). Individual liberties, in our understanding, comprise rights that ensure physical integrity, as well as those that facilitate free conduct of life.

To illustrate this point: In its 2008 manifesto, the Italian *Lega Nord* (LN/Northern League) proposed several measures restricting the liberties of Muslims. One proposition was to make the construction (or enlargement) of mosques dependent on approval by a local referendum. Thus, the individual right to free exercise and practice of one's own religion would have been sidelined by majoritarian rule (Albertazzi and Mueller 2013, 345). Accordingly, we assume:

Hypothesis 3 Right-wing populist parties exert a negative effect on individual liberties.

Similar to the argument brought forward for RWPs' impact on individual liberties, we expect RWPs to harm certain liberal aspects of the rule of law. We argue that RWPs in government try to elude horizontal accountability and position themselves against the effective independence of the judiciary and the impartiality of the legal system. Constitutional courts need to act as the last safeguards repelling populist challenges to the liberal democratic order (Stanley 2016; Blauberger and Kelemen 2017). The leadership of Viktor Orbán is an example of a populist abuse of power. When *Fidesz* came to power, it limited the influence of the Constitutional Court, replaced several high-ranking judges, and abolished the possibility for citizens to directly petition the Constitutional Court (Batory 2016). Other RWPs have reduced electoral integrity, as members of RWPs have been reported to engage in electoral fraud, while RWPs themselves have repeatedly questioned the integrity of voting processes (Norris and Grömping 2017, 29).

Hypothesis 4 Right-wing populist parties exert a negative effect on the rule of law.

As much as RWPs are expected to negatively impact on the rule of law and individual liberties, we assume RWPs seek to suppress freedom of association and freedom of opinion. Whereas some RWPs claim to liberate the public sphere from cultural "elitism" such as political correctness, populist discourse is rather tailored to the creation of polarized discourses. This is exemplified by how populists view their political opponents. While non-populist parties regard the political opponent as an equal *adversary*, right-wing populists question the legitimacy of their political *foes* (Abts and Rummens 2007, 419). In the past, RWPs have engaged in suppressing media outlets and drastically worsening public perception of the media, established alternative news sources of dubious quality, and reduced funding for public broadcasters. In Poland, for instance, PiS has effectively pushed the narrative of "Poland in ruins" despite clear evidence to the contrary (Fomina and Kucharczyk 2016, 60). RWPs regularly stereotype migrants, denigrate refugees, and mock groups which they regard as non-native. Wodak (2013) has observed a process of "othering" in the public sphere for Austria during the time Haider was leader of the FPÖ. She concludes that this process was spreading in society, ranging from the media, political parties, and institutions to everyday life interactions.

Hypothesis 5 Right-wing populist parties exert a negative effect on the public sphere.

Finally, RWPs are expected to stimulate participation. Participation is understood here as the equality of participation as well as effective participation in both electoral and other forms. This effect is expected to operate in two ways. First, RWPs can fill a gap of unaddressed issues and can position themselves in-between mainstream right and right-wing extremist parties. Further, they can address voters who are dissatisfied with the working of democracy and have anti-elite and antiestablishment attitudes, as their political communication is tailored to such groups (e.g., Treib 2014). For Italy, Verbeek and Zaslove (2016, 318) assert that populism "has been partly functional [...] in contributing to establish more contestation." Hence, RWPs can be attractive to former nonvoters, raise turnout, and have therefore a positive effect on participation.

Additionally, RWPs can indirectly impact on participation, as their populist rhetoric and their right-wing issue profile provoke countermovements. Such movements, like the Committee for the Defense of Democracy (KOD) in Poland or "Pulse for Europe," are direct responses to populists in government and signs of a wider politicization of the public (Guérot 2017). We therefore assume:

Hypothesis 6 Right-wing populist parties exert a positive effect on participation.

5.3 Research Design

As we want to explore whether right-wing populist parties do have an effect on democratic quality and on democracy's subdimensions, we use a research design that is centered on the causing factor (Gschwend and Schimmelfennig 2007). We apply several panel regression models in which we hold the independent variables constant while varying on the dependent variable.

To evaluate our predictions empirically, we construct a dataset comprising all cabinets in the member states of the European Union (EU),[4] plus Norway and Switzerland from 1990 to 2014.[5] The time period is constrained by the availability of data for our main dependent variables. Nevertheless, as Huber and Schimpf (2016, 112) have argued before, this time period captures the main stages of the establishment of right-wing populist parties and is therefore suitable for analysis. For Eastern Europe, the starting year varies between 1990 and 1993, as we recognize only those cabinets which were elected after independence for a regular term (Grotz and Müller-Rommel 2015, 318).[6] The coding rules for cabinet formation and termination follow those in Woldendorp et al. (2010, 10). Further, we exclude those cabinets which lasted less than 182 days. Data for cabinets, cabinet duration, government involvement, and parties' seat shares in parliament are drawn from the dataset "Elections, Parties, Governments" (WZB 2017).

Right-wing populist parties were coded according to the classification provided by Mudde (2007). To this list, we add parties, which can be identified as right-wing populist, but are borderline cases in the sense that they do not necessarily meet the criteria of being radical, as nativism is not part of their *core* ideology (Van Kessel 2015; Mudde 2017). These parties include the *Centre Democrats* (Netherlands), *Fidesz* (Hungary), *Forza Italia* (Italy), *Law and Justice* party (Poland), *List Pim Fortuyn* (Netherlands), *True Finns Party* (Finland), and the *UK Independence Party* (UKIP). By including these parties into the analysis, we pursue a conservative approach.[7]

For an assessment of the *dependent variables* democratic quality and its partial regimes, we rely, as do most of the chapters of this volume, on the Democracy Barometer (Bühlmann et al. 2012; Merkel et al. 2016). In accordance with the scope of this chapter, the Democracy Barometer is conceptualized to measure a midrange model of democracy, based on a hierarchical aggregation of 105 indicators. According to the project, democracy consists of three core principles: freedom,

[4]Due to missing values, Romania before 1995, Croatia before 2000, and Cyprus had to be excluded from the analysis.

[5]Cabinets, which were still in office at the end of 2014, were not included in the analysis to ensure case comparability, as we include government duration in the model.

[6]The starting year for Hungary is 1990; for Bulgaria and Poland 1991; for Estonia, Lithuania, and Romania 1992; and for the Czech Republic, Latvia, Slovenia, and Slovakia 1993.

[7]The appendix includes a complete list of parties coded as right-wing populist. Please note that the Croatian HDZ is coded only until 2000 as right-wing populist.

equality, and control. These core principles are, in turn, constituted from nine functions of democracy, of which we will use *representation*, *individual liberty*, *rule of law*, *public sphere*, and *participation*.[8] The indicators for democratic quality and the democratic functions were standardized on a scale ranging from 0 to 100, giving us a nuanced measurement of the varying degree of democratic quality. As the data are provided on an annual basis, we calculated country averages. Country averages were computed by taking the mean value of all years covered by one government in one country for all variables of interest. In contrast to Huber and Schimpf (2016), we do not use a subset of democratic functions to measure the quality of democracy. Instead, we use the preconstructed measurement of the Democracy Barometer, as only the full index ensures that the balance between freedom, equality, and control is depicted adequately.

The construction of our main independent variables *seat share in parliament* and *government inclusion* follows the structure laid out in hypotheses 1a and 1b. First, we expect RWPs to exert negative and positive effects on democratic quality conditional to the degree of involvement in government. We distinguish between four different gradations of government involvement: no involvement, support party for the government, minor party in government, and government leadership, which we have combined as categories of one polytomous variable. If there was more than one right-wing populist party per cabinet period, we have used the value indicating the strongest involvement in government.[9] We added the attribute *support party* as a control, as we regard the effect of minority coalitions with RWPs' participation as primarily shaped by the coalition's major parties.

Second, to measure the electoral power of RWPs, we use here right-wing populists' *seat share in parliament*. We assume that whether a right-wing populist party is represented in parliament and how strong it is plays a role in explaining democratic quality. This allows us to distinguish between RWPs outside and inside the parliamentary opposition. We have also considered using a party's vote share to measure electoral power, but we ultimately refrained from doing so for comparative reasons. As electoral systems have varying effective thresholds for parties to enter parliament, the vote share necessary to have relevance in terms of electoral power varies by country. Further, using the vote share is problematic insofar as we do not always have full data for very small parties.[10] Nevertheless, one may reasonably argue that an RWP can already exert indirect influence before entering parliament. The *Alternative for Germany* (AfD) is such a case. The AfD was founded in 2013 and is expected to enter parliament in 2017. In the 4 years in between, however, the party has considerably influenced the German political agenda and, therefore, the

[8]For a more detailed description of the Democracy Barometer, see also Heyne in this volume.

[9]In model 1 we only distinguish between *no government involvement* and any form of involvement, whereas in model 2 we combine *minor party in government* and *government leadership* in order to explain the additional explanatory power of a more distinct measurement.

[10]Nevertheless, we have computed all models with the vote share data available and did not observe differences in terms of significant effects.

public sphere. For the reasons given above, this is an effect we do not capture here further.

Therefore, we use the summed *seat share* of right-wing populist parties in parliament. As control variables, we add government duration (in days), GDP per capita (measured in 2005 constant USD; World Bank 2016; Teorell et al. 2017), and a dummy variable for Eastern and Western European countries.

To account for the hierarchical structure of the data, we have conducted a random effects panel regression model (Singer and Willett 2003; Brüderl 2010).[11] As we are interested above all in the change caused by the rising strength of right-wing populist parties, a model which only accounts for *within*-case variance would be more suitable. In order to add also time-constant variables to our models, we have refrained from using this alternative and employed Hausman tests instead, which show no significant difference between random- and fixed-effects modeling in our case (Hausman 1978). All independent, continuous variables were centered to their country group mean (Gelman and Hill 2006). To avoid overconfidence, panel-corrected standard errors have been calculated, accounting for autocorrelation in time and country groups (Beck et al. 1995).

5.4 Empirical Results

5.4.1 Quality of Democracy

The remainder of the chapter presents the empirical results for the previously formulated hypothesis. First, we investigate the effect RWPs exert on the overall quality of democracy. In Table 5.1, the results for hypothesis 1a and 1b are summarized. We have included our main independent variable *government inclusion* in a stepwise approach (models 1–3) to show that the models are stable over varying gradations of RWPs' inclusion in government. While we find evidence for direct negative effects of RWPs (hypothesis 1b), we do not see any indications for an indirect influence of RWPs on the quality of democracy (hypothesis 1a). The best explanation in terms of detail and predicted variance is presented in the third model. It shows that there is a significant negative effect on democratic quality when RWPs are included in government. This effect remains negative when RWPs exert government leadership. Further, the inclusion of RWPs as supporters of minority governments does not impact the quality of democracy. These findings are in line with those of Huber and Schimpf (2016), even though we tested for the full index of democratic quality as conceptualized by Bühlmann et al. (2012).

We have, furthermore, refined the analysis by Huber and Schimpf (2016) and added the *seat share in parliament* as an indicator for RWPs' electoral strength. We

[11] All empirical analysis in this paper has been conducted with the statistical software environment R. The syntax used and a prepared dataset are available upon request.

Table 5.1 Effect of right-wing populism on democratic quality

	Dependent variable		
	Quality of democracy		
	(1)	(2)	(3)
Inclusion in government:			
– Part of government	−1.103***	−1.093***	−1.234**
	(0.351)	(0.360)	(0.501)
– Support government		0.220	0.234
		(0.682)	(0.686)
– Government leadership			−0.849**
			(0.426)
Seat share in parliament	0.079	0.061	0.039
	(0.392)	(0.424)	(0.411)
GDP *per capita*	0.042	0.037	0.035
	(0.442)	(0.446)	(0.448)
Government duration	0.542**	0.540**	0.550**
	(0.257)	(0.257)	(0.260)
Eastern Europe	−9.403***	−9.390***	−9.399***
	(3.083)	(3.125)	(3.115)
Intercept	62.946***	62.930***	62.937***
	(2.054)	(2.119)	(2.110)
Observations	211	211	211
R^2	0.205	0.231	0.223

Note: $^{*}p < 0.1$; $^{**}p < 0.5$; $^{***}p < 0.01$

have suggested that the mere representation of RWPs as an opposition party may exert a positive impact on democratic quality. But as the effect of RWP's seat share on democratic quality is negative, it is insignificant. Thus, the mere presence of RWPs in parliament does not negatively impact the overall quality of democracy.

5.4.2 *Representation*

Before we turn to a discussion of the regression results for RWPs' effect on substantial representation and the representation of minorities, we take a look at RWPs' position in the party system. In addition to mobilization through political discontent and anti-elite attitudes, RWPs seek convergence with potential voters on substantive political preferences (Ivarsflaten 2008; Wagner et al. 2015; Van Hauwaert and Van Kessel 2017). As an example, Fig. 5.2 illustrates the supply-side of RWPs and mainstream parties in the Dutch party system. According to Kitschelt's theory of the two-dimensionality of the competitive space in postindustrial democracies, the axes are formed by the socioeconomic left-right dimension and the libertarian-authoritarian dimension (Kitschelt 1994, 1995). Party positions have been derived from the Chapel Hill Expert Survey (Bakker et al. 2015).

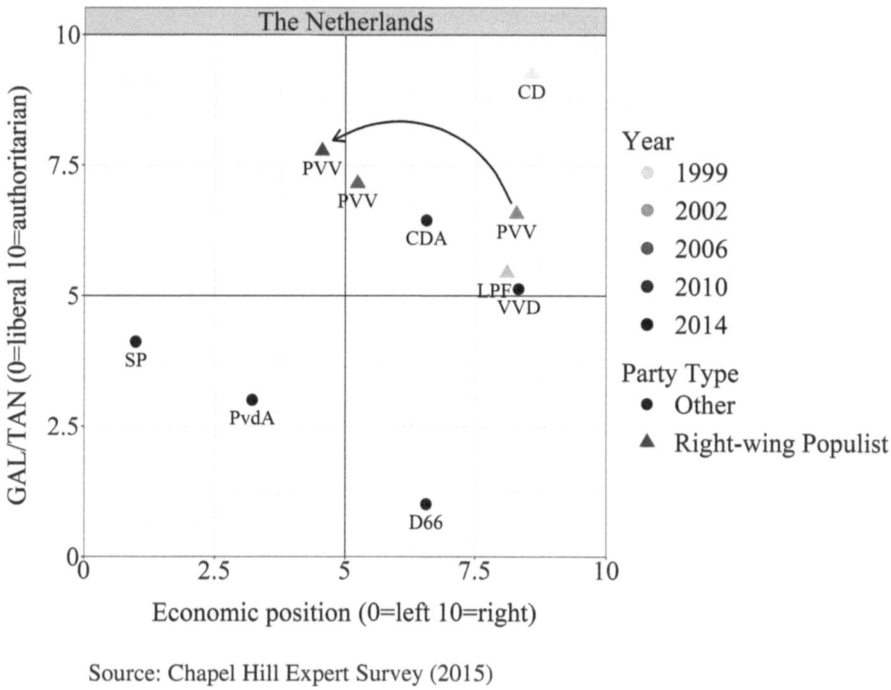

Fig. 5.2 Right-wing populist parties in the Netherland's political arena

The Dutch party system functions here as an example of RWPs' re-positioning in the party system's left-authoritarian quadrant. Especially for Western European—albeit not for all European—countries, we can observe in the Chapel Hill Data a static trend of RWPs changing from neoliberal to more left-leaning economic positions, such as protectionism and support for social programs (de Lange 2007). The figure illustrates this development: while both the LPF and the PVV started out on the economic right, the PVV as the lone surviving right-wing populist party has continuously rearranged its profile. In Western Europe, RWPs, in comparison to mainstream parties, have taken up a distinct position in the party system where they can attract voters with a left-authoritarian profile. There is also considerable demand for left-authoritarian parties, as a comparison of turnout rates depending on voters' issue positions has revealed (Hillen and Steiner 2017). Hence, RWPs seem to fill a representation gap for voters with authoritarian views and a socioeconomic interest in anti-liberal protection by the state. Röth et al. (2017) have studied the impact of RWPs in government on socioeconomic issues. They conclude that RWPs indeed refrain from welfare-state retrenchment, as they take into consideration parts of their voter base which hold particularly strong left-wing socioeconomic positions. Further, governments with RWP inclusion were less likely to have deregulatory economic policies in comparison to mainstream-right governments.

Table 5.2 Effect of right-wing populist parties on representation

	Dependent variable		
	Representation	Representation of minorities	Substantial representation
	(1)	(2)	(3)
Inclusion in government:			
– Part of government	−0.979	−0.934	−1.542
	(1.156)	(1.832)	(1.107)
– Support government	−1.689**	−3.889***	0.621
	(0.684)	(1.348)	(0.867)
– Government leadership	−1.564*	−3.032**	−1.903
	(0.895)	(1.401)	(1.544)
Seat share in parliament	0.365	0.253	0.298
	(0.604)	(1.449)	(0.984)
GDP *per capita*	4.257***	8.428***	0.497
	(0.793)	(1.742)	(0.974)
Government duration	−0.029	−0.327	0.197
	(0.394)	(0.813)	(0.492)
Eastern Europe	−11.721***	−21.126***	−2.948
	(3.322)	(7.375)	(5.312)
Intercept	60.191***	71.898***	49.194***
	(2.517)	(6.018)	(4.202)
Observations	212	212	215
R^2	0.484	0.469	0.031

Note: $^{*}p < 0.1$; $^{**}p < 0.5$; $^{***}p < 0.01$

However, the representation effect of RWPs through their distinct position in the party system should not be overstated. Particularly regarding the economic axis, RWPs have in the past tried to blur their positions vis-à-vis the voters and to lower the salience of economic issues (Rovny 2013). Other observers have suggested that the rise in support for RWPs might be at the expense of the liberal left (Markowski 2016, 1316) In addition, one must not forget RWPs' welfare chauvinism. Further, in the eyes of right-wing populists, a generous welfare state is only desirable for the native population, while non-native groups are to be excluded (Mudde and Rovira Kaltwasser 2013, 160).

In the same vein, the regression models in Table 5.2 indicate a solely negative effect of RWPs on political representation. We find a direct negative effect for minority groups when RWPs are part of government, as expected in hypothesis 2b. Also, the overall representation function is negatively influenced by RWPs in government. Contrary to the descriptive evidence above and our initial assumption, RWPs do not significantly improve the quality of representation. Thus, we reject hypothesis 2a. We can conclude that if RWPs actually fill a representation gap, as the descriptive analysis of party positions suggests, this is not reflected in our model, which takes the impact of RWPs' government inclusion and seat share on representation into consideration. Instead, RWPs lower the quality of representation for minority groups.

Table 5.3 Effect of right-wing populist parties on functions of democratic quality

	Dependent variable			
	Individual liberty	Rule of law	Public sphere	Participation
	(1)	(2)	(3)	(4)
Inclusion in government:				
– Part of government	−2.125	−2.350	−1.050	0.853
	(1.644)	(1.642)	(0.855)	(0.910)
– Support government	2.153**	−2.045	−0.452	1.270
	(0.917)	(3.581)	(1.110)	(0.875)
– Government leadership	−2.272**	−0.704	−0.938*	1.015
	(1.131)	(1.446)	(0.499)	(1.521)
Seat share in parliament	−1.322	0.495	−0.731*	2.371**
	(1.143)	(1.504)	(0.412)	(1.042)
GDP *per capita*	0.061	−2.159	0.520	−6.939***
	(1.075)	(1.595)	(0.917)	(1.452)
Government duration	1.103*	0.402	0.092	−0.466
	(0.666)	(0.702)	(0.374)	(0.498)
Eastern Europe	−5.520	−22.119**	−8.112	−5.494
	(4.940)	(8.954)	(6.031)	(3.434)
Intercept	82.753***	69.332***	48.162***	54.233***
	(3.278)	(4.898)	(4.262)	(2.429)
Observations	213	212	212	215
R^2	0.116	0.150	0.033	0.544

Notes: $^{*}p < 0.1$; $^{**}p < 0.5$; $^{***}p < 0.01$

5.4.3 *Selected Functions of Democracy*

We now turn to the effects RWPs have on other selected functions of democracy. The results are displayed in Table 5.3. As expected, RWPs negatively influence individual liberties (hypothesis 3). The effect is significant for RWPs having government leadership, but it does not increase with RWPs' representation in parliament. Hence, we only observe indications for RWPs' direct effect on individual liberties, but not for any form of indirect effects.

Contrary to the expected causal relationship in hypothesis 4, we cannot find support for a significant negative impact of RWPs on the rule of law, neither when RWPs are part of government, nor when in opposition. While the coefficients point in the right direction, this non-effect remains stable when we test only for the influence of RWPs on the rule of law's sub-function *equality before the law*. In this sub-function, we would have expected the largest effect of RWPs. Given the vast amount of case study literature describing how RWPs challenge constitutional courts and horizontal accountability, this is a new finding. In part, it contradicts the results of Huber and Schimpf (2016), who observe a small negative impact of

RWPs in opposition on the rule of law. The finding highlights that RWPs' verbal attacks on the independent court system were apparently not sufficient to harm the rule of law in a substantive way. Further, the European Court of Justice (ECJ) and other judicial mechanisms seem to have played a crucial role in safeguarding member states from democratic backsliding (Batory 2016; Blauberger and Kelemen 2017). For this analysis, we conclude that between 1990 and 2014, RWPs have not affected the rule of law.

In line with our earlier assumption, we find a negative link between the representation of RWPs in parliament and the public sphere (hypothesis 5). The effect increases when RWPs exercise government leadership. Nevertheless, RWPs' populist rhetoric alone is sufficient to undermine the partial regime of the public sphere.

The single most positive effect of RWPs we can assert is on participation. In accordance with our line of argumentation in hypothesis 6, RWPs' increasing electoral strength has a positive effect on political participation. However, we cannot say whether this effect is caused directly by RWPs' attractiveness for otherwise unrepresented voters or whether it is predominantly caused by the indirect mobilization of countermovements. Support for the first explanation was given by Hillen and Steiner (2017), who suggest that the emergence of the *Finns Party* as a left-authoritarian party increased turnout among voters with left-authoritarian issue positions. Whether countermovements of non-populist party supporters play an additional role for the positive development of participation remains unresolved here.

5.5 Conclusion

The purpose of this chapter was to ask whether right-wing populism constitutes a threat to democracy. Our empirical analysis reveals mixed results. First, we were able to confirm and refine the results of Huber and Schimpf (2016), who asserted that RWPs reduce democratic quality when in government, but not when in opposition. We add that this remains true even when we account for the electoral strength of RWPs. Second, a closer investigation of RWPs' allegedly positive representation function shows that, in fact, right-wing populist parties take up a distinct position in the electoral arena and address otherwise unrepresented left-authoritarian voters. However, this positioning strategy fails to enhance substantial or descriptive representation in a meaningful way. Third, the results for selected subdimensions of democratic quality demonstrate a more negative effect of RWPs in- and outside government. While the electoral strength of RWPs tends to enhance participation, they prove to be harmful for the public sphere and individual liberties. For the rule of law, we were not able to confirm the expected negative effects.

Do these results indicate an ongoing crisis of democracy? Overall, democracy is obviously not automatically in danger of re-autocratization under the threat of right-wing populists. While the quality of democracy declines under the government involvement of RWPs, the basic democratic norms and procedures are not deeply affected if RWPs do not dominate government as it is the case in Poland and Hungary. However, there is a real danger for democracies becoming less liberal. While the input dimension of democracy (especially the participation of the electorate, i.e., the sovereignty of the people) seems to be strengthened in part by the mere existence of populist parties (which may indicate, in a positive reading, a repoliticization of the democratic polity), the liberal dimension of democracy comes under pressure. Although this is not the case in all temporary democracies with RWPs in government, the current cases of Poland and Hungary nevertheless show that democracy is not immune to the dangers of re-autocratization if populists dominate governments and are willing and able to curtail the liberal components of modern democracy, especially the rule of law and the institutions of checks and balances. In a word: Right-wing populists do not pose a direct threat to democracy as long as they are checked by the majority of democratic parties and stick to the democratic rules of the game. However, a severe crisis of democracy is to be expected if this is no longer the case. Poland and Hungary today are the writing on the wall.

Appendix

Right-wing populist parties

Country	Initials	Party name	Years included (first and last election results recognized)
Austria	FPÖ	Freedom Party of Austria	1990–2013
	BZÖ	Alliance for the Future of Austria	2006–2013
Belgium	VB	Flemish Interest	1991–2014
	FN/NF	National Front	1991–2010
Bulgaria	Ataka	Attack Coalition	2005–2014
Croatia	HDZ	Croatian Democratic Union	1990–2000
	HSP	Croatian Party of Rights	1992–1995
	HSP/ZDS	Croatian Party of Rights/Zagorje Democratic Party	2003
	HSP AS	Croatian Party of Rights Dr. Ante Starcevic	2011
Czech Republic	SPR-RSC	Rally for the Republic – Republican Party of Czechoslovakia	1992–2010
	Úsvit	Dawn of Direct Democracy	2013
Denmark	DF	Danish People's Party	1998–2011
Estonia	ERSP	Estonian National Independence Party	1992
	EK	Estonian Citizens Coalition	1992
Finland	PS	True Finns	1991–2011
France	FN	National Front	1993–2012
Great Britain	UKIP	United Kingdom Independence Party	1997–2010

(continued)

Country	Initials	Party name	Years included (first and last election results recognized)
Greece	LAOS	Popular Orthodox Rally	2007–2012
Hungary	FIDESZ-MPP	Fidesz-Hungarian Civic Union	1990–2014
	MIéP	Hungarian Justice and Life Party	1994–1998
	Jobbik	The Movement for a Better Hungary	2010–2014
Italy	LV	Venetian League	1992–2001
	LN	Northern League-Federal Italy	1992–2013
	Casa	House of Freedom	1994–2001
	MS	Social Movement-Flame Tricolore	1996–2006
	FI	Forward Italy	2006
	M5S	Five Star Movement	2013
Latvia	TB	Union For Homeland and Freedom	1993–1995
	NA	National Alliance "All For Latvia!"—"For Fatherland and Freedom/LNNK"	2010–2014
Netherlands	CD	Centre Democrats	1994–1998
	LPF	List Pim Fortuyn	2002–2003
	PVV	Party for Freedom	2006–2012
Poland	PX	Party X	1991
	KPN	Confederation for Independent Poland	1991–1993
	ROP	Movement for Rebuilding Poland	1997
	PiS	Law and Justice	2001–2011
	LPR	League of Polish Families	2001–2007
Romania	PUNR	Party of Romanian National Unity	1992–1996
	PRM	Greater Romania Party	1992–2008
Slovakia	SNS	Slovak National Party	1990–2010
	OLaNO	Ordinary People and Independent Personalities	2012
Slovenia	SNS	Slovenian National Party	1996–2008
Sweden	NyD	New Democracy	1991–1998
	SD	Sweden Democrats	1991–2014
Switzerland	SD	Swiss Democrats	1991–2007
	FPS	Freedom Party	1991–2003
	SVP/UDC	Swiss People's Party	1991–2011

References

Abts, K., & Rummens, S. (2007). Populism versus democracy. *Political Studies, 55*(2), 405–424. https://doi.org/10.1111/j.1467-9248.2007.00657.x.

Akkerman, T. (2012). Comparing radical right parties in government: Immigration and integration policies in nine countries (19962010). *West European Politics, 35*(3), 511–529. https://doi.org/10.1080/01402382.2012.665738.

Akkerman, T. (2015). Immigration policy and electoral competition in Western Europe: A fine-grained analysis of party positions over the past two decades. *Party Politics, 21*(1), 54–67. https://doi.org/10.1177/1354068812462928.

Akkerman, T. (2016). The party for freedom: Balancing between mission, votes and office. In T. Akkerman, S. L. de Lange, & M. Rooduijn (Eds.), *Radical right-wing populist parties in Western Europe: Into the mainstream?* (pp. 145–168). London: Routledge.

Akkerman, T., & de Lange, S. L. (2012). Radical right parties in office: Incumbency records and the electoral cost of governing. *Government and Opposition, 47*(4), 574–596. https://doi.org/10.1111/j.1477-7053.2012.01375.x.

Akkerman, T., de Lange, S. L., & Rooduijn, M. (2016). Into the mainstream? A comparative analysis of the programmatic profiles of radical right-wing populist parties in Western Europe over time. In T. Akkerman, S. L. de Lange, & M. Rooduijn (Eds.), *Radical right-wing populist parties in Western Europe: Into the mainstream?* (pp. 31–52). London: Routledge.

Albertazzi, D., & McDonnell, D. (Eds.). (2008). *Twenty-first century populism: The spectre of western European democracy*. Basingstoke: Palgrave Macmillan.

Albertazzi, D., McDonnell, D., & Newell, J. L. (2011). Di Lotta E Di Governo: The Lega Nord and Rifondazione Comunista in office. *Party Politics, 17*(4), 471–487. https://doi.org/10.1177/1354068811400523.

Albertazzi, D., & Mueller, S. (2013). Populism and liberal democracy: Populists in government in Austria, Italy, Poland and Switzerland. *Government and Opposition, 48*(3), 343–371. https://doi.org/10.1017/gov.2013.12.

Alonso, S., & Claro da Fonseca, S. (2012). Immigration, left and right. *Party Politics, 18*(6), 865–884. https://doi.org/10.1177/1354068810393265.

Arditi, B. (2005). Populism as an internal periphery of democratic politics. In F. Panizza (Ed.), *Populism and the mirror of democracy* (pp. 72–98). London: Verso.

Aslanidis, P. (2016). Is populism an ideology? A refutation and a new perspective. *Political Studies, 64*(1_suppl), 88–104. https://doi.org/10.1111/1467-9248.12224.

Bakker, R., de Vries, C., Edwards, E., Hooghe, L., Jolly, S., Marks, G., Polk, J., Rovny, J., Steenbergen, M., & Vachudova, M. A. (2015). Measuring party positions in Europe: The Chapel Hill expert survey trend file, 19992010. *Party Politics, 21*(1), 143–152. https://doi.org/10.1177/1354068812462931.

Batory, A. (2016). Populists in government? Hungary's "System of National Cooperation". *Democratization, 23*(2), 283–303. https://doi.org/10.1080/13510347.2015.1076214.

Beck, J. N., Beck, N., Katz, J. N., & Katz, N. (1995). What to do (and not to do) with time-series cross-section data. *American Political Science Review, 100*(4), 634–647.

Betz, H.-G. (1994). *Radical right-wing populism in Western Europe*. Basingstoke: Palgrave Macmillan.

Blauberger, M., & Kelemen, R. D. (2017). Can courts rescue national democracy? Judicial safeguards against democratic backsliding in the EU. *Journal of European Public Policy, 24*(3), 321–336. https://doi.org/10.1080/13501763.2016.1229357.

Bolin, N., Lidén, G., & Nyhlén, J. (2014). Do anti-immigration parties matter? The case of the Sweden democrats and local refugee policy. *Scandinavian Political Studies, 37*(3), 323–343. https://doi.org/10.1111/1467-9477.12031.

Brüderl, J. (2010). Kausalanalyse mit Paneldaten. In H. Best & C. Wolf (Eds.), *Handbuch der sozialwissenschaftlichen Datenanalyse* (pp. 963–994). Wiesbaden: VS Verlag für Sozialwissenschaften.

Bühlmann, M., Merkel, W., Müller, L., & Weßels, B. (2012). The democracy barometer: A new instrument to measure the quality of democracy and its potential for comparative research. *European Political Science, 11*(4), 519–536. https://doi.org/10.1057/eps.2011.46.

Canovan, M. (1999). Trust the people! Populism and the two faces of democracy. *Political Studies, 47*(1), 2–16.
Canovan, M. (2004). Populism for political theorists? *Journal of Political Ideologies, 9*(3), 241–252. https://doi.org/10.1080/1356931042000263500.
de Lange, S. L. (2007). A new winning formula? The programmatic appeal of the radical right. *Party Politics, 13*(4), 411–435.
de Lange, S. L. (2012). New alliances: Why mainstream parties govern with radical right-wing populist parties. *Political Studies, 60*(4), 899–918. https://doi.org/10.1111/j.1467-9248.2012.00947.x.
Decker, F. (Ed.). (2006). *Populismus: Gefahr für die Demokratie oder nützliches Korrektiv?* Wiesbaden: VS Verlag für Sozialwissenschaften.
Fomina, J., & Kucharczyk, J. (2016). Populism and protest in Poland. *Journal of Democracy, 27* (4), 58–68.
Gelman, A., & Hill, J. (2006). *Data analysis using regression and multilevel/hierarchical models*. Cambridge: Cambridge University Press.
Golder, M. (2016). Far right parties in Europe. *Annual Review of Political Science, 19*(1), 477–497. https://doi.org/10.1146/annurev-polisci-042814-012441.
Grotz, F., & Müller-Rommel, F. (2015). Schwache Regierungschefs? Politische Erfahrung und Amtsdauer von Premierministern in Mittel- und Osteuropa. *Zeitschrift für Parlamentsfragen, 46*(2), 310–327. https://doi.org/10.5771/0340-1758-2015-2-310.
Gschwend, T., & Schimmelfennig, F. (2007). *Research design in political science: How to practice what they preach*. Basingstoke: Palgrave Macmillan.
Guérot, U. (2017). *Der neue Bürgerkrieg: das offene Europa und seine Feinde*. Berlin: Ullstein.
Hausman, J. (1978). Specification tests in econometrics. *Econometrica, 46*(6), 1251–1257.
Heinisch, R. (2003). Success in opposition failure in government: Explaining the performance of right-wing populist parties in public office. *West European Politics, 26*(3), 91–130. https://doi.org/10.1080/01402380312331280608.
Heinisch, R., & Hauser, K. (2016). The mainstreaming of the Austrian freedom party: The more things change. In T. Akkerman, S. L. de Lange, & M. Rooduijn (Eds.), *Radical right-wing populist parties in Western Europe: Into the mainstream?* (pp. 73–93). London: Routledge.
Hillen, S., & Steiner, N. D. (2017). Left-authoritarians and voter turnout in West European countries. https://papers.ssrn.com/sol3/papers.cfm?abstract_id=2947782. Accessed 12 Sept 2017.
Huber, R. A., & Schimpf, C. H. (2015). Friend or foe? Testing the influence of populism on democratic quality in Latin America: Friend or foe? Populism and democracy. *Political Studies*, n/a–n/a. doi: https://doi.org/10.1111/1467-9248.12219. http://journals.sagepub.com/doi/full/10.1111/1467-9248.12219. Accessed 12 Sept 2017.
Huber, R. A., & Schimpf, C. H. (2016). A drunken guest in Europe?: The influence of populist radical right parties on democratic quality. *Zeitschrift für Vergleichende Politikwissenschaft, 10*(2), 103–129. https://doi.org/10.1007/s12286-016-0302-0.
Inglehart, R. F., & Norris, P. (2016). Trump, Brexit, and the rise of populism: Economic have-Nots and cultural backlash. HKS Working Paper No, RWP16-026. https://papers.ssrn.com/sol3/papers.cfm?abstract_id=2818659. Accessed 12 Sept 2017
Ivarsflaten, E. (2008). What unites right-wing populists in Western Europe?: Re-examining grievance mobilization models in seven successful cases. *Comparative Political Studies, 41* (1), 3–23. https://doi.org/10.1177/0010414006294168.
Kitschelt, H. (1994). *The transformation of European Social Democracy*. Cambridge: Cambridge University Press.
Kitschelt, H. (1995). *The radical right in Western Europe: A comparative analysis*. Ann Arbor: University of Michigan Press.
Laclau, E. (2005a). *On populist reason*. London: Verso.
Laclau, E. (2005b). Populism: What's in a name? In F. Panizza (Ed.), *Populism and the mirror of democracy* (pp. 32–47). London: Verso.

Laclau, E., & Mouffe, C. (1985). *Hegemony and socialist strategy: Towards a radical democratic politics*. London: Verso.
Lewandowsky, M. (2012). Rechtspopulismus als Herausforderung für die Demokratie in der Bundesrepublik Deutschland. In T. Mörschel & C. Krell (Eds.), *Demokratie in Deutschland* (pp. 389–411). Wiesbaden: VS Verlag für Sozialwissenschaften.
MacRea, D., & Gellner, E. (1969). Populism as an ideology. In G. Ionescu (Ed.), *Populism: Its meanings and national characteristics* (pp. 153–164). London: Weidenfeld & Nicolson.
Markowski, R. (2016). The polish parliamentary election of 2015: A free and fair election that results in unfair political consequences. *West European Politics, 39*(6), 1–12. https://doi.org/10.1080/01402382.2016.1177305.
Mazzoleni, O. (2016). Staying away from the mainstream: The case of the Swiss People's party. In T. Akkerman, S. L. de Lange, & M. Rooduijn (Eds.), *Radical right-wing populist parties in Western Europe: Into the mainstream?* (pp. 193–207). London: Routledge.
Mény, Y., & Surel, Y. (2002). The constitutive ambiguity of populism. In Y. Mény & Y. Surel (Eds.), *Democracies and the populist challenge* (pp. 1–21). Basingstoke: Palgrave Macmillan.
Merkel, W. (2004). Embedded and defective democracies. *Democratization, 11*(5), 33–58.
Merkel, W., Bochsler, D., Bousbah, K., Bühlmann, M., Giebler, H., Hänni, M., Heyne, L., Müller, L., Ruth, S., & Weßels, B. (2016). *Democracy barometer. Methodology. Version 5*. Aarau: Zentrum für Demokratie.
Mouffe, C. (2000). *The democratic paradox*. London: Verso.
Mouffe, C. (2005). *On the political. Thinking in action*. London: Routledge.
Mouffe, C., & Wagner, E. (2013). *Agonistics: Thinking the world politically*. London: Verso.
Mudde, C. (2004). The populist zeitgeist. *Government and Opposition, 39*(4), 542–563.
Mudde, C. (2007). *Populist radical right parties in Europe*. Cambridge: Cambridge University Press.
Mudde, C. (2013). Three decades of populist radical right parties in Western Europe: So what? *European Journal of Political Research, 52*(1), 1–19. https://doi.org/10.1111/j.1475-6765.2012.02065.x.
Mudde, C. (2017). Introduction to the populist radical right. In C. Mudde (Ed.), *The populist radical right: A reader* (pp. 1–10). London: Routledge.
Mudde, C., & Rovira Kaltwasser, C. (2012). Populism: Corrective and threat to democracy. In C. Mudde & C. Rovira Kaltwasser (Eds.), *Populism in Europe and the Americas: Threat or corrective for democracy?* (pp. 205–222). Cambridge: Cambridge University Press.
Mudde, C., & Rovira Kaltwasser, C. (2013). Exclusionary vs. inclusionary populism: Comparing contemporary Europe and Latin America. *Government and Opposition, 48*(2), 147–174. https://doi.org/10.1017/gov.2012.11.
Mudde, C., & Rovira Kaltwasser, C. (2017). *Populism: A very short introduction*. Oxford: Oxford University Press.
Müller, J.-W. (2016). *Was ist populismus? Ein Essay*. Berlin: Suhrkamp.
Norris, P., & Grömping, M. (2017). *Populist Threats to electoral integrity: The year in elections, 2016-2017*. HKS Working Paper No. RWP17-018. https://papers.ssrn.com/sol3/papers.cfm?abstract_id=2965729. Accessed 28 Aug 2017.
Otjes, S., & Louwerse, T. (2015). Populists in parliament: Comparing left-wing and right-wing populism in the Netherlands: Populists in parliament. *Political Studies, 63*(1), 60–79. https://doi.org/10.1111/1467-9248.12089.
Panizza, F. (2005). Populism and the mirror of democracy—introduction. In F. Panizza (Ed.), *Populism and the mirror of democracy* (pp. 1–31). London: Verso.
Pedahzur, A., & Weinberg, L. (2001). Modern European democracy and its enemies: The threat of the extreme right. *Totalitarian Movements and Political Religions, 2*(1), 52–72. https://doi.org/10.1080/714005438.
Rooduijn, M., de Lange, S. L., & van der Brug, W. (2014). A populist zeitgeist? Programmatic contagion by populist parties in Western Europe. *Party Politics, 20*(4), 563–575. https://doi.org/10.1177/1354068811436065.

Röth, L., Afonso, A., & Spies, D. C. (2017). The impact of populist radical right parties on socio-economic policies. *European Political Science Review*, published online: 13 June 2017. doi: https://doi.org/10.1017/S1755773917000133.

Rovira Kaltwasser, C. (2011). Populismus in vergleichender Perspektive. *Berliner Debatte Initial, 22*(1), 4–11.

Rovira Kaltwasser, C. (2012). The ambivalence of populism: Threat and corrective for democracy. *Democratization, 19*(2), 184–208. https://doi.org/10.1080/13510347.2011.572619.

Rovira Kaltwasser, C., & Taggart, P. (2016). Dealing with populists in government: A framework for analysis. *Democratization, 23*(2), 201–220. https://doi.org/10.1080/13510347.2015.1058785.

Rovny, J. (2013). Where do radical right parties stand? Position blurring in multidimensional competition. *European Political Science Review, 5*, 1), 1–1),26. https://doi.org/10.1017/S1755773911000282.

Schain, M. A. (2006). The extreme-right and immigration policy-making: Measuring direct and indirect effects. *West European Politics, 29*(2), 270–289. https://doi.org/10.1080/01402380500512619.

Singer, J. D., & Willett, J. B. (2003). *Applied longitudinal data analysis*. Oxford: Oxford University Press. https://doi.org/10.1093/acprof:oso/9780195152968.001.0001.

Stanley, B. (2016). Confrontation by default and confrontation by design: Strategic and institutional responses to Poland's populist coalition government. *Democratization, 23*(2), 263–282. https://doi.org/10.1080/13510347.2015.1058782.

Stavrakakis, Y., & Katsambekis, G. (2014). Left-wing populism in the European periphery: The case of SYRIZA. *Journal of Political Ideologies, 19*(2), 119–142. https://doi.org/10.1080/13569317.2014.909266.

Stavrakakis, Y., Katsambekis, G., Nikisianis, N., Kioupkiolis, A., & Siomos, T. (2017). Extreme right-wing populism in Europe: Revisiting a reified association. *Critical Discourse Studies, 14*(4), 420–439. https://doi.org/10.1080/17405904.2017.1309325.

Taggart, P. (2000). *Populism*. Philadelphia, PA: Open University Press.

Taggart, P. (2002). Populism and the pathology of representative politics. In Y. Mény & Y. Surel (Eds.), *Democracies and the populist challenge* (pp. 62–80). Basingstoke: Palgrave Macmillan. doi: 10.1057/9781403920072.

Taggart, P. (2004). Populism and representative politics in contemporary Europe. *Journal of Political Ideologies, 9*(3), 269–288. https://doi.org/10.1080/1356931042000263528.

Tännsjö, T. (1992). *Populist democracy: A defence*. London: Routledge.

Teorell, J., Dahlberg, S., Holmberg, S., Rothstein, B., Khomenko, A., & Svensson, R. (2017). QoG standard dataset 2017. The quality of government institute, University of Gothenburg. doi: https://doi.org/10.18157/QoGStdJan17.

Treib, O. (2014). The voter says no, but nobody listens: Causes and consequences of the Eurosceptic vote in the 2014 European elections. *Journal of European Public Policy, 21*(10), 1541–1554. https://doi.org/10.1080/13501763.2014.941534.

Van Hauwaert, S. M., & Van Kessel, S. (2017). Beyond protest and discontent: A cross-national analysis of the effect of populist attitudes and issue positions on populist party support. *European Journal of Political Research*, first published 8 June 2017. doi:https://doi.org/10.1111/1475-6765.12216.

Van Kessel, S. (2015). *Populist parties in Europe: Agents of discontent?* Basingstoke: Palgrave Macmillan.

Van Spanje, J. (2010). Contagious parties anti-immigration parties and their impact on other parties' immigration stances in contemporary Western Europe. *Party Politics, 16*(5), 563–586.

Verbeek, B., & Zaslove, A. (2016). Italy: A case of mutating populism? *Democratization, 23*(2), 304–323. https://doi.org/10.1080/13510347.2015.1076213.

Wagner, A., Lewandowsky, M., & Giebler, H. (2015). Alles neu macht der Mai? In M. Kaeding & N. Switek (Eds.), *Die Europawahl 2014* (pp. 137–148). Wiesbaden: Springer VS.

Weyland, K. (2001). Clarifying a contested concept: Populism in the study of Latin American politics. *Comparative Politics, 34*(1), 1–22. https://doi.org/10.2307/422412.

Wodak, R. (2013). "Anything goes"—the Haiderization of Europe. In R. Wodak, M. Khosravinik, & B. Mral (Eds.), *Rightwing populism in Europe: Politics and discourse* (pp. 23–38). London: Bloomsbury.

Wodak, R. (2015). *The politics of fear: What right-wing populist discourses mean.* Beverly Hills, CA: Sage.

Woldendorp, J., Keman, H., & Budge, I. (2010). *Party government in 48 democracies (1945–1998): Composition, duration, personnel.* Dordrecht: Kluwer Academic.

World Bank. (2016). World development indicators. Washington, DC: The World Bank. http://data.worldbank.org/data-catalog/world-development-indicators. Accessed 23 May 2017.

WZB. (2017). *Databank "elections, parties, governments" of the research unit "democracy and democratization"*. Berlin: WZB Berlin Social Science Center.

Part II
Representation

Chapter 6
Inequality in Political Representation: Is the Lower Social Stratum Worse Represented?

Pola Lehmann, Sven Regel, and Sara Schlote

6.1 Introduction

This chapter focuses on a key aspect of representative democracies: the representation of citizens by parliamentarians. In modern democracies, representation is the crucial factor safeguarding popular sovereignty, the fundamental principle of democracy, without involving all citizens in the day-to-day political process. The power of parliamentarians to make decisions and take political action is legitimated by their status as representatives of the people. In free and fair elections, the electorate gives parliamentarians a mandate to represent their interests (Powell 2000, 89ff.). Recurring elections ensure the responsiveness of MPs. Only through regular elections can citizens exercise control over parliamentarians and choose them in accordance with their preferences.

Another principle is innate to democracy: equality. There is widespread consensus in society and among scholars that the principle of equality applies for all citizens regardless of their position in society and accordingly all citizens must be involved equally in the political process (Schumpeter 1942, Chap. 21; Dahl 1971, 3, 1989, 109 and 228; Habermas 2001).

It is already apparent that the equality principle is no longer secured when it comes to participation in elections (Schäfer and Schoen 2013, 100ff.). With this in mind, Merkel and Petring posit that one segment of the population, namely, the lower third of society, has in recent years come increasingly to suffer systematic underrepresentation (Merkel and Petring 2012, 93ff.). They argue that the declining voter turnout

P. Lehmann (✉) · S. Regel
Department of Democracy and Democratization, WZB Berlin Social Science Center, Berlin, Germany
e-mail: pola.lehmann@wzb.eu; sven.regel@wzb.eu

S. Schlote
Social Democratic Party of Germany (SPD), Berlin, Germany
e-mail: sara-schlote@gmx.de

W. Merkel, S. Kneip (eds.), *Democracy and Crisis*,
https://doi.org/10.1007/978-3-319-72559-8_6

does not only produce an imbalance in participation but that this deficiency also leads to worse substantive representation of the preferences of the lower third of society.

If this is true, if a segment of the population is systematically worse represented than everyone else, this would violate the principle of the formal equality of all citizens. There is at least good reason to ask whether lasting violation of such a key principle does not contribute to a crisis of democracy. However, it is as yet no more than surmise that a decline in turnout in the lower social stratum brings a decline in representation of this stratum's preferences in parliament and government. It has yet to be shown that the interests of this section of the population are not adequately represented in parliament. We test this thesis on the basis of data on citizen and parliamentarian preferences. We examine whether inequality in representation can indeed be demonstrated and whether the preferences of the lower social stratum are indeed worse represented by parliamentarians.

6.2 The Underrepresented Lower Social Stratum?

6.2.1 Models of Social Stratification

The literature on the social stratification of society offers a wide range of models. Mere reference to the lower social stratum therefore fails to provide clarity on whose representation is at stake. Is it the poorest members of the population? The uneducated? We should therefore begin by considering the various stratification models to establish a basis for deciding who counts as lower social stratum.

When assigning people to social strata, socioeconomic aspects are the main factors. Economic and educational factors are the most important determinants of social stratification. To combine these two indicators, people are often assigned to a social stratum in terms of occupational groups, since a person's occupation can function very well as a variable bracketing income and education (Bourdieu 1984; Geißler 2010, 37). The complexity of such socioeconomic models varies. For instance, the German discussion about a *shrinking middle stratum* is generally based only on income levels (see ISG 2011, 3). But the majority of models are based on a combination of income and education. There are, of course, many other stratification models.[1]

[1]These are, for example, the so-called social milieu models. The traditional indicators are supplemented by a number of indicators vertical to income and educational hierarchies. They include gender, age, ethnic and regional origin, and marital status (Geißler 2010, 42). Second, there are the social milieu models, which add subjective indicators such as lifestyles and life attitudes to the objective ones (ibid., 45). A classical example of such a classification is the Sinus-Milieus, where on a second axis, traditionalists, modernizers, individualists, and people open to reorientation are distinguished from one another (SINUS 2011, 14). A recent model focuses on inclusion and exclusion. In its basic form, it is bipolar in structure, concentrating on a small group of extremely disadvantaged people who have lost their place in society through unemployment, poverty, a lack of prospects, and a damaged self-image (Geißler 2010, 49).

Table 6.1 Stratification model

Income	*Very high*	Middle stratum	Middle stratum	Upper stratum	Upper stratum
	Rather high	Middle stratum	Middle stratum	Middle stratum	Upper stratum
	Medium	Middle stratum	Middle stratum	Middle stratum	Middle stratum
	Rather low	Lower stratum	Lower stratum	Middle stratum	Middle stratum
	Very low	Lower stratum	Lower stratum	Middle stratum	Middle stratum
		None	*Low*	*Medium*	*High*
		Education			

Source: Own presentation

If studies address the representation of the lower social stratum at all, most take reference to the socioeconomically worse-off members of society. Table 6.1 describes the model chosen for this analysis, which is two-dimensional, comprising the indicators income and education. As a rule, the segment of the population on the margins of society is regarded as the lower social stratum. Such marginalization is usually caused by resource poverty. Low income and a lack of education are the core factors in resource scarcity. It is implausible that one of the two resources is more important than the other or that a deficit on one dimension cannot be at least partially compensated for by the other dimension. People are therefore classified as lower social stratum only if they suffer from resource poverty on both dimensions.

6.2.2 *Specific Preferences, Lack of Participation, and Weak Representation*

If a lack of participation by a societal group is to result in weak representation, this group's preferences must differ from those of other groups in society.

In the United States, as Gilens (2005) and Ura and Ellies (2008) show, preferences vary from one income group to the next. However, the two studies examine the question not on an aggregated left-right axis but on the basis of single issues or on a conservative-liberal axis based on issues. As long ago as 1972, Verba and Nie showed what bias arises in the United States through the group of strongly participatory citizens, whose composition is not representative of society. First, they point out that stronger participation leads to stronger responsiveness of the representatives to participatory citizens. Second, they show that the attitudes of politically more active citizens in the United States are disproportionately conservative, but also that to a disproportionately high degree, this group comes from socioeconomically better placed segments of the population in which, once again, certain attitudes are disproportionately widespread. In short, it can be said that representatives lend a particularly willing ear to rich and well-educated citizens and to those with a conservative outlook (Verba and Nie 1972, 286f. and 296f.). However, it should be added that Verba and Nie measure the responsiveness of congressmen and women in terms of the perception of problems common to representatives and citizens (ibid., 302). They can show at best indirectly that—as far as preferences about how these problems ought to be tackled—representatives react responsively to citizens who are active and thus on average better-off.

There are, on the other hand, seldom studies that evaluate this puzzle comparatively between countries. An article by Rosset et al. (2011) is an exception. Using survey data they show that the level of income inequality in a country influences the quality of preference representation of the lower strata.

6.3 Theoretical Basis

6.3.1 Substantive Representation

In representative democracy, the demos is not directly involved in making political decisions; it delegates its interests to representatives and exercises power through the most perfect possible representation. To this end, citizens have to participate on an equal footing in the political process; but they do not have to be present in parliament themselves (Dahl 1989, 29f. and 109). Instead they select their representatives in elections.

The majority of studies on the representation of marginalized sections of the population are concerned with descriptive representation (Dovi 2007, 22; see also Diamond and Hartstock 1981, 717–721; Sapiro 1981; Gould 1996; Phillips 1998; Williams 1998; Mansbridge 1999; Young 2000). Studies on descriptive representation examine the extent to which the descriptive characteristics of societal groups, such as social stratum, gender, or ethnic origin, are reflected by their representatives. Furthermore they analyze the extent to which such descriptive representation leads to decisions reflecting the presumed interests of the group (see Mansbridge 1999, 641; Young 2000, 254). Few such studies have investigated the effects of such descriptive representation on the preference representation of given social strata by members of parliament. One exception is Young (2000, 354). She shows that descriptive representation does not guarantee better preference representation. In a 1985 study, Weßels also comes to the conclusion that matching social characteristics between MPs and voters have no decisive influence on issue congruence. He identifies parties as the decisive factor for congruence, which is reinforced if there is congruence between the social characteristics of party voters and those of parliamentarians (Weßels 1985). This finding naturally says nothing about whether descriptive representation should not be completely neglected for reasons of fairness (Mansbridge 1999, 641). Rebenstorf and Weßels (1989), for example, show that the quality of descriptive representation does at least influence how well citizens from various social groups feel themselves to be represented.

However, we understand representation not in a descriptive sense; our focus is on substantive representation. Substantive representation implies that electing a representative is not enough: he or she must also represent the preferences of voters and react responsively to them (Pitkin 1967, 115f.). This means that the voter preferences have to be equally represented (Hamilton and Madison 1788; Dahl 1989, 109). Naturally, the preferences of parliamentarians cannot translate one-to-one into parliamentary output. There are a number of reasons. First, a compromise has to be found between different preferences. In finding such a compromise, not only the preferences of MPs can play a role but also other institutional and noninstitutional veto players or international and supranational contractual agreements (Tsebelis 2002, 6–8). Second, voters of opposition parties do not always see their preferences taken into account in the legislation adopted. These parties can nevertheless exert a certain influence by at least introducing the preferences of their constituencies into the discussion that precedes adoption (Huber and Powell 1994, 300). Ultimately, MPs have to translate the will of citizens not in purely delegative terms; they must act freely in keeping with these preferences (Burke 1774).

Despite these and other possible factors that prevent the exact translation of single preferences, similar policy preferences are one of the best indications that parliamentarians will act in parliament as representatives of those who voted for them. Behavioral research shows a strong correlation between attitudes and action (Weßels 1999, 140). In their influential 1963 article, Miller and Stokes also showed that the attitudes of MPs in general policy areas influence their decisions on very specific policies (Miller and Stokes 1963, 48).

The greatest possible congruence between the preferences of citizens and those of parliamentarians is thus not a sufficient but a necessary condition for functioning representation. Input representation contributes to MPs "[...] taking the interests of their voters as the basis for their voting behavior" (Weßels 1993, 103; transl. BW). The outcome of the discussion process will, however, not be equally good for every citizen at all times. For the abovementioned reasons, it is clear that preferences are not always reflected to the same degree in the policy output of parliament. A high level of congruence therefore does not guarantee decision-making representation, but it is a good start (Holmberg 1991, 293).[2]

A high level of congruence means that there are as few political attitudes among citizens as possible that are not represented at all in parliament and thus have hardly any prospect of finding a hearing. The logical conclusion is that, if there is a continuously lower degree of congruence between preferences of one section of the population with the representatives than of other sections of the population with the representatives, they will have less chance of being represented in parliamentary decisions.

[2]Huber and Powell (1994), too, identify this link between MP preferences and their later action as the idea behind the *proportionate influence vision*. However, the study points in a somewhat different direction than ours, so that their findings cannot be directly transferred. But they are a further indication that there is good reason to posit a link between MP preferences and parliamentary output.

6.3.2 *Responsible Party Model*

So far, we have largely ignored the question of whether representatives are individual or collective actors. In democracies with majority voting systems, it is often assumed that there are direct representational ties between the citizens of a constituency and their member of parliament. In countries with proportional voting systems, it is assumed that the relationship between citizens and their MP operates through parties (Dalton 2002, 230). In fact, parties play the key role in conveying preferences between representatives and those represented in all systems. This reflection gave rise to the *responsible party model* (RPM). It assumes that parliamentarians are delegates of their parties and do not regard the constituency as their primary frame of reference (Weßels 1991, 329). As a rule, it is the parties that decide who may be candidate for parliament; they draw up the party program and organize themselves in parliamentary parties with strong party discipline. Much more than individual members of parliament, it is parties that are the main actors in modern representative systems (Dalton 2000). The RPM brings together key principles that have to be fulfilled if we are to speak of a representative democracy:

- "Voters do have a choice, i.e., they can choose between at least two parties with different policy proposals.
- The internal cohesion, or party discipline, of political parties is sufficient to enable them to implement their policy.
- Voters do have policy preferences.
- Voters are aware of the differences between the programs of different political parties.
- Voters do vote according to their policy preferences, i.e., they choose the party that represents their policy preferences best" (Schmitt and Thomassen 1999, 113ff.).

It makes sense to take these RPM considerations into account when analyzing the representation of the lower social stratum because its voters may well fulfil criteria three to five of the RPM worse than others. If the lower social stratum has particular difficulty in recognizing the positions of parties and the differences between them, and thus in voting for a party whose preferences are congruent with their own, or if parties know that the danger of being punished by voters from the lower social stratum for their policy is low, these could be reasons for representing them less well.

6.4 Hypotheses

The thesis that the lower social stratum is worse represented in parliament than other strata of society is to be examined in what follows on the basis of survey data. We begin by investigating whether—independently of other variables decisive for the quality of representation—the lower social stratum is worse represented than the rest of the population. This requires examination of how well preferences of the lower social stratum are represented in parliament. But the quality of representation for comparative groups also has to be ascertained. A low level of representation of the lower stratum can also be a mere indicator of overall poor representation in a country. From the point of view of democratic theory, such a case would naturally be questionable; but it would not point to a specific problem of the lower stratum but raise other questions. We are not concerned with what level of representation is good or bad but whether sections of the population are systematically worse represented than others, thus violating the ideal of equality. We first examine the following hypothesis:

H1 The preferences of the lower social stratum are worse represented in parliament than the preferences of the middle and upper strata.

However, if we consider not only the initial thesis but also its derivation, this hypothesis can be differentiated. Merkel and Petring (2012) posit worse representation above all because they assume lower political participation by the lower social stratum. An analysis of bad representation of the lower social stratum should therefore at least address the question of turnout. Two developments are conceivable: first, that voter turnout within the lower social stratum is lower than in other segments of the population, and, second, that this difference affects the quality of representation more strongly than in other population groups:

H2 Citizens from the lower social stratum turn out to vote less than citizens from other strata and are less represented than the latter.

There are two assumptions behind this hypothesis, which first need to be examined separately.

H2a Citizens from the lower stratum turn out to vote less than the rest of the population.

H2b If members of single strata vote less, they are less represented than citizens from other strata who vote more.

Finally, an analysis of the quality of representation in European parliamentary democracies can hardly neglect one of the most important actors in the everyday of representation: political parties. If citizens are to be represented above all by the party they vote for, and if the lower social stratum is worse represented than others, whether the connection between parties and citizens of the lower stratum functions worse than the connection between parties and members of other strata has to be investigated.

H3 Voters of the lower stratum are worse represented by their respective party than voters from other strata.

6.5 Data and Operationalization

6.5.1 Data Basis

We draw on two sets of data in which citizens and parliamentarians are questioned about their preferences. The data on citizens come from the *Comparative Study of Electoral Systems* (CSES 2011). This is an international comparative project that combines questions from national post-electoral studies across a number of countries in the CSES data set. For our study, the third wave has been used, because they are from the same legislative periods as the MP surveys. The third wave covers post-election studies in the countries under examination between 2006 and 2011.[3]

The data on parliamentarians come from PARTIREP (2012). In the framework of PARTIREP, a survey of parliamentarians from 15 countries was carried out. This survey was conducted between March 2009 and the summer of 2010.[4] The response rate in parliaments varied. In order to avoid distortions that could arise because of the response rate, MP data were weighted controlling for the election result and party membership. A combination of CSES and PARTIREP permits analysis in only eight countries (Germany, Ireland, the Netherlands, Norway, Austria, Poland, Portugal, and Switzerland), since these countries alone were included in both studies.

Both surveys provide data on the self-positioning of respondents on a left-right dimension. For this purpose, respondents had to state where they see their own position between 0 (left) and 10 (right) on an 11-point scale. Positions on single issues are not contained in the CSES data set. Later analyses can therefore be carried out only on the aggregate left-right dimension. The CSES data set also contains important information on the socioeconomic situations of respondents, including their income quintile and level of education. PARTIREP provides information on the party membership of parliamentarians and CSES information on which parties citizens voted for at the last election.

6.5.2 Operationalization of Social Stratification

First of all, citizen respondents have to be classified in terms of social stratification. In Sect. 2.1 we explained why we chose a conceptualization of social strata combining income and educational characteristics. On the basis of this theoretical concept, we assigned respondents to social strata for the purposes of the analysis.

For operationalization purposes, we drew on two variables from the CSES data set: income (C2020) and education (C2003). The income variable divides

[3]In cases where surveys were carried out on two elections in a country, we used data that comes from the same legislative period as the data on parliamentarians.

[4]Members of regional and national parliaments were asked to participate in the study. For the following analysis, only data on members of national parliaments were used.

respondents into household income quintiles. However, household income is a very inexact quantity, for an income that could place a single in the well-earning middle social stratum is likely to scarcely to meet the needs of a five-member family. For this reason the number of household members (C2021) is taken into account.[5]

In addition to income, education is used to assign people to social strata. The education variable codes respondents' standard of education on an eight-point scale. However, the use of this scale differs widely from country to country. All countries use only some of the scale elements and in the individual form of scale have coded the variance of educational qualifications differently. The different national codings have, as far as possible, been assigned to one of the four following categories: (1) no educational qualifications, (2) lower and intermediate secondary education and/or vocational training qualifications, (3) upper secondary education and/or advanced vocational training qualifications, and (4) university degree.[6]

6.5.3 Operationalization of Congruence Measurement

In order to measure how representative parliamentarians are as a whole and not only individual members of parliament or governments, a measure of congruence is needed that includes the distribution of individual preferences. For this purpose, it is possible to compare the distribution of citizens' and parliamentarians' preferences (Golder and Stramski 2010). The more similar the distributions of the two groups are, the more representative parliament is:

$$\text{Congruence}(a,b) = \sum_{i=0}^{n-1} \min\left\{ \frac{\text{Respondent}_{\text{ai}}}{\sum_{k=0}^{n-1} \text{Respondent}_{\text{ak}}}, \frac{\text{Respondent}_{\text{bi}}}{\sum_{k=0}^{n-1} \text{Respondent}_{\text{bk}}} \right\}$$

where *a* and *b* are different groups of respondents, *n* is the number of discrete values on the ideology scale, and $\text{respondents}_{\text{ai}}$ is the number of respondents in group *a* for value *i* on the ideology scale.[7]

[5]Since the income variable states only quintiles and no exact household incomes, the mean income within the quintile is estimated, and for each respondent, this value is divided by the number of household members.

[6]In the case of four countries (Netherlands, Norway, Austria, Switzerland), no satisfactory categorization was possible because of the way these categories have been aggregated by the CSES country experts. For these four countries, the income variable was used more restrictively in defining classes in order to take account of differences in the coding of educational qualifications.

[7]This method is not influenced by whether attitudes are normally distributed, because it takes the complete distribution into account and not only aggregated values (Golder and Stramski 2010, 95). Moreover, since all the distributions used in this analysis overlap, this formula, slightly simplified in comparison to the use of differences of cumulative distribution functions, can be used.

6.6 Results

How are the preferences of parliamentarians and citizens distributed across the individual social strata? What influence does social strata affiliation have on the quality of representation and to what extent does the electoral turnout of respondents differentiate in this regard? What special roles do parties play in the representation of citizens?

6.6.1 Description

The distribution of the left-right self-positioning of citizens and parliamentarians is shown in Fig. 6.1. Before citizens' preferences are compared with those of parliamentarians, it is useful to look at the distributions separately and identify peculiarities to allow the comparison to be better assessed.[8]

All citizen respondents in the individual countries are distributed across the entire left-right spectrum. The greatest number of citizens in all countries places themselves in the center. The remaining voters position themselves to the right and left of center, but, with the exception of Germany and Austria, a majority of these citizens see themselves as right of center. This trend is strongest in Poland; indeed, the absolute majority of the complete sample is right of center. Portugal and with some reservations Austria are the two countries in which distribution is most even.

The distribution of parliamentarians differs strongly from country to country. Only in Austria and, less markedly, in Norway are parliamentarians relatively evenly distributed on the left and right sides of the left-right spectrum. Left and right positions are thus relatively equally represented in parliament. In all other countries, there is a clear trend for parliamentarians to be positioned on the left or the right. There is a trend toward the left in Germany, Ireland, the Netherlands, and Portugal, whereas in Poland and Switzerland, most members of parliament place themselves on the right.

In comparison with citizens, it is interesting to see that parliamentarians much more rarely position themselves exactly in the center (i.e., 5 on the scale). With the exception of Germans, most members of parliament place themselves either on the left or the right. In this they differ from citizens, who more frequently take a position in the center. This could be because parliamentarians are more interested in differentiating themselves, marking themselves off from members of other parties, so that they more often choose positions on one of the two sides. Parliamentarians want to

[8]We have not for all respondents observations on all variables used in this analysis. These citizens are therefore excluded from the study. Most of the answers that are lacking are to questions on income and on left-right self-positioning. The number of cases is therefore considerably reduced especially for Portugal and Ireland. And in the party-specific analysis in Sect. 6.3, only respondents who state their concrete choice of party could be taken into consideration.

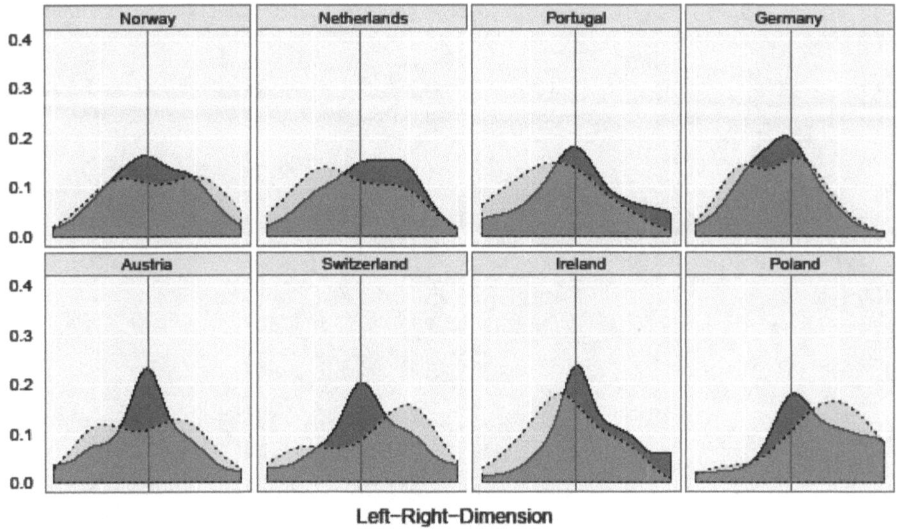

Fig. 6.1 Left-right self-positioning of citizens (solid line) and parliamentarians (dashed line). Source: Own calculations on the basis of CSES and PARTIREP

make citizens a distinguishable offer in order to gain their votes; they are more interested than voters in distinguishing themselves from one another. As a rule, the majority of parties are positioned either on the left or right of the spectrum, and their MPs accordingly place themselves on the appropriate side. In their daily professional lives, they are also more often confronted by the question of where they position themselves politically. A citizen who does not face the question so frequently and is therefore perhaps more uncertain or indifferent about his position will therefore more probably opt for the center than will a parliamentarian.

If we examine the distribution of citizens' preferences individually for each social stratum, we find firstly that the differences in the distribution of the preferences of all respondents are not extremely great (see Fig. 6.2). Social stratum does not appear to be the determining variable for preferences, but preferences are very heterogeneously distributed within strata. As among other citizens, there are people in the lower social stratum who position themselves on the left, on the right, and in the center. Country-specific patterns are reproduced within strata. That is to say, that if the relative majority of all respondents in a country take left wing positions, this dominance of the left is also reflected in the individual social strata. The same is true for the dominance of right-wing positions. The sole exception, to a low degree, is Norway, whose lower social stratum is almost normally distributed, whereas the middle and upper strata show a slight tendency to take right-wing positions. In all countries, social stratum affiliation brings only small shifts in preference distribution. In no case are there striking differences from the totality of respondents.

Basically it is possible that these observations arise only because differences in preferences on single issues between social strata balance out on the aggregated

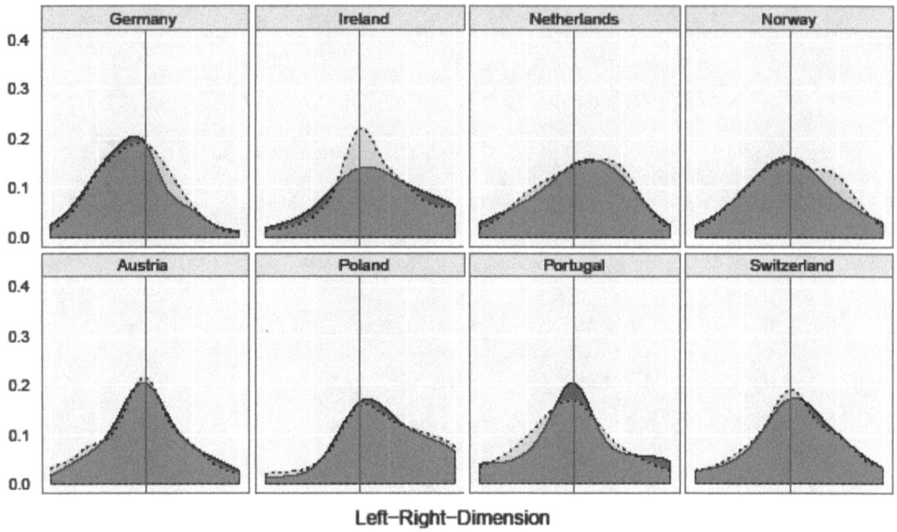

Fig. 6.2 Left-right self-positioning of the lower social stratum (solid line) and middle and upper strata (dashed line). Source: Own calculations on the basis of CSES

left-right dimension. Unfortunately, the CSES data set provides no internationally comparable statements of preferences on issues. However, the *German Longitudinal Election Study* (GLES, Rattinger et al. 2012), which supplies the database for German CSES data, addresses three issues. Thus, the possibility of greater preference differences at the issue level can be tested at least for Germany. In this case, results similar to those for the left-right dimension are to be found for two issues: the socioeconomic question[9] and the nuclear power issue.[10] For these two issues, there are no great differences between social strata. The situation is different for the third question, covering the libertarian-authoritarian dimension, which addresses immigration.[11] Here there are stratum-specific differences in preferences. The lower social stratum is much more in favor of limiting immigration than the middle and upper strata.

[9]"Some people would like to see lower taxes even if that means some reduction in health, education, and social benefits; others would like to see more government spending on health, education, and social benefits even if it means some increases in taxes." (11-point scale).

[10]"Should more nuclear power stations be built or should all nuclear power stations be closed down today?" (11-point scale).

[11]"We now turn to the issue of immigration. Should laws on immigration be relaxed or be made tougher?" (11-point scale).

6.6.2 Congruence

What has so far been said shows that the preferences of citizens and parliamentarians do not coincide exactly. But how congruent is the distribution of voter and MP preferences in fact, and what differences are there for the congruence of the different social strata?

Figure 6.3 shows how high the congruence is between the preferences of members of parliament and citizens from the different social strata in the countries under study. It is apparent that the level of congruence between social strata differs more strongly from country to country than within single countries. There are nevertheless stratum-specific differences, and in all countries they are to the disadvantage of the lower social stratum. In Ireland, the difference in the quality of representation between individual strata is, for example, relatively low; in Norway and Portugal it is more prominent. But all social strata in these countries are better represented than every stratum in Ireland. That citizens from the lower social stratum are worse represented than citizens from other strata (hypothesis 1) is hence true in all countries.

It has been shown that the theory that the lower social stratum is worse represented than others derives from observation that the lower social stratum participates less in politics and the conclusion that this affects the quality of representation. In this analysis, participation is measured in terms of voter turnout, so that turnout first has to be examined separately for each social stratum (see Table 6.2).

It is clear that social stratum affiliation has a strong influence. In seven of the eight countries, the lower social stratum votes less frequently than other strata. This

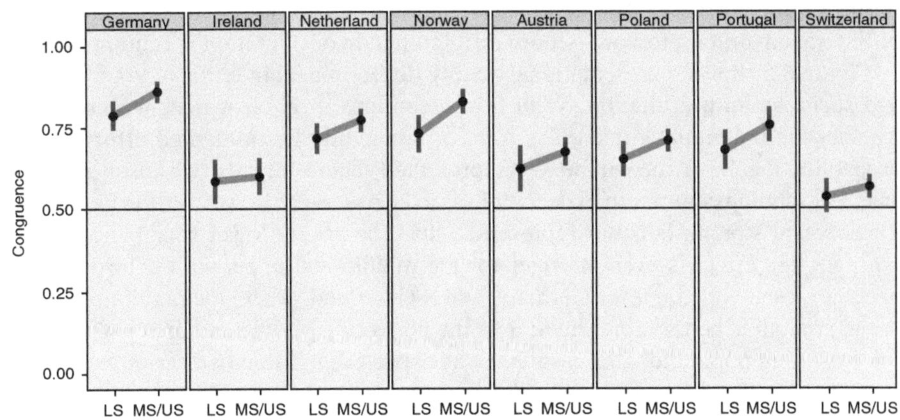

Fig. 6.3 Congruence of different social strata with parliamentarians. Note: On the y-axis the level of congruence is plotted, on the x-axis the lower social stratum versus the middle and upper stratum. The line between the points shows no continuous increase of representation between strata. It links only the congruence values of the different strata in a country. Consequently, the difference in congruence between social strata in a country is low if the line is very flat and higher, the more diagonal the line becomes. The vertical lines show bootstrapped 90% confidence intervals. Source: Own calculations on the basis of CSES and PARTIREP

Table 6.2 Voter turnout by country and social stratum, in %

	AUT	DEU	IRL	NLD	NOR	POL	PRT	CHE
Lower stratum	80	65	89	88	81	51	72	59
Middle and upper stratum	87	86	88	95	92	77	75	71

Source: Own calculations on the basis of CSES

is most dramatic in Poland and Germany. In these countries turnover falls by 26 percentage points in Poland and 21 in Germany. But the other countries, too, show strong differences in voter turnout from stratum to stratum. Only in Ireland, where overall turnout is relatively high, do members of the lower social stratum go to the polls even a little more frequently. With one exception, hypothesis 2a is therefore confirmed.

But are these sometimes huge differences in participation reflected by correspondingly large differences in the quality of democratic representation? Figure 6.4 shows that this is mostly not the case. As Fig. 6.3 has shown, the quality of representation is worse for the lower social stratum than for the middle and upper strata in all countries. However, if we compare this with how strongly voter turnout falls in individual cases, the drop in the quality of representation is moderate. Ireland, whose lower social stratum votes slightly more frequently than the middle and upper strata, is the exception. But there are also scarcely measurable differences in congruence. Thus hypothesis 2b, which states that lower turnout is accompanied by worse representation, is also confirmed with one exception.

But this finding does not yet allow us to conclude that voting has no influence on the quality of representation. In order to determine how well or badly a given social stratum is represented—despite the more or less frequent failure of some members of this social stratum to vote—more differentiated consideration is required.

Figure 6.5 shows representational quality differentiated in terms of voter turnout and social stratum affiliation. With few exceptions, it is clear that, within strata, whether the individual citizen is a voter or a nonvoter has a marked effect on the probability that he or she will be well represented. There are only two cases in which an effect running contrary to expectations is to be observed. In Austria, the nonvoting lower social stratum is better represented than the voting lower social stratum. In Portugal this effect is even stronger for the middle and upper strata. Two further peculiarities are apparent for Germany and Switzerland, where the nonvoting lower social stratum is better represented than the nonvoting middle and upper strata. But for the voting population, the results are as expected; in these two countries, voters from the middle and upper strata are better represented than voters from the lower social stratum.

But the findings also show that voting alone changes nothing with regard to the worse representation of the lower social stratum. The voting lower social stratum is always

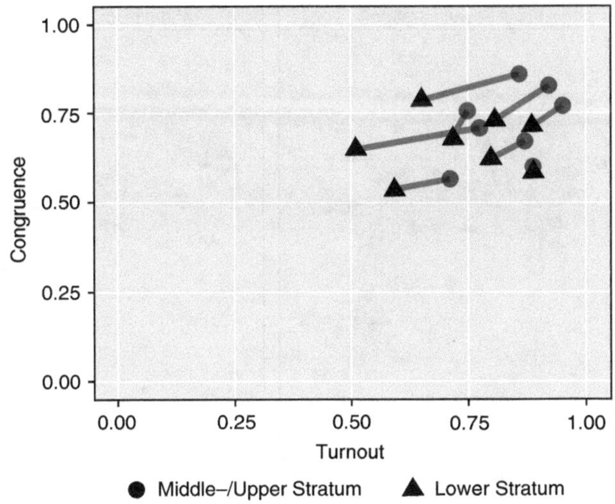

Fig. 6.4 Congruence of different social strata with parliamentarians in terms of voter turnout. Note: The level of voter turnout is plotted on the x-axis and congruence of strata with parliamentarians on the y-axis. The triangles represent the lower class in a single country. The position of a triangle indicates the level of lower class voter turnout in the given country and the level of congruence of preferences of the lower social stratum with those of parliamentarians. The circles give the same information for the middle and upper strata in a country. The connecting lines relate the lower social stratum to the middle and upper strata of a country. Source: Own calculations on the basis of CSES and PARTIREP

worse represented than other voters. If this mechanism proves to be permanent, it would provide no good incentive for a lower social stratum that goes less often to the polls anyway to change this habit.

6.6.3 Responsible Party Model

The results so far have shown that the data does indeed provide evidence in favor of the thesis that the lower social stratum is underrepresented. But how do the results look if representation is considered in terms of parties?[12] The findings shown in Fig. 6.6 are clear; only four parties represent their voters from this stratum better than their voters from the middle and upper strata. For another four parties, the quality of representation does not depend on social strata. But the vast majority of parties represent their voters from the middle and upper social stratum better than those from the lower stratum, thus confirming hypothesis 3.

[12]Individual citizens are assigned to the party which they stated they voted for at the last election (variable C3023_LH_PL in CSES).

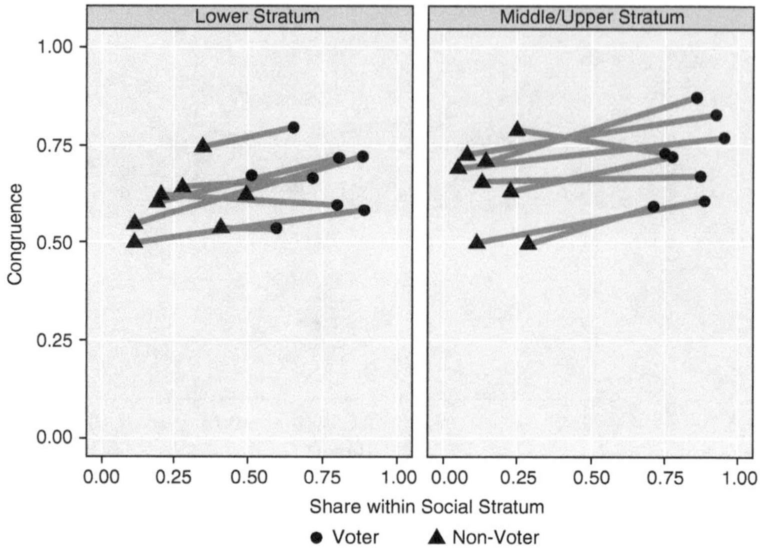

Fig. 6.5 Voter turnout and the representation of voters and nonvoters by social stratum. Note: Congruence is plotted on the *y*-axis. The figure on the left shows congruence differentiated in terms of nonvoters (triangle) and voters (circle) of the lower social stratum. On the right we see the same for the middle and upper strata: first for the nonvoters of a social stratum and then for the voters of the same social stratum. Plotted on the *x*-axis is how voters and nonvoters are distributed in percentage terms in the given social stratum. Source: Own calculations on the basis of CSES and PARTIREP

6.7 Conclusion and Outlook

This chapter has investigated how the quality of representation of citizens from the lower social stratum differs from that of citizens in other strata. A look at the distribution of preferences by stratum shows that social strata affiliation does not determine preferences. In the eight countries examined, people from the same social stratum showed widely differing preferences. Nevertheless, the analysis has shown that the lower strata are worse represented than the middle and upper strata in all the cases under study. However, differences in the quality of representation from country to country are greater than differences between strata within a given country.

Why is the lower social stratum underrepresented? It was posited that lower participation by the lower stratum is an important explanatory factor. And, indeed, with one exception, the lower social stratum votes less frequently than the middle and upper strata, and the level of voter turnout in a social stratum influences the quality of their representation. However, this correlation is not as strong as could be supposed. It cannot be shown that nonvoting has a disproportionate influence on the representational quality of the lower social stratum.

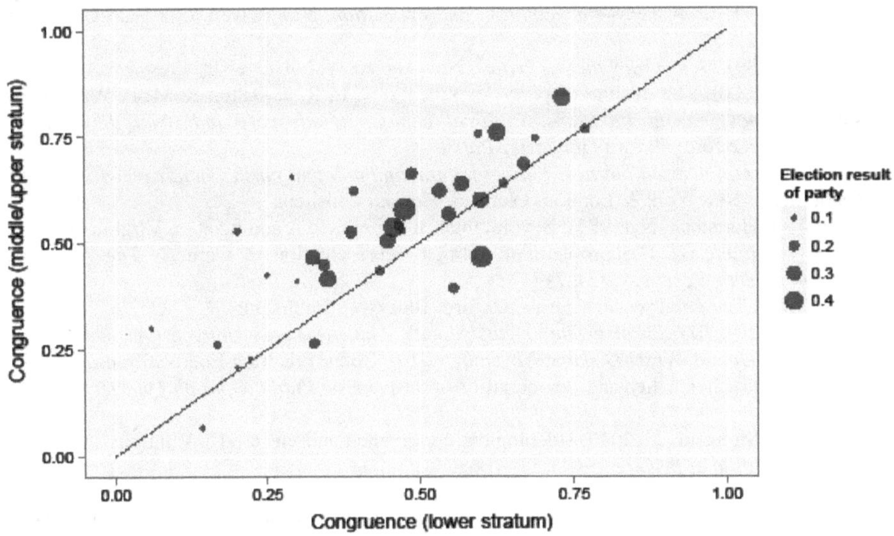

Fig. 6.6 Congruence between voters and the parties for which they voted. Note: The axes refer to congruence between the preferences of MPs of a party with the preferences of voters of this party from the middle and upper strata (*y*-axis) and the preferences of voters of this party from the lower stratum (*x*-axis). The size of the individual points indicates the percentage of the vote gained by the party at the last election. All parties above the diagonal line have greater congruence with their voters of the middle and upper social strata than with their voters of the lower social stratum.

Finally, given the importance of parties in the chain of representation, we examined how well or badly individual parties represent the various strata. Here, too, our analysis points to problems. With few exceptions, parties represent their voters from the middle and upper strata better than their voters from the lower social stratum.

Strikingly, a look at the absolute quality of representation for the lower social stratum shows no evidence of a crisis. But from a relative point of view, it is clear that the lower social stratum is worse off than the middle and upper strata in all respects. Should this relative difference increase over time, it would have to be considered a danger to democracy because it would harm the democratic principle of equality.

References

Bourdieu, P. (1984). *Distinction. A social critique of the judgement of taste*. Cambridge, MA: Harvard University Press.

Burke, E. (1774). *Speech to the electors of Bristol*. http://press-pubs.uchicago.edu/founders/documents/v1ch13s7.html. Accessed 13 July 2013.

Comparative Study of Electoral Systems (CSES) (2011). *CSES Module 3 full release* [dataset]. 27 March 2013. www.cses.org. Accessed 14 May 2013.

Dahl, R. A. (1971). *Polyarchy. Participation and opposition.* New Haven, CT: Yale University Press.
Dahl, R. A. (1989). *Democracy and its critics.* New Haven: Yale University Press.
Dalton, R. J. (2000). The decline of party identifications. In R. J. Dalton & M. P. Wattenberg (Eds.), *Parties without Partisans. Political change in advanced industrial democracies* (pp. 19–36). Oxford: Oxford University Press.
Dalton, R. J. (2002). *Citizen politics: Public opinion and political parties in advanced industrial democracies.* New York & London: Chatham House Publishers.
Diamond, I., & Hartstock, N. (1981). Beyond interest in politics: A comment on Virginia Sapiro's 'When are interests? The problem of political representation of women'. *The American Political Science Review, 75*(3), 717–721.
Dovi, S. (2007). *The good representative.* Oxford: Blackwell Publishing.
Geißler, R. (2010). *Die Sozialstruktur Deutschlands. Aktuelle Entwicklungen und theoretische Erklärungsmodelle. WISO Diskurs, November 2010.* Bonn: Friedrich-Ebert-Stiftung.
Gilens, M. (2005). Inequality and democratic responsiveness. *Public Opinion Quarterly, 69*(5), 778–796.
Golder, M., & Stramski, J. (2010). Ideological congruence and electoral institutions. *American Journal of Political Science, 54*(1), 90–106.
Gould, C. (1996). Diversity and democracy: Representing differences. In S. Benhabib (Ed.), *Democracy and difference: Contesting the boundaries of the political* (pp. 171–186). Princeton, NJ: Princeton University Press.
Habermas, J. (2001). *Between facts and norms. Contribution to a discourse theory of law and democracy.* Cambridge, MA: MIT Press.
Hamilton, A., & Madison, J. (1788). Federalist No. 57. In A. Hamilton, J. Madison, & J. Jay (Eds.), *The Federalist Papers.* http://thomas.loc.gov/home/histdox/fed_57.html. Accessed 3 Feb 2013.
Holmberg, S. (1991). Political representation in Sweden. In H.-D. Klingemann, R. Stöss, & B. Weßels (Eds.), *Politische Klasse und politische Institutionen* (pp. 290–324). Opladen: Westdeutscher Verlag.
Huber, J. D., & Powell, G. B. (1994). Congruence between Citizens and policy-makers in two visions of liberal democracy. *World Politics, 46*(3), 291–326.
Institut für Sozialforschung und Gesellschaftspolitik (ISG) (2011). *Überprüfung der These einer "schrumpfenden Mittelschicht" in Deutschland.* Expertise im Auftrag des Bundesministeriums für Arbeit und Soziales: Köln: ISG.
Mansbridge, J. (1999). Should blacks represent blacks and women represent women? A contingent 'Yes. *The Journal of Politics, 61*(3), 628–657.
Merkel, W., & Petring, A. (2012). Politische Partizipation und demokratische Inklusion. In T. Mörschel & C. Krell (Eds.), *Demokratie in Deutschland. Zustand—Herausforderungen—Perspektiven* (pp. 93–119). VS Verlag für Sozialwissenschaften: Wiesbaden.
Miller, W. E., & Stokes, D. E. (1963). Constituency influence in Congress. *The American Political Science Review, 57*(1), 45–56.
PARTIREP (2012). *Comparative MP Survey.* Dataset. 1 September 2012. http://www.partirep.eu/. Accessed 20 May 2013.
Phillips, A. (1998). *Feminism and politics.* Oxford: Oxford University Press.
Pitkin, H. F. (1967). *The concept of representation.* Berkeley, CA: University of California Press.
Powell, G. B. (2000). *Elections as instruments of democracy. Majoritarian and proportional visions.* New Haven, CT: Yale University Press.
Rattinger, H., Roßteutscher, S., Schmitt-Beck, R., & Weßels, B. (2012). *Vor- und Nachwahl-Querschnitt (Kumulation) (GLES 2009).* GESIS Datenarchiv, Köln. ZA5302 Datenfile Version 6.0.0, doi: https://doi.org/10.4232/1.11373.
Rebenstorf, H., & Weßels, B. (1989). Wie wünschen sich die Wähler ihre Abgeordneten? Ergebnisse einer repräsentativen Bevölkerungsumfrage zum Problem der sozialen Repräsentativität des Deutschen Bundestages. *Zeitschrift für Parlamentsfragen, 20*(3), 408–424.

Rosset, J., Giger, N., & Bernauer, J. (2011). *Political representation of the poor and economic inequality: A comparative analysis*. Paper, Drei-Länder-Tagung. Basel, 13–14 January 2011.
Sapiro, V. (1981). When are interest interesting? *American Political Science Review, 75*(3), 701–716.
Schäfer, A., & Schoen, H. (2013). Mehr Demokratie, aber nur für wenige? Der Zielkonflikt zwischen mehr Beteiligung und politischer Gleichheit. *Leviathan, 41*, 94–120.
Schmitt, H., & Thomassen, J. (1999). Distinctiveness and cohesion of parties. In H. Schmitt & J. Thomassen (Eds.), *Political representation and legitimacy in the European Union* (pp. 111–128). Oxford: Oxford University Press.
Schumpeter, J. A. (1942). *Capitalism, socialism and democracy*. New York, NY: Harper Press.
SINUS. (2011). *Informationen zu den Sinus-Milieus 2011*. Heidelberg: SINUS-Markt- und Sozialforschung GmbH.
Tsebelis, G. (2002). *Veto players. How political institutions work*. New York, NY: Russell Sage Foundation.
Ura, J. D., & Ellies, C. R. (2008). Income, preferences, and the dynamics of policy responsiveness. *Political Science and Politics, 41*(4), 785–794.
Verba, S., & Nie, N. H. (1972). *Participation in America. Political democracy and social equality*. New York, NY: Harper & Row.
Williams, M. (1998). *Voice, trust, and memory: Marginalized groups and the failings of liberals representation*. Princeton, NJ: Princeton University Press.
Weßels, B. (1985). Wählerschaft und Führungsschicht: Probleme politischer Repräsentation. Ein Forschungsbericht. Freie Universität Berlin. *Information aus Lehre und. Forschung, 2*.
Weßels, B. (1991). Abgeordnete und Bürger: Parteien und Wahlkreiskommunikation als Faktoren politischer Repräsentation. In H.-D. Klingemann, R. Stöss, & B. Weßels (Eds.), *Politische Klasse und politische Institutionen* (pp. 325–356). Opladen: Westdeutscher Verlag.
Weßels, B. (1993). Politische Repräsentation als Prozess einer gesellschaftlich-parlamentarischen Kommunikation. In D. Herzog, H. Rebenstorf, & B. Weßels (Eds.), *Parlament und Gesellschaft* (pp. 99–137). Opladen: Westdeutscher Verlag.
Weßels, B. (1999). System characteristics matter: Empirical evidence from ten representation studies. In W. E. Miller, R. Pierce, J. Thomassen, R. Herrera, S. Holmberg, P. Esaiasson, & B. Weßels (Eds.), *Policy representation in Western democracies* (pp. 137–161). Oxford: Oxford University Press.
Young, I. M. (2000). *Inclusion and democracy*. Oxford: Oxford University Press.

Chapter 7
Decline or Change? Party Types and the Crisis of Representative Democracy

Heiko Giebler, Onawa Promise Lacewell, Sven Regel, and Annika Werner

7.1 Introduction

The decline of parties, crucial actors in representative democracies over the past three decades, has been of great concern for party development scholars and democracy scholars alike. Such scholars point to decreasing vote shares for established parties, the rise of third parties and niche parties, the increasingly key role played by nonparty actors in fulfilling roles traditionally the purview of parties, and decreasing party membership levels as red flags signaling the end of the party era. These observed developments are often discussed as leading to a range of distortions in the functioning of democracy. However, the assumptions underlying such causalities remain largely theoretically derived, and the causal mechanisms linking party decline and democratic malaise (or, in other words, a crisis of democracy) remain empirically untested. This chapter presents a first step toward such an empirical test and aims to link the developments in party and party system evolution to the fulfillment of the basic functions of political parties, namely, mobilization, representation, and forming and sustaining stable governments in democracies. To do so, we deduce a measurable concept focusing on size, political program, and societal rootedness which encompasses the most important party

H. Giebler (✉) · S. Regel
Department of Democracy and Democratization, WZB Berlin Social Science Center, Berlin, Germany
e-mail: heiko.giebler@wzb.eu; sven.regel@wzb.eu

O. P. Lacewell
MPB Research, Kreuzlingen, Switzerland
e-mail: onawa.lacewell@myprivatebanking.com

A. Werner
Centre for Governance and Public Policy, Griffith University, Brisbane, Australia
e-mail: a.werner@griffith.edu.au

W. Merkel, S. Kneip (eds.), *Democracy and Crisis*,
https://doi.org/10.1007/978-3-319-72559-8_7

types in Western democracies. The importance of these party types is based, on the one hand, on the roles these parties play in their national context. We concentrate on *large parties*, which form the backbone of their respective party systems. On the other hand, the importance of the party types is deduced from their empirical frequency. On this basis and connecting to the typology of Gunther and Diamond (2001, 2003), we can identify the three most important party types: *mass-based*, *catch-all*, and *programmatic parties*.

For the differentiation of the three party types, we use the most comprehensive dataset of party membership collected to date, which includes membership figures for 15 countries for the time period between the 1960s and 2010s. We also employ an innovative approach to measuring programmatic clarity of party manifestos, and develop a party size measure which is not biased by the nature of the electoral system. This enables us not only to gain insights into the development of political parties and the validity of the literature on their crisis but to provide crucial information on the linkages between party development, party types, and the fulfillment of elementary functions for democracy by political parties. In this way, we go beyond normative claims on the crisis of democracy induced by the crisis of political parties. Our findings suggest that the emergence and vanishing of certain party types does indeed have an impact on the "health" of democracy. At the same time, these effects are much smaller than and not necessarily as negative as the public and scientific discourses would have us believe.

7.2 Theory

7.2.1 Parties and Their Functions in Democracies

Any discussion of the decline of political parties and the subsequent crisis of democracy has a natural beginning in the general concept of political parties. Universally, parties share the unique role of brokering relationships between the mass of citizens and governments. This crucial role is evidenced in the very definition of political parties, from Schumpeter's general view that a "party is a group whose members act in concert in the competitive struggle for political power" to Sartori's (1976) even more abstract definition that "a party is a part-of-a whole." Schattschneider (1942, p. 1) went so far as to claim that "[. . .] modern democracy is unthinkable except in terms of parties." While the concept of a political party is broad, the purpose of parties in democracies can be defined rather narrowly as seeking to control the apparatus of government on the part of their supporters (Schumpeter 1942; Epstein 1967; LaPalombara 2007).

In the parlance of the embedded democracy concept (Merkel et al. 2003), parties form the crucial actor of the second partial regime (political participation) and, as such, are crucial to this conceptualization of democracy. Moreover, they are of major relevance for democratically representative elections, which highlights their importance for the first partial regime (electoral regime). Gunther and Diamond

(2001) provide a useful outline of seven key functions parties perform in democracies: candidate nomination, electoral mobilization, issue structuring, societal representation, interest aggregation, forming and sustaining governments, and social integration. Whether all seven functions are equally important to democracy is debatable. However, it seems clear that, were these functions to be interrupted or left unfulfilled, the very survival of representative democracy could be at stake.

Given the traditional emphasis on political parties in democracies, it is unsurprising that an observed weakening of political parties in modern democracies would be seen as a sign of crisis within the democracy itself. There are three of the democratic functions—mobilization, representation, and government formation/stability—that are deemed particularly relevant by the literature on the crisis of democracy (Chap. 1). Thus, these functions are suitable to test the relationship between the often decried decline of (established) parties and the central topic of this book, the crisis of representative democracy.

7.2.2 *Looking Through Rose-Colored Glasses: Parties and Party Decline from the Golden Age of Party Politics*

The current literature decrying the decline of the role of political parties in modern democracies is set against a backdrop of a strong period of party politics in Western European democracies beginning sometime after the Second World War (Dalton and Wattenberg 2000; Mair 2006; LaPalombara 2007). The supposed golden age of parties occurred during the 1950s, 1960s, and 1970s and was characterized by large parties which dominated political competition, winning major shares of electoral votes and comprising either the major government or opposition parties in most countries. Around the mid-1970s, this golden age ended, and a surge of literature proclaimed the "decline of political parties" (see, for instance, Lawson and Merkl 1988; Reiter 1989; LaPalombara 2007; Dalton and Wattenberg 2000).

This is not to say, however, that the idea that political parties were in decline first occurred during the demise of this golden age. Even during this period, scholars such as Otto Kirchheimer (1965) cautioned against the trend toward an increasingly catch all nature in traditional mass-integration parties and claimed that this trend would lead to parties "losing ideological baggage" as they moved toward the middle of the political spectrum, de-emphasized their traditional class clientele, and formed stronger ties to interest groups. Dennis (1966, p. 613) observed that "anti-party norms and images are present as a living part of the political culture in many Western political systems." Also in the 1960s, scholars began to seek explanations for a perceived decline of parties (Fraenkel 1964; Haas 1964; Reiter 1989, p. 326). Despite these early discussions of signs of decline in Western European party systems, the pattern of party politics during this golden age did, supposedly, lead to high levels of mobilization, increased representation, and high levels of government stability. In this sense, despite the signs of decline already evident during this period, established parties performed well on a functional basis.

Internal and External Pressures on Traditional Parties at the End of the Golden Age

In the 1970s, formerly dominant large parties began to come under both internal pressure from intraparty fractions and external pressure from new parties on both the right and the left of the ideological spectrum.[1] The most obvious manifestation of this pressure was the decreasing share of the vote for large parties. These electoral losses led to much discussed shifts in party tactics in the 1990s when parties such as the British Labour Party and the German Social Democrats began to pursue "Third Way" strategies (Giddons 2000; Merkel et al. 2008; Allen 2009; Poguntke 2014) as party leaders fought desperately to stop the hemorrhaging of traditionally core voters.

Nevertheless, the decline of large parties after the golden age is shown by more than just lost votes. Internally, decreasing membership numbers (Mair and van Biezen 2001; van Biezen et al. 2012) throughout the period also reveal pressure leading to a decrease in social rootedness—a characteristic of most traditional mass parties through the golden age. While there is debate about whether the decline of reported membership figures is indeed fully indicative of a net loss of active members,[2] the decline is so dramatic that it unarguably poses a challenge to parties that had, in the past, relied on members as a source of party strength and financial support.

Externally, large parties had to deal with a changing landscape of political competition, when serious opposition from postmodernist, or New Politics movements such as ecology movements, began to erode the traditional basis of support for large parties. Rather quickly, such movements established themselves as important players in party systems. One need only to think of the Green parties, new left parties, or radical right parties that mushroomed in many party systems throughout the 1980s, 1990s, and early 2000s for an indication of this trend (e.g., Adams et al. 2006; Spoon 2009; Wagner 2012). While the specific type of niche parties that developed was highly dependent on the national context (Kitschelt 1993), virtually every party system was affected, and thus no formerly dominant party was left unchallenged. The example of Germany is particularly salient in that a stable 2.5 party system dominated by the SPD and the CDU/CSU in the 1960s and 1970s gave

[1]The literature discusses a wealth of developments that is either deemed reason or indicator for the decline of parties. It is, however, important to distinguish between challenges to parties that they need to react to and signs of their decline. Therefore, we do not discuss developments like the decrease of party identification and partisanship (Dalton 2000; LaPalombara 2007), the emergence of sub- or supranational government (e.g., Strøm 2000), or the role of media and new technology (Dalton and Wattenberg 2000; LaPalombara 2007) at this point.

[2]Scarrow (2000), for instance, discussed other reasons for a nominal decline of membership numbers, while scholars like Heidar and Saglie (2003) highlight that the raw numbers are under-complex indicators, and issues such as the ratio of active and passive members as well as the role of members need to be taken into account.

way, rather quickly, to today's five-party system where both traditional large parties fight to maintain their relevance (Poguntke 2014).

Similar stories have been repeated throughout Western democracies, leading to increasing unease among party scholars that democracy in general is threatened by this trend. There are many hypothesized reasons for the general upheaval that began to plague Western European party systems during the mid- to late 1970s (Reiter 1989, p. 329). The decline of traditional parties and the rise of niche and small party movements are but one symptom of general unrest. Into this framework came what are now well-known theories of post-materialism (Inglehart 1977) and the unfreezing of party systems (Mair 1989) as well as a general discussion about the rise and fall of traditional social cleavages versus new cleavages (Bartolini 2007; Bornschier 2010; Kriesi et al. 2012). Generally, though, it is clear that the traditional cleavage structures underlying Western European societies and political systems in the decades before the 1970s—namely, the four identified by Lipset and Rokkan (1967)—began to weaken at some point in the mid- to late 1970s. The decreased salience of class and the secular cleavages, specifically, directly influenced the constituencies of the very parties who dominated the golden age as these parties relied on traditional social groups for voters.

7.2.3 *Lions, Tigers, and Bears: Distinguishing Different Types of Large Parties*

This standard summation of the decline of parties from the golden age period is not without critics, however (Daalder 1992). As Ignazi (1996) points out, much of the literature equated the decline of large parties with an overall decline. However, equating large parties with parties in general is problematic. As early as 1989, Reiter notes that the observed decline in large parties is really a shift in support from traditional mass parties to minor parties and that this shift may, in fact, be an indicator of hope that newer, smaller parties may eventually become larger, major parties fulfilling the same role as their predecessors. Reiter goes on to summarize the problematic nature of equating large parties to parties generally by stating that "using the rise of minor parties as an indicator of party decline reflects the major-party bias of many political scientists, who equate partisanship with major-party-sanship" (Reiter 1989, p .327). If we take Ignazi and Reiter's point to heart—that what really happened after the golden age was not a general decline of parties but a decline of large parties—then it is useful to, first, differentiate between large and small parties.

A quick glance at Western European democracies shows us a vast array of different types of traditional party actor. Much of the literature focuses on the rise and fall of *catch-all parties* but clearly not even this standard party type developed in all countries, as Kirchheimer (1965, p. 30) points out, because the historical development of some countries did not render *catch-all parties* useful. For example, the British parties came under scant pressure from new parties because of the majoritarian electoral system but had to deal with increased internal disruptions—particularly obvious in the case of the Labour Party. The traditional parties in the Netherlands, on the other hand, had to cope with internal pressures similar to those of the British parties, but the proportional nature of the electoral system led to an increasing number of new parties, i.e., external pressure, as well. Furthermore, we know from party development literature that such pressure led parties to alter their behavior (e.g., Kitschelt 1993; Katz and Mair 1995; Poguntke 2014). Parties modified their own organization to counter internal pressure or repositioned themselves within the context of political competition to counter external pressure. Such behavioral "corrections" also contributed, in part, to their electoral decline, for instance, when—in Germany—the moderate left party (SPD) moved to the center of the political spectrum, while one or more competing parties remained in the left spectrum. Depending on original party type, national contexts, and subsequent behavior alteration that took place, the type of party that developed after the golden age could be very different. Strategically, a party facing a general decline in social rootedness as evidenced by falling party membership in addition to decreasing shares of the vote must make a choice to secure the survival of the party. One choice, based on a purely Downsian model of party competition, would be for the party to diversify its ideological stance in order to try to capture as many nontraditional members as possible. Another possibility, in case of relatively homogenous societies (such as those found in many Scandinavian countries), would be to tighten the ideological cohesiveness of the party around the median party voter position.

The types of party that developed from the demise of the golden age, then, may be very different beasts. It is important to note at this juncture that we take a primarily functional rather than developmental view of parties. While factors such as national context may help explain why different parties developed in different party systems (Kirchheimer 1965; Lipset and Rokkan 1967), we do not take a "parties as biographies" approach in this chapter. Doing so would demand that we trace the decline of parties already in place in the 1960s across time. Therefore, we do not focus on whether the German Social Democratic Party, for example, maintained its vote share across time or whether it had or has a crisis in terms of popular support. We do so because, e.g., all catch-all parties will show similar features and behaviors and will have similar effects on national democracy. From such a functional perspective, it is utterly irrelevant whether it is one and the same catch-all party or whether it is party A in a political system until the 1980s and party B from the 1980s onward.

Furthermore, we argue that it is not sufficient to distinguish only between large and small parties. It is also necessary to provide a typology that further differentiates between types of large party. Put simply, in the context of the supposed decline of large parties, it may be important to understand whether certain types of large party lend themselves more readily to the lack of fulfillment of the three functions of mobilization, representation, and government stability than do others. This approach is in concordance with recent research on party types and their consequences for (a crisis of) democracy (Bardi et al. 2014).

Party Types and Democratic Functions

The link between party decline, or large party decline to be more specific, and supposed consequences of such a decline for democracy is normatively precise but lacks rigorous empirical testing (e.g., Kirchheimer 1954; Kirchheimer 1965; Crozier et al. 1975; Crouch 2004). Generally, scholars pinpoint those aspects of democracy most threatened when parties are no longer able to mobilize voters, represent voters, or form stable governments. Once parties stop fulfilling these functions, the implications are far ranging: governments become unstable and citizens experience alienation and, as a result, may stop participating in politics. While such conclusions seem to be plausible, well-theorized outcomes of large party decline, the causal mechanisms underlying them remain unclear. Somehow, the (de)evolution of modern parties is subsequently connected to the end of party competition and, hence, the complete breakdown of representation mechanisms (Blyth and Katz 2005). Additionally, decreasing partisanship among voters is supposed to lead directly not only to a decrease in the effectiveness of government (Allen 2009; Whiteley 2009) but perhaps to the end of party government (LaPalombara 2007, p. 148). LaPalombara (2007) provides a comprehensive discussion of the alleged ills facing democracies if parties decline. Among them are the end of societal change, decline in public confidence, and the end of responsible government as well as accountability. However, the precise relationship between large party decline and democratic malaise has remained argumentative. Moreover, large parties are more or less seen as a homogenous group of political actors, which divorces the party development literature from the party decline literature.

This section introduces a typology of large party types that is also empirically testable, provides a clear definitional distinction between party types, and is directly linked to the fulfillment of democratic functions. Based on this typology, we are able to address the two guiding questions of this chapter: first, what kind of developments regarding political parties has taken place in the last five decades in Western democracies? Second, how do these developments contribute to an increasing or decreasing fulfillment of the core functions of political parties and, in consequence, to a crisis of democracy?

Instead of creating a new typology from the ground up, we choose to use a subset of Gunther and Diamond's (2001, 2003) party typology. There are five types of party included in this definition: *elite*, *mass-based*, *electoralist*, *ethnic*, and *movement*. *Elite parties* were parties of the prewar period, primarily and are, according to Gunther and Diamond, the predecessors of postwar *mass parties*. Therefore we would not expect to find them in modern democracies. Likewise, *ethnic* and *movement parties* are both very specific party types that deal with niche, or single, issues. As such, we would not expect them to overlap with what we consider traditional established parties in Western European democracies. Given this, we begin with the assumption that electorally large parties will fall under one of the two types in modern democracies: *mass-based* or *electoralist*—both of which have clearly distinct profiles. The main distinction between these two types is the role of party members (Gunther and Diamond 2001, 10f.). While *mass-based parties* rely on a strong link between themselves and the societal group they focus on, i.e., have many members, *electoralist parties* are free of such ties and are more focused on pursuing voters independent of social groups. For *electoralist parties*, then, party membership comes low on the list of concerns.[3] Programmatically, mass-based parties attempt to mobilize member voters with tailored policy programs that are ideologically congruent to members' interests (Gunther and Diamond 2001, p. 17).

With a focus on party programs, the conceptualization by Gunther and Diamond includes an important further subdivision of *electoralist parties* into two distinct subtypes: *catch-all parties* and *programmatic parties*. While both subtypes have low linkages to party members, they differ in their programmatic clarity. *Catch-all parties* follow a purely vote maximizing strategy, which means that they will take only vague programmatic policy positions and will also obscure their true positions in favor of appealing to a broader spectrum of voters. While *catch-all parties* have the potential to aggregate the interest of a large group of citizens, they are likely to avoid programmatic commitment (Gunther and Diamond 2001, p. 27). *Programmatic parties*, on the other hand, present themselves with a clear programmatic profile that is easily identifiable and ideologically sound—similar to *mass parties*. While programmatic parties, too, aim at vote maximization, they do so by focusing mainly on their ideologically homogenous core voters. As Gunther and Diamond (ibid.) put it: "It [the programmatic party] has much more of a distinct, consistent, and coherent programmatic or ideological agenda than does the ideal-type catch-all party, and it clearly incorporates those ideological or programmatic appeals in its electoral campaigns and its legislative and government agenda." Thus, they do not obscure their profiles by claiming contradictory policy positions or by hedging their bets and supporting both positions of a bi-positional issue as we would expect from catch-all parties.

These two features of large parties—party membership and programmatic clarity—allow us to distinguish between three types of large party commonly found in Western European democracies: mass-integration parties, catch-all parties, and programmatic parties. Table 7.1 summarizes this typology of large parties.

Party Types and Their Performance

While party membership and programmatic clarity provide a clear way to distinguish the three party types definitionally, it is also possible to distinguish between the three in terms of how, and to what extent, they fulfill the three key democratic functions identified previously.

According to Gunther and Diamond (2003, p. 178), *mass parties* are "characterized by a large base of dues-paying members who remain active in party affairs

[3]The party development literature refers to the "role" of party members within the party organization, i.e., their involvement in candidate selection or program development. As the collection of such data is notoriously difficult, the "role" is usually substituted with the "number" of party members, assuming that members leave the party if their role diminishes. We follow this approach.

Table 7.1 Scheme of party types and characteristics

	Mass party	Programmatic party	Catch-all party
Programmatic clarity	High	High	Low
Party membership	High	Low	Low

[. . .].” Hence, *mass parties* are specifically well suited to the task of electoral mobilization and societal representation as they are capable of drawing from their strong member base. However, these parties might have difficulties to form and sustain governments, as their primary goal will be the implementation of the maximal version of their ideological-driven program, which tends to estrange centrist parties and those with opposing ideologies (Gunther and Diamond 2001, p. 17). It is also necessary to take into account that, in terms of electoral mobilization and societal representation, *mass parties* will only be strong in fulfilling these two functions when it comes to *their* voting constituencies and not necessarily those constituents falling outside these bounds.

Catch-all parties, like the *programmatic parties* discussed below, fall under the classification of electoralist parties as their main goal is building, and winning, electoral campaigns. *Catch-all parties* are “distinguished by [their] shallow organization, superficial and vague ideology, and overwhelmingly electoral orientation” (Gunther and Diamond 2003, p. 185). In other words, they are purely vote-maximizing parties who try to be “open to everyone.” Despite not having the large membership base enjoyed by mass parties, we expect that *catch-all parties* (given their electoral orientation) will be well suited to fulfilling the task of electoral mobilization. Kirchheimer (1965) acknowledges that catch-all parties are excellent at voter mobilization given the primary focus on electoral campaigning.[4] Nevertheless, such parties are necessarily less capable of aiding societal representation as they lack clear policy positions and vertical integration into society. Political decisions, that these parties make, necessarily conflict with some positions of their very heterogeneous voters. Finally, their ability to form and sustain coalitions should be strong as *catch-all parties* are inherently flexible in their policy orientation and can accommodate potential coalition partners in order to sustain their power (ibid.).

Turning to the democratic functions best fulfilled by the second type of electoralist party included in our typology—*programmatic parties*—we would expect that such parties, given their electoralist nature, will be relatively good at electoral mobilization. Furthermore, their combination of a lack of a core membership base and programmatic clarity leads us to predict that these parties will have a harder time fulfilling the functions of societal representation than *mass parties* but should be better than their *catch-all* counterparts. While their primary aim is to win elections, they pursue this goal with the help of a clearly defined party program (Gunther and Diamond 2001, p. 27). Hence, their ability to form governments

[4]However, other scholars such as Panebianco (1988) question just how good catch-all parties can be at electoral mobilization when they lack a clear societal base to mobilize.

should range somewhere between that of *catch-all* and *mass parties*, as they should be less bound by their members or mid-level functionaries than the latter. The *programmatic party*, therefore, can be seen as a midpoint between the two other types. These parties have the organizational structures common to *catch-all parties* combined with strong ideological stances reminiscent of *mass parties*. Whereas *catch-all parties* and *mass parties* are both very good at fulfilling one or two of the three functions, they also fall short on at least one. *Programmatic parties*, on the other hand, are moderately good at fulfilling most functions but not extremely good at fulfilling any specific function.

7.3 Measurement

Following from the theoretical framework, we develop a two-stage measurement approach to identify and distinguish mass parties, programmatic parties, and catch-all parties. In the first stage, we differentiate small from large parties, while the second stage uses party membership information as well as the parties' programmatic profiles to distinguish different party types. The underlying research question makes it necessary to define these measures in a way that is applicable not only to a wide range of different democratic systems but, more importantly, to a long time period. Hence, we present our approach in detail in both formal and substantive terms. Obviously, such a large-scale comparative approach does not come without costs or, in other words, a certain level of abstraction and simplification. Nevertheless, we are convinced that the measurement outlined below taps into the core elements of the party types in question, thereby complying with standards of content validity for political science concepts.

7.3.1 Stage One: Large versus Small Parties

We subset out large versus small parties by applying a vote share threshold that is relative to the number and size of the other parties in the party system.[5] Why rely on such a relative measure and not on a simple, absolute measure? Basically, we argue that the concepts "large" and "small" are in themselves relative, which, in consequence, has to be taken into account. Electoral systems have a strong impact on party size and the effective number of parties because they either encourage or discourage "voting with the heart" (Oppenhuis et al. 1996).[6] Hence, the electoral

[5]The information on electoral results is taken from the department's database (WZB 2014).

[6]Beyond this psychological effect, their vote-to-seat translation rules mechanically favor larger parties to different degrees (Duverger 1963). As we are using vote shares, the latter effect is of no direct importance.

support of parties is not just a result of their own appeal to voters but of an appeal induced by electoral system incentives. Therefore, any absolute measure of size is biased in favor of democracies with low district magnitudes because in these democracies vote concentration is more likely and subsequently leads to a reduction of the party system to only large parties. Moreover, the functional role of a party as a large party depends on the size of all other parties in the system.

Examples might help to clarify this argument: assume that in one country the largest party receives 30% of the vote and the remaining votes are equally distributed between four other parties (18% each). In the second country, the largest party wins only 29% of the vote but there are five other parties with equal vote shares (14% each). If one would apply an absolute threshold set to, e.g., 30%, the largest party in the first example would be classified as a large party, while there is no large party in the second example. Such a result seems hard to defend; in the latter example, the largest parties receive more than twice the number of votes than all other contenders. The ratio is much smaller in the first example. To prevent such a bias as well as logical shortcomings, we develop the following relative measure of party size (RMPS) based on the parties' vote shares that is fully comparable between systems and over time[7]:

$$\mathrm{RMPS}_{ik} = \frac{\sum_{j=1}^{n_k} \frac{\mathrm{voteshare}_{ik}}{\mathrm{voteshare}_{jk}} - 1}{\sum_{l=1}^{n_k} \left(\sum_{j=1}^{n_k} \frac{\mathrm{voteshare}_{lk}}{\mathrm{voteshare}_{jk}} - 1 \right)} \tag{7.1}$$

where i represents the party, k represents the election, n represents the total number of parties competing, and j/l are running numbers from 1 to n. For each party in each election, we calculate the ratios between the party's vote share and the vote share of all other competing parties.[8] The sum of these ratios is then divided by the respective values for all parties to generate a common scale that resembles the party's relative weight. The range of this scale is $0 < RMPS_{ik} < 1$, and we define parties as large if their value is above 0.25.

7.3.2 Stage Two: Differentiating Large Parties

As shown in Table 7.1, information on the party membership base and programmatic clarity is sufficient to differentiate between the three types of large parties.

[7] The number of competing parties n has to be larger than one which, obviously, is a precondition for democratic elections.

[8] We subtract one in the equation to eliminate the party's eigenvalue.

Party Membership Base

The core characteristic of *mass integration parties* is a strong reliance on party members. Hence, building on existing work (Katz and Mair 1992; Mair and van Biezen 2001; van Biezen et al. 2012), we collected information on party membership figures for as many parties and time points as possible. Unfortunately, it is not feasible to get a full time-series dataset for all parties. Therefore, we interpolate some of the missing data points: (a) in the case of the availability of two sequential points in time, we linearly interpolate the missing values in between, and (b) at the two temporal endpoints, we use the last available pair of real values for a linear interpolation beyond the temporal endpoints. In order to secure validity, we apply a minimum quality criterion by only allowing interpolation for missing data within a maximal distance of 10 years to the next "real" data point.

The party membership base (PMB) is calculated in a very straightforward manner:

$$\mathrm{PMB}_{ik} = \frac{\mathrm{members}_{ik}}{\mathrm{electorate}_{k}} \tag{7.2}$$

where i represents the party and k represents the election. We divide the number of party members by the total number of eligible voters in the respective election. The range of this measure runs from 0 (no members) to 1 (in the implausible case that all eligible voters in a country are members of one and the same party). The threshold is set to 0.05 which refers to a situation in which 5% of the eligible population are members of the respective party. We refrain from using other measures, for example, the party members to party voter ratio, because they are not suited for comparison over time. While the denominator in our equation is rather stable over time—or, at least, follows a stable trend—electoral success is rather volatile. If one were to include electoral success, changes in PMB_{ik} could occur due to changes in membership figures but also because of electoral outcomes. A parallel decrease in votes and members would not influence such an indicator and fails to reflect decreasing societal rootedness. Our measure, on the other hand, is only sensitive to the numbers we are truly interested in—party membership figures.

Programmatic Clarity

In order to measure the programmatic clarity of parties, we employ one of the most-used and well-known sources of party programmatic data, the Manifesto Project Dataset (Volkens et al. 2012, 2013), which provides content analytical data on party policy positions derived from electoral manifestos.[9] Within the coding scheme of the Manifesto Project are 13 pairs of antipodal policy, meaning that there is a positive and a negative category for one policy area (Werner et al. 2011). These 13 pairs concern most of the core policy questions in Western European party competition.[10]

---

[9] Regarding the relevance of electoral manifestos, see also Merz and Regel (2013).

[10] In detail, they cover foreign special relationships, military, European Union, internationalism, constitutionalism, political centralization, economic protectionism, welfare state, national way of life, education, multiculturalism, morality, and labor groups.

A high level of programmatic clarity (PC) is evident if a party only mentions one side of each of these policy areas. Likewise, a party that makes statements for both sides of these areas obscures its position and is thus programmatically unclear. The same is true if a party makes no statements at all regarding one of these 13 core policy areas.

In order to assess the overall clarity of a program, we build an index over all 13 pairs. Furthermore, the relevance of a single policy category depends on contextual factors, both internal and external to the polity. In other words, salient policies at the heart of political competition between parties are neither constant over time nor do they have to be present in all countries. Again, contextualization of our measure becomes necessary. We do this by calculating election-specific weights for each of the policy categories. In a first step, all 26 policy categories (13 pairs)—measured as proportions of all statements in the party's manifesto—are rescaled that

$$\sum_{j=1}^{n} \text{position}_{ijk}^{+} + \sum_{j=1}^{n} \text{position}_{ijk}^{-} = 1 \tag{7.3}$$

where n represents the total number of policy categories, j represents the single policy category, i represents the party, and k represents the election.

Now, the empirical values of the 26 policy categories no longer represent the proportion of the overall manifesto but of the 13 core policy areas (reflected by the 13 pairs). We then calculate the weight W_{jk} as the weighted[11] salience of the policy over all parties running in the election:

$$W_{jk} = \sum_{i=1}^{n} (\text{position}_{ijk}^{+} + \text{position}_{ijk}^{-}) * \text{RMPS}_{ik} \tag{7.4}$$

where n represents the total number of parties, j represents the policy area, i represents the party, and k represents the election. This means that if a policy area is never mentioned in all party manifestos of one election, the weight of the policy area becomes zero.

Finally, we calculate the programmatic clarity as

$$\text{PC}_{ik} = \sum_{j=1}^{n} \left(\frac{|\ \text{position}_{ijk}^{+} - \text{position}_{ijk}^{-}\ |}{\text{position}_{ijk}^{+} + \text{position}_{ijk}^{-}} * W_{jk} \right) \tag{7.5}$$

where n represents the total number of policy areas, j represents the policy area, i represents the party, and k represents election. Hence, for each of the 13 pairs, we

[11] In this case, weighted refers to acknowledgment of the parties' electoral size, measured as the RMPS.

calculate a clarity value as the ratio of the absolute difference between positive and negative statements divided by the overall proportion of positive and negative statements. For example, a party presenting only positive statements receives a value of 1, while a party with an equal number of positive and negative statements receives a programmatic clarity value of 0. This value is then multiplied with the overall weight of the issue in the election. As a result, parties with a clear profile regarding salient policy areas have higher levels of programmatic clarity. If a policy area is not salient in an election, clarity in this area is of either small or no importance for the overall score. The scale of this measure runs from 0 (no clarity) to 1 (full clarity). We define the threshold of programmatic clarity to 0.75. In somewhat abstract terms, this represents a party that has a clear position on 75% of the 13 core policy areas.

7.3.3 Thresholds

To prevent any argument that our thresholds to measure party types are set arbitrarily, we refer on the one hand to the high face validity of our classification presented in the following section. Moreover, we ran a set of simulations to emphasize the quality of our thresholds. The simulations follow the simple idea that reasonable changes regarding the thresholds should not lead to major changes regarding the classification of parties being large, having a large membership base or showing high programmatic clarity. If we would encounter such changes, neither the descriptive nor the causal analysis could be considered to be reliable and robust. For each of the three thresholds, we drew 1000 random values from a normal distribution where the mean of the distribution is equal to the respective threshold and the standard deviation is equal to 5% of the respective mean. For example, in the case of programmatic clarity, we drew from a distribution with a mean of 0.75 and a standard deviation of 0.0375. In other words, 95.4% of the draws are values between 0.675 and 0.825. All these 1000 values are then used as simulated thresholds to calculate whether a party is above or below the threshold. Hence, for each party in each election, we get 1000 comparisons between the original party classification, for example, as a large party, and the classifications based on the simulated thresholds, either large party or small party. We then calculate the proportion of deviations from the original classification. For all three measures, the error probability, meaning the deviation from the original classification based on the described thresholds, is below 3%. We see this as a strong indicator in favor of the selected thresholds and thus the validity of the following analyses.

7.4 Party Types: Descriptives

The first portion of the analysis is devoted to a more detailed look at the descriptives and examines variations in party types within countries and across time. The dataset includes parties from 15 Western European democracies beginning in the 1960s and continuing through 2010s. These countries are Sweden, Norway, Denmark, Finland, the Netherlands, France, Italy, Spain, Greece, Portugal, Germany, Austria, Switzerland, the United Kingdom, and Ireland. In other words, we are looking at established democracies in Western Europe which constitute the empirical core of the crisis of political party literature.[12] We refrain from extending our sample to countries from other regions, for example, Eastern Europe, because parties and party systems are radically different from their Western counterparts. Even parties and party systems in other older democracies like the USA or Japan are hardly comparable with the historical development we have witnessed in Western Europe (Duverger 1963). The analysis below shows how the measurement developed previously assigns parties into party types and whether there are noticeable patterns across countries and time with regard to party development.

7.4.1 *Distribution of Party Types*

To begin, in Table 7.2 we present the percentages of the party types across time as well as the average cumulative vote shares for all four types per decade. A few interesting conclusions are immediately apparent. First, we can see that the majority of parties in the sample are *programmatic parties* with just over 60% of the observations falling into this party-type category. The rest of the observations are spread almost evenly between the *catch-all and mass party* categories. Second, we see that the share of *programmatic parties* has increased steadily over the decades, while the share of mass parties has declined equally steadily. Whereas 36% of the observations in the 1960s could be labeled as *mass parties*, by the 2000s fewer than 10% of the observations fell into this category. The inverse is true for *programmatic parties*, and the trend is even stronger: by the 2000s, over 70% of the parties under observation could be classified as *programmatic parties*. Interestingly, we see that the share of *catch-all parties* has somewhat increased in the 1970s and 1980s, decreased drastically in the 1990s just to increase again in the first half of the 2000s. Obviously, there is no clear pattern when it comes to this party type. More importantly, there is no validation at all of the domination of catch-all parties in Western party systems.

[12]Unfortunately, we are not able to include Luxembourg (due to missing information on party membership), Belgium (due to the special nature of government formation and the electoral system), and microstates like Liechtenstein or Andorra.

Table 7.2 Share of party types per decade, in %

	1965–1969	1970s	1980s	1990s	2000–2005	Average
Catch-all party	0.10	0.25	0.20	0.12	0.19	0.18
Mass party	0.36	0.14	0.11	0.06	0.09	0.13
Programmatic party	0.42	0.53	0.61	0.76	0.72	0.63
Rest party	0.11	0.08	0.08	0.06	0.00	0.07
Average cumulative vote share	60.70	59.40	60.99	50.45	52.71	56.78

Source: Own calculations

The table also presents all observations that cannot be classified with our scheme. It represents parties showing high membership figures but low programmatic clarity that can also not be classified as one of the other party types of the initial classification scheme of Gunther and Diamond (2001, 2003). It has to be clarified during analysis whether this category represents a party type not covered by our typology or whether this is a transitional category—some kind of evolutionary intermediate step—only. As we see in the analysis below, this category is not heavily populated with only around six parties at different points in time.

The last row gives the average cumulative vote shares of all types of large parties based on the relative vote share presented above in the measurement section.[13] Clearly, the numbers are very stable for the period between 1965 and 1989, which covers the golden age of political parties. Roughly 60% of the relative share of the vote falls to large parties. There is a sharp drop in the 1990s consistent with the literature on party system development: large parties lose more and more votes, smaller parties grow in importance, and the overall party system fragmentation increases. Nevertheless, large parties still represent the majority of voters.

The second step of this descriptive analysis looks at cross-country variation in our typology of large parties. Figure. 7.1 includes all countries in the sample with the party membership variable on the x-axis and the programmatic clarity variable on the y-axis. For each subplot representing a country, the black vertical lines indicate the threshold for high versus low party membership, and the black horizontal line indicates the threshold between high versus low programmatic clarity. In all, these thresholds divide the graph into four quadrants with one large party type each—the three substantive types as well as the rest type.

As we can see from Fig. 7.1, there is variation in the types of large party found in the country sample.[14] First, we see that there are two countries with a single type of large party only: Italy and Spain. In both countries, we only see *programmatic parties*, although in Italy these *programmatic parties* are on the threshold of being *mass parties* but fail to obtain the membership numbers necessary to become actual *mass parties*. Second, the largest group of countries in the figure is the group where

[13]To calculate the values for each time period, we add the relative vote shares of all large parties in a country, calculate the total overall countries, and divide this number by the total number of countries.

[14]The shade of the dots does not carry information but is created by overlapping dots.

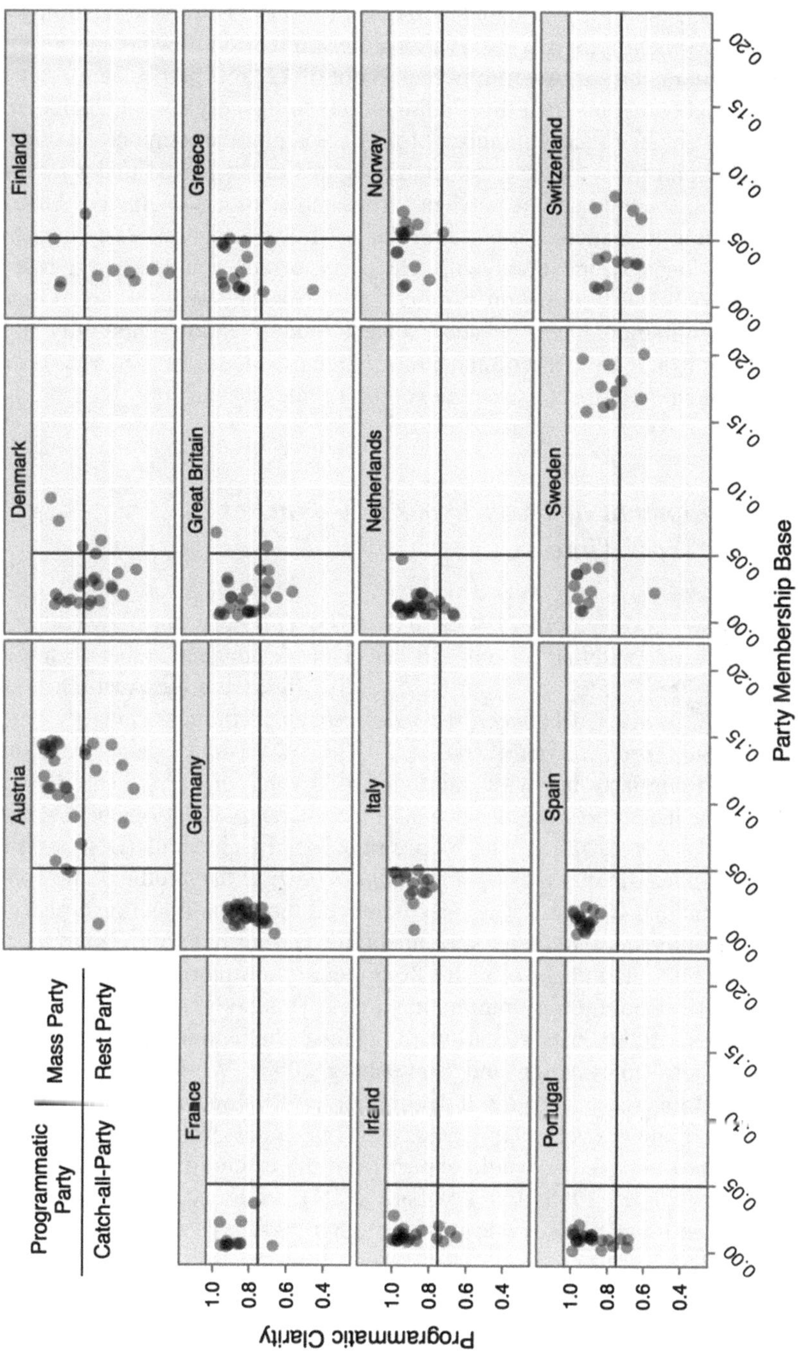

Fig. 7.1 Party types of large parties by countries. Source: Authors' own figure

both *catch-all* and *programmatic parties* exist simultaneously: Germany, the United Kingdom, Portugal, Greece, Finland, and the Netherlands. Third, and regarding the problematic rest category, these observations are limited to a few countries. They feature most prominently in Austria; in fact, 8 out of 17 "rest parties" are Austrian parties. One might conclude that this finding points to the very special character of Austria when it comes to party membership. There is no other democratic country showing higher and more stable membership figures in the period under research than Austria. This special relation between parties and members might give Austrian parties more room to maneuver regarding their political program. Party members have by definition a strong bond with the party, which can lead to a blurred perception of political action and political performance (Wagner and Giebler 2014). Moreover, in more recent decades, societal modernization supposedly diversified membership at least to a certain degree, which might also be seen as a starting point for a weakening of the Austrian *mass parties*' ideological core.

7.4.2 Development of Party Types in Countries and Across Time

Figure. 7.2 shows the development of large parties over time, grouped by countries, and reveals several patterns.[15] First, we see a close connection between *mass parties* and our "rest" category. Both the Swedish (Sda) and the Austrian Social Democrats (SPÖ) switched between the *mass party* and the rest category before developing into *programmatic parties*. The Danish Social Democrats (SD) developed similarly but with interludes as a *catch-all party*. The Austrian ÖVP, too, has switched between the two high membership categories but seems to have stabilized as a *mass party*. The Norwegian Social Democrats (DNA), on the other hand, morphed directly into *a programmatic party* in the middle of the 1980s. Overall, it seems that the "rest" category is indeed mostly a transitional phase of *mass party* development in very specific contexts. Furthermore, *mass parties* generally went through a phase of reshuffling identity during the 1970s and 1980s before most developed into programmatic parties. This both confirms and contradicts the theses of the critics that warn against the end of the golden age (a.o. Kirchheimer 1965; Dalton and Wattenberg 2000). While the mass parties have indeed lost this status because of declining membership numbers, this has not coincided with higher levels of programmatic vagueness and the obscuring of programmatic positions as we would expect from the catch-all party development literature (Kirchheimer 1965; LaPalombara 2007), as especially programmatic parties have been founded or developed from other party types.

[15]The figure displays parties only when they meet the criterion of being a "large" party. There are two explanations for parties not being represented for the whole time frame: they might not have run during the respective election or they might have been/become a small party.

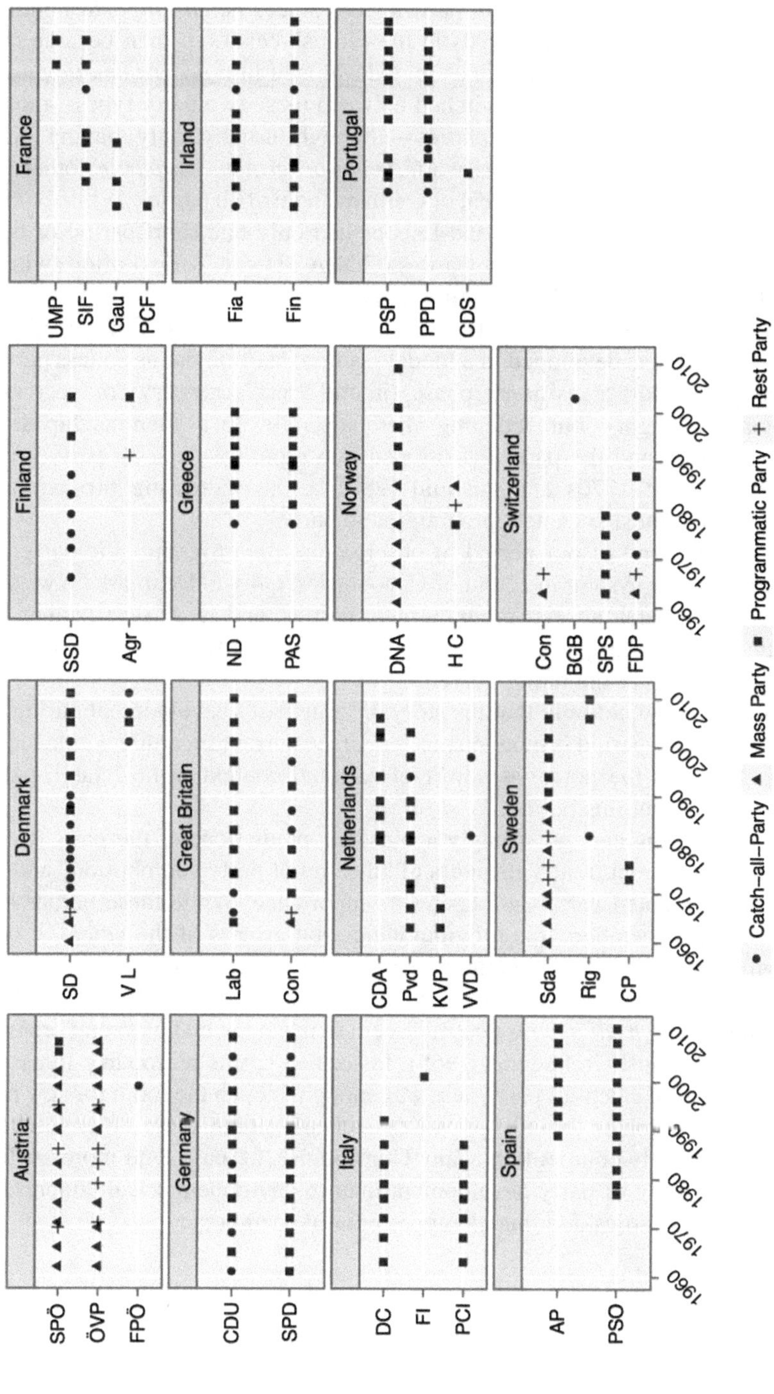

Fig. 7.2 Development of party types of large parties over time. Source: Authors' own figure

A second trend is apparent if we look at the development of *catch-all parties*. In Greece, Portugal, and Finland, large parties were indeed *catch-all parties* until the beginning of the 1980s (or the 1990s in the Finnish case) but then became more programmatically clear and concise as they developed into *programmatic parties*. A large number of other parties switched between these two party types—most of the British, Irish, and German parties—although usually only having single instances of being *catch-all parties* while being *programmatic parties* otherwise. Interesting is the similar development of German and British parties. While both the German Social Democrats (SPD) and Labour had only one short period of being *catch-all parties*, both conservative parties (CDU/CSU and Tories) often switched between being catch-all and programmatic parties. Indeed, the British Conservatives oscillated between two party types over nearly the whole period. Finally, the Swiss liberal FDP has developed in a model fashion: starting out as a mass party, it went through a short transitional phase (in the "rest" category) of decreasing programmatic category but retaining members. But then membership levels decreased as well, and the party transitioned into a purely catch-all party for the period between the 1970s and the mid-1980s before increasing programmatic clarity again and, thus, became a programmatic party.

Overall, at the end of our period of observation, the programmatic party type dominated the party system in 12 out of 15 countries. Only in Denmark do we see a balance between catch-all and programmatic parties, and in Austria neither programmatic nor catch-all parties playing a role as mass parties and "rest" category parties (see above) are the major players.

Such trends show not only that the story of large party development during and after the golden age period is more nuanced than the current literature would lead us to believe but also the potential power of national context in how large parties transform throughout this period.

Overall, these findings go strongly against the predictions of the party decline literature that we are currently in an era of "the end of party competition" and that programmatic-oriented parties are losing in importance. While these parties have indeed lost many members, the programmatic arbitrariness of the *catch-all party* type often bemoaned in the literature seems to have been just one step in party development. In direct contradiction to the dire warnings of Kirchheimer, the development of *catch-all parties* does not seem to mean the end of strong programmatic representation (Kirchheimer 1965). Instead, it seems reasonable to assume that short periods of catch-all party-ness was enough to open the room for new party actors, which then forced those large parties to clearly situate themselves within the (programmatic) party competition again. Our findings, at least, lend more credibility to such a reading of party development than to any nonempirical "doomsday" interpretations of parties and thus the representative democracy.

7.5 Analysis: Party Types and Democratic Functions

7.5.1 Mobilization

Decreasing turnout levels are seen as one of the most obvious manifestations of the crisis of democracy. It is argued that they would signal disenchantment with politics and political apathy and decreases the legitimacy of parliaments and governments. However, are developments regarding party types in any way connected to this? Are some party types indeed better or worse in mobilizing the electorate? We use a regression model to validate whether party types or, more concretely, *mass parties* and *catch-all parties* indeed had a positive effect on turnout figures.[16] In other words: the model measures the impact of the number of mass parties and catch-all parties in the previous term ($t-1$) on the current turnout ($t0$). Relying on a time lag seems to be a reasonable approach to verify the mobilization capacities of these party types, while ignoring such a time lag would result in endogeneity problems. Obviously, aggregate turnout is affected by many different factors (for an overview see Franklin 2004; Blais 2006). Hence, we introduce several control variables to prevent an *omitted-variable bias*. These are (a) the closeness of the election (vote share difference between the largest and the second largest party), (b) the natural logarithm of the size of the electorate, (c) the effective number of parties (as a proxy for both the nature of the electoral system as well as of the supply side), and (d) compulsory voting (whether the country has compulsory voting or a history of compulsory voting). Additionally, we introduce dummy variables representing decades to control for time effects.[17] Finally, the model also includes an indicator representing the number of parties falling into the rest category. Recall that the latter and *mass parties* share high membership figures, while only *mass parties* show high programmatic clarity. By including the number of parties falling into the rest category, we can validate our claim that high turnout is not a mere consequence of high party membership figures but a feature of a specific party type.

Table 7.3 presents the results of the regression analysis.[18] The number of *mass parties* in the term period before the respective election has a significant effect on the turnout level. Holding all other predictors constant at their means, for each mass party in the system, turnout increases by about 4% points. The existence of parties falling into the rest category also has a positive sign, but the effect is not significant. Therefore, the positive effect of *mass parties* is not simply due to membership figures. There is no significant impact of *catch-all parties* on turnout. The assumption *that catch-all parties* have a positive effect on turnout due to their sophisticated mobilization strategies and campaign machines can be rejected. *Programmatic parties* do not significantly affect electoral turnout. They are neither good nor bad when it comes to voter mobilization.

[16]Hence, the cases in this analysis are elections.

[17]The hierarchical data structure makes it necessary to calculate cluster-adjusted standard errors.

[18]As the controls are of no primary interest, we have omitted them from the table with the exception of the decade dummies.

Table 7.3 Party types and electoral mobilization

	(1)
Number of mass parties ($t-1$)	0.04** (0.01)
Number of catch-all parties ($t-1$)	0.01 (0.76)
Number of programmatic parties ($t-1$)	0.00 (0.80)
Number of rest parties ($t-1$)	0.03 (0.25)
Decades (base category: 1960s)	
– 1970s	−0.03 (0.17)
– 1980s	−0.04 (0.10)
– 1990s	−0.10*** (0.00)
– 2000s	−0.11*** (0.01)
– 2010s	−0.09 (0.15)
_cons	0.68** (0.02)
N	190
R^2	0.28

Note: P-values in brackets; *$p < 0.1$; **$p < 0.05$; ***$p < 0.01$

Moreover, we can show that this effect holds even when controlling for decade. This is important due to the development trend of mass parties, which our initial descriptive analysis shows to disappear over time. Finally, the model explains about 28% of the variation in turnout, while leaving out the mass party variable decreases the R^2 value to 0.25. Hence, including the information on the number of mass parties in the previous legislative term makes a significant explanatory contribution to predicting electoral turnout.

7.5.2 Representation

While the discussion on what exactly representation means and who can and should represent whom in a democracy is long and complex (see, e.g., Pitkin 1972; Rehfeld 2009; Mansbridge 2011), it is still possible to claim that one of the core representative mechanisms in modern party democracies is between a political party and its supporters. This link is, for example, described within the framework of the *responsible party model* (Thomassen 1994; Thomassen and Schmitt 1997; Mair 2008) where—in a nutshell—parties present their political profiles and voters choose the party offering the profile that best fits their own interests and vote for them on election day. The parties, then, take responsibility to implement their policy proposals should they be elected to parliament and are held accountable for their actions at the next election by their constituents. One way of assessing how well parties perform in this process is to examine the degree of congruence they create between the policy profile they put forth in a given election and the policy interests of their potential supporters (e.g., Adams and Ezrow 2009; Powell 2009; Golder and Stramski 2010). To assess congruence we use a combined dataset of party left–right positions based on the Manifesto Project Dataset and of party supporters' left–right self-positioning from Eurobarometer as well as CSES 1–3[19] surveys.[20] We rescale the survey respondents onto the theoretical party position scale, ranging from -100 (left) to 100 (right). The next step is to then calculate the distance between the party's position and the mean position of their respective supporters in order to assess the congruence between a party and their own supporters. Thus for this analysis, a case is a single party at a single point in time. This allows us to verify whether *mass parties* indeed represent their own supporters better than *catch-all* and *programmatic parties*, as the theory suggested.

Before we come to this model, however, we compare the distribution of supporters by comparing the standard deviation of left–right self-positioning of the parties' supporters between the party types. A simple ANOVA analysis, checking whether the party types have significantly different means, finds as expected. The supporters of catch-all parties have an average standard deviation of 32.98 scale points. In comparison, the average distribution of mass party supporters is 3.03 scale points smaller (significant with $p < 0.1$), while programmatic parties and the parties of the rest type do not vary significantly.[21] This result gives a first hint that *catch-all parties* could indeed have a harder time representing their supporters than mass parties, given that their supporters are more dispersed along the left–right scale. This is not unexpected given the diffuse policy supply catch-all parties provide.

Indeed, this result is confirmed by the analysis explaining the parties' distances to the average left–right position of their supporters. In order to avoid the *omitted variable problem*, we include controls for the most likely variables influencing representation: (a) the electoral system, (b) effective number of parties, (c) the polarization of the party system, (d) the absolute number of large parties, as well as (e) variables for time effects. Furthermore, standard errors are clustered by country to take the data structure into account. Table 7.4 shows the results of the analysis, omitting the results for the controls.

While the effect is only significant at the $p < 0.10$ level, we do find that *mass parties* are indeed closer to their average supporter than *catch-all parties* by 15 scale points. The results for *programmatic parties* are not significant, but the beta coefficient is in the expected direction and size: *programmatic parties* have a

[19]The Comparative Study of Electoral Systems (CSES) is the largest comparative project dealing with election studies. A jointly developed questionnaire is used in a variety of national election studies. On this basis a comparable dataset covering multiple democracies was created (www.cses.org).

[20]In order to avoid the problem that the "left-right" dimension might have different meanings in different countries (Benoit and Laver 2006) and/or at different points in time, we use the method of Simon Franzmann and Andre Kaiser (2006) to calculate country- and time-specific party left-right positions from Manifesto data. We can then combine these positions with the respective country- and time-specific survey results and only need the much less comprehensive assumption that citizens and parties in one country, at one point in time, share the same understanding of the political competition.

[21]$F(3, 181) = 2.56, p > F = 0.056$.

Table 7.4 Party types and representation

	(1)
Party type (base category: catch-all party)	
– Mass party	−15.19* (8.45)
– Programmatic party	−4.14 (7.07)
– Rest party	−2.64 (9.53)
Decades (base category: 1970s)	
– 1980s	−5.52 (4.51)
– 1990s	−12.41* (5.85)
– 2000s	−12.05* (6.70)
_cons	31.63* (16.79)
N	184
R^2	0.15

Note: Robust standard errors in brackets. *$p < 0.1$; **$p < 0.05$; ***$p < 0.01$

slight tendency to be better at representing their supporters than *catch-all parties* but not at the level of *mass parties*. These results confirm our theoretical proposition that the social rootedness and clear programmatic profile of *mass parties* lead to a strong representation link between these parties and their supporters. At the same time, the supporters of *mass parties* come from a significantly narrower left–right spectrum than those of *catch-all parties*. Hence, *catch-all parties* successfully appeal to a broader audience, drawing in supporters from a much broader segment of society. However, these are then significantly worse represented. With the disappearance of *mass parties*, the performance of parties regarding representation has been reduced, which is a bigger problem for representative democracy. But as *mass parties* are mostly substituted by *programmatic parties*, this effect is not dramatic enough to use the term crisis.

7.5.3 Government Stability

In general, both types of electoralist party should be able to sustain governments better than *mass-based parties*, simply because their actions are more focused on office-seeking than policy-seeking. Moreover, their organizational structure gives more power to party elites, which increases the capacity for strategic behavior. At the same time, *catch-all parties* should be even better at sustaining governments because they are less constrained by a clear political program than *programmatic parties*. In other words, *catch-all parties* are more flexible in reacting to internal and external developments and more able to reach a compromise with coalition partners. Does the configuration of governments in terms of the three party types under analysis have an effect on government stability?

Government stability here refers to the continuity of a government between two regular elections with instability being defined as either a change in the composition of the government (either the full government or the set of parties comprising the

Table 7.5 Party types and government stability

	(1)
Party type (base category: rest-party government)	
– Mass party government	0.96 (0.20)
– Catch-all party government	1.12^{**} (0.02)
– Programmatic party government	0.53 (0.37)
Decades (base category: 1960s)	
– 1970s	0.15 (0.78)
– 1980s	0.73 (0.31)
– 1990s	2.00^{**} (0.04)
– 2000s	1.37^{*} (0.09)
_cons	−0.73 (0.22)
N	148
Pseudo R^2	0.13

Note: *P*-values in brackets. $^{*}p < 0.1$; $^{**}p < 0.05$; $^{***}p < 0.01$

government) or when the prime minister changes (Müller and Strøm 2000, p. 12). Such a definition is commonly agreed upon in the literature (Budge and Keman 1990; Lijphart 1999; Conrad and Golder 2010). To be clear, however, the ending of the government by a regular election is not instability but part of the natural, stable transition of power in democracies.[22] The unit of observation for this analysis is the first government in a country for each legislative term. As the dependent variable, we built a binary indicator: a government is considered to be stable if it lasts for at least 75% of the regular term.

The different party types are measured on the level of governments. Therefore, three dummy variables were created, each showing a value of one if the respective party type is present in the government. The fourth type of large parties, those falling into the rest category, are used as the base category.[23] Furthermore, we introduce three control variables: (a) the number of parties in government, (b) a dummy variable distinguishing minority from majority governments, and (c) the maximum left–right distance of all parties in government. Following from the literature (e.g., Taylor and Herman 1971; Immergut 1990; Lijphart 1999; Tsebelis 2002), these indicators have been shown to have an impact on government stability because they affect a government's ability to act and to establish policy programs. Again, the model includes variables controlling for time effects. The regression results are shown in Table 7.5.[24]

First of all, we see a clear temporal effect: governments have become more stable in the 1990s and 2000s in comparison with governments in the 1960s,

[22]Similar to the other parts of our analysis, we use cluster-corrected regression analysis to test the impact of different party types.

[23]Consequently, governments containing more than one party type had to be excluded from the analysis. Fortunately, only nine governments were lost due to this restriction.

[24]Control variables are omitted from the table.

holding all other factors constant. The question whether this is caused by the increased experience of democracy or other factors cannot be resolved in this paper. At minimum, one can conclude that, in contrast to electoral turnout, there is not an overall downward trend endangering the efficiency of elected governments and, as a consequence, a crisis of the democracy phenomenon. Regarding our variables of interest—the party types—we get a result more or less consistent with theoretical expectations. Governments including at least one catch-all party have a much higher probability of surviving than the baseline category representing rest parties. In fact, holding all other independent variables on their empirical mean, the probability of a government being stable increases from 35% to 57% if a *catch-all party* is part of the government. The coefficients for *mass parties* and *programmatic parties* are positive but both are far from statistically significant. In other words, and consistent with our assumptions, only the purest type of an electoralist party in our analysis, the *catch-all party*, plays a relevant role in regard to government stability.

7.6 Conclusion

Much has been written about the decline of political parties and the more or less devastating effects of this decline for the functioning of modern representative democracies. In this chapter, we have raised the point that this literature is full of untested propositions and "doomsday" predictions that have little, if any, empirical support. Therefore, we set out to take a first step toward a rigorous empirical test of whether and how much a "decline of parties" exists and contributes to a "crisis of democracy."

In order to do this, we concentrate on the major players among political parties when it comes to the fulfillment of their democratic functions: large parties. In a second step, we subset large parties into three party types: *mass*, *catch-all*, and *programmatic parties*. For this we develop a two-dimensional conceptualization focusing on party membership and programmatic clarity. Looking at the large parties in 15 Western European countries from the 1960s to 2010s, we find that the *programmatic party* type dominates most systems. *Mass parties*, on the other hand, have declined steadily over time and are by now only a dominant feature in the Austrian party system. Given this development, it is safe to say that the age of the *mass party* is very likely past, as we cannot conceive how these parties would be able to win back large numbers of members. We also show that while the *catch-all party* type has not decreased in numbers to the extent that *mass parties* have, they have also not mushroomed as predicted by scholars such as Kirchheimer. Thus, while the strong vertical link between society and political parties in the form of *mass parties* has indeed diminished substantially in most countries, a complete depoliticization and de-ideologization of party competition in the form of *catch-all parties* have also not taken place in most systems. Thus, we were able to show that there is no general decline of large parties, but we did find changes among party types.

Furthermore, we analyze whether the existence or disappearance of certain (large) party types has an effect on the three key functions parties fulfill in democracy: mobilization, representation, and government stability. With regard to mobilization, our results show that, controlling for several other factors, *mass parties* have a positive impact on turnout levels. In contrast to Kirchheimer's argument regarding the powerful campaign machines of *catch-all parties*, these parties do not affect turnout. This is not just a relevant finding, but it might also be another piece to complete the puzzle of decreasing turnout rates in advanced democracies. *Mass parties* have clearly been on the retreat for several decades, and this has a negative effect on citizens' electoral participation—obviously more severe in countries with a formerly strong tradition of *mass parties*. At the same time, neither the development of *catch-all parties* nor the large number of *programmatic parties* can fill this void. A programmatic profile still needs to be communicated to the voters, and for this process party members still seem to play an important role.

Turning to fulfillment of the representation function, the results are in line with expectations. Specifically, we show that *mass parties* are better at fulfilling this function than their *catch-all counterparts*: *mass parties* are closer to the average supporter than *catch-all parties*. At the same time, we show that *catch-all parties* do appeal to a broader audience than do *mass parties*—something we would expect given the well-documented nature of these parties programmatically. For the purposes of representation, however, the decline of the *mass party* is troubling as we show that these parties were clearly better at fulfilling the representative function than *catch-all parties*. On the other hand, the most common party type identified by our classification—the *programmatic party*—is better than *catch-all parties* at representing although still much worse than mass parties. With this finding we confirm that *programmatic parties* are functioning as the C-students of modern party systems with regard to key democratic functions.

Finally, our analysis shows that different party types in power do affect the durability of governments. Governments including a *catch-all party* are much more stable than governments without. At least in this regard, they outperform the other party types; whether this is enough to outweigh their effects on turnout and representation seems questionable. On the other hand, forming stable governments has traditionally been seen as one of the weaknesses of *mass parties*, but we find no empirical evidence that they perform worse than *programmatic parties*.

While the three functions of parties assessed in this chapter are arguably crucial for democracies, they are not the only functions parties fulfill. As presented above, Gunther and Diamond (2001, 2003) list additional functions for some of which we can draw cautious conclusions. For example, the fact that a large, and even growing, proportion of parties under investigation are *programmatic parties* shows that programmatic clarity remains a stable feature of political competition, which, in turn, is likely to have a positive effect on the capability of parties to fulfill other democratic functions. While we could not test this proposition directly in this chapter, we can argue that issue structuring is a given outcome if roughly three in four large parties in a party system have high programmatic clarity. A less positive picture emerges if we think about large party development with regard to parties' social integration function. In this regard, we see, for instance, a clear pattern of decreasing party membership numbers, which may still affect democracy indirectly, e.g., through decreased societal rootedness. If we assume that one of the main integration mechanisms is via party membership and that the continuous "learning" of democratic values and procedures as well as a political sense of belonging, which membership provides, is still highly relevant for fostering democracy, the picture looks grim. This function is clearly only fulfilled by one of the three large party types we identify: *mass parties*. Hence, we must draw similar conclusions as we do for mobilization: as *mass parties* seem to be irreversibly vanishing, the fulfillment of this function becomes increasingly difficult. Nonetheless, the process we are observing is clearly better characterized as a development of party systems and party types than as a crisis of democracy provoked by the decline of political parties in general.

References

Adams, J., & Ezrow, L. (2009). Who do European parties represent? How Western European parties represent the policy preferences of opinion leaders. *The Journal of Politics, 71*(1), 206–223.

Adams, J., Clark, M., Ezrow, L., & Glasgow, G. (2006). Are niche parties fundamentally different from mainstream parties? The causes and the electoral consequences of Western European parties' policy shifts, 1976–1998. *American Journal of Political Science, 50*(3), 513–529.

Allen, C. S. (2009). 'Empty nets': Social democracy and the 'catch-all party thesis' in Germany and Sweden. *Party Politics, 15*(5), 635–654.

Bartolini, S. (2007). *The political mobilization of the European left 1860–1980: The class cleavage*. New York, NY: Cambridge University Press.

Bardi, L., Bartolini, S., & Trechsel, A. H. (2014). Responsive and responsible? The role of parties in twenty-first century politics. *West European Politics, 37*(2), 235–252.

Benoit, K., & Laver, M. (2006). *Party policy in modern democracies*. London: Routledge.

Blais, A. (2006). What affects voter turnout? *Annual Review of Political Science, 9*, 111–125.

Blyth, M., & Katz, R. (2005). From catch-all politics to cartelisation: The political economy of the cartel party. *West European Politics, 28*(1), 33–60.

Bornschier, S. (2010). *Cleavage politics and the populist right: The new cultural conflict in Western Europe*. Philadelphia, PA: Temple University Press.

Budge, I., & Keman, H. (1990). *Parties and democracy: Government formation and government functioning in twenty states*. Oxford: Oxford University Press.

Conrad, C. R., & Golder, S. N. (2010). Measuring government duration and stability in Central Eastern European democracies. *European Journal of Political Research, 9*(1), 119–150.

Crouch, C. (2004). *Post-democracy*. Cambridge: Polity Press.

Crozier, M. J., Huntington, S. P., & Watanuki, J. (1975). *The crisis of democracy. Report on the governability of democracies to the trilateral commission*. New York, NY: New York University Press.

Daalder, H. (1992). A crisis of party? *Scandinavian Political Studies, 15*(4), 269–286.

Dalton, R. J. (2000). The decline of party identification. In R. J. Dalton & P. M. Wattenberg (Eds.), *Parties without partisans. Political change in advanced industrial democracies* (pp. 19–36). Oxford: Oxford University Press.

Dalton, R. J., & Wattenberg, P. M. (Eds.). (2000). *Parties without partisans. Political change in advanced industrial democracies*. Oxford: Oxford University Press.

Dennis, J. (1966). Support for the party system by the mass public. *American Political Science Review, 60*(3), 600–615.

Duverger, M. (1963). *Political parties: Their organization and activity in the modern state*. New York, NY: Wiley.

Epstein, L. D. (1967). *Political parties in western democracies*. New York, NY: Praeger.

Fraenkel, C. (1964). Bureaucracy and democracy in the New Europe. In S. R. Graubard (Ed.), *A new Europe?* (pp. 538–559). Boston, MA: Houghton Mifflin Harcourt.

Franklin, M. (2004). *Voter turnout and the dynamics of electoral competition in established democracies since 1945*. Cambridge: Cambridge University Press.

Franzmann, S., & Kaiser, A. (2006). Locating political parties in policy space. A reanalysis of party manifesto data. *Party Politics, 12*(2), 163–188.

Giddons, A. (2000). *The third way and its critics*. Oxford: Polity Press.

Golder, M., & Stramski, J. (2010). Ideological congruence and electoral institutions. *American Journal of Political Science, 54*(1), 90–106.

Gunther, R., & Diamond, L. (2001). Types and functions of parties. In L. Diamond & R. Gunther (Eds.), *Political parties and democracy* (pp. 3–39). Baltimore, MD: Johns Hopkins University Press.

Gunther, R., & Diamond, L. (2003). Species of political parties: A new typology. *Party Politics, 9* (2), 167–199.

Haas, E. B. (1964). Technology, pluralism and the new Europe. In S. R. Graubard (Ed.), *A new Europe?* (pp. 62–88). Boston, MA: Houghton Mifflin Harcourt.

Heidar, K., & Saglie, J. (2003). A decline of linkage? Intra-party participation in Norway, 1991–2000. *European Journal of Political Research, 42*(6), 761–786.

Ignazi, P. (1996). The crisis of parties and the rise of new political parties. *Party Politics, 2*(4), 549–566.

Immergut, E. M. (1990). Institutions, veto-points, and policy results: A comparative analysis of health care. *Journal of Public Policy, 10*(4), 391–416.

Inglehart, R. (1977). *The silent revolution: Changing values and political style among western publics*. Princeton, NJ: Princeton University Press.

Katz, R. S., & Mair, P. (1992). The membership of political parties in European democracies, 1960–1990. *European Journal of Political Research, 22*(3), 329–345.

Katz, R. S., & Mair, P. (1995). Changing models of party organization and party democracy. The emergence of the cartel party. *Party Politics, 1*(1), 5–28.

Kirchheimer, O. (1953/54). Parteistruktur und Massendemokratie in Europa. *Archiv des öffentlichen Rechts, 79*(3), 301–325.

Kirchheimer, O. (1965). Der Wandel des westeuropäischen Parteiensystems. *Politische Vierteljahresschrift, 6*(1), 20–41.

Kitschelt, H. (1993). The green phenomenon in Western party systems. In S. Kamieniecki (Ed.), *Environmental politics in the international arena: Movements, parties, organizations, and policy* (pp. 93–112). Albany, NY: SUNY Press.

Kriesi, H. P., Grande, E., Dolezal, M., Helbing, M., Hölinger, D., Hutter, S., & Wüst, B. (2012). *Political conflict in Western Europe*. Cambridge: Cambridge University Press.

LaPalombara, J. (2007). Reflections on political parties and political development, four decades later. *Party Politics, 13*(2), 141–154.

Lawson, K., & Merkl, P. H. (1988). *When parties fail*. Princeton, NJ: Princeton University Press.

Lijphart, A. (1999). *Patterns of democracy: Government forms and performance in thirty-six countries*. New Haven, CT: Yale University Press.

Lipset, S. M., & Rokkan, S. (1967). *Cleavage structures, party systems, and voter alignments*. New York, NY: The Free Press.

Mair, P. (1989). Continuity, change and the vulnerability of party. *West European Politics, 12*(4), 169–187.
Mair, P., & van Biezen, I. (2001). Party membership in twenty European democracies, 1980–2000. *Party Politics, 7*(1), 5–21.
Mair, P. (2006). Ruling the void: The hollowing of western democracy. *New Left Review, 42*, 25–51.
Mair, P. (2008). The challenge to party government. *West European Politics, 31*(1–2), 211–234.
Mansbridge, J. (2011). Clarifying the concept of representation. *American Political Science Review, 105*(3), 621–630.
Merkel, W., Puhle, H. J., Croissant, A., Eicher, C., & Thiery, P. (2003). *Defekte Demokratien. Band 1: Theorie*. Opladen: Leske + Budrich.
Merkel, W., Petring, A., Henkes, C., & Egle, C. (2008). *Social democracy in power: The capacity to reform*. Abingdon: Routledge.
Merz, N., & Regel, S. (2013). Die Programmatik der Parteien. In O. Niedermayer (Ed.), *Handbuch Parteienforschung* (pp. 211–238). Wiesbaden: Springer VS.
Müller, W., & Strøm, K. (2000). *Coalition governments in Western Europe*. Oxford: Oxford University Press.
Oppenhuis, E., van der Eijk, C., & Franklin, M. N. (1996). The party context: outcomes. In C. van der Eijk & M. N. Franklin (Eds.), *Choosing Europe? The European electorate and national politics in the face of the union* (pp. 287–305). Ann Arbor, MI: University of Michigan Press.
Panebianco, A. (1988). *Political parties: Organization and power*. Cambridge: Cambridge University Press.
Pitkin, H. F. (1972). *The concept of representation*. Berkeley, CA: University of California Press.
Poguntke, T. (2014). Towards a new party system: The vanishing hold of the catch-all parties in Germany. *Party Politics, 20*(6), 950–963.
Powell, G. B., Jr. (2009). The ideological congruence controversy: The impact of alternative measures, data, and time periods on the effects of election rules. *Comparative Political Studies, 42*(12), 1475–1497.
Rehfeld, A. (2009). Representation rethought: On trustees, delegates, and gyroscopes in the study of political representation and democracy. *American Political Science Review, 103*(2), 214–230.
Reiter, H. L. (1989). Party decline in the west a skeptic's view. *Journal of Theoretical Politics, 1* (3), 325–348.
Sartori, G. (1976). *Parties and party systems*. Cambridge: Cambridge University Press.
Scarrow, S. E. (2000). Parties without members? Party organization in a changing electoral environment. In R. J. Dalton & P. M. Wattenberg (Eds.), *Parties without partisans. Political change in advanced industrial democracies* (pp. 79–101). Oxford: Oxford University Press.
Schattschneider, E. E. (1942). *Party government*. New York, NY: Rinehart Press.
Schumpeter, J. A. (1942). *Capitalism, socialism and democracy*. New York, NY: Harper Press.
Spoon, J. (2009). Holding their own: Explaining the persistence of green parties in France and the UK. *Party Politics, 15*(5), 615–634.
Strøm, K. (2000). Parties at the core of government. In R. J. Dalton & P. M. Wattenberg (Eds.), *Parties without partisans. Political change in advanced industrial democracies* (pp. 180–207). Oxford: Oxford University Press.
Taylor, M., & Herman, V. M. (1971). Party systems and government stability. *American Political Science Review, 65*(1), 28–37.
Thomassen, J. (1994). Empirical research into political representation: Failing democracy or failing models. In K. M. Jennings & T. E. Nann (Eds.), *Elections at home and abroad: Essays in honor of Warren Miller* (pp. 237–265). Michigan: University of Michigan Press.
Thomassen, J., & Schmitt, H. (1997). Policy representation. *European Journal of Political Research, 32*(2), 165–184.
Tsebelis, G. (2002). *Veto players: How political institutions work*. Princeton, NJ: Princeton University Press.

van Biezen, I., Mair, P., & Poguntke, T. (2012). Going, going, ... gone? The decline of party membership in contemporary Europe. *European Journal of Political Research, 51*(1), 24–56.

Volkens, A., Lacewell, O. P., Lehmann, P., Regel, S., Schultze, H., & Werner, A. (2012). *The manifesto data collection. Manifesto project (MRG/CMP/MARPOR)*. Berlin: WZB Berlin Social Science Center.

Volkens, A., Bara, J., Budge, I., & McDonald, M. D. (Eds.). (2013). *Mapping policy preferences from texts III. Statistical solutions for manifesto analysts*. Oxford: Oxford University Press.

Wagner, A., & Giebler, H. (2014). It's the responsibility, stupid! Determinanten der Verantwortlichkeitszuschreibung zwischen Europäischer Union und nationaler Regierung für die wirtschaftliche Lage. *Zeitschrift für Vergleichende Politikwissenschaft, 8*(5), 123–142.

Wagner, M. (2012). Defining and measuring niche parties. *Party Politics, 18*(6), 845–864.

Werner, A., Lacewell, O.P., & Volkens, A. (2011). *Manifesto coding handbook. 4th revised version*. Accessed April 10, 2017, from www.manifesto-project.wzb.eu

Whiteley, P. (2009). Where have all the members gone? The dynamics of party membership in Britain. *Parliamentary Affairs, 62*(2), 242–257.

WZB. (2014). *Database "elections, parties, governments" of the research unit "democracy and democratization"*. Berlin: WZB Berlin Social Science Center.

Chapter 8
Parties, Do You See the Signs? Popular Opinions on Inequality and Responsiveness of Political Parties

Alexander Petring

Elections are the institutional heart of democratic systems. Even a minimalist definition of democracy cannot bypass the electoral process. This can also be said of midrange definitions, such as that offered by the embedded democracy concept underlying this chapter. The electoral regime has a representational function and is expected to produce accountability and responsibility and ensure responsiveness. Whereas democratic accountability means above all that (governing) parties make their decisions transparent and thus give voters the opportunity to sanction them positively or negatively for their actions at the next election, responsiveness is concerned with the extent to which single parties or the party system as a whole meets the needs and interests of voters programmatically and through (governmental) action (Kriesi 2013, p. 613). From a processual perspective, it could be argued that responsiveness comes before accountability. This is the case at least when responsiveness is placed at the point in time when governments make and announce decisions for future policy measures. When these measures are then implemented, accountability is called for and finally also responsibility for the consequences of these decisions. In turn, however, evaluation of these measures by voters is a point of reference for the responsive behavior of parties. Ideally, we therefore have permanent feedback between accountability and responsiveness. From a normative point of view, the two are therefore necessary conditions for a functioning democracy.

This chapter will be looking at the extent to which voter attitudes to social inequality have changed over the past three decades and whether parties have reacted programmatically to these attitudes—in other words, have parties been responsive with respect to social inequality? For democracy theory this is anything but trivial. For we know that socioeconomic inequality generally translates into

A. Petring (✉)
Research & Analysis, Social Democratic Party of Germany (SPD), Berlin, Germany
e-mail: alexander.petring@spd.de

W. Merkel, S. Kneip (eds.), *Democracy and Crisis*,
https://doi.org/10.1007/978-3-319-72559-8_8

political inequality and thus violates one of the core principles of democracy (see the introduction in Chap. 3).

From a democracy theory perspective, however, finding the right measure of responsiveness is not easy. Taken to extremes, responsiveness would be pure populism. We would be dealing with parties without any programmatic core, guided only by more or less short-term moods. In the medium term, this would bring no reliability and consequently no accountability. The long-term formative task of parties and government would be lost to view. The positions which had induced the voter to opt for a particular party could be reversed only weeks or months later. For democratic theory, well-grounded responsiveness is thus built on a relatively stable and clearly recognizable programmatic/ideological core, which is, however, sensitive to changes in attitude and hence has to ensure the permanent translation of principles into concrete programs.[1]

8.1 The Status of Research

Responsiveness is a comparatively young technical term in political science (Uppendahl 1981). Following Elmer Eric Schattschneider (1942), it gained greater normative-theoretical prominence above all through Hannah Pitkin (1967) and Amitai Etzioni (1968). The increasing importance of the responsiveness concept in political science has been essentially accompanied by the abandonment of elitist concepts of representation in democracy theory.

In empirical representation research, the "responsible party model" (Schattschneider 1942; Thomassen and Schmitt 1999b) is the classical point of departure for studies on responsiveness. According to this model, the democratic legitimation chain runs from (the majority of) the population to parliament, which installs and oversees the government (Thomassen and Schmitt 1999b, p. 15). If this model of democracy is to work, three minimal conditions have to be met: (1) a range of parties has to stand for election that differ programmatically, (2) internal cohesion or party discipline has to be sufficiently strong to enable parties to implement their programs, and (3) the voters have to make rational decisions. This means that they have personal policy preferences and knowledge of the policy differences between parties and opt for the party whose program comes closest to their own preferences.

The question of responsiveness is examined under the "responsible party model" by looking at the congruence of voter positions with the positions of parliamentarians or parties (Thomassen and Schmitt 1999a). Although this sort of

[1]That this distinction is difficult to make has been shown by Angela Merkel's phaseout of the nuclear phaseout, following soon afterward by the phaseout of the phaseout of the phaseout. Was this still a responsive behavior or already what democracy theory must regard as problematic populism?

operationalization is obvious, the model cannot itself explain how exactly congruence is to be established between preferences. A mechanism would have to be identified by which parties and parliamentarians gain knowledge of voter preferences and react to them.[2] At the level of the party system, for example, this feedback can conceivably be provided by changes in the election results of individual parties. However, responsiveness is also implemented at the level of single parties—otherwise party programs would be completely static. A feedback loop between voters and individual parties or parliamentarians is thus an implicit component of the model—but it has not been explicitly formulated. Moreover, it is not clear whether responsiveness and congruence are to be understood as identical or discrete concepts (see also Bartels 2008, p. 4).

G. Bingham Powell takes a view of the chain of responsiveness similar to that of the RPM (Powell 2004). But he adds the connection between governments and policy outcomes as a further, final link in the democratic responsiveness chain (see also Schattschneider 1942). For Powell, responsiveness is to be sought in all links of the chain and in its entirety. For him, empirical examination therefore requires an analysis that covers citizen preferences, parties, and government action (output and outcomes)—over all policy areas (Powell 2004, p. 101).

Of these three levels, we will be looking at only the first two—and we will be doing so with one reservation. Responsiveness is to be examined only with regard to social inequality. A study that tackles all policy areas individually and in their entirety is beyond the scope of this chapter. There are a number of reasons for neglecting governmental action in this analysis. A serious overview of legislative measures that influence the development of social inequality is an empirically ambitious project that would have to cover an extended period of time and a number of countries. It would require examination of the relationship between government outputs and outcomes. In addition to the cases in which deliberately produced outputs lead to the desired outcomes, there are situations, much more problematic from the responsiveness point of view, in which measures do not lead to the desired results or in which inaction produces a desired result.[3] In short, we are using the narrower responsiveness concept, which is underlying the responsible party concept, but with parties not parliamentarians as reference category, and, furthermore, ignoring the question of congruence between voters and parties or parliamentarians.

Responsiveness accordingly requires the party system to take up and represent changing attitudes among the population. Responsiveness is thus procedural in nature. Because (unlike congruence) it is geared to change, it is a characteristic of political systems that can be observed only over time. The processual dimension of responsiveness makes empirical investigation difficult, because information is required on a number of points in time. Another problem arises from the question of where we can actually pinpoint responsiveness or the lack thereof. The beginning

[2]Nowadays this happens above all through surveys commissioned at brief and regular intervals by parties.

[3]To say nothing of the problem of ascribing given outcomes to individual outputs.

of the responsiveness chain is relatively easy to identify: the attitudes of citizens. But what is to react to (changing) attitudes? Single parties? The party system as a whole? And if the party system of a country as a whole is to be the addressee of demands for responsiveness, can responsive behavior by one party be set off against the nonresponsive behavior of another?

On the conceptual basis of embedded democracy, we can ascertain a latent crisis of democracy if a majority of parties prove to be unresponsive to changing preferences over a longer period. That such a latent state of crisis had long been reached was notably asserted by Katz and Mair (1995). In their thesis of the cartel party, they claim an ever stronger turn toward the state, stronger ties between parties, and, as a result, the increasing similarity of all parties and overall weakening links between parties and civil society (Katz and Mair 2009, 755ff.; Blyth and Katz 2005, 45f.). Other authors claim that in the field of redistributive policy, that is, above all in social and fiscal policy, left-of-center parties in particular have at the latest since the 1990s proved unable to respond to the wishes of their core clientele in the light of globalization (Huber and Stephens 2001; Pierson 2001; for an overview see also Haeusermann and Geering 2011). However, the cartel party thesis is also compatible with other diagnoses of crisis. Thus, Katz and Mair point to Bernard Manin's thesis of "audience democracy," according to which politics does not go beyond spectacle and substantive positions play no role or at best a very subordinate one (Katz and Mair 2009, p. 755). From here it is not far to post-democracy, in which apathetic citizens consume the public spectacle, while "real" politics is hatched out by political and economic elites in back rooms (Crouch 2004, p. 4). However, there is so far no systematic empirical evidence (beyond isolated cases) for the general validity of these strong theses.

8.2 The Empirical Basis

Aggravated by the financial, bank, and debt crises, material inequality has in recent years become an increasingly important social policy issue in established democracies, too. One reason is the trend toward growing income and wealth inequality in many industrial societies since the 1980s (See Chap. 11).

From antiquity to the present day, there has been criticism that at a certain stage (whenever) increasing inequality endangers the stability of political systems (and hinders democratization; see, e.g., Lipset 1959, 1994). Plato recommended not allowing the wealth ratio between rich and poor to exceed 4:1 if stable conditions were to be maintained: "Should anyone acquire more than this—whether by discovery or gift or money-making, or through gaining a sum exceeding the due measure by some other such piece of luck, if he makes the surplus over to the State and the gods who keep the State, he shall be well-esteemed and free from penalty."[4]

[4]Plato. Plato in Twelve Volumes, Vols. 10 and 11 translated by R.G. Bury. Cambridge, MA, Harvard University Press; London, William Heinemann Ltd. 1967 and 1968. 744e.

But from a democratic point of view, such questions are quite irrelevant. To examine responsiveness at the citizen-party level means rather to focus on the congruence between changes in the attitudes of citizens and changes in party programs. For this purpose we require information about citizen attitudes and about the content of party programs and promises. Because there is a temporal, dynamic dimension to the responsiveness concept, this information has to be available about at least two points in time. Moreover, the data should be available on more than a single democracy, so that any statements about democracy as such have at least some prospect of tenable generalization.

We begin with the attitudes of citizens. Four surveys in the framework of the *International Social Survey Programme* (ISSP) conducted between 1987 and 2009 asked citizens whether they consider income inequality in their country to be too great and whether they felt that it was the task of the government to change this.[5] The good thing about these surveys is that they provide information going back to the 1980s as well as data that are recent enough—the last survey date being 2009—to come after the outbreak of the financial and economic crisis of 2007. Also on the debit side is that the surveys reflect not only the situation in a single country but permit a comparative study across countries. These positive aspects are, however, accompanied by a number of problematic ones. It is unfortunate that data were collected at only four time points: 1987, 1992, 1999, and 2009. Furthermore, the intervals between studies are not identical, but vary from 5 to 7 and even 10 years.[6] There are weaknesses not only in the temporal dimension but also in the spatial dimension. The group of countries under study varies in two regards. First, more and more countries were added. Second, not all the countries in which attitudes were recorded were included in all succeeding surveys. Data on all four points in time are thus available only for Austria, Germany, the UK, Hungary, Poland, and the USA. For all other countries, survey data are not available for all 4 years (between 10 [1987] and 36 [2009] countries participated in the ISSP). Besides these temporal and spatial reservations, there are also methodological problems in the narrower sense of the term. Thus, population weightings to correct socioeconomic representativeness were given for only a minority of countries. Still more problematic is that the wording of the question on respondent party preferences varies from country to country and to some extent even within a country over time. Most frequently, respondents were asked what party they voted for at the last election. Sometimes voting intentions for the next elections were asked for, the "Sunday question" was put ("If there was a general election next Sunday . . ."), or respondents were asked whether they related closely to a particular party. In this

[5]On a scale from 1 to 5 (1 strongly agree, 2 agree, 3 neither agree nor disagree, 4 disagree, 5 strongly disagree), respondents were asked to express their agreement or disagreement with the two statements: "Differences in income in [COUNTRY] are too large" and "It is the responsibility of the government to reduce the differences in income between people with high incomes and those with low incomes."

[6]This longer period of time is particularly problematic in assessing whether the attitudes of respondents in 2009 already reflect experience with the financial crisis.

chapter, these varying formulations are treated as equivalent. This is relatively unproblematic, because identification with a party is empirically closely connected with voting for that party. Although, to be exact, we are dealing with different concepts (identification with a party and voting intentions or finally electoral choice), the two variables are so closely interwoven that the questions put can be treated as identical.

On programmatic positions we have the data from the Manifesto Project (see https://manifesto-project.wzb.eu/). Since the end of the 1970s, this project has recorded party positions on the basis of election manifestos. In spring 2014, information was available on 3611 election manifestos of 916 parties for 629 elections in 55 countries. The data show the relative frequency of arguments and positions in a total of 56 categories ranging from disarmament to social policy and international cooperation. Of particular interest for this chapter are the categories "welfare state expansion" and "welfare state limitation." They correspond to the question from the ISSP surveys on whether it is the task of the government to reduce differences in income. With the exception of education policy, all statements are recorded that have to do with the introduction, expansion, termination, or cutback of social policy programs. In addition to fiscal policy, social policy is a key tool for correcting primary distribution by the market and thus relates closely to the inequality issue. Since the Manifesto Project deals mainly with the programs of parties represented in parliament, information is not available for all parties named by ISSP respondents. The resulting gaps in collating this data with the ISSP data are, however, small.

8.3 Responsiveness in Young and Old Democracies

There are three steps to the empirical analysis. First, citizen attitudes and changes in them are examined over the past 25 years. The following subsection addresses programmatic shifts by parties. Finally, the two levels are combined in search of an answer to the responsiveness question.

8.3.1 Citizen Attitudes Toward Income Inequality and Redistribution

In 22 countries, attitudes among the population show some notable differences but nevertheless have much in common: in all countries and at all points in time, a clear majority of at least 59% of respondents agrees that differences in income in their country are too large (see Table 8.1). Nonetheless, variance between countries and, to some extent, over the two decades under study is considerable. In Hungary, Portugal, and Bulgaria, over 95% of respondents take this view (at least

Table 8.1 Percentages of respondents that find differences in income in their country too large

Country	1987	1992	1999	2009
Hungary	76.3	83.9	93.2	97.1
Portugal			95.9	95.4
Slovenia		86.4	91.0	95.3
Bulgaria		96.5	96.8	94.2
Slovakia			93.7	92.0
Spain			89.3	91.2
France			86.8	91.0
Germany	75.9	88.5	82.2	89.6
Poland	81.6	85.4	89.3	88.3
Austria	89.9	82.1	86.3	88.3
Switzerland	67.5			87.4
Czech Republic			87.8	84.4
Israel			89.8	83.9
Japan			69.1	77.9
Britain	75.8	81.1	81.3	77.1
Australia	60.7	63.1	70.9	74.0
Sweden		59.5	71.1	73.1
United States of America	59.1	77.2	66.2	66.5
New Zealand		73.3	73.2	64.9
Norway		70.8	72.5	60.7
Canada		70.6	68.2	
Italy	87.0	89.4		

Source: ISSP (1987–2009), own calculations

sometimes), whereas in the USA, Australia, and Norway, the agreement rate is at times only just under 60%. In Hungary and Switzerland, the increase from 1987 to 2009, at about 20%, is greatest; in Austria and the UK, agreement rates changed least.[7]

In international comparison, these attitudes do not relate in any way to the statistics on "real" inequality, for example, Gini coefficients. In other words, the proportion of people who find income differences too large is not systematically

[7]The percentages given in Table 8.1 conceal further differences. If we differentiate between the two agreement categories combined there ("agree," "strongly agree"), we find that in some countries most agreement comes under the weaker category. This is particularly the case for the USA, Britain, Australia, New Zealand, and Canada, but also for Norway and Sweden—thus for the countries that show comparatively low rates of agreement overall. The countries with the highest percentages in the strong agreement category are Portugal (60%), Slovakia (62%), France (68%), and Hungary (77%). These values are all from the 2009 survey, and the increase in a sense of inequality is reflected overall in an increasing number of respondents who choose the strong agreement category. In the eight countries for which there are data on both 1987 and 2009, the average rate of agreement in the weak category fell from 44% to 39%, whereas the share of respondents in the strong agreement category rose from 29% to 45%. For a more detailed international comparative analysis of attitudes to inequality, see, e.g., Osberg and Smeeding (2006).

Table 8.2 Percentage of respondents who consider it the task of the government to reduce differences in income

Country	1987	1992	1999	2009
Portugal			90.4	92.0
Slovenia		80.0	84.8	90.7
Hungary	79.5	74.6	80.1	83.6
Bulgaria		81.4	85.0	82.1
Spain			79.3	79.6
Poland	70.3	77.4	85.2	78.8
Israel			80.9	78.1
France			63.5	77.2
Slovakia			74.5	75.4
Austria	80.7	69.5	72.7	74.6
Germany	60.5	73.4	61.2	65.5
Czech Republic			71.9	64.2
Switzerland	42.7			62.9
Britain	63.9	65.2	67.5	60.6
Sweden		52.9	59.5	58.0
Japan			52.6	54.4
Norway		60.1	61.9	52.0
Australia	44.1	42.5	49.7	51.3
New Zealand		53.1	49.4	42.4
United States of America	32.7	38.2	35.3	32.6
Canada		47.9	45.4	
Italy	81.8	79.9		

Source: ISSP (1987–2009), own calculations

higher in countries where income inequality is really high than in countries where such inequality is comparatively low. This is, however, hardly surprising, for two conditions have to be met if this is to be so. First, the majority of respondents have to take conditions in other countries as the point of reference for their assessment of inequality. Second, they would have to have concrete information about income inequality in these other countries. The (rare) studies on attitudes toward justice/fairness assume, on the contrary, that it is above all national cultures (e.g., religion) and the differing importance of individual characteristics (e.g., gender, class, income, profession) that can explain differences between countries in assessing justice (Osberg and Smeeding 2006, 468ff.).

Besides being asked to assess inequality, citizens were also asked whether they consider it the task of the government to reduce differences in income (see Table 8.2). In contrast to the preceding question, we find that there are some countries at certain points in time in which a majority favors no political measures against inequality. This is the case throughout in the USA and Canada and at least at certain time points in Switzerland, New Zealand, and Australia.

Although in the eight countries for which we have survey data for both 1987 and 2009 there is an average rise from 59% to 63%, this increase is markedly lower than for the question on income inequality (from 73% to 84%). Moreover, the number of

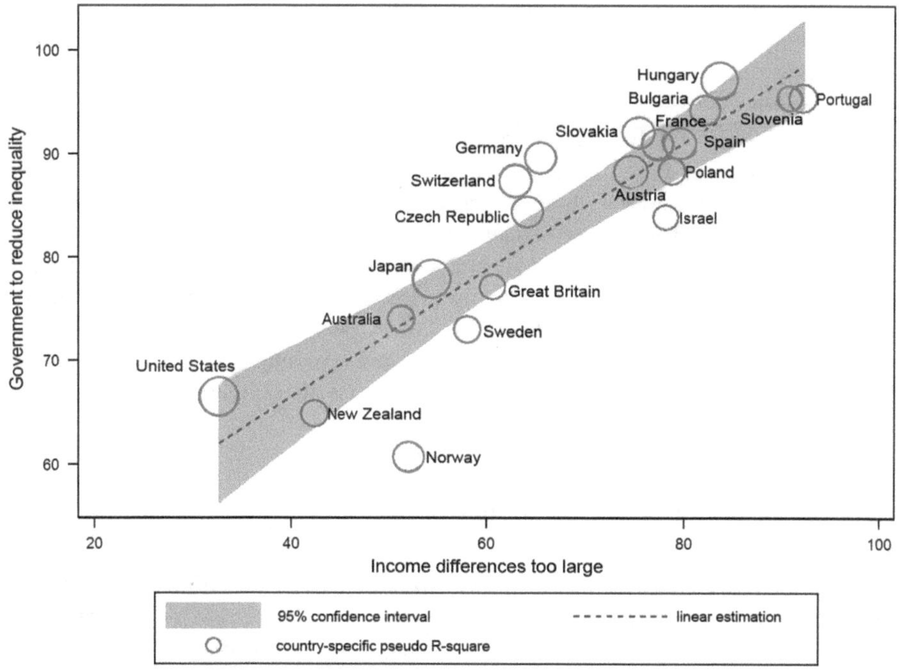

Fig. 8.1 Connection between dissatisfaction with income distribution and the demand for government action against inequality, 2009. Note: The dashed line with the gray 95% confidence interval is the line of regression for the connection at the country level. The size of the circles indicates the quality of the model at the microlevel (pseudo R-squared of an ordinal logistic regression) in the countries concerned, which ranges from 8.3% in the USA to 23.5% in Slovenia. Small circles show a relatively strong link; large circles show a weaker connection. Source: ISSP (1987–2009), own calculations

countries in which a relative majority of respondents is in the stronger agreement category is much smaller. In 2009 this was the case only for Hungary, France, Israel, Bulgaria, Portugal, and Slovenia.

Despite the overall lower agreement rates for the second question, in most countries and at most points in time, there was a majority in favor of government action to reduce income inequality. It is likely that agreement rates for a government redistribution policy increase in proportion to dissatisfaction with the distribution of income. And the correlation between the two values at the macro level (between the given agreement rates at the national level) is comparatively high. With a bivariate regression at the national level for 2009, 81% of variance in attitudes toward government responsibility can be explained in terms of attitudes toward income inequality (see Fig. 8.1).

At the individual level this link is markedly weaker.[8] The explained variance ranges from 8.3% (USA) to 23.5% (Slovenia). On this subject, too, there is surprisingly little literature that explains such differences between countries with respect to attitudes toward governmental redistribution. For the 20 countries in the early 2000s, Philipp Rehm has established a link between attitudes toward unemployment benefits and the uneven distribution of the risk of becoming unemployed (Rehm 2011). In countries where the risk of becoming unemployed is relatively evenly distributed across different occupational groups, support for generous wage-replacement benefits was higher than in countries where this risk differed strongly from one occupational group to another. However, it seems likely that for the general differences between countries in attitudes toward government redistribution measures, differing societal attitudes toward government action in general and differing societal discourses justifying inequality are also important.

8.3.2 *Party Programs on Redistribution*

Social and fiscal policy are thc two most important tools available to the government for redistribution purposes. Unfortunately, the Manifesto data contain no category covering statements on fiscal policy in this regard. But there are the two categories already mentioned, which cover negative and positive statements relating to social policy. The balance is computed of these two categories to determine the social policy position.[9] Party responsiveness in the sense of a reaction to changes in attitude among voters implies a temporal sequence in which programmatic shifts follow changes in attitude. For this reason, party positions on social policy in the years of ISSP surveys—if they happened to be election years in the given country—or in the year of the next election are taken as the basis. In some cases, however, no election took place after 2009 or party manifestos were not coded. This is the case for Austria, Australia, Canada, Switzerland, France, Israel, Italy, Japan, New Zealand, and Poland, so that for these countries information on the development of programs of parties represented in parliament is available for only three time points.

The box plot in Fig. 8.2 shows the programmatic median of party systems of the countries under study and 50% of the observation points in the boxes. The whiskers cover 1.5 times the interquartile range[10]; party program positions beyond are shown by points.

[8]The question is thus whether the connection can also be established at the respondent level. Can the level of dissatisfaction with income inequality be explained by a preference for government redistribution measures?

[9]For a discussion on problems in using Manifesto data in general and on determining positions in particular, see Budge (2001), as well as Franzmann and Kaiser (2006).

[10]The interquartile range is the difference between the upper and lower quartiles (75%–25%). It thus shows the range of this 50% of all values that are closest to the median.

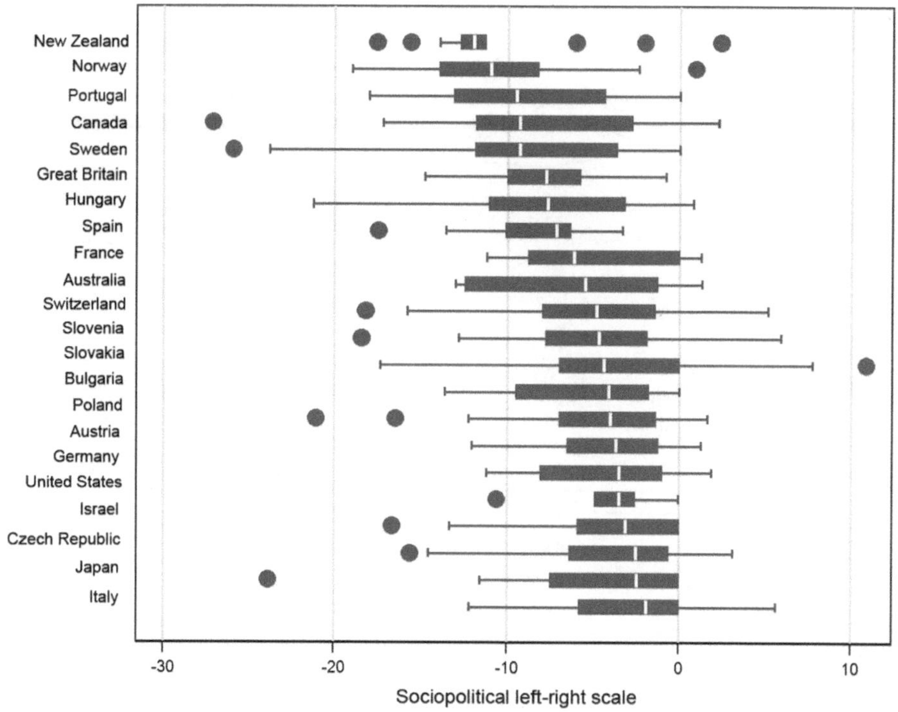

Fig. 8.2 Unweighted social policy positions of parties in parliament at the closest time points after ISSP surveys, 1987, 1992, 1999, and 2009. Source: Volkens et al. (2013), own calculations

As to be expected in social policy, there are few parties that express any determination to reduce social measures. In all countries, 50% of all party programs adopt neutral or pro-welfare state positions at the three or four time points of observation. Slovakia, Sweden, and Hungary have a very broad programmatic range on social policy. The USA with its two-party system is, not surprisingly, most homogeneous in this regard.

Across the four observation time points and different party families, a somewhat more instructive picture emerges. As Fig. 8.3 shows, all party families, with the exception of ethnic/regional parties, shift to the left—albeit it not continuously. Moreover, left-wing parties, that is to say, social democrats and (post) communists shift programmatically more than Christian democrats, conservatives, and liberals.[11] The ideological variance between party families with regard to social policy was greater in 2009 than in 1987.

[11]There are two reasons for the at first glance surprising finding that social democrats are mostly to the left (if only slightly) of communist parties. In the first place, only a relatively limited section of party programs is shown. More important, however, is that the communist parties in this sample are above all successors to the former Eastern European governing parties before the collapse of the Soviet Union. Here we adopt the coding of the Manifesto Project.

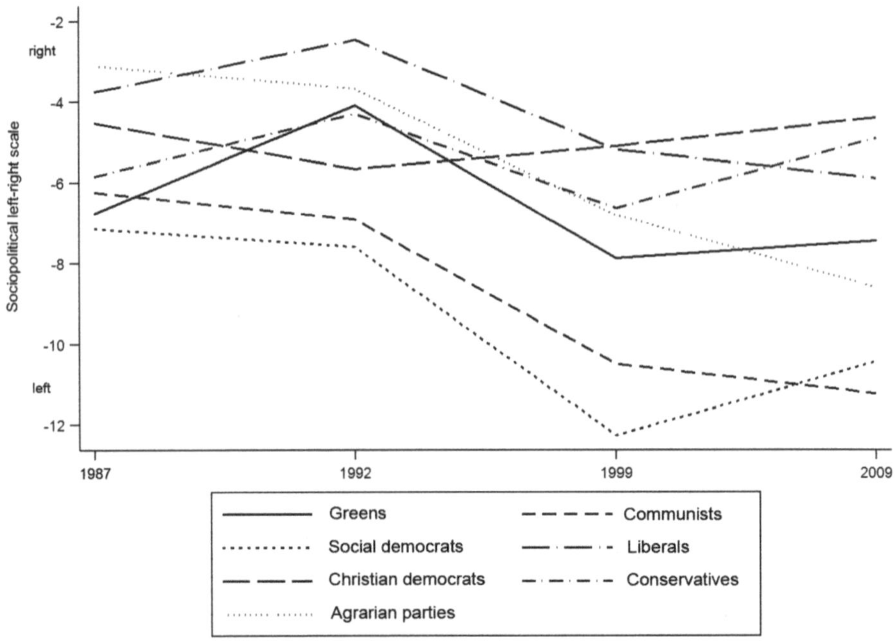

Fig. 8.3 Party family left-right positions on social policy over time. Source: Volkens et al. (2013), own calculations

Both for the democracies under study overall and for individual countries, there is hence no justification for saying that there are no or no longer any differences between parties' programs on social policy. Moreover, the congruence between voters and parties on social policy is relatively high in the different countries. Voters of left-wing parties (that is to say, of parties that take a positive stance on social policy measures) demand more government commitment to redistribution than voters of conservative or liberal parties.[12]

8.3.3 Democratic Responsiveness: Strategic Party Reactions to Changing Citizen Attitudes

The responsiveness of parties in matters of income inequality should be apparent from their attitudes toward policy measures against inequality. If citizens demand stronger policy measures to reduce differences in income, responsive parties can be

[12]The relevant findings are not presented here because we are addressing responsiveness and not congruence. In the field of labor market policy, however, Haeusermann and Geering (2011) come to the same conclusion with respect to the congruence between voter attitudes and party programs.

expected to react by placing greater emphasis on redistribution in their programs (and later, in the event of participation in government, by the introduction of concrete measures).

As we have seen in the first section of this chapter, responsiveness can be examined on two levels: that of the entire party system and that of individual parties and their supporters. The question is the extent to which redistribution positions differ among party supporters. Statistically significant differences in attitude between the supporters of different parties within a country are shown both by visual inspection of the confidence intervals of supporter-specific mean values for the issue of governmental redistribution and by statistical variance analysis of these mean values.[13] This result is not very surprising; after all, in most established democracies, the left-right dimension is still a key structuring shortcut for voters (Mair 2007).

However, if we examine changes in party supporter attitudes over time, we no longer find statistically significant differences between the supporters of different parties in any of the countries under study. This means that the slightly growing demand for governmental redistribution is not systematically concentrated among the supporters of individual parties. Investigating how parties have reacted to changes among their supporters faces the problem already mentioned of differences in the scaling of the data sources used. While in the ISSP surveys citizens were able to express their views on government redistribution policy on a 5-point scale, the Manifesto Project measures party programs in terms of percentages, which in the case of the difference between two categories (welfare-state expansion—welfare-state limitation) results in a scale that theoretically can accommodate values between −100 and +100. From an empirical point of view, these extremes are far from exhausted, as Fig. 8.2 has already shown. The problem is now that it simply cannot be determined what value at the individual attitude level corresponds to what concrete value on the party program scale. For example, it cannot be ascertained whether the welfare-state value of 2.7 for the SPD in 2012 compared with the average value of 0.65 on the scale from −2 to +2 for SPD supporters in the 2009 survey is too high, too low, or precisely right from the responsiveness perspective.

Recalling the processual nature of the responsiveness concept, however, offers a possibility of dealing with this problem to at least some extent. For if it is impossible to say exactly what attitude value corresponds to what programmatic position, it can at least be said that a stronger desire for governmental redistribution is likely to be accompanied from a responsiveness perspective by stronger emphasis on the issue in the party program (and vice versa). A comparison of direction is thus

[13]However, attitudes do not differ significantly between all groups of party supporters. In Germany, for example, there are no significant differences between supporters of the CDU/CSU and the FDP, but there are between those of the CDU/CSU and the SPD, the Greens, and the Left Party. There are also statistically significant differences between the SPD and the Left Party.

Table 8.3 Responsive and nonresponsive parties, 1982–2009

Country	Responsive	Nonresponsive	Responsiveness rate	Share of the vote of responsive parties
Norway	10	4	71.43	79.20
Sweden	8	6	57.14	64.04
Austria	4	3	57.14	57.34
Germany	7	5	58.33	48.84
Britain	5	3	62.50	48.44
USA	3	3	50.00	48.06
Hungary	3	2	60.00	38.94
New Zealand	1	1	50.00	38.74
Portugal	1	1	50.00	37.73
Australia	4	5	44.44	29.28
Czech Republic	1	2	33.33	22.09
Slovakia	1	2	33.33	15.42
Slovenia	1	1	50.00	0.00
Poland	0	1	0.00	0.00

Source: Volkens et al. (2013), ISSP (1987–2009), own calculations

possible. However, owing to the lack of data, this congruence in the shifts of party supporters and parties can be assessed only for a limited number of parties.

The overall picture is inconsistent and permits no clear conclusions. The responsiveness rate—the percentage of responsive parties among all parties—ranges from over 70% in Norway to 0% in Poland (albeit for only the one party on which data were available). Beyond these two extremes, the camps of responsive and nonresponsive parties are approximately equal in size in all other countries. Owing to data restrictions, not all parties represented in parliament at all three theoretically possible time points (the earliest time point serves as a point of reference for voter and party shifts and is thus left out of account) could be taken into consideration. More informative than the responsiveness rate is therefore the relative share of the vote represented by responsive parties. The basis for this share of the vote differs depending on the number of time points for which information is available.[14] A "standardized" statistic is to be found in the last column of Table 8.3. Norway heads the field with 79%, followed by Sweden with 64%. But in Sweden, Austria, Germany, Britain, and the USA, too, responsive parties represent around half of all votes cast. In the lower half of the table, we find, with the exception of Australia, countries in which the number of parties on which information is available is so small that no generalized statement can be made about them.

[14]If, as for Germany, data is available for all points in time, there are three elections on which information about responsive and nonresponsive parties could be obtained. The basis is accordingly 300, since the total share of the vote of all parties in the three elections was 300%. In a country on which data is available for only two time points, such as New Zealand, statements on the responsiveness of parties could be made only for one election—the basis is thus 100%.

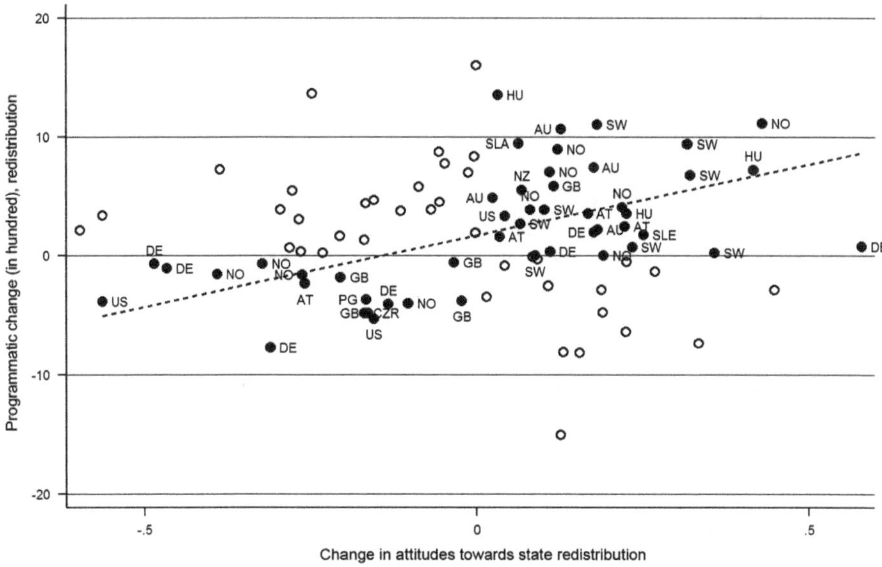

Fig. 8.4 Changes in the attitudes of party supporters and programmatic reactions by the relevant parties, 1987–2009. Note: The dashed line indicates only the group of responsive parties (filled-in points). Source: Volkens et al. (2013), ISSP (1987–2009), own calculations

Overall, no clear pattern was therefore apparent. Figure 8.4 shows this result. The filled-in points show responsive parties; the dashed line is the estimated link only for the group of these parties responsive to changes in attitude among their supporters. If we look only at this group of responsive parties, we can at least say which parties react with above-average responsiveness and which, although responsive, react with below-average responsiveness to changes in the attitudes of their supporters. Among the six parties in government that react most strongly to the inequality issue are two Norwegian parties (social democrat and right-wing populist) and two Swedish parties (social democratic and Christian democratic), thus representing societies in which redistribution issues have traditionally played a major role (Esping-Andersen 1990).[15]

This party-political pattern, according to which chiefly center and center-left parties are generally responsive to redistribution issues—thus depending on whether there is an increasing or decreasing demand—is confirmed overall (see Table 8.4). Greens, social democrats, and Christian democrats head the list.

However, left-of-center parties are by no means more open to stronger redistribution than right-of-center parties. On the contrary, precisely parties with a right-wing stance on economic and social issues prove to be responsive to growing

[15]They are joined by the Hungarian socialists and the Slovakian Christian democrats.

Table 8.4 Share of responsive and nonresponsive parties by party family, 1982–2009

Party family	Responsive	Of which for more redistribution	Nonresponsive	Responsiveness rate
Greens	4	2	1	80
Social democrats	15	8	7	65.22
Christian democrats	7	5	5	58.33
Liberals	5	4	5	54.55
Communists	3	1	3	50
Conservatives	8	6	9	47.06
Agrarian parties	3	3	6	33.33

Source: Volkens et al. (2013), ISSP (1987–2009), own calculations

redistribution demands on the part of their supporters. Left-of-center parties, by contrast, react responsively in about half of cases to demands for less redistribution. In this classical left-right question, parties therefore seem to rely largely on their traditional image as being for or against redistribution and see no reason for programmatic reactions if their supporters shift in accordance with this image. Only if supporters change their attitudes, shifting in the direction of the opposing political camp, do parties feel obliged to react. Thus, if supporters of a social democrat party express strong demands for governmental redistribution, the party can in many cases rest on its laurels as "credible defender of the welfare state" (Kitschelt 2001). If, however, supporters want less redistribution, those responsible in the party must fear losing voters to the Christian democratic or liberal competition and will accordingly reduce the programmatic position of the party on redistribution.

This need not necessarily lead to convergence between party programs. It is likely only in a two-party system and with an electorate that is unimodally distributed around a programmatic midpoint. The only case of a clear two-party system in the sample and period under study is anyway to be found only in the USA, and the assumption of a normal distribution of voters is also largely true (Fiorina and Abrams 2008). This has nevertheless not led to congruence between election programs (Lacewell 2016) and at the level of political elites has even resulted in increasing polarization (Fiorina and Abrams 2008).[16]

[16]For an overview of programmatic shift in 24 democracies in the 1980s and 1990s, see also Budge and Klingemann (2001).

8.4 Conclusion

No comprehensive conclusion about the responsiveness of parties in established democracies can be drawn on the basis of the data used, of limitation to the subject of economic inequality, and of the number of countries and period under study. However, well-founded opinions can be expressed on some positions in the crisis debate, such as those stated in the introduction to this book and at the beginning of this chapter. The analysis has not been able to confirm some arguments advanced by the probably most prominent exponents of crisis: the assertion made in connection with the cartel thesis of the progressive convergence between both party programs and supporter attitudes. At the national level there are significant differences in attitude toward inequality and redistribution between the supporters of different parties—especially between left- and right-wing parties. Nor is there overall convergence between party programs on redistribution issues. To this extent, the crisis scenario advanced by proponents of the cartel party, globalization, and post-democracy theses is not confirmed.

However, there is also no justification for ascribing comprehensive effectiveness to the responsiveness mechanism. Overall, no stable connection could be established between changes in attitude and changes in party programs. Nevertheless, there are examples of responsive behavior in all countries in the period under review. However, it seems likely that corresponding programmatic changes are strongly guided by strategic considerations generated by national party competition. The propensity for responsiveness seems to be greater if a party's own voters appear to be moving in the direction of the opposing political camp. Is such strategic behavior by parties to be criticized from a democracy theory point of view?

The double orientation of parties on votes and content is hardly a new insight (see, e.g., Strøm 1990). If rational compromise is taken to be a key characteristic of democracy (in contrast to fundamental positioning), it is to be welcomed if parties continue to show stable differences in their basic attitude toward redistribution policy. A largely volatile party system would be just as problematic from a democratic theory point of view as a completely unresponsive behavior by parties. Finally, programmatic stability is necessary to allow parties to develop stable links with civil society groups and to ensure that voters are at least to some extent represented not only at election time but throughout the legislative period and that the need for voters to inform themselves does not increase too much from election to election.

If on the basis of this basic ideological stability parties engage in selective responsive behavior in an effort to gain a majority enabling them to enter government, this could be regarded as a dubious compromise, as a betrayal of their "true" convictions. Although such compromises may not be in keeping with the ideal positions of core party supporters, they can lend the party scope for political action and concrete decisions. And the voters who finally vote for a party see these concrete decisions as better than the alternatives up for election. Here, too, democracy proves once again, citing Churchill, to be "the worst form of government except all those other forms that have been tried from time to time."

References

Bartels, L. M. (2008, August). *The opinion-policy disconnect: cross-national spending preferences and democratic representation*. Paper read at and prepared for the Annual Meeting of the American Political Science Association, Boston.

Blyth, M., & Katz, R. (2005). From catch-all politics to cartelisation: The political economy of the cartel party. *West European Politics, 28*(1), 33–60.

Budge, I. (2001). Theory and measurement of party policy positions. In I. Budge, H.-D. Klingemann, A. Volkens, J. Bara, & E. Tanenbaum (Eds.), *Mapping policy preferences. estimates for parties, electors, and governments 1945–1998* (pp. 75–90). Oxford: Oxford University Press.

Budge, I., & Klingemann, H.-D. (2001). Finally! Comparative over-time mapping of party policy movement. In I. Budge, H.-D. Klingemann, A. Volkens, J. Bara, & E. Tanenbaum (Eds.), *Mapping policy preferences. Estimates for parties, electors, and governments 1945–1998* (pp. 19–50). Oxford: Oxford University Press.

Crouch, C. (2004). *Post-democracy*. Cambridge: Polity Press.

Esping-Andersen, G. (1990). *The three worlds of welfare capitalism*. Cambridge: Polity Press.

Etzioni, A. (1968). *The active society: A theory of societal and political processes*. London: Collier-Macmillan.

Fiorina, M. P., & Abrams, S. J. (2008). Political polarization in the American public. *Annual Review of Political Science, 11*, 563–588.

Franzmann, S., & Kaiser, A. (2006). Locating political parties in policy space a reanalysis of party manifesto data. *Party Politics, 12*(2), 163–188.

Haeusermann, S., & Geering, D. (2011, September). *Policy congruence and distributive politics: Matching voter preferences and party positions on labor market policy*. Paper read at APSA 2011 Annual Meeting Paper, Seattle.

Huber, E., & Stephens, J. D. (2001). *Development and crisis of the welfare state. Parties and policies in global markets*. Chicago, IL: The University of Chicago Press.

Katz, R. S., & Mair, P. (1995). Changing models of party organization and party democracy the emergence of the Cartel party. *Party Politics, 1*(1), 5–28.

Katz, R. S., & Mair, P. (2009). The Cartel party thesis: A restatement. *Perspectives on Politics, 7* (4), 753–766.

Kitschelt, H. (2001). Partisan competition and welfare state retrenchment. When do politicians choose unpopular policies? In P. Pierson (Ed.), *The New Politics of the Welfare State* (pp. 265–302). Oxford: Oxford University Press.

Lacewell, O. P. (2016). Divided we fall? Polarization in the 2012 U.S. Presidential elections. In C. Bieber & K. Kamps (Eds.), *Die US-Präsidentschaftswahl 2012: Analysen der Politik- und Kommunikationswissenschaft* (pp. 85–108). Wiesbaden: Springer VS.

Lipset, S. M. (1959). Some social requisites of democracy: Economic development and political legitimacy. *The American Political Science Review, 53*(1), 69–105.

Lipset, S. M. (1994). The social requisites of democracy revisited: 1993 Presidential address. *American Sociological Review, 59*(1), 1–22.

Mair, P. (2007). Left-right orientations. In R. J. Dalton & H.-D. Klingemann (Eds.), *The Oxford handbook of political behavior* (pp. 206–222). Oxford: Oxford University Press.

Osberg, L., & Smeeding, T. (2006). "Fair" inequality? Attitudes toward pay differentials: The United States in comparative perspective. *American Sociological Review, 71*(3), 450–473.
Pierson, P. (Ed.). (2001). *The new politics of the welfare state*. Oxford: Oxford University Press.
Pitkin, H. F. (1967). *The concept of representation*. Berkeley, CA: University of California Press.
Powell, G. B., Jr. (2004). The chain of responsiveness. *Journal of Democracy, 15*(4), 91–105.
Rehm, P. (2011). Social policy by popular demand. *World Politics, 63*(2), 271–299.
Schattschneider, E. E. (1942). *Party government*. New York: Holt, Rinehart & Winston.
Strøm, K. (1990). A behavioral theory of competitive political parties. *American Journal of Political Science, 34*(2), 565–598.
Thomassen, J., & Schmitt, H. (1999a). Issue congruence. In H. Schmitt & J. Thomassen (Eds.), *Political representation and legitimacy in the European Union* (pp. 186–208). Oxford: Oxford University Press.
Thomassen, J., & Schmitt, H. (1999b). Political representation and legitimacy in the European Union. In H. Schmitt & J. Thomassen (Eds.), *Political representation and legitimacy in the European Union* (pp. 3–21). Oxford: Oxford University Press.
Uppendahl, H. (1981). Repräsentation und Responsivität. Bausteine einer Theorie responsiver Demokratie. *Zeitschrift für Parlamentsfragen, 12*(1), 123–134.
Volkens, A., Lehmann, P., Merz, N., Regel, S., Werner, A., Lacewell, O., & Schultze, H. (2013). *The manifesto data collection. Manifesto Project (MRG/CMP/MARPOR)*. Version 2013b. Berlin: WZB Berlin Social Science Center.

Chapter 9
Democracy Without Choice: Citizens' Perceptions of Government's Autonomy During the Eurozone Crisis

Rubén Ruiz-Rufino and Sonia Alonso

9.1 Introduction

In this chapter we aim to give the theory of democratic choice a chance. Our objective is to show that citizens truly care about the autonomy of their governments to be responsive to their preferences, or, to put it differently, we expect citizens to react critically when governments are unresponsive because their policy autonomy is compromised. We assess this statement by looking at how citizen satisfaction with the way democracy works (SWD) is affected when the degree of their national government's autonomy is compromised by external impositions. Citizens hold certain prior beliefs about the degree to which governments are free to be responsive to their preferences. Such beliefs about governments' degree of autonomy, however, are not constant across time but change when exposed to new information through a process of Bayesian updating (Gerber and Green 1998; Bartels 2002; Bullock 2009; Dinas 2013). We argue that the bailout decisions

 This is a slightly revised reprint of an article that originally appeared in the *European Journal of Political Research* (EJPR), 56(2):320–345. Wiley and Sons granted permission for reprint in this volume. Our thanks go to John Wiley and Sons and both authors.
This article has benefited from comments from many colleagues. We are especially grateful to Shaun Hargreaves Heap, Kostas Matakos, Gabriel Leon, Miguel Almunia, Lee Savage, Edoardo Bresanelli, Damien Bol, Alexander Afonso, Anna Gwizada, and José María Maravall. We have also greatly benefited from the detailed comments of the EJPR anonymous reviewers.

R. Ruiz-Rufino (✉)
Department of Political Economy, King's College London, London, UK
e-mail: ruben.ruiz_rufino@kcl.ac.uk

S. Alonso
School of Foreign Service, Georgetown University in Qatar, Doha, Qatar
e-mail: sa1197@georgetown.edu

W. Merkel, S. Kneip (eds.), *Democracy and Crisis*,
https://doi.org/10.1007/978-3-319-72559-8_9

of the so-called *Troika* (the IMF, the European Commission, and the European Central Bank) in Cyprus, Greece, Ireland, and Portugal, as well as the partial interventions in Spain and Italy, were events that transformed the prior beliefs of citizens about the policy autonomy of national governments inside the Eurozone. The resulting posterior belief was that governments were not free to be responsive to their citizens and consequently elections served no longer as mechanisms to bring about policy change. The main implication of this theory is that variations in levels of SWD are produced not *exclusively* by variations in a government's economic performance but *also* by variations in democratic choice.

Most scholars in political science would agree with the statement that democracy is about choice. Even the so-called minimalist conceptions of democracy would make no objection to this: "Only voting that facilitates popular choice is democratic" (Riker 1982, p. 5). In the absence of choice between programmatic alternatives, voting only serves to "ratify choices made elsewhere" (Przeworski 2010, p. 117). The very logic of electoral competition encourages parties to offer alternative platforms at election time in the hope of maximizing their votes. Even if the structure of competition is such that parties appeal to the median voter, the logic of voting generally impedes the belief that party platforms are completely identical (Downs 1957, p. 41).

Choice in democracy does not deal exclusively with citizens and elections; elected governments must also be autonomous to act upon their mandate by choosing among alternative policy paths. According to democratic theory, if the constraints on national governmental autonomy were such that elected governments would apply the same policies irrespective of their electoral promises, then voting would no longer be an act of selecting among different choices (Mair 2013; Maravall 2013). Elections, however, are believed to be an appropriate enough mechanism to ensure that elected officials, out of fear of the next election, will "restrain from deploying the force of government against citizens to make them support unpopular policies that officials believe necessary" (Riker 1982, p. 9). Government autonomy and democratic mandates can, however, be at odds with each other. Governments always face a trade-off between responsiveness to the preferences of their own citizens and responsibility toward previously acquired commitments, such as international treaties or financial obligations (Kydland and Prescott 1977; Held 1995; Garrett 1998; Mair 2011; Rodrik 2011; Friedman 2012; Stiglitz 2012).

We know little about how losses in a government's autonomy to act on its democratic mandate affect citizens' attitudes toward the way democracy works. From a normative point of view, citizens should find the usurpation of a democratically elected government's autonomy illegitimate and, therefore, undemocratic. However, citizens do not seem to act as democratic theory would expect them to. For example, governments' loss of policy autonomy has been present since the establishment of the Economic and Monetary Union of the European Union (EMU), and yet Eurozone citizens only felt dissatisfied with the functioning of democracy after the economic and financial crisis hit Europe in 2008 (Jones 2009). During the preceding period of economic boom, satisfaction with democracy actually grew under a context where restrictive fiscal and monetary rules existed for everyone.

If citizens truly relied on democratic normative standards when judging the functioning of extant democracies, they would not find democratic satisfaction in the fact that national governments have less, not more, policy autonomy inside the EMU. Allegedly, the fact that they do implies that citizens do not care about their government's autonomy and democratic choice as long as things are going well for them. This is precisely how political economy arguments explain satisfaction with democracy despite losses in national governmental autonomy, namely, as a consequence of good economic performance. Citizens do not pay attention to how much autonomy and choice they have at home, as long as they enjoy high levels of economic growth, low unemployment, and wealth redistribution (Scharpf 1997, 1999).

Our alternative explanation based on political learning is also consistent with the observation that, prior to the 2008 financial and economic crisis, citizens were satisfied with national democracy even though national governments had suffered losses of autonomy as a result of the monetary union. Our theory explains this puzzle as follows. Citizens' prior belief about the degree of their respective national government's autonomy did not change just after joining the European Economic and Monetary Union (EMU). More concretely, before Greece's first bailout loan in May 2010, citizens living within the EMU did not perceive the degree to which their governments had lost policy autonomy for three interrelated reasons. First, EU fiscal rules, like those imposed by the Stability and Growth Pact, were weakly enforced providing large room for deviant governments to respond to their electoral interests at home. Second, most of the economies that joined the Euro had lived an expansive economic cycle before 2008, when it was impossible to test the robustness of the new monetary institutions in the event of a crisis (De Grauwe 2010). The institutional shortcomings of the Euro had been theorized openly in the press[1] or at academic levels (De Grauwe 2006, 2010) but had never been empirically tested given that Europe had lived in relative economic stability since the adoption of the currency. Last, but not least, financial markets were on the side of the Euro and did not act as an external financial enforcer of EMU rules. International financial market pressure was still absent.

Citizens' beliefs about their government autonomy as one that is responsive to their mandates did not change between 2002 and 2010 because no objective fact occurred in this period that made an update of beliefs necessary. Citizens only perceived their own lack of choice to decide between policy alternatives when a series of "information shocks" (most notably, the bailouts and partial interventions of Eurozone peripheral countries) led them to update their prior political beliefs. National governments of the Eurozone periphery, under pressure by speculative financial markets and with their hands tied by the monetary union, were forced to

[1]See, for example, *The Economist* 9 April 1998.

choose responsibility over responsiveness, turning against their democratic mandates in order to avoid disaster.

Our argument goes beyond the conclusions put forward by Polavieja (2013) by locating the origin of high levels of dissatisfaction with democracy not in the combined effect of bad economic performance and the *objective* lack of policy autonomy but, instead, on the citizens' *perception* of this constrained autonomy through a process of political learning. In this respect, we build on Armingeon and Guthmann (2014) and Armingeon et al.'s (2016) explanatory models, based on citizen perceptions of the lack of national government autonomy. These authors theorize and test, as we do, that citizens care about democratic choice and that they perceived the absence of choice during the Great Recession. However, they cannot explain why SWD, for example, grew in countries like Germany, also subject to losses in government autonomy. If citizens care about autonomy and Germany is a member of EMU, why are German citizens satisfied with the way democracy works in their country? Armingeon and Guthmann (2014) and Armingeon et al. (2016) fail to provide an explanation that connects democratic choice with the differences in SWD across Eurozone countries. We propose that this causal mechanism is political learning.

Our theoretical claims find empirical confirmation after analyzing variations in the level of SWD in Eurobarometer surveys conducted between 2002 and 2014. We first provide qualitative evidence to illustrate our mechanisms at work, and then we use a two-step statistical analysis that combines individual and aggregate data. Individually we estimate the correlates of SWD for all respondents in each country. At the aggregate level, we use our individual-level predictions to conduct a series of difference-in-difference analyses only in countries that belong to the Eurozone, where fiscal and monetary rules are held constant.

In the following sections, we first develop a theoretical model, and then we test it empirically using both individual and aggregated data. Finally we offer some concluding remarks.

9.2 Political Economy and Democratic Choice

Until recently, democratic choice was not part of political economy explanations to understand cross-country variations in levels of SWD. Starting with Polavieja (2013), however, increasing research is being done that incorporates democratic choice as a factor that, combined with economic performance, affects satisfaction with democracy (Armingeon and Guthmann 2014; Armingeon et al. 2016).

Polavieja (2013) shows how the constrained autonomy of Eurozone governments has a negative impact on SWD. Using the combined effect of GDP contraction between 2004 and 2010 and EMU membership as the main causal mechanisms, he shows that the direct impact of the recession on SWD differs by membership in the EMU. His analysis concludes that the larger the GDP contraction between 2004 and 2010 inside the Eurozone, the deeper the fall in SWD. This finding, however, is not observed outside the Eurozone, where levels of SWD remain relatively stable irrespective of the size of GDP contraction (Polavieja 2013, p. 296). We agree with the interpretation put forward by Polavieja (2013) as a plausible explanation for this finding. According to Polavieja's interpretation, citizens perceive the incapacity of their governments to combat the deep economic recession, and this is why economic performance and SWD are more strongly correlated inside the EMU than outside it. Our objective in this chapter is to take this interpretation further both theoretically and empirically.

In order to do this, we build on Armingeon and Guthmann (2014) and Armingeon et al. (2016), who have also tried to isolate the effect that the absence of democratic choice has on SWD within the context of the Great Recession. Armingeon and Guthmann (2014) look at the extent to which a constrained democracy accounts for decreasing levels in SWD (Armingeon and Guthmann 2014, p. 424). Their answer is that the erosion of SWD is due not only to the economic crisis but also to the accompanying loss of governmental autonomy. Always, according to their analysis, the loss of governmental autonomy is objectively reflected in IMF conditionality and, more importantly, subjectively perceived by the citizens via the mass media. However, the statistical results of their model show that the strength of the IMF conditionality variable does not provide strong support for their argument. The relevant coefficient is either not significant or mildly significant (10%) after controlling for economic variables such as austerity (Armingeon and Guthmann 2014, p. 434).

Armingeon et al. (2016) start with a discussion of input and output democratic legitimacy, the former being the realm of choice and the latter being the domain of economic performance. They defend that a loss of legitimacy in either choice or performance will likely bring about erosion in democratic support. We agree with this and build from it, focusing the rest of our chapter on one element of input legitimacy: the level of autonomy of national governments to respond to the preferences of citizens. Where we disagree with Armingeon et al. (2016) is, again, in the causal mechanism that connects the objective loss of autonomy by national governments with citizens' perceptions of it. This will be better understood if we look at the way these authors proceed empirically.

Armingeon et al. (2016, p. 13) use an interaction between EMU membership and the annual change in nominal unit labor costs (ULC), which is a way of measuring the degree of internal devaluation suffered by Eurozone countries during the crisis. The hypothesis being tested is that a Eurozone country that goes through a process of internal devaluation will suffer a considerable erosion of democratic support as a result of a combined loss of output (i.e., a reduction in wages) and input (i.e., a reduction in democratic choice) legitimacy, whereas a country outside the EMU will suffer a loss of output legitimacy, but input legitimacy will be intact and, therefore, the erosion of democratic support will not be as large. This interaction, however, does not really capture what the authors claim, namely, the compounded loss of input and output legitimacy. The interaction is just showing that SWD diminishes as a result of internal devaluation policies to a greater extent among Eurozone countries than among countries outside the EMU, an argument that goes

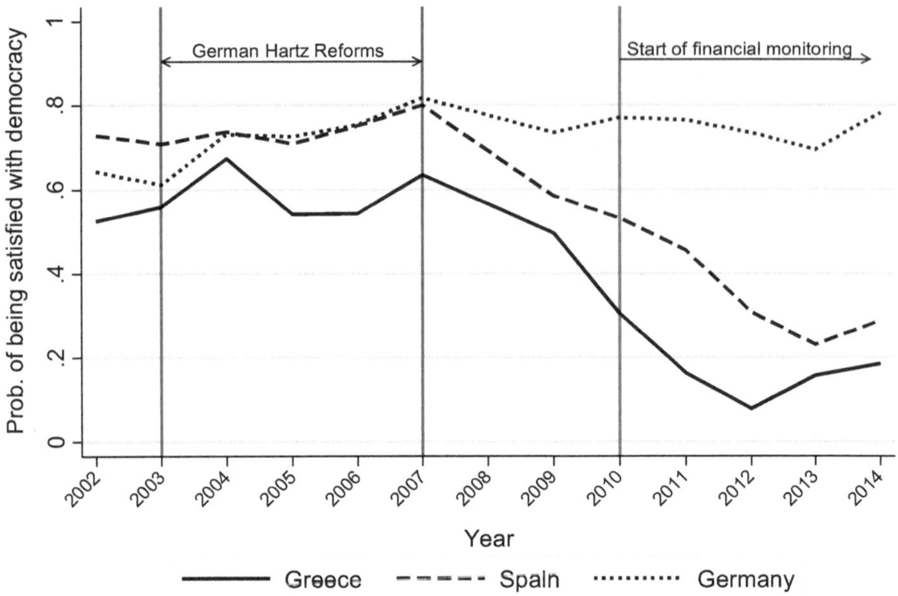

Fig. 9.1 Evolution of satisfaction with democracy in Spain, Germany, and Greece between 2002 and 2014

much in line with Polavieja's analysis (2013) but not beyond it because it does not address the different levels of SWD found among EMU countries. These differences, in our view, are the result of citizens' perceptions about how much autonomy their national governments truly have, and citizens' perceptions, in turn, are formed through a process of political learning that does not take place everywhere inside the Eurozone but only in some countries.

Armingeon et al. (2016) use EMU membership as a proxy for Eurozone citizen perception of the loss of national government autonomy. However, the empirical evidence shows that EMU membership cannot be treated as a proxy measure of citizen perception. It is easy to see why if we look at Germany between 2003 and 2007, when the so-called Hartz reforms took place. During this period, the ruling SPD implemented the Agenda 2010 program that envisaged a series of economic policies in order to increase the country's level of competitiveness. A key action in this package was the Hartz reforms which completely altered the functioning of the German labor market. The implementation of this new regulation brought a de facto internal devaluation in wages that generated great inequality among salaries (OECD 2009). As Fig. 9.1 shows, during this period, the probability of being satisfied with the way democracy works in Germany actually increased, inconsistent with the expectations of Armingeon et al.'s hypothesis for an EMU country. A deeper internal devaluation was also observed in both Greece and Spain between 2010 and 2014. On this occasion, however, SWD plummeted in these two countries in clear contrast with Germany between 2003 and 2007. The only difference between the German internal devaluation and the one that took place in Greece and Spain is that they are not related to their final outcome—an increase in the levels of inequality—but rather to the origin of the decision: German internal devaluation was part of a policy adopted by de facto democratically elected German politicians whereas the Greek and Spanish devaluations were imposed by external unelected institutions (the so-called Troika).

According to our proposed explanatory mechanism, SWD increased because internal devaluation was the result of a decision taken by the German government with the support of a majority of German citizens. The decision was in line with EMU rules, but the fact remains that it was a popular and freely adopted decision of the German government. In other words, what we are trying to say is that Germany, an EMU member tied by EMU rules, went through a process of self-inflicted austerity that actually improved SWD. Therefore, the variable EMU membership cannot capture the real loss of national governments' autonomy as *objectively* experienced by governments and as *subjectively* perceived by citizens. As a consequence, when national governments' preferences are aligned with EMU rules, as in the German case, citizens do not need to update their beliefs about their government's level of autonomy as being responsive to its citizens. By contrast, when national preferences are not aligned with EMU rules, as happened, for instance, in the signature of a Memorandum of Understanding (MoU) setting up the conditions to accept a financial bailout, the *objective* lack of autonomy that national governments really have is openly disclosed. It is at this point that citizens learn and update their beliefs. This happened in Greece and Spain (Fig. 9.1), as well as in the other bailed-out countries, but not in Germany.

Whether democratic choice is an essential component of citizens' understanding of democracy is still an open question, since there is a scarcity of individual data with which to test it. For this reason, we need to rely on proxies. The sixth round of the European Social Survey contains several items that address this topic in some detail (Ferrin and Kriesi 2016). According to the ESS data, citizens value that (a) parties offer clear alternative platforms during elections and (b) that rascals who do not do a good job are kicked out of office. Moreover, when citizens are confronted with a situation in which the government wants to do one thing and the majority of the people prefers another, a large majority of European respondents (66%) believes that in a democracy the government should change its plan in order to be responsive to the preferences of the people. Only 17% think that the government should stick to its plan regardless of the popular will (see Table 9.7 in the Appendix). Choice is therefore a fundamental attribute of democracy, both at election time and afterward. Accountability is another.

Moreover, if our argument about the importance of choice for citizens was to be corroborated by reality, we should see that the preference for responsiveness is strong everywhere, not just in the bailed-out countries. Data from round 6 of the

European Social Survey[2] confirms this expectation. There is only one country in which respondents give priority to the government's criterion over the preferences of the people in case of disagreement: Denmark. Everywhere else, a majority of citizens considers that in the presence of disagreement between the government and the people, priority should be given to what the majority of the people think. These majorities are as high as 79% in Spain or 75% in Germany. At the same time, we would also expect worse evaluations of the existing levels of responsiveness in bailed-out countries than in countries that have not been intervened in and whose preferences are better aligned with EMU rules. This expectation is also partially confirmed by the round 6 ESS data (see Table 9.8 in the Appendix). The perceived level of government's responsiveness in a particular country is measured along a scale that goes from "government never responsive" (value 0) to "government always responsive" (value 10). Bailed-out countries show lower scores (i.e., more negative evaluations of responsiveness) than core Euro countries with pro-austerity publics, with the only exception of Germany, where respondents negatively evaluate the level of responsiveness of the German government.

9.3 The Political Learning of Democratic Choice: Testable Hypotheses

Political surveys in Europe do not ask respondents their opinion about the level of autonomy that their respective national governments ought to have in order to be responsive to the majoritarian preferences of society. Therefore, we cannot measure it directly. However, we can rely on existing research about Bayesian political learning to define a plausible causal mechanism linking democratic choice to satisfaction with democracy that can then be tested. We know from the literature on Bayesian learning that citizens update prior political beliefs when exposed to new information (Gerber and Green 1998; Bartels 2002; Bullock 2009). In fact, Bayesian approaches are increasingly used as a normative standard "by which to judge reactions to political information" (Bullock 2009, p. 1123).[3] Bayesian learning has been applied by public opinion scholars to study evaluations of politicians and governments as well as public opinion change in reaction to concrete political events (Dinas 2013).

To our knowledge, however, there is no research about political learning in relation to the levels of democratic choice over policy. Therefore, and for lack of better information, we will assume that citizens hold a prior belief about the degree

[2]Fieldwork for this survey was carried out between the end of 2012 and the beginning of 2013, 2 years into the bailouts and with the economic recession still at large.

[3]Even if many critics find these models wanting due to the fact that people have partisan and ideological biases that forestall a truly Bayesian belief updating, Bullock (2009) has demonstrated that the presence of partisan bias is compatible with Bayesian learning.

to which their national governments are autonomous in choosing among policy alternatives in their countries, if only because we know that they value democratic choice from a normative point of view (Ferrin and Kriesi 2016). In the absence of contradicting evidence, these prior beliefs are likely to be normally distributed around the median belief. The median belief is that governments are ultimately free to comply with their democratic mandates and when they fail to do so they are held accountable to their voters. This existing distribution of beliefs, on the other hand, will change if some new political information emerges concerning the degree of democratic choice and, with it, its median belief will change too.

In our view, the economic interventions of the Troika in Greece, Ireland, Portugal, and Cyprus, as well as the partial interventions in Spain and Italy, were events that transformed citizens' prior beliefs about the autonomy of national governments inside the Eurozone. The resulting posterior median belief was that governments were not free to be responsive to their citizens and, as a consequence, elections could not bring about policy change. As information providers, these events were of such magnitude (both in terms of quantity and quality of information) that we will consider them "information shocks" (Dinas 2013). This is not a far-fetched proposition. It is a well-known fact that in periods of crisis people follow political information more closely and are open to look for new ways of understanding personal and collective interests than in periods of relative stability (Matakos and Xefteris 2015).

If our classification of the external intervention events in the Eurozone periphery as "information shocks" has any validity, we should be able to see that citizens were more generally informed about the European Union in the years after the outbreak of the crisis than in the preceding period. Indeed this is what Eurobarometer data show, as reflected in Fig. 9.2. Citizens' level of *objective* knowledge (i.e., information) about the European Central Bank and the European Commission[4] increased after the outbreak of the crisis. More importantly for our argument, citizens from the Eurozone periphery surpassed citizens from the rest of the Eurozone in their knowledge about European institutions at that very moment too. This means that the citizens more hardly hit by the debt crisis were those who increased their level of information the most. It is therefore not implausible to conclude that voters were paying a lot of attention to events at the time when the bailouts hit their respective countries and that, as a result of this new information, they updated their political beliefs about democratic choice in their countries.

Troika interventions only happened in a few countries within the Eurozone (concretely, in Cyprus, Greece, Ireland, Italy, Portugal, and Spain), and, therefore, only citizens from these countries had reasons to update their beliefs. This is not to

[4]The exact questions are as follows: "Have you heard of the European Commission?" "Have you heard of the European Central Bank?" The questions, therefore, measure *objective* knowledge: whether the respondent knows about the *existence* of these institutions.

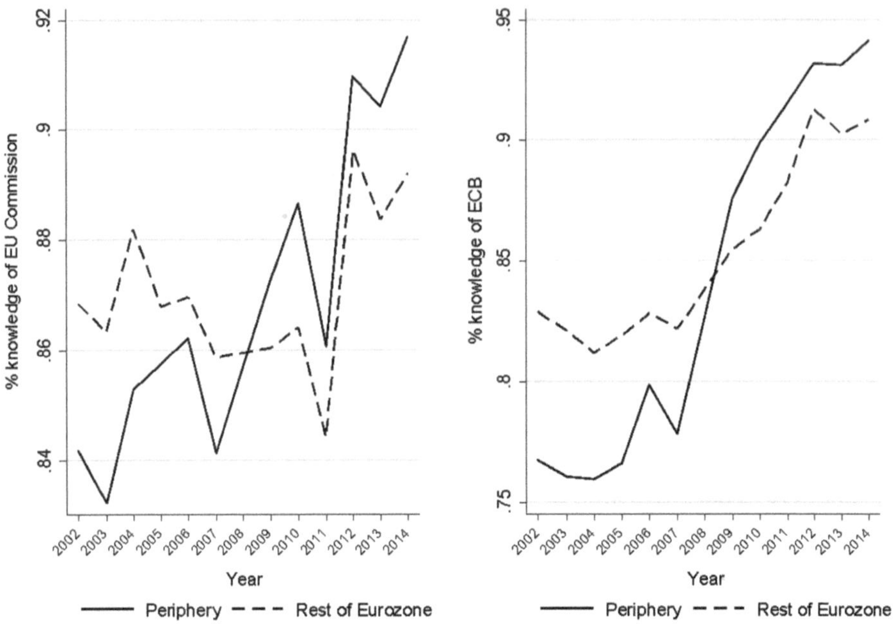

Fig. 9.2 Knowledge of European institutions in Eurozone countries

deny that citizens from non-intervened in countries might also update their beliefs as a result of what is happening to their neighbors,[5] but we expect this to happen to a much lesser degree. If our hypothesis is confirmed, we should expect that the belief updating happens progressively as the different bailouts are observed.

9.4 Data and Method

We empirically test our argument by using both individual and aggregate data. The individual data come from the Eurobarometer surveys. We have created a dataset using all Eurobarometers that asked about satisfaction with democracy at the national level from 2002 to 2014.[6] The sample size is 152,196 individuals from 13 European countries that joined the Eurozone between 1999 and 2002.[7]

[5]In this respect, we expect some countries outside the intervened in group to have more amenable citizens to belief updating than others as a result of past political experience. France, for example, already had the experience of being forced into line during the second half of the 1980s, when the Mitterrand government was constrained into taking a monetary policy that was compatible with the prevailing European orthodoxy (Moss 2000).

[6]The list of Eurobarometers (EB) used in our dataset is the following: EB58.1, EB60.1, EB62, EB63.4, EB65.2, EB68.2, EB72.4, EB73.4, EB76.3, EB78.1, EB80.1, and EB81.4.

[7]We also include Cyprus who joined the Eurozone in 2008 (see fn 11).

Following the convention used in previous studies (Armingeon and Guthmann 2014; Armingeon et al. 2016), our dependent variable is binary where 1 indicates satisfaction with democracy and 0, dissatisfaction.[8] About 58.8% of the sample declares some level of satisfaction with the way democracy works in their country of origin, but more importantly, levels of SWD vary greatly across countries and years.

The empirical strategy that we follow is a two-step regression approach (Jusko and Shively 2005; Polavieja 2013). This is an adequate method to deal with individual data clustered in countries that also has a time-series structure (Gelman 2005). Thus, we can take into account the temporal dimension as well as the impact of specific national factors in the evolution of SWD. In the first step, we apply logit models using pooled individual data to calculate the predicted probability of an individual being satisfied with democracy for each country and year of interest. These predicted probabilities are calculated from 2002 to 2014, and, according to our theory, they should reflect the effects of the updating of beliefs regarding the functioning of democracy. In the second step, we use these predicted probabilities as the dependent variable in a new dataset that includes members of the Eurozone since 2002.[9] In this second dataset, the unit of analysis is country-year and the number of observations is 154.

9.4.1 Stage One: Individual Analysis

We begin our empirical analysis by using individual data to calculate a first-step logit regression model. As explained above, we use the logit coefficients to estimate the following probability $\left(\widehat{SWD}\right)$:

$$\Pr(SWD = 1|X) = \widehat{SWD}_{c,t} = \frac{1}{1 + e^{-\left(\beta_0 + \beta_i X_{i,c,t}\right)}}$$

[8]The original EB question has four categories: "very satisfied," "fairly satisfied" "not very satisfied," and "not at all satisfied." Since we are just interested in explaining temporal cross-country variation of levels of SWD, a binary variable is better suited for our analysis (see also Armingeon and Guthmann 2014). This decision is further justified by the distribution of the original SWD variable whereby about 80% of the cases are concentrated in the categories "fairly satisfied" and "not very satisfied."

[9]The reason for doing this is to have a group of countries with a sufficiently large time span where the Eurozone rules have applied and been held constant. The countries considered joined the Eurozone between 1999 and 2002: France, Belgium, Netherlands, Germany, Italy, Luxembourg, Ireland, Greece, Spain, Portugal, Finland and Austria. To further test our hypotheses we also include Cyprus, which joined the Eurozone in 2008. The rationale behind this is that Cyprus was bailed out in 2013. This is also the logic behind the exclusion of Malta, Slovenia, and Slovakia. In any case, the analysis does not change if these three countries are included.

where X is a vector containing the set of explanatory variables and subscripts i, c, and t refer to individual i in country c and year t, respectively. The predicted probability of SWD is calculated keeping the relevant explanatory variables at their means.

As Polavieja (2013) shows, SWD can be explained at the individual level by analyzing variables reflecting an individual's socioeconomic attributes like education or occupation. Some studies include other control variables like satisfaction with the economy or assessment of national economy (Anderson and Guillory 1997; Blais and Gelineau 2007; Armingeon and Guthmann 2014; Cordero and Simón 2016). Since the direction of the causality regarding these variables and our dependent variable is unclear, we prefer to keep them out of the analysis to avoid any possible source of endogeneity[10]. In particular, we estimate predicted probabilities from the following model:

$$\widehat{SWD}_{c,t} = \beta_0 + \beta_1 Educ_{i,c,t} + \beta_2 Occup_{i,c,t} + \beta_3 Age_{i,c,t} + \beta_4 Sex_{i,c,t} + \vartheta_c + \tau_t + u_{i,c,t},$$

where *Education* is measured using the age in which the respondent finished her studies.[11] *Occupation* uses the EB's own occupation scale and has eight categories.[12] The regressions also use Gender and Age as independent variables.[13] Finally, we also control for country fixed effects and time trends. Table 9.1 shows the estimated coefficients for the different models.

[10]The EBs used in this analysis do not include the question "satisfaction with economy." Instead, they include a question asking the respondents to indicate their views on the economy. Such a variable has three categories: better, worse, and same. We decided to exclude this variable from the individual analysis to reduce the level of endogeneity. It is unclear which direction the causality between SWD and expectations on the economy takes. It could be argued that expectations on the economy do actually explain SWD, but it could also be argued the other way round. If that is the case, the coefficients would be biased and would contaminate our analysis. We analyzed this issue by running an auxiliary regression (ordinal logit) using expectations on the economy as the dependent variable and SWD as an independent variable, keeping all other variables as controls. In such a model, SWD is strongly significant and the direction of the coefficients is the one we would expect. More satisfaction with democracy increases the probability of having better economic expectations ($SWD = 0.03^{***}$).

[11]This variable is also categorical and has ten values: "up to 14 years" (base), "15 years," "16 years," "17 years," "18 years," "19 years," "20 years," "21 years," "22 years and older," and "still studying."

[12]The base category is "self-employed" followed by "managers," "other white collars," "manual workers," "house person," "unemployed," "retired," and "student."

[13]The models displayed here do not include ideology as a control variable. This is because ideology was not included in all the EB analyzed here. We have, however, run the same regressions including ideology for the EB which included this variable, and the results are essentially the same to the one reported here.

Table 9.1 Individual factors explaining satisfaction with democracy in the Eurozone countries, 2002–2014

Variables	Base Model	Country FE	Country + Year FE
Education: 15 years	0.468*** (0.0267)	−0.0775*** (0.0291)	−0.0476 (0.0293)
Education: 16 years	0.431*** (0.0240)	−0.0956*** (0.0263)	−0.0544** (0.0265)
Education: 17 years	0.539*** (0.0263)	−0.0226 (0.0285)	0.0164 (0.0288)
Education: 18 years	0.426*** (0.0214)	0.0185 (0.0234)	0.0785*** (0.0236)
Education: 19 years	0.519*** (0.0265)	0.0789*** (0.0288)	0.139*** (0.0290)
Education: 20 years	0.638*** (0.0302)	0.133*** (0.0324)	0.193*** (0.0326)
Education: 21 years	0.868*** (0.0332)	0.257*** (0.0353)	0.322*** (0.0357)
Education: 22+ years	0.786*** (0.0222)	0.252*** (0.0246)	0.304*** (0.0249)
Education: still studying	0.173 (0.128)	−0.315** (0.137)	−0.374*** (0.144)
Occupation: managers	0.423*** (0.0271)	0.223*** (0.0284)	0.213*** (0.0286)
Occupation: other white collars	0.152*** (0.0251)	0.0694*** (0.0262)	0.0685*** (0.0263)
Occupation: manual workers	0.0944*** (0.0225)	−0.101*** (0.0238)	−0.0995*** (0.0238)
Occupation: house persons	0.173*** (0.0271)	0.0367 (0.0283)	0.00528 (0.0284)
Occupation: unemployed	−0.555*** (0.0274)	−0.665*** (0.0286)	−0.596*** (0.0289)
Occupation: retired	0.0851*** (0.0254)	−0.0830*** (0.0268)	−0.0838*** (0.0269)
Occupation: students	0.755*** (0.130)	0.586*** (0.139)	0.737*** (0.146)
Female	−0.0767*** (0.0125)	−0.0771*** (0.0129)	−0.0777*** (0.0130)
Age	0.00526*** (0.000563)	0.000522 (0.000591)	0.00188*** (0.000597)
Constant	−0.430*** (0.0374)	0.186*** (0.0459)	0.163*** (0.0497)
Observations	122,993	122,993	122,993

Note: Robust standard errors in parentheses. *** $p < 0.01$; ** $p < 0.05$; * $p < 0.1$

The three models in Table 9.1 show a high level of consistency between the direction and statistical significance of the coefficients.[14] Model 3 shows the estimated results considering both country and year fixed effects. Predicted probabilities using this model show that SWD decreased between 2007 (before the crisis) and 2014 (after the crisis) for all levels of education. However, the probability of being satisfied with democracy is significantly smaller among citizens with less education and people who are still studying, holding all other variables at their means. A similar picture is seen when predicted probabilities are calculated for each occupation. Overall, levels of SWD decreased in 2014 compared with 2007 for all

[14]We also used the weights generated by the EB with similar results.

the categories included in this variable. However, some occupations are more resilient to the effects of the crisis than others. The comparison between managers and unemployed individuals between 2007 and 2014 provides a useful illustration here. Individuals holding a managerial occupation had a probability of being satisfied with democracy of 70% in 2007 while such probability decreased to 57% in 2014. For an unemployed individual the same probability was 53% in 2007 and 38% in 2014.

In the particular time frame analyzed here, these coefficients reflect how economic policies used during the financial crisis may have hit citizens differently. Highly educated people with managerial jobs have suffered the harshness of the crisis less than low-skilled unemployed workers or those who are already retired. For these social groups, voting can become an important political tool to replace governments delivering policies which may have negative effects on their lives.

9.4.2 Stage Two: Country-Level Analysis

To test our main hypothesis, the second stage of our empirical strategy involves a cross-country, cross-year analysis of SWD. As explained above, a Troika direct intervention in a Eurozone country[15] becomes an "information shock" that citizens observe and use to produce a belief update. This is exactly the effect that we aim to isolate in this part of the analysis. To do so, we perform a series of difference-in-difference analyses following the waves of "information shocks" that took place between 2010 and 2013 and comparing the effects of each previous diff-in-diff test with the next. To do so, we split the sample of countries into two groups depending on whether a given country has been under a Troika intervention or not. The idea of a diff-in-diff analysis is, precisely, to estimate if the difference in change of SWD for these two groups of countries differs substantially before and after citizens have been exposed to the "information shock" (Angrist and Pischke 2008, 2014). To do that, we first estimate SWD in countries that were not monitored by the Troika both before and after a particular "information shock" is observed.

$$\begin{aligned}\delta_1 &= E(SWD|Shock = 0, Exposure = 0)\\ &\quad -E(SWD|Shock = 0, Exposure = 1)\end{aligned}$$

Second, we estimate the same values for countries that were exposed to an "information shock."

[15]Let us recall that a Troika intervention is defined as either the signature of a MoU (Greece and Ireland in 2010, Portugal in 2011, and Cyprus in 2013), the signature of a partial MoU (Spain in 2012), or an explicit threat from the ECB to let the country under attack by financial markets fall unless it implements an austerity package (Spain and Italy in 2011).

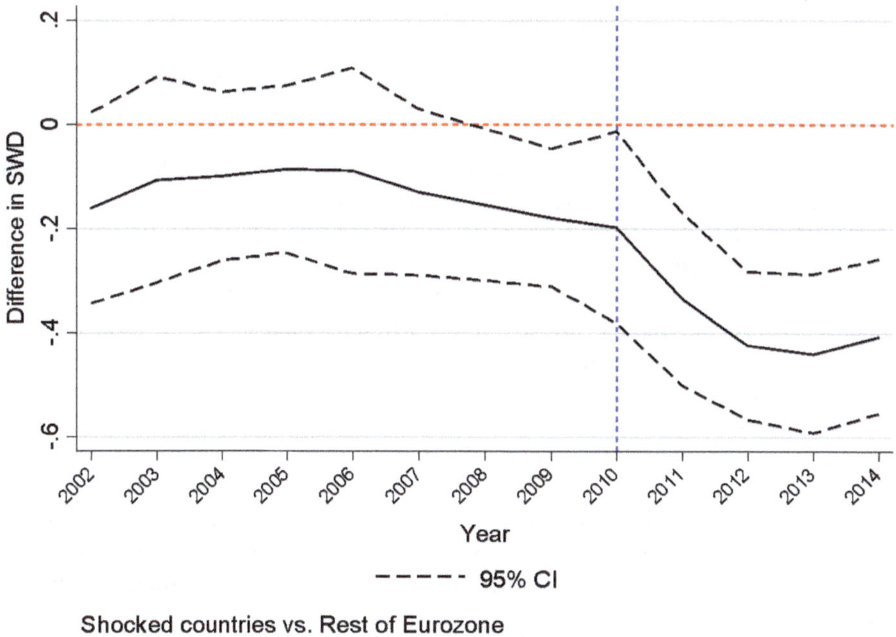

Fig. 9.3 Mean test of SWD between "shocked" countries and the rest of the Eurozone

$$\delta_2 = E(SWD|Shock = 1, Exposure = 0)$$
$$-E(SWD|Shock = 1, Exposure = 1)$$

Finally, we estimate the difference of these values:

$$\delta_{dd} = \delta_1 - \delta_2$$

We expect the second difference, δ_2, to be much larger than the first difference, δ_1, resulting in a negative diff-in-diff coefficient. Figure. 9.3 illustrates this idea. The solid line shows the result of comparing the mean of SWD in countries that received information shocks and those that did not. Between 2002 and 2007, the differences in SWD between these two groups of countries were statistically the same. Only after 2009[16] are such differences statistically different from zero. However, it is in 2010 when a sharp decrease is observed between countries receiving an information shock and the rest of the Eurozone.

[16]Eurobarometers did not ask about SWD in 2008.

To estimate the diff-in-diff analysis, we use the following general model:

$$\widehat{SWD}_{c,t} = \beta_0 + \gamma_1 Shock_c + \gamma_2 Exposure_t + \delta_{dd} Shock_c * Exposure_t \\ + \beta_1 Deficit_{c,t} + \beta_2 SWD_{c,t-1} + \omega_c + \varphi_t + \varepsilon_{c,t}$$

where *Shock* is a binary variable indicating that a given country c has suffered an intervention by the Troika. According to our theory, these scenarios trigger an "information shock" used by citizens to update their beliefs on the functioning of democracy. *Exposure* is a binary variable indicating whether year t marks the moment in which the countries were exposed to the effect of "information shock." To test our theory, we use three different values of *Exposure*, one for each of the years in which one or more information shocks took place: 2010, 2011, and 2012.[17] In each of these years, citizens from different countries were exposed to "information shocks" as a consequence of their countries being intervened in by European institutions. If our theory is correct, we should observe a sustained negative and significant coefficient in the interaction term of these two variables during the periods in which the treatment is applied. In other words, the gap in SWD between the two groups of countries should be significantly large every time an information shock is observed and should increase as information shocks accumulate.

To make sure that the effect of the "information shocks" is isolated, we include a series of control variables. First, *Deficit* is a control variable indicating the level of fiscal deficit as percentage of GDP in country c in year t.[18] Second, we also include the lagged value of SWD for each country to control for the effect of previous satisfaction on current perceptions of SWD. Finally, our model also controls for time trends operationalized as the interaction between country, ω, and year, φ, values.[19] We expect this interaction to absorb all the country- and time-specific combined variation observed within countries and years. Finally, errors are robust to control for heteroscedasticity. Table 9.2 summarizes the descriptive information of these variables.

9.5 SWD in a Context of Economic Crisis

Previous work on explaining public attitudes like SWD have given significant weight to the importance of the economy (Norris 1999; Waldron-Moore 1999). In fact, Fig. 9.3 suggests a clear relationship between economic downturn and SWD.

[17]Cyprus signed a MoU in 2013 but this year is excluded from the analysis given that the series ends in 2014.

[18]Data comes from Eurostat and it indicates the general government deficit (−) and surplus (+).

[19]Angrist and Pischke (2014) indicate that this interaction is required when the data has a pooled cross-country time-series structure like this one.

Table 9.2 Satisfaction with democracy, level of fiscal deficit, and income in Eurozone countries, 2002–2014

	SWD				Deficit				Income			
	Mean	SD	Min	Max	Mean	SD	Min	Max	Mean	SD	Min	Max
Monitored countries												
2002	0.52	0.2	0.31	0.73	−1.77	1.64	−3.3	−0.3	2.16	1.26	1.05	3.41
2003	0.53	0.19	0.32	0.73	−3.06	3.37	−7.8	0.7	1.66	2.26	−1	3.95
2004	0.62	0.15	0.4	0.81	−3.48	3.78	−8.8	1.4	2.9	1.38	1.44	4.74
2005	0.59	0.13	0.42	0.74	−2.71	3.41	−6.2	1.3	2.8	2.74	0.55	0.663
2006	0.6	0.17	0.31	0.79	−1.63	3.57	−5.9	2.8	1.73	1.74	−0.14	3.97
2007	0.6	0.17	0.38	0.8	−0.95	3.6	−6.7	3.2	2.64	2.25	1.21	6.39
2009	0.53	0.08	0.42	0.62	−10.1	4.11	−15.2	−5.3	0.99	1.92	−1.86	3.43
2010	0.45	0.12	0.28	0.58	−12.18	10.32	−32.3	−4.2	−3.3	4.25	−10.5	0.7
2011	0.37	0.14	0.16	0.59	−8.13	3.25	−12.5	−3.5	−4.24	4.03	−10.56	−0.56
2012	0.27	0.13	0.07	0.48	−6.95	2.64	−10.4	−3	−5.17	3.05	−9.75	−1.15
2013	0.25	0.13	0.12	0.51	−6.26	3.27	−12.4	−2.9	−2.18	2.5	−6.56	−0.49
2014	0.3	0.12	0.18	0.55	−5.41	2.32	−8.9	−3	−0.07	1.08	−1.6	1.24
Rest Eurozone												
2002	0.68	0.08	0.58	0.79	−0.55	2.91	−3.9	4.1	1.17	0.148	−0.46	3.02
2003	0.63	0.11	0.45	0.79	−1.68	2.39	−4.2	2.4	1.15	1.34	−0.35	3.41
2004	0.72	0.1	0.58	0.85	−1.82	2.39	−4.8	2.2	1.41	1.53	0.02	3.93
2005	0.67	0.12	0.48	0.83	−1.31	2.22	−3.4	2.6	1.21	1.31	−0.08	3.65

(continued)

Table 9.2 (continued)

	SWD				Deficit				Income			
	Mean	SD	Min	Max	Mean	SD	Min	Max	Mean	SD	Min	Max
2006	0.69	0.15	0.45	0.84	−0.1	2.29	−2.5	3.9	2.25	0.79	0.99	3.27
2007	0.73	0.08	0.61	0.81	0.85	2.78	−2.5	5.1	2.06	0.92	0.4	2.99
2009	0.71	0.12	0.53	0.91	−4.21	2.26	−7.2	−0.5	1.04	0.89	−0.09	1.89
2010	0.65	0.16	0.41	0.88	−3.92	1.96	−6.8	−0.5	0.48	1.26	−0.95	2.36
2011	0.71	0.12	0.52	0.88	−2.51	2.08	−5.1	0.5	0.44	0.61	−0.5	1.03
2012	0.69	0.1	0.57	0.86	−2.42	1.96	−4.8	0.2	0.27	0.98	−1.08	1.79
2013	0.69	0.11	0.47	0.8	−1.8	1.67	−4.1	0.7	−0.29	0.79	−1.51	0.6
2014	0.71	0.11	0.52	0.86	−1.01	2.69	−3.9	3.3	0.71	0.82	−0.76	1.49

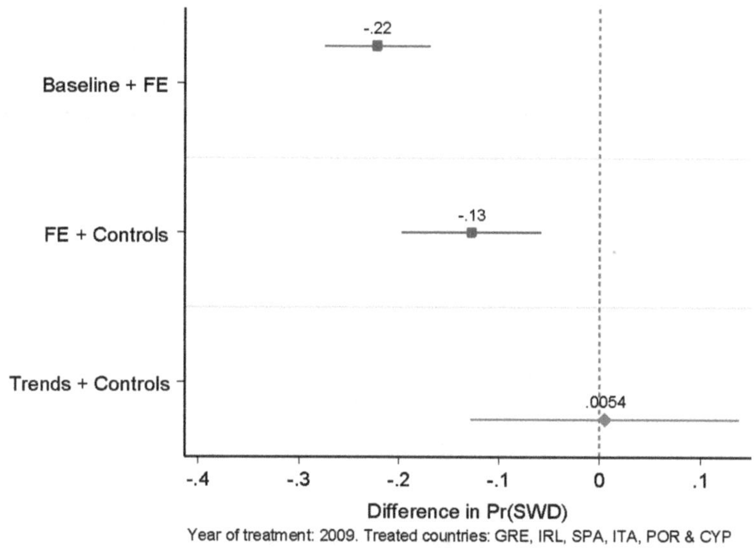

Fig. 9.4 The effect of the crisis in SWD (year of treatment: 2009)

There is ample evidence suggesting that the 2008 financial crisis had an impact on voters (Bellucci 2014; Bellucci et al. 2012; Lewis-Beck and Nadeau 2012), and some authors have also referred to the impact of austerity measures to explain current cross-country variations of SWD (Polavieja 2013; Armingeon and Guthmann 2014; Freire et al. 2014; Cordero and Simón 2016).

Both our theoretical framework and our data, however, do not support this hypothesis in its entirety. Theoretically, the economic policies in response to the 2008 financial crisis cannot explain, by and of themselves, the increasing gap existing between countries that were financially intervened in and countries that were not. Austerity packages were adopted by the German and Dutch governments, and SWD, although affected, did not plummet. The difference between Germany and the Netherlands, on the one hand, and intervened in countries, on the other, is that austerity was not only harsher and clearly failing to produce results among the latter but also imposed by European institutions; in Germany and the Netherlands, on the other hand, it was self-imposed. Our data clearly rejects the hypothesis that economic conditions already existing in 2009 are the key drivers of the decreasing level of SWD. To show this we set the year of *Exposure* in our model at 2009.[20]

Figure. 9.4 shows the diff-in-diff coefficients calculated using the diff-in-diff model explained above.[21] The first value in the upper region of the figure

[20]Data from 2009 comes from EB 72.4, which was conducted between October and November 2009. Using data from the last term of 2009 enhances the logic to use 2009. Unfortunately, the Eurobarometers did not ask about SWD in October/November 2008.

[21]Table 9.5 in the Appendix shows all information regarding this model.

corresponds to a model containing fixed effects; the second value in the middle adds the controls. The coefficients are negative and statistically significant. However, when time trends are introduced and the model controls for all idiosyncratic particularities within countries and between years, the effect disappears completely (third value in the lower right region of the figure). For us, this is an indication that although the crisis was, already in 2009, eroding citizens' SWD, as expected by the political economy thesis, it was not sufficient to explain the emerging gap between intervened in countries and the rest of the Eurozone.

9.6 Troika Interventions as Information Shocks

The key argument of this article is that citizens in countries whose economies were intervened by supranational institutions underwent a process of political learning through belief updating about the way democracy works. As explained above, such process of learning was triggered by information shocks.

The first "information shock" that triggered a belief update was the Memorandum of Understanding signed by the Greek government with the Troika on 3 May 2010 that tied its hands for years to come. At this point, only Greek citizens updated their beliefs and learnt from the information shock. The Greek crisis, however, soon spread across the rest of the most fragile Eurozone economies. Ireland and Portugal were the next to fall. Ireland signed the Memorandum of Understanding with the Troika a few months after Greece, on 28 November 2010. It was followed by Portugal on 3 May 2011. These two bailouts are the second and third "information shocks," pushing larger numbers of citizens to update their beliefs.

We consider the ECB interventions in Spain and Italy in May 2011 to be "information shocks" too. They were the result of forceful impositions from European institutions, even if they did not imply signing a MoU with the Troika. The ECB offered to save Italy and Spain from a fiscal meltdown if they agreed to follow the ECB instructions and apply austerity policies. In return, the ECB would alleviate the pressure of international markets by a massive purchase of Italian and Spanish bonds in the secondary market. On 12–13 May 2011, the Prime Minister of Spain announced in parliament a policy switch toward austerity that would cost him his political career and his party, the Socialist Party, the government. Immediately after, on 13 May 2011, the ECB made a massive purchase of Spanish and Italian bonds in the secondary market that put a stop to attacks by international markets on their sovereign debt. On 2 September 2011, a constitutional reform was approved by the incumbent party, PSOE, with the support of the main opposition party, Popular Party, which fixed a budget deficit limit of 0.4% of GDP and a budget debt maximum of 60% of GDP for all Spanish public administrations. A few days later, on 14 September 2011, the Italian Senate approved the law on a balanced budget. Unlike Spain, however, the Italian lower chamber rejected the law on 10 October 2011, triggering an institutional crisis that only ended with the formation of an

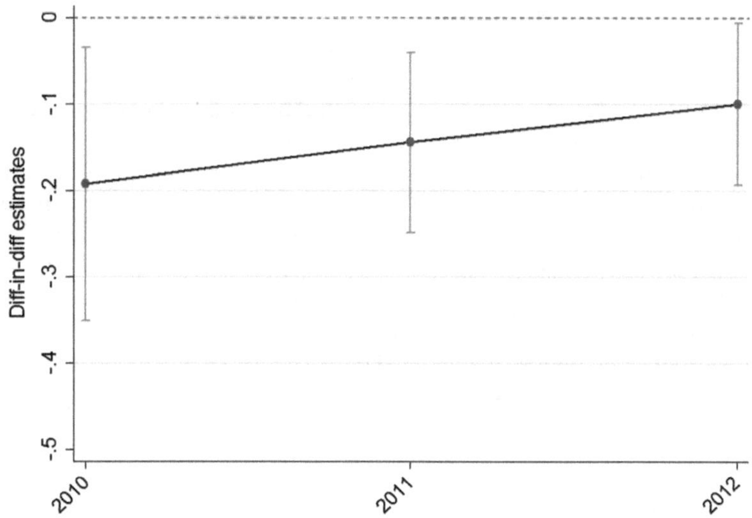

Fig. 9.5 Diff-in-diff coefficients

externally imposed technocratic government, headed by Mario Monti (Bellucci 2014).

Greece needed a second bailout package in 2011, and Spain also requested financial assistance to bail out its banking system, signing a MoU with the Troika, on 15 November 2012. The last country to sign a MoU with the Troika was Cyprus, on 16 March 2013. The MoUs replaced party manifestos as the roadmaps of policy. These documents set out in great detail the conditions that each of these countries needed to meet as part of their financial assistance. In many respects, the MoUs were contracts that bound future elected governments. If the countries did not abide by these agreements they would not get the money they needed to keep their economies and their states afloat. Citizens from intervened in countries voted in elections but did not get to choose among alternative economic policies because economic policy had already been determined by the MoU contract.[22]

Figure 9.5 shows the diff-in-diff coefficients and their 95% confidence intervals estimated in a sequential way as countries of the Eurozone periphery were being intervened in one after another. The 2010 model only includes Greece as the country receiving the information shock, since the Eurobarometer's fieldwork took place at the end of May 2010, and, therefore, only Greece had been bailed out at that point (Ireland signed the MoU in November 2010). The next model uses

[22]The Prime Minister of Spain, Mariano Rajoy, bluntly admitted that: "We Spaniards cannot choose, we do not have the freedom to do so." See interview in Spanish newspaper *EL PAIS* on 11.7.2012.

2011 as the year of the treatment since it includes those countries bailed out up until the time when the Eurobarometer's fieldwork took place.[23] Finally, the model using the year 2012 as the treatment (i.e., "information shock") includes the same countries as in the year 2011 since only Spain requested a bailout in 2012 to face the financial situation of the Spanish banking sector.[24]

The values plotted in Fig. 9.5 show strong empirical support for our main claim. The difference in the levels of SWD between countries exposed to information shocks as a consequence of European intervention and countries not receiving such treatment is always negative and statistically significant. These coefficients are controlled for previous levels of satisfaction with democracy, for the level of existing deficit in their country, and also for country fixed effects and time trends. All are conditions that impose a high level of restrictions in the model and that try to isolate the effect of information shocks from other potential confounders.

9.7 Robustness Tests

We run a series of robustness tests to evaluate the consistency of our main findings. The first test assumes that there is some level of information spillover once Greece signed the MoU in May 2010. The logic is the following: after the signature of the MoU, not only did Greek citizens update their beliefs about the functioning of democracy but also citizens from countries affected by major structural economic problems (Armingeon and Guthmann 2014). The Greek bailout was broadly discussed and commented in newspapers and became a topic of debate in the Eurozone during that period. If this spillover hypothesis is true, a different analysis should be conducted. Instead of using a sequential treatment as the one described in Fig. 9.5, now the year of treatment becomes 2010, and the two groups are the non-intervened in Eurozone countries, on the one hand, and all the intervened in Eurozone countries, on the other.

Model 1 in Table 9.3 shows the various diff-in-diff coefficients when all intervened in countries are treated.[25] The coefficients show that it is only after 2011 when the difference is statistically significant. As previously mentioned, by that year most of the countries had either signed a MoU (Greece, Ireland, and Portugal) or had their economies indirectly but explicitly intervened in by EU institutions (Italy and Spain). Model 2 excludes Greece from the analysis, and, again, the differences are statistically significant after 2011. Finally, Model 3 includes only Greece in the treatment, eliminating Portugal, Ireland, Spain, and Italy. The coefficient is statistically significant in 2010, the year in which Greece

[23]Countries include Portugal, Greece, Spain, and Italy. We also include Ireland since the MoU was signed at the end of 2010.

[24]The Appendix shows the table containing all the details of these models.

[25]Full models are available upon request.

Table 9.3 Robustness tests: diff-in-diff estimates

	Model 1	Model 2	Model 3	Model 4
	Spillover	No GRE	Only GRE	Income
Diff-in-diff estimates				
2010	−0.06 (−0.05)	−0.03 (0.05)	−0.238** (0.100)	−0.163*** (0.032)
2011	−0.168*** (0.05)	−0.161*** (0.05)	−0.242** (0.123)	−0.154** (0.06)
2012	−0.117** (0.04)	−0.144*** (0.04)	−0.052 (0.129)	−0.136*** (0.04)
FE Trends	Yes	Yes	Yes	Yes

Actual statistical significance is $p > 0.054$

signed the first MoU. It is also significant in 2011 when Greece signed its second MoU. The results of these three models suggest that no information spillover occurred and that, just as our theory predicts, citizens updated their beliefs about the functioning of democracy just when they observed the consequences of the Troika intervention in their own countries.

Finally, Model 4 adds a new control variable to the analysis, disposable income. This variable comes from the OCDE and refers to the annual growth rate (%) of household disposable income between 2002 and 2014.[26] Model 4 is limited only to countries that belong to this organization, thus excluding Cyprus from the analysis. Luxembourg is also excluded from the analysis due to data availability. Adding this new variable imposes another restriction to the model by controlling for the socioeconomic conditions of citizens. The coefficients in Table 9.3 show the expected direction and significance, thereby providing further support to our theory.

Our last robustness test uses the original categories of the SWD variable as coded by the Eurobarometers. If our theory and data are correct, a changed specification of the dependent variable that returns it to its original categories should not alter our results. Using an ordered logit model, we re-estimated the model, and we calculated the predicted probabilities of those being "fairly satisfied" with the way democracy works. The reasons why we focus on this particular category are that (a) it represents the largest category in the original SWD variable and that (b) if both our theory and data are correct, we should observe a similar pattern when analyzing this variable, i.e., we should expect a significant gap in the values of this category depending on whether a country signed a MoU or not. The results are shown in Table 9.6 in the Appendix and confirm the findings obtained with our original dichotomous specification of the dependent variable.[27]

[26]Data can be accessed at https://data.oecd.org/hha/household-disposable-income.htm.

[27]We also re-estimated the models using the category "not very satisfied" with the way democracy works.

9.8 Concluding Remarks

In this chapter we analyze how losses in a government's autonomy to act on its democratic mandate affect its citizen's attitudes toward the way democracy works. To explore this question, we have focused on the evolution of SWD in the countries that were part of the Eurozone from its inception in 2001. The Eurozone financial and debt crisis provides a critical test for the study of citizens' attitudes toward the absence of democratic choice. The question is intriguing given the sharp decrease in the levels of satisfaction with democracy in countries that were rather enthusiastic about the European project to begin with. In line with previous research, our results show that bad economic outcomes downgrade the levels of satisfaction with democracy across countries. However, bad economic performance does not suffice alone to explain the collapse of SWD in some countries within the Eurozone and not in others.

Our argument links changes in levels of SWD with the availability of policy choices that is assumed to exist in a democracy. When citizens observe that democracy is a system in which parties lose elections but winners are unwilling or unable to implement alternative policies to those that were rejected at the ballot box, then satisfaction with democracy decreases. This, we show, is the main mechanism explaining the sharp fall in levels of satisfaction with democracy across several Eurozone countries during the Great Recession. One of the many negative externalities of this crisis has been to show the fragility of some institutional designs that had been economically outperforming in the years before the crisis. In this context, as the financial crisis became a currency crisis within the Eurozone, these countries faced serious financial challenges that forced them to require financial assistance programs. It was the acceptance of the conditions of such programs that served as an information release mechanism to citizens in these countries; voters soon found out that voting was no longer about choosing since the room to decide on domestic policies was curtailed by the impositions of the bailout conditions.

The findings of this research go in line with the theoretical trilemma put forward by Rodrik (2011) and according to which nation-states cannot enjoy simultaneously high levels of globalization, national democracy, and state sovereignty. Increasingly the solution out of this trilemma is globalization and state sovereignty at the expense of national democracy. It also agrees with some previous research on the potential pitfalls of the institutional design of the Eurozone, in particular the lack of further political integration (De Grauwe 2013).

Whether a democracy without choices but with popular support is really a democracy or not is open for debate. What is sure, however, is that a democracy with neither choices nor popular support is open for tumult and instability. The performance of democracies is based on both procedures and results. When procedures (i.e., regular competitive elections and choice) guarantee voters the change of policies that they may find ineffective, then procedures and policy change reinforce one another as sources of regime adhesion. However, if procedures do not serve as a mechanism to produce the policy change preferred by the majority, then democracy will be eroded on both fronts, as procedures and as content.

Appendix

Table 9.4 Diff-in-diff analysis in 2009

	2009		
Variables	Baseline	Baseline + controls	Trend
Diff-in-diff	−0.222*** (0.0268)	−0.127*** (0.0352)	0.00542 (0.0674)
Shock	0.0706* (0.0357)	0.0341 (0.0377)	66.88*** (23.55)
2009	0.00614 (0.0327)	0.0596** (0.0235)	−0.0498 (0.0423)
Deficit		0.00168 (0.00233)	0.000972 (0.00172)
SWD_t1		0.532*** (0.117)	0.291** (0.114)
Constant	0.530*** (0.0282)	0.218*** (0.0698)	−4.241 (12.35)
FE	Yes	Yes	No
FE trend	No	No	Yes
Observations	154	141	141
R-squared	0.842	0.894	0.895

Note: Robust standard errors in parentheses. *** $p < 0.01$; ** $p < 0.05$; * $p < 0.1$

Table 9.5 Diff-in-diff results for sequential treatment

Variables	2010			2011			2012		
	Baseline	Baseline + controls	Trend	Baseline	Baseline + controls	Trend	Baseline	Baseline + controls	Trend
Diff-in-Diff	−0.303*** (0.0373)	−0.166*** (0.0578)	−0.192** (0.0799)	−0.225*** (0.0304)	−0.126*** (0.0355)	−0.144*** (0.0528)	−0.222*** (0.0347)	−0.103*** (0.0357)	−0.0993** (0.0473)
Shock	−0.0229 (0.0272)	0.0193 (0.0410)	31.10 (21.60)	−0.162*** (0.0291)	−0.0628 (0.0395)	−11.60 (17.99)	−0.182*** (0.0265)	−0.0726* (0.0411)	1.553 (16.25)
2010	−0.0660* (0.0387)	0.0254 (0.0236)	−0.0638** (0.0282)						
2011				−0.000730 (0.0349)	0.0537** (0.0238)	−0.0122 (0.0388)			
2012							−0.00283 (0.0357)	0.0483* (0.0244)	−0.0284 (0.0275)
Deficit		0.00595 (0.00360)	0.00197 (0.00166)		0.00531** (0.00263)	0.00531*** (0.00151)		0.00565* (0.00310)	0.00568*** (0.00199)
SWD_t1		0.565*** (0.128)	0.188* (0.0986)		0.500*** (0.124)	0.125 (0.102)		0.530*** (0.138)	0.137 (0.101)
Constant	0.565*** (0.0266)	0.235*** (0.0829)	−6.725 (10.10)	0.545*** (0.0260)	0.258*** (0.0765)	5.559 (10.72)	0.553*** (0.0256)	0.249*** (0.0852)	2.704 (8.861)
Fixed effects	Yes	Yes	No	Yes	Yes	No	Yes	Yes	No
FE trends	No	No	Yes	No	No	Yes	No	No	Yes
Observations	154	141	141	154	141	141	154	141	141
R-squared	0.802	0.886	0.906	0.833	0.892	0.907	0.819	0.884	0.904

Note: Robust standard errors in parentheses. *** $p < 0.01$; ** $p < 0.05$; * $p < 0.1$

Table 9.6 Diff-in-diff results for category "fairly satisfied with the way democracy works"

	2010			2011			2012		
Variables	Baseline	Baseline + controls	Trend	Baseline	Baseline + controls	Trend	Baseline	Baseline + controls	Trend
Diff-in-Diff	−0.212*** (0.0250)	−0.126*** (0.0322)	−0.135** (0.0534)	−0.159*** (0.0227)	−0.0882*** (0.0230)	−0.0827** (0.0352)	−0.158*** (0.0263)	−0.0815*** (0.0262)	−0.0660* (0.0333)
Shock	−0.0979*** (0.0184)	−0.0216 (0.0291)	16.24 (13.51)	−0.174*** (0.0236)	−0.0836** (0.0345)	−5.873 (13.91)	−0.188*** (0.0214)	−0.0863** (0.0345)	0.236 (12.86)
2010	−0.0486* (0.0267)	−0.000661 (0.0209)	−0.0339* (0.0188)						
2011				−0.00247 (0.0259)	0.0163 (0.0214)	−0.0283 (0.0185)			
2012							−0.00328 (0.0265)	0.0164 (0.0220)	−0.0333** (0.0151)
Deficit		0.00527** (0.00265)	0.000792 (0.00111)		0.00482** (0.00205)	0.00293*** (0.000997)		0.00509** (0.00232)	0.00334** (0.00129)
SWD_t1		0.516*** (0.0854)	0.226*** (0.0854)		0.438*** (0.0885)	0.124 (0.0881)		0.467*** (0.0955)	0.114 (0.0964)
Constant	0.513*** (0.0195)	0.264*** (0.0547)	1.487 (8.383)	0.498*** (0.0197)	0.295*** (0.0531)	3.437 (7.982)	0.504*** (0.0191)	0.285*** (0.0570)	3.404 (7.611)
Fixed effects	Yes	Yes	No	Yes	Yes	No	Yes	Yes	No
FE trends	No	No	Yes	No	No	Yes	No	No	Yes
Observations	154	141	141	154	141	141	154	141	141
R-squared	0.835	0.900	0.922	0.860	0.903	0.927	0.850	0.900	0.925

Note: Robust standard errors in parentheses. *** $p < 0.01$; ** $p < 0.05$; * $p < 0.1$

Table 9.7 Citizens' preferences—responsiveness versus responsibility (European Social Survey, Round 6, 2013)

"Sometimes the government disagrees with what most people think is best for the country. Which one of the statements on this card describes what you think is best for democracy in general?"	Frequency	%
"The government should change its planned policies in response to what most people think."	35977	65.8
"The government should stick to its planned policies regardless of what most people think."	9298	17.01
"It depends on the circumstances."	6607	12.08
Refusal	100	0.18
Don't know	2633	4.82
No answer	58	0.11
Total	54673	100

Table 9.8 Evaluation of level of responsiveness in respondent's country (European Social Survey, Round 6, 2013)

	<= 5 (0–10 scale)	Mean	SD
Cyprus	55.2	4.1	2.6
Spain	70.2	3	2.6
Ireland	49	4.4	2.4
Italy	65	3.5	2.5
Portugal	68.5	3.4	3.4
Germany	62.9	4	2.6
Denmark	24.1	5.7	2.1
Finland	39	5	2
Netherlands	38.4	5.1	2

Note: 0–10 scale, from never responsive to always responsive

References

Anderson, C. J., & Guillory, C. A. (1997). Political institutions and satisfaction with democracy: A cross-national analysis of consensus and majoritarian systems. *The American Political Science Review, 91*, 66–81.

Angrist, J., & Pischke, J. S. (2008). *Mostly harmless econometrics: An empiricist's companion.* Princeton, NJ: Princeton University Press.

Angrist, J. D., & Pischke, J. S. (2014). *Mastering 'metrics:' The path from cause to effect.* Princeton, NJ: Princeton University Press.

Armingeon, K., & Guthmann, K. (2014). Democracy in crisis? The declining support for national democracy in European countries, 2007–2011. *European Journal of Political Research, 53*, 423–442.

Armingeon, K., Guthmann, K., & Weisstanner, D. (2016). How the Euro divides the union: The effect of economic adjustment on support for democracy in Europe. *Socio-Economic Review, 14*(1), 1–26.

Bartels, L. M. (2002). Beyond the running tally: Partisan bias in political perceptions. *Political Behavior, 24*, 117–150.

Bellucci, P. (2014). The political consequences of blame attribution for the economic crisis in the 2013 Italian national election. *Journal of Elections, Public Opinion and Parties, 24*, 243–263.

Bellucci, P., Costa Lobo, M., & Lewis-Beck, M. S. (2012). Economic crisis and elections: The European periphery. *Electoral Studies, 31*, 469–471.

Blais, A., & Gelineau, F. (2007). Winning, losing and satisfaction with democracy. *Political Studies, 55*, 425–441.

Bullock, J. G. (2009). Partisan bias and the Bayesian ideal in the study of public opinion. *The Journal of Politics, 71*, 1109–1124.

Cordero, G., & Simón, P. (2016). Economic crisis and support for democracy in Europe. *West European Politics, 39*(2), 305–325.

De Grauwe, P. (2006). What have we learnt about monetary integration since the Maastricht Treaty? *JCMS: Journal of Common Market Studies, 44*, 711–730.

De Grauwe, P. (2010). The fragility of the Eurozone's institutions. *Open Economies Review, 10*, 167–174.

De Grauwe, P. (2013). *Design failures in the Eurozone. Can they be fixed?* LEQS Paper 57/2013.

Dinas, E. (2013). Opening "openness to change:" Political events and the increased sensitivity of young adults. *Political Research Quarterly, 66*, 868–882.

Downs, A. (1957). *An economic theory of democracy*. New York, NY: Harper & Row.

Ferrin, M., & Kriesi, H. P. (Eds.). (2016). *How Europeans view and evaluate democracy?* Oxford: Oxford University Press.

Freire, A., Lisi, M., Andreadis, I., & Leite Viegas, J. M. (2014). Political representation in bailed-out Southern Europe: Greece and Portugal compared. *South European Society and Politics, 19*, 413–433.

Friedman, T. L. (2012). *The Lexus and the olive tree: Understanding globalization*. London: Picador.

Garrett, G. (1998). Global markets and national politics: Collision course or virtuous circle? *International Organization, 52*, 787–824.

Gelman, A. (2005). Two-stage regression and multilevel modelling: A commentary. *Political Analysis, 13*, 459–461.

Gerber, A., & Green, D. P. (1998). Rational learning and partisan attitudes. *American Journal of Political Science, 42*, 794–818.

Held, D. (1995). *Democracy and the global order: From the modern state to cosmopolitan governance*. Stanford, CA: Stanford University Press.

Jones, E. (2009). Output legitimacy and the global financial crisis: Perceptions matter. *JCMS: Journal of Common Market Studies, 47*, 1085–1105.

Jusko, K. L., & Shively, W. P. (2005). Applying a two-step strategy to the analysis of cross-national public opinion data. *Political Analysis, 13*, 327–344.

Kydland, F. E., & Prescott, E. C. (1977). Rules rather than discretion: The inconsistency of optimal plans. *Journal of Political Economy, 85*, 473–491.

Lewis-Beck, M. S., & Nadeau, R. (2012). Pigs or not? Economic voting in Southern Europe. *Electoral Studies, 31*, 472–477.

Mair, P. (2011). The election in context. In M. Gallagher & M. Marsh (Eds.), *How Ireland voted 2011: The full story of Ireland's earthquake election* (pp. 283–297). Basingstoke: Palgrave Macmillan.

Mair, P. (2013). *Ruling the void: The hollowing of western democracy*. London: Verso.

Maravall, J. M. (2013). *Las Promesas Politicas*. Barcelona: Galaxia Gutenberg.

Matakos, K., & Xefteris, D. (2015). Citizens or clients? Evidence on opportunistic voting from a natural experiment in Greece. *Political Science Research and Methods, 4*(3), 1–39.

Moss, B. (2000). *The single European currency in national perspective: A community in crisis?* London: Palgrave Macmillan UK.

Norris, P. (1999). *Critical citizens: Global support for democratic government*. Oxford: Oxford University Press.

OECD. (2009). *The political economy of reform: Lessons from pensions, product markets and labour markets in ten OECD countries*. Accessed April 11, 2017, from http://www.oecd.org/site/sgemrh/46190166.pdf

Polavieja, J. (2013). Economic crisis, political legitimacy, and social cohesion. In D. Gallie (Ed.), *Economic crisis, quality of work and social integration: The European experience* (pp. 256–278). Oxford: Oxford University Press.

Przeworski, A. (2010). *Democracy and the limits of self-government*. New York, NY: Cambridge University Press.

Riker, W. H. (1982). *Liberalism against populism: A confrontation between the theory of democracy and the theory of social choice*. Long Grove, IL: Waveland Press.

Rodrik, D. (2011). *The globalization paradox: Democracy and the future of the world economy*. Oxford: Oxford University Press.

Scharpf, F. W. (1997). Economic integration, democracy and the welfare state. *Journal of European Public Policy, 4*, 18–36.

Scharpf, F. W. (1999). *Governing in Europe: Effective and democratic?* Oxford: Oxford University Press.

Stiglitz, J. (2012). *The price of inequality*. London: Penguin Books Limited.

Waldron-Moore, P. (1999). Eastern Europe at the crossroads of democratic transition: Evaluating support for democratic institutions, satisfaction with democratic government, and consolidation of democratic regimes. *Comparative Political Studies, 32*, 32–62.

Part III
Governance

Chapter 10
Globalization and Democracy: Does Denationalization Affect the Quality of Democracy?

Lea Heyne

10.1 Introduction

In the debate on a legitimacy crisis of established democracies, globalization is a frequent buzzword—mostly in the context of a critical view on the internationalization of economics, politics, and society. The notion that globalization poses an imminent and serious threat to democracy is very widespread not only among political scientists but also in a wider public. Yet the evidence brought forward in this regard is often merely impressionistic and seldom empirically founded. For instance, globalization is held responsible for decreasing national sovereignty and autonomy, for capital flight, low-wage job competition, and declining social and living standards—and, as a result, for a popular backlash against free trade and growing hostility toward immigrants. Indeed, the electoral success of right-wing populist parties with nationalistic and protectionist programs in Europe shows that, especially in times of economic crisis, the concept of the further dissolution of boundaries is encountering considerable resistance.

At the same time, the social sciences seem to disagree on whether how and by what mechanisms globalization is affecting the quality of national democracies. Whereas several authors have argued that globalization is responsible for hollowing out democracy (Streeck 1998, 2013; Sassen 2007), others claim that internationalization has largely positive effects on democratic quality (Keohane et al. 2009; Bühlmann 2010). In this chapter, I use the Democracy Barometer (Bochsler et al. 2014), an index of democratic quality, as a starting point for the theoretical and empirical assessment of the possible effects of globalization on democratic quality. After a short definition of both globalization and democratic quality, I examine the main arguments brought forward in the debate for both negative and positive effects. I then test the hypotheses derived from

L. Heyne (✉)
NCCR Democracy, University of Zurich, Zurich, Switzerland
e-mail: lea.heyne@zda.uzh.ch

W. Merkel, S. Kneip (eds.), *Democracy and Crisis*,
https://doi.org/10.1007/978-3-319-72559-8_10

these different theoretical approaches empirically, using data from the Democracy Barometer (DB) and the KOF[1] index of globalization (Dreher 2005). The results suggest that different forms of globalization also differ in their impact on democracy and that the three democratic principles, freedom, equality, and control, are not equally strongly affected.

10.2 Democracy and Globalization, Two Controversial Concepts

10.2.1 Democracy and Democratic Quality

Like the other contributions in this volume, this chapter leans on a middle range definition of democracy, as proposed by the concept of "embedded democracy" (Merkel 2004, 2010).[2] Democracy is understood as a combination of liberal and participatory elements, whereas outcomes of democratic policies such as social justice are explicitly not part of the definition (Bühlmann et al. 2012, 3ff.). In order to assess the actual quality of democratic structures, my analysis relies on the Democracy Barometer. This instrument is based on the premise that a democratic system tries to establish a balance between the normative and interdependent values of freedom and equality. In order to maintain such a balance, any democratic system needs a third dimension, namely, control, a dimension that is all the more important for a democracy because the institutionalized checks on political authorities distinguish democratic systems from autocracies. These three fundamental principles—freedom, equality, and control—thus form the basis of any democratic system, and the degree to which they are fulfilled determines the level of democratic quality (see Fig. 10.1). *Freedom* in the sense of negative freedom is first of all defined by the absence of heteronomy, which means that individual rights have to be protected and guaranteed by the rule of law. These rights, which have developed over time, include the freedom of opinion and religion, the protection of life, and property rights (ibid., 5). In order to guarantee the freedom of opinion and expression, a good democracy also needs to have a free and diverse public sphere which allows citizens to gather and exchange information and opinions. *Equality*, the next principle, is to be understood as political equality and means that all citizens are treated equal in the political process and have the same access to political power. Political equality thus aims at the equal formulation, equal consideration, and equal inclusion of all citizens' preferences. However, preferences can be given equal consideration only if political representation is as equal as possible and if political processes are transparent and comprehensible to every citizen (ibid., 6). *Control*, lastly, can be seen as a means to establish and maintain the fragile equilibrium between the two first principles. Vertically, control is exercised through elections themselves, as they allow citizens to make decisions about the balance between freedom and equality. Horizontally,

[1]KOF stands for the Swiss Economic Institute (Konjunkturforschungsstelle) of the ETH Zürich.

[2]This concept is also the basis for the Democracy Barometer (DB).

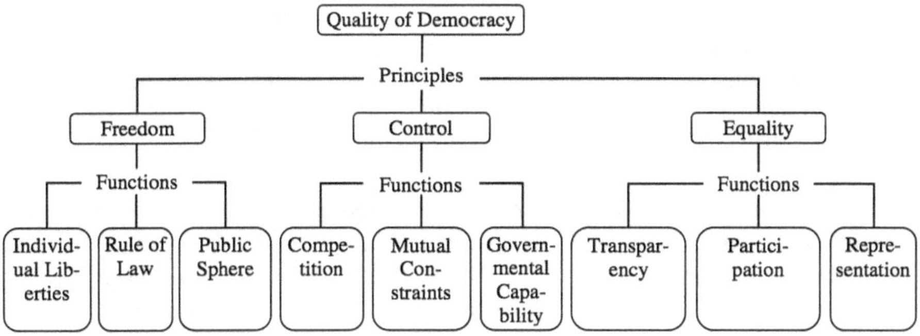

Fig. 10.1 Democratic quality in the Democracy Barometer. Source: Democracy Barometer

control takes place through the classical institutional checks and balances. Furthermore, governments need to have a certain efficiency so that they can actually implement democratic decisions—if the elected representatives have no real capability to govern, they cannot be responsive to the citizens (ibid., 8).

10.2.2 Globalization

Globalization, as Zimmerling has put it, has been "the major buzzword of the past decade or so in the social sciences, as well as in a wider public" (Zimmerling 2005, 62). It is a phenomenon that has triggered a veritable flood of analyses, articles, books, and papers since it found its way into the academic and political debate (Guillén 2001, 240). Yet, whereas everyone seems to agree that globalization is an important, if not the most important phenomenon of the current world order, there is surprisingly little consensus on what it actually is, and even less on how exactly it works or what it causes. Or, as Brennan (2005, 27) has put it, globalization, like democracy, is a term that often carries more emotional than descriptive or analytical freight. Given the blurred conceptualization of globalization, some authors even avoid using the term altogether, opting for such alternatives as "denationalization" (Zürn 1998) or "transnationalization" (Mau 2007).

In general, globalization refers to the idea of a shrinking world or a world growing together and to the belief that there has recently been an unprecedented increase in cross-border interdependence and integration. One of the most systematic accounts of the concept and its processes is offered by Held et al. (1999, 16), who define globalization as "a process (or set of processes) which embodies a transformation in the spatial organization of social relations and transactions—assessed in terms of their extensity, intensity, velocity and impact—generating transcontinental or interregional flows and networks of activity, interaction, and the exercise of power." According to them, the impact of globalization can take four forms: decisional (on the relative costs and benefits of given options), institutional (on the "choosability" of certain options; "agenda-setting"), distributive (on the relative material and political positions of groups), and structural (on behavioral and organizational patterns) (ibid., 18). Importantly, globalization is associated with a "stretching" of power relations, so that sites of power become increasingly distant from the subjects or locales which experience its consequences (McGrew 1997, 8).

Concerning the actual extent and impact of contemporary globalization processes, three different currents of opinion can be identified. The so-called *hyperglobalists* share the belief that globalization consists not only in remarkable quantitative change but also in qualitative changes in social relations and interactions, which inevitably leads to a "new epoch in human history" (Zimmerling 2005, 62). *Globalization skeptics*, on the other hand, basically state that globalization is a myth, as recent economic developments are neither new in quality nor truly global in reach, but rather selective, asymmetrical, and fragmentative in their effects (Krasner 1993). Skeptics not only reject the idea that economic internationalization erodes national sovereignty but also assert that processes of globalization are not morally desirable (McGrew 1997, 11). The third view is the *transformationalist* one, which holds a middle ground between the two others and affirms that while globalization does exist and is a historically unprecedented and new kind of process, its future course is by no means foreseeable or inevitable and depends strongly on the choices made by conscious actors (Zimmerling 2005, 66). Since most globalization scholars more or less agree with this approach, my analysis will also be based on a transformationalist view.

When it comes to where globalization processes happen, the areas mostly mentioned are the economy (exchange, production, capital flows), communications (information, ideas, knowledge), ecology (environmental problems, global public goods), culture (beliefs, values, institutions), security (arms trade, conflict resolution, military interventions), and politics ("global governance," inter-/supranational organizations, international law). In all these issue areas, globalization can be expected to operate in ways that may be potentially relevant for national democracy, but the most important areas are clearly the economy and politics. So far, economic issues have undoubtedly received the greatest attention from globalization scholars, "so much so that when the term 'globalization' is used alone, without further specification, a reference to economic globalization is usually assumed" (ibid., 67). There is a widespread belief that the economy is the area in which globalization is not only most advanced but also where it has the greatest impact on the everyday life of most people and that economic globalization has served as a sort of starting point and trigger for other forms. In the following analysis, I address three dimensions of globalization: economic, political, and social.

Economic globalization describes the following phenomena: the internationalization of production by multinational corporations (Goodhart 2001, 529), the reduction of tariff and trade restrictions (Cerny 1999, 55), the liberalization of national labor markets (Cox 1997, 52), as well as the establishment of a largely unregulated global financial market (Held 1998, 64). In sum, these developments lead to a considerable decrease of effective state autonomy in economic and financial matters. *Political globalization* refers to the establishment of new forms of multilateral and multinational politics, accompanied by distinctive styles of collective decision-making. They include transnational NGOs such as Amnesty International, intergovernmental organizations like the UN, the WTO, and the IMF, and regional supranational authorities like the EU. Furthermore, there is the growing power of international regulatory regimes in a variety of policy areas (Goodhart 2001, 530), as well as an increase in the emphasis on collective defense and cooperative security (Held 1998, 70). *Social globalization*, lastly, includes new communication trends such as the spread of English as a lingua franca and the internationalization of telecommunications and media conglomerates but also the increasing cross-border movement of people, through both tourism and migration.

10.3 Globalization: Threat or Benefit for the Quality of Democracy?

At least three different contexts of democracy are commonly focused on when the actual or possible impact of globalization on democracy is discussed. The first context is the *currently nondemocratic (or partly democratic)* states, where the main issue is the effects of globalization on their prospects for democratization or democratic consolidation. There is an exhaustive literature on the relationship between globalization and democratization, mostly concerned with the impact of economic globalization (in terms of openness of national markets) on nondemocratic (or inadequately democratic) countries. A second context is the *international system* as a whole, where discussion mainly revolves around the possible need for democratization as a consequence of globalization. The democratization (or rather the democratic deficiency) of global governance is a frequently discussed topic in the international relations literature, especially in the growing literature on "cosmopolitanism" and global democracy. The third area is *established democracies*, where the main question is how globalization affects their political stability and the evolution of their systemic quality. This last context is the one relevant for this contribution, in which I focus on the three democratic principles, freedom, equality, and control, in order to localize possible effects more precisely.

10.3.1 Democratization Through Globalization?

Positive Effects of Globalization on Democratic Freedom

An argument regularly advanced by transformationalists is that globalization furthers the emergence of new progressive political forces and stimulates democratic energy in the form of NGOs, INGOs, social movements, etc. These civil society movements, which are transnational in organization and scope, promote human rights (women's rights, LGBT rights, the rights of political, ethnic or religious minorities) and, in broad terms, pursue a policy of emancipation (Streeck 1998, 16). The increase in this kind of organization has been interpreted as the emergence of a global civil society, which operates "above the individual and below the state, but across national boundaries," and which seeks to make states as well as the international community of states accountable for their actions (McGrew 1997, 13). Even though this evolving global civil society also stands in a rather ambiguous relationship to territorial forms of democracy pursuing a policy of emancipation that transcends national frontiers, one can presume that the developments fostered by their activity—the better protection of human rights—are positive for national democracy, as well. In this context, Dickenson (1997, 117) has claimed that globalization "may make democracy real for women in a way that the liberal democratic nation-states have failed to do" by achieving the recognition of women's rights as universal human rights. As Cerny (1999, 6) has remarked, if democracy is seen merely as pluralism and individual independence, then the complexities of globalization can certainly create myriad niches which may foster diversity and autonomy. The argument made here thus implies that *political globalization* enhances national democratic quality through the pressure exerted by a transnational civil society on countries to improve individual liberties and the rule of law, especially for minorities.

Another view argues that globalization reduces information costs (by facilitating communication, transport, etc.) and thus increases information flows and hence also the level of information among citizens. A prosperous democracy requires well-informed actors, and, with increasing globalization, citizens have access to more information, supplied not just by their own governments but also by other independent sources (Li and Reuveny 2003, 34). According to this argument, *social globalization* (in terms of increased contact and communication), by expanding the degree and the quality of available information on politics, strengthens the quality of the public sphere as such, as well as citizens' level of information.

Positive Effects of Globalization on Democratic Control
The American political scientists Keohane, Macedo, and Moravcik have informed the notion of *democracy-enhancing multilateralism* (Keohane et al. 2009). They state that multilateral institutions can enhance the quality of national democratic processes, even in well-functioning democracies, in several ways: by restricting the power of special interest factions and improving the quality of democratic deliberation while also increasing capacities to achieve important public purposes. For instance, multilateral trade norms and institutions have altered domestic practices by generally enhancing executive and judicial power, reshaping the incentives of legislators, and shifting the salience of issues, which, according to the authors, empowers previously powerless diffuse interests (ibid., 11). Institutions like GATT or the WTO are thus thought to provide mechanisms by which democratic publics can limit the influence of special interest groups, as they commit governments to a set of multilateral rules and practices that reflect broad public interests and thus enhance democratic processes with respect, for instance (ibid., 16). Furthermore, Keohane et al. claim that individual democracies can utilize information and expertise more effectively when they participate in multilateral institutions and networks. They argue that "the wider scope, greater diversity, expert staffs, and political insulation of multilateral forums can enhance the epistemic basis of political decision-making by expanding the range of information available to national politicians and public" (ibid., 18). The authors thus propose that processes of public deliberation gain in legitimacy and transparency by including the views of outsiders, both those affected by national public

decisions and those who may have insights to contribute from their distinct experience. Applied to the concept of democratic quality, this hypothesis would imply that *political globalization* has a positive impact on democratic control, as membership in multilateral institutions and treaties is assumed to enhance the efficiency and agency of democratic governments and to reduce the influence of special interests groups to the advantage of the public interest.

In a similar vein, authors have argued that competition with other jurisdictions makes it more difficult for governments to implement political schemes that benefit some citizens at the expense of others. This assumes that, due to increased mobility, "competition among jurisdictions offers citizens and jurisdiction-users effective protection against exploitation, be it in favor of privileged groups or of those who hold the reins of political decision-making power" (Vanberg 2002, 30). The issue at the core of the "competition of jurisdictions" argument is thus mobility and exit, namely, the question whether mobile factors are ready to pay the price demanded for jurisdiction services or prefer to forego these services in favor of alternative options. Accordingly, when it comes to the ability of governments to act in the common interests of all citizens, competition among jurisdictions can be expected to assist governments as well as citizens in finding out which jurisdiction characteristics and services best serve the common interests of all citizens, and how these jurisdictions can be provided most efficiently (ibid., 30ff.). In doing so, competition among jurisdictions can help to improve democracy by forcing (or motivating) governments to better adapt institutions and rules to the needs of their citizens. *Social globalization*, more precisely, the increased spread of ideas, information, and people across national borders, should hence also strengthen the control function by supporting competition and a balance of powers.

Positive Effects of Globalization on Democratic Equality

The main argument cited when it comes to a positive impact of globalization on democratic quality concerns the effects of economic development. The view that globalization fosters democracy thus rests on an indirect causal linkage, which is as follows: (1) globalization is conducive to economic development and growth and (2) economic development and growth foster democracy (Lopéz-Córdova and Meissner 2008, 544). Based on the modernization theory (Przeworski et al. 2000) and Lipset's (1959) theory of social prerequisites for democracy, scholars argue that a country's economic well-being positively contributes to its regime quality by enhancing the stability and legitimacy of a democracy. The wealthier a country is and the lower its probability of economic crisis, the higher are human development and the quality of life (Inglehart and Welzel 2005). This includes, for example, a higher income level, a better quality of social and health care, access to education for all inhabitants, and an innovative and productive economy. Accordingly, economic globalization should have a positive impact on democratic quality by steering economic growth and development within nation-states, which then fosters human development and increases the living standards of the population. However, these are not yet primary factors of democratic quality but only social preconditions. Still, political equality should also be strongly related to the fulfillment of these prerequisites: Increased wealth and societal development (i.e., by spreading education) positively affect the equality of participation by citizens, in institutionalized ways (elections) and in non-institutionalized ways (demonstrations, petitions, etc.). Furthermore, better living conditions could also increase transparency by minimizing incentives for corruption. Hence, following this argument, *economic globalization* should increase democratic quality by enhancing the political equality of citizens through a rise in human development.

10.3.2 Denationalization as a Loss of Democracy?

Negative Effects of Globalization on Democratic Freedom

The security trap argument contends that the loss of control over criminals and terrorists implied in the opening of borders and the advance of communication technologies creates a need, for the sake of security, of more controls and monitoring within states and thus a negative effect on the liberal quality of democratic systems (Zimmerling 2005, 74). The notion that in recent decades, aggravated by the terrorist attacks of 9/11, freedom rights have been largely dismantled in liberal democracies is commonly brought forward in the literature on globalization and democracy. Civil rights such as informational self-determination and the freedom of speech, of movement, and of association have, according to this argument, suffered from the international war on terrorism. Further, it is often argued that intelligence services have vastly enlarged their scope of action and competences, thus shifting the pendulum away from freedom and toward more surveillance. In this context, Busch (2011) claims that the distinction between police, intelligence services, and military is becoming more and more blurred and that data exchange between the security agencies of different countries is increasing without being subject to democratic control. Both tendencies seem to be confirmed by the recent NSA scandal.

In general, many political analysts assert that policy fields such as migration, visas and asylum, border protection, surveillance, and especially protection against terrorism have undergone a gradual process of "securitization" (Buzan and Wæver 2003). The theory of securitization is commonly used as a theoretical tool to understand "how security is invoked to legitimize contentious legislation, policies or practices that would otherwise not have been deemed legitimate" (Neal 2009, 335). In other words, securitization explains the attempt to move a topic away from normal politics into an area of security in order to legitimate extraordinary means against a perceived existential threat (Bigo 2006, 74ff.). Globalization, by increasing international terrorism, trafficking, and other crimes, has raised concerns about collective security among the populations of developed democracies and has thus served as a rationale for securitization. Hence, it has not only supplied the justification for governments to enhance control and surveillance over their own citizens but has also provided them with the means to do so: more and more effective surveillance technologies working on a global scale. In recent decades, governments have tightened security provisions, created new surveillance instruments, and reduced individual freedom rights in the name of security—often with the implicit or explicit consent of their citizens. On the one hand, one could argue that by reacting to the demands raised by their citizens, governments actually fulfill their democratic function of responsiveness, so that their action would rather be indicative of good democratic quality. On the other hand, civil liberties are an essential element of democratic quality and governance, and constraining these individual liberties is a breach of human rights and endangers the functioning of democracy as such, so that such restrictions cannot be justified democratically. Accordingly, *economic* as well as *social globalization* could negatively affect democratic freedom.

Negative Effects of Globalization on Democratic Control
Potential dangers for the control function in established democracies are often to be found in the growing incongruence of democratic decision-making: while classic territorial democracy assumes a "symmetrical and congruent relationship between decision-makers and the recipients of political decisions" (Held 2000, 290), globalization calls this principle into question. As a result of growing global interdependencies and denationalization, citizens of democratic states can be affected by decisions in which they have no stake (Kriesi et al. 2013, 4). They might be decisions by other national authorities (such as immigration or taxation laws) but also decisions at the supra- or international level, taken by institutions such as the EU, the WTO, or the IMF (Lavenex 2013, 106). These actors are not democratically accountable to national electorates—or, in the case of the EU, only to a very limited extent. Additionally, there is a trend toward a change in the nature of governance and shift from the interventionist to the regulatory state, along with a move from value-based politics within majoritarian elected representative bodies toward technocratic, science, and expert-based practices in non-majoritarian and nonelected bodies, especially in EU politics. These functional channels replace electoral channels of participation but are not democratically legitimized (see Papadopoulos 2010). Moreover, democratic governments are subject to a growing number of international treaties and agreements, making it more and more difficult for them to respond to the needs of their own citizens. Another aspect is the diminishing impact of national democratic legislatures on economic affairs—as Held (1998, 67ff.) argues, the liberalization and deregulation of global financial and trade movements have shifted the balance of power between capital and (democratic) politics in favor of the former. The reduction of state controls and the expansion of exit options for capital in financial markets relative to national capital controls, national banking regulations, and national investment strategies have significantly lowered the impact of democratically elected governments on economic and financial matters. Not only institutions such as the IMF and the World Bank but also private actors are able to shape state policies both internally and externally but remain largely unobstructed by democratic control and accountability (Cox 1997, 60). Streeck has raised the concern that, due to the existence of sectoral and functional exit options from the nation-state, the capacity of democratic states to govern is decreasing, making democracy more dispensable for those who are mobile and increasingly inefficient for those who are not (Streeck 1998, 37).

A similar argument claims that the abovementioned processes not only weaken the power to govern and the autonomy of democratic administration but also create a power imbalance within democratic institutions: some parts of the liberal state (including the executive branch of government and some of the key agencies under its control) actually gain in power; at the same time, the various policies promoting corporate economic globalization have the effect of eliminating oversight functions and thus hollowing out the legislature (Sassen 2007). It is widely assumed that internationalization strengthens the relative governmental influence on the executive branch (Moravcsik 1993) to the detriment of legislatures, which are less strongly represented at the international level. Examples for this development are institutions such as the G20, the Troika, or the ECB, which have gained even greater importance since the fiscal crisis. These institutions are all dominated by the (elected) executives of the relevant countries. Putnam (1988) refers to government representatives as "gatekeepers" in international negotiations, as they are the only ones participating in both the international and national arenas. Legislatures, it is argued, are losing influence relative to executives as they are increasingly excluded from important decision-making forums. Lavenex (2013, 118) argues that this leads to a problem of inclusion, as directly legitimated, universal representatives of a political community—parliamentarians—can no longer fully participate in the policy-making process. Similarly, Streeck (1998, 10) has claimed that globalization might serve to promote an "international alliance of national executives" at the expense of national democracy. In sum, the control principle can be weakened by both *political* and *economic globalization*, as democratic governments (voluntarily) give up political control over economic and societal matters and thus face a loss of autonomy vis-à-vis nondemocratic actors.

Negative Effects of Globalization on Democratic Equality

Arguments that internationalization has a negative impact on the equality principle claim that economic globalization harms the social equality of industrialized societies. Economic globalization, promoting the idea of competitiveness in world markets as a primary goal and criterion for national politics, is thus seen as a cause for growing inequalities in democratic societies. The argument goes as follows: the massive deregulation of economic and financial controls, the privatization of public sector enterprises, and public debt reduction notably through cuts in social expenditure adapted during the 1980s and 1990s represented a complete reversal in the set of policies classically pursued by advanced capitalist countries. As a result of this "U-turn in public policies" (Cox 1997, 50), social polarization in the advanced capitalist countries increased, resulting in higher unemployment and decreased social services. Economic globalization accordingly triggered a downward spiral of tax reduction, wage competition, and capital mobility and has led democratic governments to implement social policy measures that divide the population into winners and losers: the establishment of a "two-thirds society," as the structural changes from economic globalization, particularly its effects on employment, induces structural marginalization and exclusion from many spheres of social life for a section of the population (Sassen 1996). Kupchan states that "for the better part of two decades, middle-class wages in the world's leading democracies have been stagnant, and economic inequality has been rising sharply as globalization has handsomely rewarded its winners but left its many losers behind" (Kupchan 2012, 1).

The "losers" of globalization are hence those whose life chances were traditionally protected by national borders and who perceive the weakening of these borders as a threat to their social status and security, as a reduction of their life chances. The winners are those who benefit from the new opportunities resulting from globalization and whose life chances are enhanced (Kriesi et al. 2008, 5ff.). Kriesi et al. assert that mobility has become a powerful factor for social stratification and suggest that, paradoxically, "the lowering and unbundling of national boundaries render them more salient, as they are weakened and reassessed, their political importance increases" (ibid., 9). This perspective highlights the social costs of growing economic and cultural interdependence for at least parts of society in established welfare states, and their resort to borders as a means of protection (see Zürn 1998). Accordingly, growing insecurities lead to negative attitudes toward globalization and a shift to protectionism and are part of a more complex syndrome of an "exclusive nationalist backlash," which includes economic protectionism, xenophobic reactions to immigrants, and a strong aversion to international institutions (Zürn and Ecker-Ehrhardt 2013, 79). The formation of new cleavages between winners and losers of globalization as a structural conflict constitutes potentials for political mobilization within national political contexts—for instance, it gives rise to new radical parties promoting ethnic nationalism, right-wing populism, separatist nationalism, or religious fundamentalism and leads to a general fragmentation of party systems (Loch and Heitmeyer 2001, 15ff.).

But how exactly do such developments affect the quality of democratic equality? Social equality or the inclusiveness of the welfare state as such are, as we have seen, not included in the definition of democracy used in this analysis. But political structures are linked to the underlying social basis, and hence growing social inequality or even exclusion of sections of the population from equal participation in society should also affect democratic equality: Both the equal representation of interests and the participation of all citizens in democratic decision-making could be impacted. Moreover, cultural alienation and social disintegration of sections of the population can have a negative effect on political involvement and endanger the stability of party systems by giving rise to populist anti-system parties. Accordingly, *economic globalization* can be associated with a decline in democratic equality.

10.4 Empirics: How Globalization Affects Democratic Quality

10.4.1 Data

In order to test the theoretical arguments described in the last section, the empirical analysis looks at the relationships between globalization and democratic quality. Each of the three democratic principles is tested separately for the impact of economic, political, and social globalization to determine where the positive hypothesis that globalization increases democratic quality holds true and where the negative hypothesis that denationalization harms "democraticness" proves valid. Given the broad theoretical assumptions and complexity of the phenomena observed, I believe that both postulates will show a certain validity.

For my analysis, I use data from the Democracy Barometer (Bochsler et al. 2014) as well as the KOF index of globalization (Dreher 2005). As mentioned in Sect. 10.2.1, the Democracy Barometer assesses the quality of established democracies using three basic principles—freedom, equality, and control—which are guaranteed by nine functions. Each of these functions is empirically measured by two components, each component by subcomponents, and each subcomponent by several indicators. Overall, the dataset uses 105 variables measuring both rules in law (constitution) and rules in use (constitutional reality) (Bühlmann et al. 2012, 17ff.). The Democracy Barometer data is available for the period from 1990 to 2010 for 30 established democracies,[3] and these countries are also the sample for my analysis. One of the most recent and comprehensive indices of globalization is the KOF index, developed by scholars from the ETH Zürich. It measures three main dimensions of globalization: economic, social, and political integration, using 23 variables. *Economic globalization* consists of two components, measuring firstly actual flows such as trade, foreign direct investment and portfolio investment, as well as income payments to foreign nationals and capital employed (both in % of GDP) to proxy for the extent a country employs foreign people and capital in its production processes. Second, it includes restrictions on trade and capital using hidden import barriers, mean tariff rates, taxes on international trade (as a share of current revenue), and an index of capital controls (Dreher 2005, 3). To proxy the degree of *political globalization*, the KOF uses the number of embassies in a country, the number of international organizations to which the country belongs, the number of international treaties it has ratified, and the number of UN peace missions in which it has participated. The index of *social globalization* is composed of data on migration, tourism, information flows, as well as cultural exchange (ibid.).

If the pessimistic assumption that globalization is weakening national democracy applies, this should be reflected in the Democracy Barometer data. Similarly, a positive effect of internationalization on democratic quality should be measurable. When looking at the development of democracy since 1990, we witness a generally positive trend: on average, the quality of democracy in the 30 blueprint countries increased slightly from 1990 to 2010, from 56.9 to 59.1 points. The only two countries where the overall quality of democracy has decreased by more than 1 point from 1990 to 2010 are Italy (−7.2 points) and Hungary (−3.4 points). All others have maintained or improved their democratic quality in this period. All in all, this picture neither supports the pessimist crisis of democracy hypothesis nor the optimist premise of increased

[3]Australia, Austria, Belgium, Canada, Costa Rica, Cyprus, the Czech Republic, Denmark, Finland, France, Germany, Hungary, Iceland, Ireland, Italy, Japan, Luxembourg, Malta, the Netherlands, New Zealand, Norway, Poland, Portugal, Slovenia, South Africa, Spain, Sweden, Switzerland, the United Kingdom, and the United States.

democratization through internationalization. However, when looking more closely at the development of democratic quality in different countries over time, it is obvious that the variance between countries is considerable (Fig. 10.2): Whereas some, such as Denmark and Switzerland, have maintained a high level of democratic quality, others (Poland) have remarkably increased their democratic performance, and still others have witnessed a general decrease (Italy) or an increase followed by a decrease in democratic quality (United States). Some countries show an almost linear development, and others have experienced several ups and downs in the level of democratic quality. This raises the question whether these differences both between and within countries over time can be explained by the impact of globalization. In other words, how much of the variance in democratic quality can be explained by globalization factors?

10.4.2 Method

To empirically test the relationship between the quality of democracy and globalization, I use multilevel analysis (MLA), a method for analyzing time-series cross-sectional data—that is, data collected on different subjects (in these case countries) at different points in time.

Conceptually, multilevel models can be seen as a hierarchical system of regression equations, thus as an extension of linear regression models (see Hox 2010).

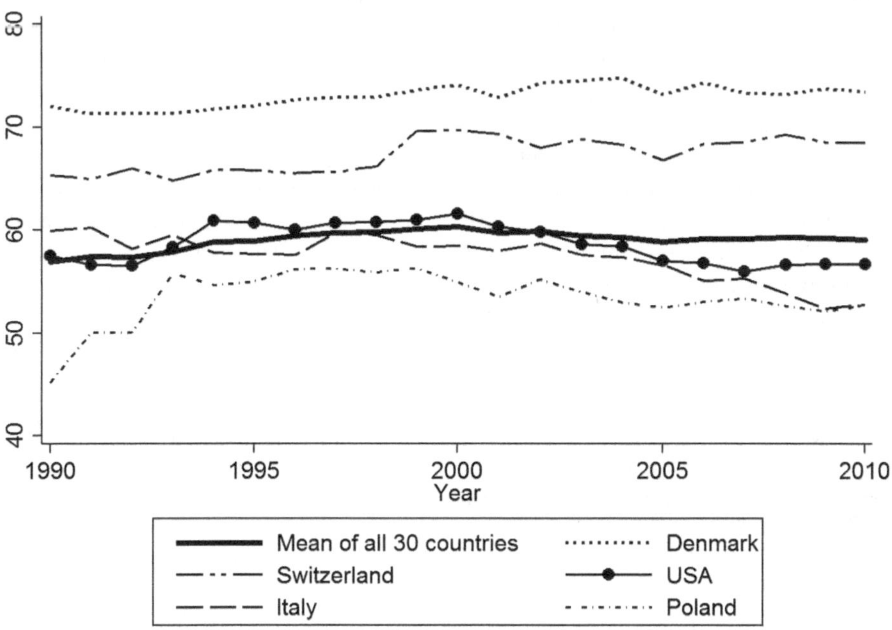

Fig. 10.2 The development of democratic quality in 30 countries. Source: Democracy Barometer

The idea of using MLA for time-series cross-sectional data is to treat observations over time as nested within units (i.e., countries), supposing in this case that the development of the quality of democracy over time (level 1) also differs from country to country (level 2). MLA is thus a suitable approach to determine whether globalization factors can account for some of the variance in the development of democratic quality in different countries over time. More concretely, I use a model commonly called the random-effects model, which allows time-invariant variables to be included and to distinguish between variation within a country and between countries (for details see Rabe-Hesketh and Skrondal 2012, 247ff.). Like linear regression, multilevel models are based on several assumptions about data, notably the normality, linearity, and homoscedasticity of the dependent variable (Hox 2010, 23ff.). Inspection of the residual terms of the Democratic Quality Index shows that none of these assumptions is violated. Furthermore, when using time-series data, we need to correct for autocorrelation of residuals, which I do by using robust standard errors based on the sandwich estimator (Rabe-Hesketh and Skrondal 2012, 326).

In addition to the Democracy Barometer index of democratic quality with its sub-indices of freedom, control, and equality as a dependent (or output) variable and the KOF index of economic, political, and social globalization as an independent (or input) variable (presented in Sects. 10.2.1 and 10.2.2), I use different control variables. The idea here is to control for factors that might have an external influence on democratic quality and thus blur the analysis.[4] First of all, based on modernization theory, economic well-being is presumed to have a positive influence on democratic quality—the wealthier a country is and the fewer economic crises it has experienced, the more likely it will be to develop high regime quality (Przeworski et al. 2000). Accordingly, I use the GDP per capita as a control variable for wealth and development.[5] To account for the impact of economic crises, I use the inflation rate as a measure.[6] I also rely on two country characteristics as control variables, the size of a country and its stability, i.e., the age of a democratic regime.[7] As Bühlmann (2010, 39) has pointed out, most authors suggest a negative connection between country size and quality of democracy, whereas the age of a democratic system is expected to positively influence its democratic quality, since younger democracies are less stable and more prone to political crisis. As the availability of the Democracy Barometer data suggests, my analysis will include the 30 blueprint democracies for the time period from 1990 to 2010. To analyze whether differences in the development of the

[4]For a list of all variables used as well as the data sources, see Table 10.5 in the Appendix.

[5]GDP per capita based on purchasing power parity (PPP). PPP GDP is gross domestic product converted into international dollars using purchasing power parity rates. The data can be found in the World Development Indicators (WDI).

[6]Inflation as measured by the annual growth rate of the GDP implicit deflator shows the rate of price change in the economy as a whole (Source: WDI).

[7]I use the mean of the logged population size between 1990 and 2010 (Source: WDI). Age of democracy is based on a corresponding variable in the Polity IV database. I also use the mean for the period 1990–2010.

quality of democracy among established democratic regimes can be explained by globalization, I look first at the impact of the three globalization factors on the overall quality of democracy index and then at the subindices for the three democratic principles freedom, control, and equality. For all four analyses, I use a stepwise procedure. First, I compare the impact of the different measures of globalization. Second, I check the robustness of this impact by including the control variables. The standard model takes the following form (see Rabe-Hesketh and Skrondal 2012, 265ff.): $Y_{ij} = \beta_0 + \beta X_{ij} + \alpha W_j + \mu_{ij} + \varepsilon_{ij}$. Y, the outcome variable (the Democratic Quality Index or its sub-indices freedom, control, equality) in a country j at time i can be explained by an overall intercept (β_0), time-dependent variables (the X variables and their respective coefficient β, e.g., the globalization indices), time-independent country properties (the W variables and their respective coefficient α; e.g., the age and size of democracy), as well as a between-entity residual term μ_{ij} (variation between countries) and a within-entity residual term ε_{ij} (variation within countries).

10.4.3 Results

The Impact of Globalization on Democratic Quality

The first model in Table 10.1 shows the impact of economic, political, and social globalization on the quality of national democracies. All three indicators have a significant impact on democratic quality, which means that, even controlling for the other indices, each remains significant. When it comes to the direction and size of this impact, the most remarkable difference between the three indicators is that, while social and political globalization seems to have a positive impact on democratic quality, the impact of economic globalization is negative. It is, however, also clearly smaller than the impact of political and social globalization. In Model 2, I add the modernization theory control variables, that is, GDP per capita and inflation. Whereas the wealth of a country as measured by GDP per capita does not have a significant effect, a high inflation rate seems to negatively affect the quality of democracy. But most importantly, all three globalization indices remain significant when controlling for these variables, although the coefficients for political and social globalization decrease slightly. In Model 3, I also add the time-invariant country attributes population size and age of democracy as control variables. In line with theoretical expectations, democracy seems to develop better in smaller and "older" democracies. Furthermore, the three globalization indices maintain their significance: the negative impact of economic openness as well as the positive impact of political and social integration on democratic quality persists.

The Impact of Globalization on the Freedom Principle

The next step was to test the same models on the subindices of democratic quality. When it comes to the impact of globalization on the freedom principle, the results show a similar pattern to those concerned with overall quality: In Model 1 we can see a significant impact of all three globalization indices on the freedom principle,

Table 10.1 The impact of globalization on democratic quality

	Model 1	Model 2	Model 3
Economic globalization	-0.060^{**} (0.025)	-0.069^{***} (0.025)	-0.071^{***} (0.026)
Political globalization	0.138^{***} (0.025)	0.117^{***} (0.026)	0.122^{***} (0.027)
Social globalization	0.122^{***} (0.030)	0.107^{***} (0.032)	0.107^{***} (0.032)
GDP per capita		0.051 (0.039)	0.046 (0.039)
Inflation		-0.101^{**} (0.045)	-0.098^{**} (0.045)
Population size			-0.242^{*} (0.140)
Age of democracy			0.325^{**} (0.146)
Constant	0.351^{***} (0.040)	0.374^{***} (0.041)	0.385^{***} (0.087)
Time-level random effects	0.196^{***} (0.025)	0.194^{***} (0.025)	0.176^{***} (0.023)
Country-level random effects	0.044^{***} (0.001)	0.044^{***} (0.001)	0.044^{***} (0.001)
Number of observations	620	620	620
Log-likelihood	965.25	968.35	971.33

Note: $^{***}p < 0.01$; $^{**}p < 0.05$; $^{*}p < 0.1$. Standard errors in brackets. All variables have been rescaled on a scale from 0 to 1, where 0 indicates the lowest value and 1 the highest value of the variable. All models estimated using STATA

with a negative influence of economic globalization and a positive one for political and social globalization. This impact also remains significant after controlling for wealth and economic crises (Model 2). These two control variables are both significant: economic crises in the form of inflation have a negative impact on the development of the freedom principle, and wealth (contrary to the theory) is also negatively related to performance at the level of freedom. Model 3 shows that the country-related control variables population size and age of democracy are both significant, showing the theoretically expected direction. Most importantly, however, all three globalization indices again remain significant after controlling for these variables (see Table 10.2).

The Impact of Globalization on the Control Principle

The next subindex of democratic quality is the control principle. Model 1 shows a significant negative impact of economic globalization on control, but on a lower significance level than in the previous models. Political globalization does not show a significant effect, whereas social globalization relates positively to democratic control to a significant degree. When it comes to the control variables, Model 2 shows that GDP per capita does not significantly affect the control principle, while inflation has a negative impact. In Model 3, the control variables age and size of a democracy do not display significant effects, whereas the significance of the two globalization indices persists (see Table 10.3).

The Impact of Globalization on the Equality Principle

The last component of the analysis is the equality principle. Again, the effects of the three globalization indices differ: According to Model 1, only two of the three globalization indices are significant when it comes to equality, political and social globalization, which both have a positive effect. Economic globalization is not

Table 10.2 The impact of globalization on the freedom principle

	Model 1	Model 2	Model 3
Economic globalization	-0.074^{**} (0.030)	-0.074^{**} (0.030)	-0.078^{***} (0.030)
Political globalization	0.115^{***} (0.030)	0.091^{***} (0.031)	0.099^{***} (0.031)
Social globalization	0.077^{**} (0.035)	0.111^{***} (0.037)	0.110^{***} (0.037)
GDP per capita		-0.116^{**} (0.046)	-0.120^{***} (0.046)
Inflation		-0.183^{***} (0.053)	-0.179^{***} (0.053)
Population size			-0.450^{***} (0.162)
Age of democracy			0.409^{**} (0.169)
Constant	0.460^{***} (0.047)	0.500^{***} (0.049)	0.589^{***} (0.100)
Time-level random effects	0.231^{***} (0.030)	0.238^{***} (0.031)	0.203^{***} (0.026)
Country-level random effects	0.052^{***} (0.002)	0.051^{***} (0.001)	0.051^{***} (0.001)
Number of observations	620	620	620
Log-likelihood	862.76	872.52	877.32

Notes: $^{***}p < 0.01$; $^{**}p < 0.05$; $^{*}p < 0.1$. Standard errors in brackets. All variables have been rescaled on a scale from 0 to 1, where 0 indicates the lowest value and 1 the highest value of the variable. All models estimated using STATA

significant in this model. Models 2 and 3 show the theoretically expected effects for the economic control variables (positive effects of GDP, negative effects of economic crises on equality), whereas the country-specific control variables are not significant. The positive effect of political globalization on equality remains significant, whereas social globalization is no longer significant in Models 2 and 3 (see Table 10.4).

10.5 Interpretation

First of all, the empirical analysis makes it clear that, as expected, the relationship between globalization and democratic quality is complex and multilayered. Different aspects of globalization indeed seem to have a varying impact on the three democratic principles. When looking at the overall Democratic Quality Index, strong economic globalization, that is, economic openness and integration into the world market, seems to relate negatively to a high level of democratic quality. This effect is independent of wealth differences, economic crises, and the size and age of a democracy. Political globalization, the degree to which a country is integrated into supra- and international institutions, as well as social globalization, flows of information, culture, and migration, are positively linked to a high level of democratic quality, again, independently of the control variables mentioned. Globalization can therefore not be said to have a uniformly positive or negative effect on democratic quality but seems to work in different directions. Given the complexity of processes commonly assembled under this label, this is hardly surprising.

But how can these results be interpreted in relation to the theoretical hypotheses about the effects of globalization on the three democratic principles presented in

Table 10.3 The impact of globalization on the control principle

	Model 1	Model 2	Model 3
Economic globalization	−0.077* (0.042)	−0.076* (0.043)	−0.072* (0.043)
Political globalization	−0.005 (0.042)	0.025 (0.044)	0.021 (0.045)
Social globalization	0.094* (0.050)	0.106** (0.053)	0.105** (0.053)
GDP per capita		−0.039 (0.066)	−0.042 (0.066)
Inflation		−0.159** (0.076)	−0.158** (0.076)
Population size			0.076 (0.166)
Age of democracy			0.098 (0.172)
Constant	0.466*** (0.048)	0.431*** (0.051)	0.360*** (0.104)
Time-level random effects	0.210*** (0.027)	0.208*** (0.027)	0.206*** (0.027)
Country-level random effects	0.074*** (0.002)	0.074*** (0.002)	0.074*** (0.002)
Number of observations	620	620	620
Log-likelihood	655.30	657.57	657.90

Note: *** $p < 0.01$; ** $p < 0.05$; * $p < 0.1$. Standard errors in brackets. All variables have been rescaled on a scale from 0 to 1, where 0 indicates the lowest value and 1 the highest value of the variable. All models estimated using STATA

Sect. 10.3? When it comes to the *freedom principle*, the positive hypothesis assumes that globalization, through the pressure exerted by a transnational civil society and the increased availability of information, increases individual liberties, the rule of law, and the public sphere. As both political and social globalization turn out to be positively correlated with a high level of freedom, the empirical results seem to support this hypothesis. The negative hypothesis, on the contrary, claims that globalization has led governments to place security over liberty and to cut back on important civil rights in the name of combating terrorism and other globalized crimes. The fact that economic globalization is actually negatively related to the level of freedom might be interpreted as a sign that this hypothesis has a certain explanatory power, too. In general, it is interesting to note that the coefficients for the impact of the different globalization indices on freedom are higher than those for control and equality, which points to the fact that the freedom principle is more strongly affected by globalization than the other principles. Accordingly, a comparatively high proportion of the positive and negative effects globalization has on democratic quality seem to reflect on the freedom principle.

At the level of *control*, the positive hypothesis is based on the notion that political globalization in the form of membership in multilateral organizations enhances governmental control because it reduces the influence of special interest factions and increases government capabilities. The nonsignificant relationship between political globalization and control cannot support this hypothesis. Moreover, globalization is presumed to shape competition between democratic jurisdictions, making it harder for inefficient and badly adapted jurisdictions to be maintained, thus also increasing the quality of democratic governance. The positive effect of social globalization could be interpreted as support for this hypothesis. The negative hypothesis asserts that the power of governments to govern is declining owing to the shift of political authority to supranational

Table 10.4 The impact of globalization on the equality principle

	Model 1	Model 2	Model 3
Economic globalization	−0.003 (0.033)	−0.034 (0.032)	−0.035 (0.033)
Political globalization	0.199*** (0.033)	0.159*** (0.034)	0.163*** (0.034)
Social globalization	0.139*** (0.039)	0.057 (0.040)	0.058 (0.040)
GDP per capita		0.282*** (0.050)	0.274*** (0.050)
Inflation		−0.131** (0.058)	−0.129** (0.058)
Population size			−0.110 (0.140)
Age of democracy			0.229 (0.146)
Constant	0.252*** (0.041)	0.283*** (0.042)	0.261*** (0.087)
Time-level random effects	0.185*** (0.024)	0.183*** (0.024)	0.175*** (0.023)
Country-level random effects	0.058*** (0.0029	0.056*** (0.002)	0.056*** (0.002)
Number of observations	620	620	620
Log-likelihood	807.23	824.32	825.59

Note: ***$p < 0.01$; **$p < 0.05$; *$p < 0.1$. Standard errors in brackets. All variables have been rescaled on a scale from 0 to 1, where 0 indicates the lowest value and 1 the highest value of the variable. All models estimated using STATA

institutions and economic actors and that globalization strengthens national executives to the detriment of legislatives, thus adversely affecting fulfillment of the control function. Indeed, the nonsignificant relationship between political globalization and control runs counter to the idea that the shift of political authority to supranational institutions is responsible for a declining control capacity of governments or for a degradation of legislative power. But the fact that economic globalization is negatively correlated with the control principle could be taken as evidence that the increasing influence of economic actors does weaken legislatives and might be responsible for a general decrease in democratic power to govern.

As far as the third democratic principle, *equality*, is concerned, the positive hypothesis assumes that globalization steers national economic growth and wealth, which, in turn, enhances democratic equality. The negative hypothesis, by contrast, states that by increasing social inequalities and causing social disintegration and alienation, globalization negatively affects political equality. Interestingly, neither of the hypotheses is supported by the data, as economic globalization does not have a significant impact on the equality principle. However, both hypotheses are indirect, assuming that economic globalization affects the social conditions of democratic societies—either positively by fueling growth and development or negatively by increasing social disparities. The fact that wealth (as measured by GDP per capita) is positively linked with a high level of equality, whereas economic crises (as measured by inflation) imply a decline in equality seems to confirm the notion that economic performance and political equality are indeed associated. The Democracy Barometer, though, measures only political equality. One could accordingly assume that either changes in social preconditions caused by globalization do not (yet) measurably affect political equality in democratic regimes. Another possible explanation would be that over the period in question (1990–2010) and across all 30 countries, the positive effect of increased growth and development through economic openness (mainly in Eastern European countries during the 1990s) somehow balance the negative effects of growing social inequalities (especially in Western European countries after 2000). Furthermore, the argument that globalization decreases the transparency of political processes, thus making citizens less capable of understanding and embracing democracy, is also not supported by the data. On the contrary, the positive relationship between political and social globalization and equality rather implies that increased information flows and political internationalization enhance equality: potential support for the positive hypothesis that by reducing information and transaction costs and by improving the situation of women, homosexuals, ethnic and religious minorities, and other groups formerly discriminated against in the political process, globalization ameliorates political equality.

Lastly, it is interesting to note that my results concerning the impact of globalization on the overall quality of democracy differ from Bühlmann's (2010) findings in a similar analysis: whereas he determines a significant positive impact of economic as well as political globalization on democratic quality, my results show a negative impact of economic globalization and a positive one for political and social globalization. As I use the same data (KOF and Democracy Barometer), these differences can most likely be explained by the fact that he used an older version of the Democracy Barometer index. His analysis thus covers only the period from 1995 to 2005, whereas I use the newer version of the Democracy Barometer running from 1990 to 2010. Also, the Democracy Barometer index has been revised and brought up to date since then, so that several components are now weighted differently. All in all, these differences in the dataset seem to change the outcome of the analysis.

10.6 Conclusion

Answering the question whether globalization is indeed a danger for the quality of democracies is not only of theoretical but also of practical relevance. Established democracies face economic and political crises that are directly or indirectly caused by globalization processes—be it the looming bankruptcy of entire states such as Greece or the growing success of nationalist and Euro-skeptical parties like the Front National in France or the Swiss People's Party (SVP) in Switzerland. In order to deal with such challenges, it is important to know whether and how democratic quality is affected by globalization. Should national sovereignty be reinforced to re-legitimate democracy, or can global crises be resolved by more economic openness and stronger international cooperation? Clearly, the relationship between globalization and democratic quality is much too complex and multifaceted to allow an explicit answer to this question. Yet, the results of my analysis can provide some indications.

The most important result of the empirical analysis is certainly that globalization processes have various effects. Whereas economic globalization interacts negatively with democratic quality, both on the overall index of democratic quality and on the three principles (however, not significantly in the case of equality), political and social globalization, although not significantly in every model, generally have a positive impact on democratic quality. This pattern shows that economic integration and openness apparently tend to be accompanied by stagnation or decline in democratic performance rather than by an increase. Thus the fear that politics cannot easily follow economics in operating on a worldwide scale and that economic considerations overwhelm, for instance, environmental or social considerations seems to be justified. There are obviously fundamental tensions between national democracy and globalized capitalism, and the loss of national autonomy in economic and financial matters is, from a democratic perspective, hardly justifiable. Political integration in international and supranational organizations, though, does not have a measurable negative impact on the quality of national democracies; on the contrary, like social globalization in the form of communication, cultural exchange and migration, it clearly shows positive effects on the performance of established democracies. Globalization hence offers potential for developing and improving democratic structures. The enlargement of the political and public spheres to the global level apparently generates greater potential for civil society control and deliberation and strengthens important democratic functions such as political freedom and equality. Notably for often discriminated groups such as women, homosexuals, and other minorities, democracy has actually visibly improved over the past two decades, and globalization seems to have contributed to this.

These effects, and this is the second interesting result, do not distribute equally across the three democratic principles. The freedom principle is most affected both positively and negatively by globalization. Individual liberties, the rule of law, and the public sphere clearly profit from political and social internationalization but are adversely affected by economic openness. Democratic control is also negatively affected by economic liberalization, but less strongly, and seems to profit from increased social globalization. Democratic equality, somewhat surprisingly from a theoretical perspective, is the least affected principle. Only political integration positively affects equality, while there are no significant negative effects. What conclusions can we draw from these results?

On the one hand, the widespread fear that globalization has brought democracy to the edge of crisis and has already destroyed most of its foundations is clearly exaggerated. Then again, the liberal paradigm that economic growth and development will quasi automatically lead to better political regimes by fueling growth and development is more than questionable, too. In general, putting presumable economic "needs" over political considerations is very likely to cause democratic deficits. And most importantly, just because there is allegedly no alternative to globalization does not mean that its course, expansion, and consequences are beyond the influence of political actors. Clearly, globalization is not just a temporary phenomenon, and, whether we like it or not, isolation and complete protectionism do not seem reasonable (or desirable) options for dealing with it. Still, democratic governments do have a range of policy options they can take—for instance, enhancing political control over economic and financial flows, reducing tax competition, and protecting their citizens against globalization-induced crises by adjusting labor markets more to the needs of citizens and strengthening instead of dismantling social security systems (see Chap. 11). Similarly, more democratic control over intelligence services and a better protection of civil liberties are politically feasible and could potentially absorb some of the negative effects of globalization on democratic quality. Further, it has become increasingly important to deal with electorate discontent and growing populism, as abstention from voting on the one hand and preferences for authoritarian solutions and nationalist, racist, or fascist discourses on the other are troubling many established democracies. Although new civil society movements are strengthened through globalization and partly fill the participation void, they cannot provide equal representation of societal interests. In order to prevent the deepening of a societal cleavage between globalization winners and losers, both political and socioeconomic equality need to be reinforced. At the same time, governments should not only take measures to counteract the negative effects of globalization but also underline the positive outcomes of internationalization, lead their electorates away from the temptation to turn in on themselves, and seek ways to reconcile them with cultural and political globalization, instead of miring down in populist discourses. In the long term, important democratic attributes such as cultural openness, political integration, and the free movement of persons will prove sustainable only if, at the same time, economic "freedoms" such as the unregulated movement of capital, goods, and services are subjected to more regulation in accordance with social and democratic criteria.

Appendix

Table 10.5 List of all variables and their sources

Variable	Source
Democratic Quality Index Freedom (Index) Control (Index) Equality (Index)	Bochsler, Daniel; Merkel, Wolfgang (project leaders); Bousbah, Karima; Bühlmann, Marc; Giebler, Heiko; Hänni, Miriam; Heyne, Lea; Müller, Lisa; Ruth, Saskia; Wessels, Bernhard (2014). Democracy Barometer. Aarau: Zentrum für Demokratie Data download via http://www.democracybarometer.org/dataset_de.html. Accessed on 10.10.2014
KOF Index of Globalization Economic globalization Political globalization Social globalization	Dreher, Axel, Noel Gaston and Pim Martens (2008), Measuring Globalisation—Gauging its Consequences. New York: Springer. (http://globalization.kof.ethz.ch) Data download via http://www.qog.pol.gu.se/data/datadownloads/qogstandarddata/. Accessed on 10.10.2014
GDP per capita Inflation Population size	World Development Indicators, The World Bank, Coverage 1960–2012, updated July 2013. (http://data.worldbank.org/data-catalog/world-development-indicators) Data download via http://www.qog.pol.gu.se/data/datadownloads/qogstandarddata/. Accessed on 10.10.2014
Age of democracy *(Original name: Durable)*	Marshall, Monty G. and Ted Robert Gurr (2012). Polity IV project: Political regime characteristics and transitions, 1800–2012. Center for Systemic Peace: University of Maryland Data download via http://www.systemicpeace.org/inscr/inscr.htm. Accessed on 10.10.2014

References

Bigo, D. (2006). *Illiberal practices of liberal regimes. The (in)security games*. Paris: L'Harmattan.

Bochsler, D., & Merkel, W., with Bousbah, K., Bühlmann, M., Giebler, H., Hänni, M., Heyne, L., Müller, L., Ruth, S., & Weßels, B. (2014). *Democracy barometer. Methodology*. Version 4. Aarau: Zentrum für Demokratie. http://www.democracybarometer.org/Data/Methodical%20Explanatory%201990-2012.pdf. Accessed 10 October 2014.

Brennan, G. (2005). Globalisation and varieties of democracy. In R. Zimmerling (Ed.), *Globalisation and democracy* (pp. 21–36). Tampere: Tampere University Press.

Bühlmann, M. (2010). *The beauty and the beast? A tale of democratic crises and globalization*. Bern: National Centre of Competence in Research Democracy. (Working Paper. Challenges to democracy in the 21st century).

Bühlmann, M., Merkel, W., Müller, L., Giebler, H., & Weßels, B. (2012). Demokratiebarometer: ein neues Instrument zur Messung von Demokratiequalität. *Zeitschrift für Vergleichende Politikwissenschaft, 6*(S1), 115–159.

Busch, A. (2011). Freiheits- und Bürgerrechte nach 9/11. In T. Jäger (Ed.), *Die Welt nach 9/11. Auswirkungen des Terrorismus auf Staatenwelt und Gesellschaft* (pp. 861–881). VS Verlag für Sozialwissenschaften: Wiesbaden.

Buzan, B., & Waever, O. (2003). *Regions and powers. A guide to the global security order*. Cambridge: Cambridge University Press.

Cerny, P. G. (1999). Globalization and the erosion of democracy. *European Journal of Political Research, 36*(1), 1–26.

Cox, R. W. (1997). *Approaches to world order*. Cambridge: Cambridge University Press.

Dickenson, D. (1997). Counting women in: Globalization, democratization and the women's movement. *The Transformation of Democracy, 7*(7), 97–120.

Dreher, A. (2005). *Does globalization affect growth? Evidence from a new Index of Globalization*. Konstanz: Thurgauer Wirtschaftsinstitut.

Goodhart, M. (2001). Democracy, globalization, and the problem of state. *Polity, 33*(4), 527–546.

Guillén, M. F. (2001). Is globalization civilizing, destructive, or feeble? A critique of five key debates in the social science literature. *Annual Review of Sociology, 27*, 235–260.

Held, D. (1998). Rethinking democracy. Globalization and democratic theory. In W. Streeck (Ed.), *Internationale Wirtschaft, nationale Demokratie. Herausforderungen für die Demokratietheorie* (pp. 59–78). Frankfurt am Main: Campus.

Held, D. (2000). *Models of democracy*. Cambridge: Polity Press.

Held, D., MacGrew, A., Goldblatt, D., & Perraton, J. (1999). *Global transformations. Politics, economics and culture*. Cambridge: Polity Press.

Hox, J. J. (2010). *Multilevel analysis. Techniques and applications*. New York, NY: Routledge.

Inglehart, R., & Welzel, C. (2005). *Modernization, cultural change, and democracy. The human development sequence*. Cambridge: Cambridge University Press.

Keohane, R. O., Macedo, S., & Moravcsik, A. (2009). Democracy-enhancing multilateralism. *International Organization, 13*(2), 1–31.

Krasner, S. D. (1993). Economic interdependence and independent statehood. In R. H. Jackson & A. James (Eds.), *States in a changing world. An analysis of regional experience* (pp. 301–321). Oxford: Oxford University Press.

Kriesi, H. P., Grande, E., Lachat, R., Dolezal, M., Bornschier, S., & Frey, T. (2008). *West European politics in the age of globalization*. Cambridge: Cambridge University Press.

Kriesi, H. P., Bochsler, D., Matthes, J., Lavenex, S., Bühlmann, M., & Esser, F. (Eds.). (2013). *Democracy in the age of globalization and mediatization*. Basingstoke: Palgrave Macmillan.

Kupchan, C. A. (2012). *The democratic Malaise. Globalization and the threat to the West*. http://www.foreignaffairs.com/articles/136783/charles-a-kupchan/the-democratic-malaise. Accessed 4 June 2014.

Lavenex, S. (2013). Globalization and the vertical challenge to democracy. In H. P. Kriesi, D. Bochsler, J. Matthes, S. Lavenex, M. Bühlmann, & F. Esser (Eds.), *Democracy in the age of globalization and mediatization* (pp. 105–134). Basingstoke: Palgrave Macmillan.

Li, Q., & Reuveny, R. (2003). Economic globalization and democracy. An empirical analysis. *British Journal of Political Science, 33*(1), 29–54.

Lipset, S. M. (1959). Some social requisites of democracy. Economic development and political legitimacy. *The American Political Science Review, 53*(1), 69–105.

Loch, D., & Heitmeyer, W. (2001). *Schattenseiten der Globalisierung. Rechtsradikalismus, Rechtspopulismus und separatistischer Regionalismus in westlichen Demokratien*. Frankfurt am Main: Suhrkamp.

López-Córdova, E., & Meissner, C. M. (2008). The impact of international trade on democracy: A long-run perspective. *World Politics, 60*(04), 539–575.

Mau, S. (2007). *Transnationale Vergesellschaftung. Die Entgrenzung sozialer Lebenswelten*. Frankfurt am Main: Campus.

McGrew, A. G. (Ed.). (1997). *The transformation of democracy? Globalization and territorial democracy*. Cambridge: Polity Press.

Merkel, W. (2004). Embedded and defective democracies. *Democratization, 11*(5), 33–58.

Merkel, W. (2010). *Systemtransformation. Eine Einführung in die Theorie und Empirie der Transformationsforschung*. Wiesbaden: VS Verlag für Sozialwissenschaften.

Moravcsik, A. (1993). Preference and power in the European Community. A liberal intergovernmentalist approach. *Journal of Common Market Studies, 31*(4), 473–524.

Neal, A. W. (2009). Securitization and risk at the EU Border. The origins of FRONTEX. *Journal of Common Market Studies, 47*(2), 333–356.

Papadopoulos, Y. (2010). Accountability and multilevel governance. More accountability, less democracy? *West European Politics, 33*(5), 1030–1049.

Przeworski, A., Alvarez, M. E., Cheibub, J. A., & Limongi, F. (2000). *Democracy and development*. In *Political Institutions and well-being in the World, 1950–1990*. Cambridge: Cambridge University Press.

Putnam, R. D. (1988). Diplomacy and domestic politics: the logic of two-level games. *International Organization, 42*(3), 427–460.

Rabe-Hesketh, S., & Skrondal, A. (2012). *Multilevel and longitudinal modeling using Stata*. College Station: Stata Press Publication.

Sassen, S. (1996). *Losing control? Sovereignty in an age of globalization*. New York, NY: Columbia University Press.

Sassen, S. (2007). *Sociology of globalization*. New York, NY: W.W. Norton.

Streeck, W. (Ed.). (1998). *Internationale Wirtschaft, nationale Demokratie. Herausforderungen für die Demokratietheorie*. Frankfurt am Main: Campus.

Streeck, W. (2013). *Gekaufte Zeit. Die vertagte Krise des demokratischen Kapitalismus*. Berlin: Suhrkamp.

Vanberg, V. (2002). Globalization, democracy and citizens' sovereignty: Can competition among governments enhance democracy? *Constitutional Political Economy, 11*(1), 87–112.

Zimmerling, R. (2005). *Globalization and democracy*. Tampere: Tampere University Press.

Zürn, M. (1998). *Regieren jenseits des Nationalstaates. Globalisierung und Denationalisierung als Chance*. Frankfurt am Main: Suhrkamp.

Zürn, M., & Ecker-Ehrhardt, M. (Eds.). (2013). *Die Politisierung der Weltpolitik. Umkämpfte internationale Institutionen*. Berlin: Suhrkamp.

Chapter 11
Is Capitalism Compatible with Democracy?

Wolfgang Merkel

11.1 Introduction

Throughout the past two centuries, capitalism and democracy have proven themselves the most successful systems of economic and political order. Following the demise of Soviet-style socialism after 1989 and the transformations of China's economy, capitalism has become the predominant system around the world. Only a few isolated countries such as North Korea have been able to resist the success of capitalism through the use of brute force. The market has become the main mechanism for economic coordination and the maximization of profits. The global competition of economic systems has been clearly won. Yet capitalism in the singular conceals the differences in the "varieties of capitalism" (Hall and Soskice 2001).[1] China's state capitalism, the Anglo-Saxon neoliberal strand of capitalism, or the Scandinavian welfare state economies differ substantially from one another. They function or malfunction rather differently in conjunction with democratic regimes.

A first German version was co-authored by Jürgen Kocka in: Wolfgang Merkel (Ed.) Demokratie und Krise (Democracy and Crisis). Wiesbaden, Springer, 2015

[1]Hall and Soskice, however, only describe two varieties of capitalism that they see represented in the context of the OECD: *liberal market economies* and *coordinated market economies*. New hybrid types of Manchester-like state capitalism in China, gangster capitalism in Russia and Ukraine during the 1990s, and crony capitalism in Southeast Asia are not taken into consideration here, since they have emerged outside the context of the OECD.

W. Merkel (✉)
Department of Democracy and Democratization, WZB Berlin Social Science Center, Berlin, Germany

Humboldt-Universität zu Berlin, Berlin, Germany
e-mail: wolfgang.merkel@wzb.eu

W. Merkel, S. Kneip (eds.), *Democracy and Crisis*,
https://doi.org/10.1007/978-3-319-72559-8_11

The success of democracy in the last quarter of the twentieth century was impressive. However, democracy's success pales in comparison to the spread of capitalism throughout the world. If we take the minimal standards of democracy as a measurement, there were 123 countries (out of around 200) that could be called "electoral democracies" in 2010 (Freedom House 2010). If the much more stringent concept of a liberal democracy is applied, only 60 countries can be classified as liberal rule of law-based democracies (Merkel 2010). Yet both electoral and liberal democracies coexist with capitalist economies. Historical evidence also confirms that no developed democracy has been able to exist without capitalism. Vice versa this is not the case. National Socialist Germany, the People's Republic of China, Singapore, and the capitalist dictatorships of Latin America or Asia in the twentieth century all demonstrate that capitalism can coexist or even flourish in the context of different forms of political government, such as democracy and dictatorship.

The impressive advancement of democracy around the world coincides with the often-cited malaise of the established democracies. Since the turn of the millennium, an ever-increasing number of theories and analyses have defined mature democracies along the lines of "diminished subtypes of democracy" (Offe 2003), "post-democracies" (Crouch 2004), "defective democracies" (Merkel 2004), or mere "façades" (Streeck 2014, p. 177). Capitalism is primarily blamed for this development. Financial capitalism in particular increases inequalities in income and political participation, curbs the powers of parliaments, and seriously constrains the capacity of national executives to govern. The latest financial crisis of 2008 and the subsequent Euro crisis have changed thinking about the complementary nature of capitalism and democracy. Both theoretical and empirical analysis reveal an increasing number of contradictions—even incompatibilities—between capitalism and democracy. Albeit with new arguments and insights, the debate contains some theoretical links with the leftist debate in the early 1970s about the legitimacy crisis of the "late capitalist state" (Offe 1972; Habermas 1975; O'Connor 1973).

How deep-seated are the incompatibilities of "varieties of capitalism" with different varieties of democracy? To what extent has capitalism in its varieties become a challenge for democracy and its normative standards? In our approach, capitalism is the challenger, the independent variable, while democracy functions as the dependent variable. Yet this independent variable is in constant change, conditioned by political, social, and economic influences. Our argument addresses the following topics:

- The main features of capitalism and democracy
- The basic different logics of the two regimes
- The (in-)compatibility of specific varieties of the two regimes
- The specifics of current financial capitalism
- Analyzing the challenges financial capitalism poses to "embedded democracies"

11.2 Three Types of Capitalism

The main difference between types of capitalism lies in the relationship between the market and the state. Three types of capitalism have prevailed at various times in democracies over the last two centuries. They are historical types but can also be read as ideal types, since the number of defining elements is reduced to the most important ones and description of their concrete properties is stylized.

Market-liberal capitalism: Its name deriving from the prevailing market principles in relations between different companies, this type was dominant in Europe and North America throughout much of the nineteenth century. State institutions largely refrained from interfering in markets (including labor markets) or in economic and social policy. Taxes and expenditures were low; the welfare state had emerged only in embryonic form.

Organized and embedded capitalism: Within the context of technological and organizational innovation, capitalism developed internal needs for coordination and regulation. Moreover, a barely regulated form of capitalism brought increasing social tensions. Together, these two factors were the driving force behind a more organized form of capitalism. This became apparent on several fronts: large businesses began to find ways of cooperating that limited competition (such as cartels, mergers, and associations) and ways to identify and represent common interests. Furthermore, the state began to interfere increasingly in the economy and society by introducing labor laws, selective subsidies, nationalization, and increasing regulation but also by creating the welfare state and expanding social policy—in Germany already in place since the 1880s (Winkler 1974; Lash and Urry 1987). The *organized capitalism* that ensued in the twentieth century took different forms: in the USA the New Deal of the 1930s and 1940s, in the Federal Republic of Germany and other European countries the social market economy, and in France and Scandinavia as distinctly Keynesian welfare state capitalism. It has, however, also existed in dictatorial varieties, as in National Socialist Germany and—again in a different form—in the state capitalism of East Asia during recent decades.[2]

Neoliberal capitalism: From the late 1970s, "neoliberal" critique gained traction, sometimes in sharp contrast to Keynesian welfare state capitalism. It stressed market mechanisms, the principle of capitalist self-regulation, and the limits of state regulation (Harvey 2007). John Maynard Keynes's concept of managing capitalism through the demand side and Karl Polanyi's idea of a socially *embedded capitalism* were replaced by Friedrich August von Hayek's understanding of the market as a *spontaneous order* and by Milton Friedman's pledge for a minimal state where state interference in the economy is restricted to modest variation in the supply of money. A new phase of capitalism began, shaped by deregulation, privatization, and partial deconstruction of the welfare state. Globalization was

[2]The labels for this type of capitalism vary: "organized capitalism," "coordinated capitalism," "Keynesian welfare state" (KWS), or "Fordism." We use the first two terms interchangeably and take KWS as a variety of "coordinated capitalism" that is particularly compatible with democracy.

advancing quickly, international financial capitalism became exceedingly important, and socioeconomic inequalities within different societies began to increase.

11.3 Three Types of Democracy

The definition of democracy is highly contested: liberal, social, pluralistic, elitist, decisionist, communitarian, cosmopolitan, republican, deliberative, participatory, feminist, critical, postmodern, and multicultural concepts of democracy all compete (Lembcke et al. 2012). From a more simplified perspective, however, three groups of democracy theories can be identified: the minimalist, middle-ground, and maximizing theories. Depending on which concept of democracy is applied, a "crisis of democracy" can seldom, often, or almost always be identified. Our point of reference is the middle-ground model of democracy, more precisely, the concept of embedded democracy.[3]

Embedded democracy consists of five partial regimes: democratic elections (A), political participation (B), civil liberties (C), the institutional protection of the separation of powers (*horizontal accountability*) (D), and the guarantee that the effective use of power by democratically elected representatives is assured de jure and de facto (E). In the democratic system, partial regimes fulfill specific functions. Each faces particular internal and external challenges. Each has its own "crisis capacity" and specific inter- and independence within embedded democracy. Whether or not a partial regime is infected by crisis and how far a crisis can expand beyond a certain partial regime depends on these factors. In what follows, we concentrate only on challenges to democracy that are caused by capitalism and its varieties.

11.4 Compatibilities and Incompatibilities

The basic logics of capitalism and democracy differ fundamentally, and there is considerable tension between the two. The basis of their legitimacy differs: unequally distributed property rights versus equal civil rights. They are dominated by different procedures: for-profit transactions in capitalism, debate, and majority decision-making in democratic politics. The clear aim of capitalist activities is the egoistic pursuit of individual advantage, even though according to Adam Smith, it can be claimed that such egoistic actions serve the common good. The realization of the common good is the aim of democratic politics; in this context, however, it is clear that the outcome of competition and cooperation between pluralist interests is coming to light only a posteriori (Fraenkel 1974[1964], p. 189). Under capitalism,

[3]Cf. more extensively, Merkel (2004).

decisions and their implementation lead to a degree of economic and social inequality (in income, wealth, power, and life chances) that is hardly acceptable in a democracy built on principles rooted in equal rights, opportunities, and duties. Vice versa, full application of democratic decision-making—general and equal participation as well as majority decisions and minority protection—is inconceivable under the rules of capitalism. Thus, capitalism is not democratic; democracy is not capitalist.

This is only one aspect; two others must be considered. On the one hand, it is a fundamental rule of liberal democracy that the reach of political decisions has to be limited: by securing basic rights (among them the right to private property since the time of John Locke and the Enlightenment), through constitutions and the rule of law, and not least through recognition of the principle that democratic decision-making is a key element of the political system. However, other partial systems must have the freedom to work according to different logics (Luhmann: "communication codes") within the framework given by a politically set and only democratically alterable constitution (Walzer 1983; Luhmann 1995).

Capitalism and democracy can easily conflict in two situations: if the distribution and use of property rights lead to an accumulation of wealth large enough to hinder politics through capitalist pressure and if democratic decisions are taken to massively limit the use of property rights. On balance, rights to property and use of capital should in general be limited and regulated by democratic governments if they threaten to eclipse or distort codes for democratic decision-making in the political sphere. Within the hierarchy of legitimacy, democratic rights can claim normative superiority as long as they do not violate human rights and abolish property rights.

On the other hand, it is also important to highlight certain affinities and congruencies between capitalism and democracy. Competition and electoral decisions play key roles in both contexts. In theory, capitalism and democracy share common enemies: the uncontrollable agglomeration of state or economic power, disorder, unpredictability, and corruption. But there is a decisive difference: whereas certain forms of capitalism produce and function with an extreme concentration of wealth and capital, democracies cannot coexist with a similar constellation and concentration of power. Finally, capitalism and democracy can support each other. Capitalism finds the going hard without a generally predictable state order, something most likely to be achieved in the long run through democratic means. It is similarly true that socially embedded capitalism is most likely to achieve sustainable growth, which in turn legitimizes and strengthens democratic institutions.

11.5 Social Welfare Capitalism: The Golden Age of Coexistence?

In the second half and especially in the third quarter of the twentieth century, an increasingly organized form of capitalism proved particularly compatible with democratic politics in Western Europe, North America, and Japan. This was the result of an increasingly expansive, interventionist welfare state that interfered with the capitalist economy by regulating, stabilizing, and equalizing it. The "Keynesian welfare state" (Offe 1984) emerged in certain Northern and Continental European countries as one form of social and coordinated capitalism. A specific system of strong interdependence developed between the state and the market, between democratic and economic institutions and the capitalist economy. Economic actors were multiply embedded, regulated, and socially obligated. The state's decision-making opened increasingly toward economic and social influence under the label of "tripartite neo-corporatism" (Schmitter 1974, 1982). Even elements of democracy were introduced into the economic system, such as codetermination and workers' councils. Several important historical factors facilitated development toward this system of a rather cooperative but nevertheless often precarious coexistence: rapid economic growth in the years following World War II, the shocking experience of the Great Recession in 1929, and political catastrophes during World War II and the interwar years. The ongoing critique of capitalism in the name of democracy, and social justice in intellectual and political debates also contributed to the social and political embedding of capitalism. A major driving force behind this development was, however, the challenge to the Western model of capitalism by a non-capitalist alternative in the form of Soviet-style *actually existing socialism*. This period proved to be the zenith of coexistence between social capitalism and social democracy in Northern and Western Europe. Yet it remained incomplete, precarious, and different from country to country (Esping-Andersen 1990; Hall and Soskice 2001).

11.6 Financial Capitalism[4]: The Breakup of Peaceful Coexistence

Since the 1970s, capitalism has changed in a way that has challenged its compatibility with democracy considerably. The turn toward neoliberalism, deregulation, and globalization and the rise of financialization have contributed significantly to these changes (Heires and Nölke 2013). The global financial crisis since 2008 has

[4]The term financial capitalism resembles Rudolf Hilferding's "Finance Capital" (*Das Finanzkapital*, Wien 1910) terminologically. Hilferding described the transformation of competitive liberal capitalism into monopolistic finance capital. However, whereas Hilferding's "organized capitalism" must be understood as a fusion of industrial, mercantile, and banking

manifested and intensified the critical elements of this new divergence: it has once more changed the relationship between the economy and the state, capitalism, and democracy. The crisis of capitalism threatens to turn into a crisis of democracy.

Beginning with Margaret Thatcher and Ronald Reagan in the early 1980s, there were concerted efforts among most capitalist economies for more deregulation and privatization, as well as (in some countries) significant cuts in welfare benefits.[5] The process was initiated and driven by Anglo-Saxon capitalism, particularly in the UK and USA. Following Friedrich von Hayek (neoclassical fiscal conservatism) and Milton Friedman (monetarism and minimal state), neoliberal theories became popular in science and journalism. They valued the self-regulating forces of the market and scorned the possibility of state intervention. The atmosphere changed: it turned away from organization, equality, and solidarity as guiding principles toward favoring free markets, productive inequality, and individualism. The decades of "organized capitalism" came to an end; the Anglo-American model of deregulated financial capitalism threatened to sideline other varieties of a more regulated, Continental capitalism. The reasons for this turn were undoubtedly the weaknesses of the Keynesian welfare state, such as the "stagflation" and sticky unemployment of the 1970s, but also the technical-organizational innovations and the beginning of the IT age. The main impetus, however, came from cross-border competition and the worldwide interconnectedness that had developed alongside globalization. Globalization put the model of organized capitalism under enormous pressure, as it had been developed within the context of the nation state. The regulating capabilities of strong nation states now faced the opposition of cross-border competition. Globalization and neoliberalism went hand in hand. The globalization of capitalism did not and should not bring with it effective global governance structures beyond the G-7 or G-20. The balance between the market and the state shifted to the disadvantage of the regulatory state and hence to the disadvantage of democracy. Legitimate democratic political regulations were dismantled into many different economic spheres, such as labor and financial markets. The supposedly more efficient market forces restructured formerly regulated markets. The already precarious "power balance" during the era of organized capitalism and the Keynesian welfare state (Korpi 1983) between capital and labor shifted in favor of capital. Globalization and deregulation were mainly the result of conscious political decisions by the USA, UK, and major capitalist international organizations such as the World Bank, International Monetary Fund (IMF), and European Union (EU).

Financial capitalism is the epitome of the kind of business that is not done through the production and exchange of goods but rather with money, conducted by brokers, banks, stock markets, investors, and capital markets. It is not a new

interests, today's financial capitalism or "financialization" of capitalism emphasizes the dominance of finance capital over all other forms of capital.

[5]Such cuts were only moderate in Scandinavia, Germany, Austria, and France but drastic within the context of Anglo-Saxon economies (USA, UK, NZ).

phenomenon. Following globalization, financial and monetary deregulation, and partial deindustrialization in some Western countries, the financial sector experienced massive expansion, particularly within the UK and the USA. Its share of total GDP in the USA rose from 10% (industrial sector 40%) in 1950 to more than 50% (industrial sector 10%) in 2000 (Heires and Nölke 2013, p. 251). The assets of banks and the profits of bankers rose exponentially. Investment banks, investment funds, and newly formed equity companies were created in large numbers. Global capital flows increased massively. A large portion of this did not serve as investment in production but funded speculation instead. Large profits were created that were not matched by any added value. The expectation of high profits—as well as the willingness to accept high risks—increased. This part of the capitalist economy was particularly deregulated and left to itself. It was equipped with new, faster technology and increasingly complex instruments. It came to be driven by strong internal competition. As such, it was unable to develop sustainable, widely accepted business rules although its overall importance for the economy increased. *Shareholder value* became the almost universal yardstick for success, and business strategies became increasingly short term. Central elements of nonmarket coordination (e.g., regulatory state and neo-corporatism) that had stabilized organized capitalism were undermined. In many segments of the economy, speculative investment capitalism replaced the previously dominant manager's capitalism. As investor George Soros already recognized in 1998, this transformation put "financial capitalism in the driver's seat" (Windolf 2005; Streeck 2009, pp. 77–89 and 230–272; Kocka 2016, pp. 96–99; Soros 1998, pp. XII and XX).

Profit seeking and investment are integral parts of both owners' and managers' capitalism. They are embedded in different functions of business leadership: the development of long-term strategies, human resource management, and the definition of social relations. The new type of financial and investment capitalism leaves most of this behind. From the outside, investment fund directors and bankers decide on the future of businesses with which they have little personal relationship. They know little more about these enterprises beyond their score on standardized indices and profit relevant market information. A radical form of differentiation or, rather, a specialization of the investment function takes place. It is expressed in the absolute focus on profit as the almost only remaining criterion for evaluating business success and financial remuneration (e.g., salary, bonuses, and shares) of equity fund managers. The internal dynamics of capitalism are increasing but so is its instability. The gap between selfish equity fund success and the public good is becoming enormous. Despite being so inherently unstable and prone to crises, changing capitalism has increased its ability to shape society. It is the driving force behind the increasing inequality of wealth and income, exemplified by the tremendously high income of today's business leaders. The ever more radical, market-oriented, and fast-paced capitalism is also the motor of labor market deregulation, bringing about an increasing number of short-term, limited, and part-time contracts.

How has this transformation from coordinated and socially embedded capitalism into deregulated financial capitalism affected democracy?

11.7 Challenges for Democracy

From the 1950s to the 1970s, capitalism was characterized by a strict regulatory framework and the expansion of interventionist Keynesian welfare states.[6] In this way, it was directly and indirectly constrained in its independence and modes of capital accumulation both a priori (e.g., regulations) and ex post (e.g., high taxes and social obligations). If a golden age of capitalist-democratic coexistence could be identified during this period, it would be that of the "social market economy"—an embedded form of capitalism—rather than capitalism itself (Polanyi 1944; Offe 1984; Hall and Soskice 2001). The postwar decades experienced decreasing socio-economic inequality, the expansion of the welfare state, and financial and labor market regulation. Labor unions were at the height of their socioeconomic and political power. Walter Korpi (1983) and Esping-Andersen (1990) have written about a "balance of class power." At no other point in time have capitalism and democracy complemented each other so well as during this short period.

However, the actual triumph of capitalism in the twentieth century was not its power-balanced coexistence with democracy but its astonishing ability to detach itself successfully from social and regulatory frameworks. With the political support of democratic governments, capitalism managed to disengage itself from major social and political responsibilities. But since the financial crisis in 2008, it has become obvious that with this triumph comes the danger of self-destruction.

"Unleashed" financial capitalism implies more problems for the functioning of embedded democracy than the capitalism that was regulated by the welfare state or Keynesianism in the first decades after the World War II. The increased "denationalization" (Zürn 1998) of the economy and political decision-making went hand in hand with increasing socioeconomic inequalities. Together they undermined two fundamental principles of democracy: (1) the core democratic principle that authoritative political decisions can be taken only by those who are legitimized by constitutional-democratic procedures and (2) the principle of political equality, which is diluted by the asymmetric distribution of socioeconomic resources among citizens, largely to the disadvantage of the lower classes of society. All OECD democracies are affected by these two developments, even if to different degrees. The more denationalization progresses, and the more capitalism loses its social ties and turns into (neo-)liberal financial capitalism, the more its negative effects on the quality of democracy can be observed, all other things being equal. I shall elaborate on this central concept in four theses.

Thesis 1: Increasing socioeconomic inequality and poverty lead to asymmetric political participation.

In 2010, economic inequality reached levels of characteristic of capitalism—at least Anglo-Saxon capitalism—before the World War I (Piketty 2014). Economic

[6]The welfare state and Keynesianism were, of course, developed to different degrees within the OECD countries (Esping-Andersen 1990; Hall and Soskice 2001).

inequality translates into social and then rapidly into political inequality. Much has been written about the connection between the availability of socioeconomic goods and their transformation into cognitive resources and political participation.[7] It is already apparent in the context of the least demanding form of political participation, namely, general elections. Election turnout is declining in Western Europe and to an even greater degree in Eastern Europe. The average turnout in Western Europe in 1975 stood at 85%; by 2012, it had declined to an average of 75%. In Eastern Europe, the decline is even more dramatic: while an average of 72% of voters cast their vote in 1991, this figure had declined to 57% in 2012. In the USA, however, even these numbers would represent a positive development. The average turnout in US congressional elections over the last three decades (1980–2012) was a mere 45.4% (WZB 2014).

General elections in which only 50% (or even less) of the electorate participate are problematic. The explicit consent for and therefore also legitimization of the elected is lower than for those representatives who were chosen in elections with a turnout of 70% or 80%. Yet there is still no democratic theory that can determine the ideal electoral turnout in democracies. The absence of half the citizens during the most important act of legitimization in a representative democracy is evidence of how (un-)important political participation in the res publica has become for the majority of citizens in the USA and most of Eastern Europe. Empirical studies show that the vast majority of those who refrain from voting also fail to engage in other forms of political participation (Przeworski 2010). Bernard Manin (1997, 222f.) called this a "democracy of spectators." Joseph Schumpeter, however, understood this state of democracy as the ideal type of an (elitist) democracy.

The crucial problem democratic theory faces is not the turnout figures themselves but the social selectivity they imply. The empirically proven rule of thumb is that the lower the electoral turnout, the higher the social exclusion within the context of elections. Undeniable evidence confirms that the lower social classes take the political exit option, while the middle and upper classes stay put.[8] Among US citizens, 80% of those with a disposable annual household income exceeding $100,000 state that they vote, compared with only 33% of those with a household income of $15,000 or less who go to the polls[9] (Bonica et al. 2013, p. 111).

[7]It is thus even more surprising that neoclassical economics and neoliberal political forces question this relationship. They see political equality fulfilled by the equal availability of political rights (see von Hayek 1978; the Free Democratic Party of Germany (FDP) and the liberal political parties in the Netherlands and Scandinavia, respectively).

[8]When asked whether their vote or political participation influence political decision-making, more than two-thirds of lower class citizens in Germany answered in the negative. When confronted with the same question, a resounding two-thirds and more of middle class citizens responded in the affirmative, stating that their voice had an impact (Merkel and Petring 2012).

[9]The exclusive character of US democracy becomes even more apparent if the 10–15% of the lower class without citizenship are taken into account. A considerably smaller section of the population (5%) at the upper end of the income scale does not have citizenship (Bonica et al. 2013, p. 110).

Increasing evidence shows that the American symptoms of lower class exclusion are ever more pertinent within the context of European societies. The electoral demos is unbalanced: the dominance of the middle classes is increasing, and participation by the lower classes is constantly decreasing. In voter turnout, most OECD countries have become "two-thirds democracies," where the lower class is largely excluded from political participation. The political principle of equality is undermined: voting tilts the policy scales in favor of top incomes (ibid.).

Declining turnout and increasing social selectivity of the electorate have become more and more prevalent in Western Europe over the last three decades. There it is slow but steady, in Eastern Europe rapid, and in the USA chronic. The primary reason can be found in the rise of socioeconomic inequality (Hacker and Pierson 2010, p. 194; Schäfer 2010; Merkel and Petring 2012; Bonica et al. 2013, p. 111). Declining turnout and increasing social selectivity of the electorate are also due to the increasingly precarious conditions faced by the lower classes on the labor market, as well as the decline of catch-all parties, labor unions, and other large collective organizations that played a crucial role in the politicization and representation of the lower classes throughout the twentieth century.

The participation-representation gap has increased in almost all OECD countries over the past decade. Citizens from the lower classes are participating less in politics than others, with considerable consequences for the representation of their interests. Parliamentary studies show that the interests of the "lower third" are less represented in parliament than those of the "upper third" of society (Lehmann et al. 2015).

Thesis 2: In open, embedded democracies, elections are increasingly unable to halt growing socioeconomic inequalities.

Considering the idea of class-oriented *economic voting*, it could be argued that all voters—or at least a considerable majority—with an income below the median would vote for political parties that fight for redistribution. This would give democracy an instrument to counterbalance severe socioeconomic inequalities. But why has this mechanism failed in recent decades? One of the reasons has already been mentioned: the lower classes, much more than the middle and upper classes, are increasingly staying home on election day. Moreover, vote-maximizing parties are tempted to abandon the lower classes as potential voters to be won over. Social democratic and other left-wing catch-all parties still sometimes claim to represent the interests of these classes in their party programs. However, this is often only lip service paid to the party's "social justice" image rather than a genuine attempt to mobilize the politically apathetic and indifferent lower classes.[10] Furthermore, party manifestos and actual policies have to be considered separately. For

[10]The financial crisis and the bottom-up redistributive effects that have become apparent within the context of the crisis seem nonetheless to have reached social democratic parties. The minimum wage and the effects of deregulation on the financial and labor markets have, after two decades, slowly made their way back to the top of party agendas.

both ideological and electoral reasons, conservative, liberal, and right-wing parties do not write normative or electoral interests into active policies of top-bottom redistribution. Left-wing parties that, when in office, wish to adopt policies to improve the situation of the lower classes—more education, minimum wages, maintenance of the welfare state, taxation of higher incomes to raise public revenues—face threats from capital owners and wealthier classes, in both discourse and reality. The main threat from these classes is to move capital and investment abroad. The financialization of capitalism and the now easier option to move financial capital across national borders has made the democratic state vulnerable. For left-wing parties, this quickly results in a conflict of interests. If investors begin to shift investments abroad, this costs jobs and results in lower economic growth, less public revenue, less social investment, and ultimately fewer votes. Fritz Scharpf fittingly defined this dilemma: "In capitalist democracies, governments depend on the confidence of their voters. But to maintain this confidence they also depend on the performance of their real economies and, increasingly, on the confidence of financial markets" (Scharpf 2011, p. 1). Not least with this in mind, the "third way" policies implemented by most social democratic parties and governments can be understood as a premature and obedient adjustment to a globalized economy. In economic and labor market policy, many social democratic parties have succumbed to the neoliberal globalization discourse of the past two decades. Redistribution issues have thus lost their main advocates in the political arena (Merkel et al. 2006).

Economic voting or class voting is not the only explanation for electoral behavior. Socioeconomic conflicts also coincide with cultural cleavages. The latter can be religious or ethnic in nature but are also manifest in attitudes on a scale from libertarianism to authoritarianism (Kitschelt 2001). Particularly the lower (middle) classes (mainly men) are receptive to authoritarian and ethnocentric policies. Examples can be found in the right-wing populist parties of Scandinavia, France, Austria, and Switzerland. In these countries, the lower class electorate has to some extent voted for authoritarian and xenophobic parties that sometimes pursue neoliberal economic policies (e.g., SVP in Switzerland and FPÖ in Austria).

During the first three quarters of the twentieth century, the right to vote and democratic elections made the ballot into a "paper stone" (Przeworski 1986). The post-revolutionary working class used it to tame and socially entrench capitalism by electing left-wing (mostly reformist social democratic) parties and to successfully establish workers' rights, a progressive tax system, and the expansion of the welfare state. This long period of social expansion witnessed a moderate redistribution of economic growth gains in most industrially advanced countries, especially after 1945. However, this trend halted and even reversed in the 1970s.[11] For top-down redistribution, the *paper stones* have lost their effectiveness to become mere *paper tigers*. Since the 1970s, democratic elections have no longer stopped the growth of

[11] In non-Anglo-Saxon countries, this shift did not happen by cutting back the welfare state but was pushed through by a tax and income policy in favor of business and the better-off.

inequality with the rich becoming richer and the poor and the lower classes sinking into social immobility.

Thesis 3: During times of financialization, the state becomes more vulnerable.

The financialization of capitalism increased the vulnerability of the state to banks, hedge funds, and large investors, making it more visible. Financialization describes a process that began in the USA and UK as its core countries. In the last two to three decades, it has changed capitalism, as well as the relationship between capital and the state in all OECD countries. Heires and Nölke (2013, p. 248) define financialization as a process that demands the deregulation of financial markets, eliminates national borders, and facilitates the introduction of new "financial products" such as derivatives and debt obligations. It brought forth the rise of hedge and pension funds and other "institutional investors." Financialization made the ideology of *shareholder value* the primary, if not only, criterion for investment decisions.

The financial sector began to occupy a dominant key position in the economy. Its profits far outgrew those of the industrial sector. Industrial producers like Porsche earned more through speculation on financial products than in its core sector, the production of cars. Financialization, however, not only increased the dependence of industrial production on the financial industry; it also increased the dependence of the state and society on this sector. Intentionally or not, the state emasculated itself by deregulating financial markets. Governments and parties dependent on economic prosperity to stay in power became reliant on the decisions of big investors and foreign creditors. The financial and Euro crisis that began in 2008 made this visible. Many governments felt obliged to respond to the calls for help from banks that claimed to be "too big to fail" (at least in Europe[12]). "System relevance" became the catchword to describe an extra-constitutional state of emergency that would in doubt justify sacrificing the freedoms of parliamentary-democratic decision-making. The fact that it was the taxpayers who had to foot the bill is yet further proof of how financial capitalism has become empowered to impose policies on state and society that lead to bottom-up redistribution, in times of both success and crisis.

Following the logic of financial capitalism, some states gave up their authoritative role as rule makers to become mere policy takers, constantly monitored by rating agencies. Every autonomous action or even discourse contradicting the new rules could lead to a lower credit rating or an increase in interest rates at which the state could borrow money on deregulated financial markets (Simmerl 2012). The combination of an international run on investment, national party competition, and neoliberal economic dogma among those governing led "[...] to free the capitalist economy and its markets once and for all—not from the governments on which they still depend in many ways, but from the kind of mass democracy that was part of the

[12]The US government followed the capitalist rules of a free market more closely when it allowed many more banks to go bankrupt then did European governments.

regime of postwar democratic capitalism" (Streeck 2014, p. 46). In the long run, this could produce a "Hayekian rival," which would be independent of democratic impositions. Should this process not be stopped, capitalism and democracy would eventually have to separate (Streeck 2014, p. 173). Even if one does not share the apocalyptic perspective of Streeck's analysis, the core argument is amazingly precise: deregulating markets has put a strain on the compatibility of capitalism and democracy and has made their incompatibilities more apparent. The gap between capitalism and democracy has become wider than during any of the democratic periods in the twentieth century. The state did not become a more proactive regulatory force despite the fact that the financial sector caused the financial crisis. Neoliberalism survived the self-inflicted crisis, which Colin Crouch has aptly termed "the strange non-death of neoliberalism" (Crouch 2011). This shows the objective state of helplessness and subjective lack of willingness of democratic governments to act in times of financialization. The current German chancellor Angela Merkel highlighted this rather openly (and probably unintentionally) when she stated that a "market conformist democracy" is what we should aim for. Had she spoken from a democratic point of view, the argument would be clear: we should not aim for "market conformist democracy" but rather for "democracy conformist capitalism." Merkel's political course is clear: it is not the market that must submit to democracy but democracy that must submit to the market. The most recent Euro crisis and the maneuvering of the European Central Bank are further proof: democracy is subordinate to the market; democracy must adjust to the market.

Thesis 4: Economic and political globalization is increasingly shifting political decision-making away from parliament to the executive.

The hallmarks of financial capitalism in an age of globalization are the speed, volume, complexity, and scope of financial transactions. By contrast, parliaments are always limited by their territorial scope and the time they need to prepare, deliberate, and pass laws. In an age of digitized computer-based financial flows, large-scale financial transactions take only a fraction of a second. American political scientist William Scheuermann (2004) speaks in general terms of an "empire of speed." German sociologist Hartmut Rosa calls this the "desynchronization" (Rosa 2012; Rosa and Scheuermann 2009) of politics and economics, democratic state decisions, and private economic transactions. The increased speed of the economy and society works in favor of political institutions that do not act deliberatively like the legislature, deliberative citizen councils, or the judiciary but act decisively like the executive. It would be naïve to assume that any political decision could keep pace with the speed of financial transactions. Yet both the demos and global elites implicitly and explicitly demand faster political decision-making. This is valid especially in times of crises that call for a strong executive (Schmitt 1996[1931]). The most recent example of this has been evident in the political discourse and actions of European governments since 2008. The demand for faster political decision-making illustrates a particular democratic paradox in times of crisis: far-reaching decisions in response to crises often have a considerable impact on welfare and redistribution. Such decisions, in particular, require reliable, democratic input legitimacy (Enderlein 2013, p. 720 and 733). Objective or assumed time constraints typically result in technocratic-executive decision-making with thin input legitimacy (Merkel 2016). Within the context of democratic regimes, the circumvention of important central democratic procedures cannot be justified by better outcomes. This, for example, is what makes Denmark different from Singapore.

11.8 Conclusion

Our theoretical and empirical analysis detects clear and distinct tensions between capitalism and democracy. It is apparent that capitalism can prosper under both democratic and authoritarian regimes but that, so far, democracy has existed only with capitalism. Nevertheless, capitalism and democracy are guided by different principles that create tensions between the two. This is expressed primarily in differing stances on equality and inequality. The level of inequality that defines specific variants of capitalism and supposedly secures productivity and profits is hardly compatible with the democratic principle of equal rights and opportunities for political participation. Socioeconomic inequality challenges the core democratic principle of equality in participation, representation, and governance.

However, capitalism per se does not exist; instead we see different "varieties of capitalism." This is equally true today as in the past. Different forms of capitalism show different degrees of compatibility with democracy. In (Western) Europe,[13] full democracy only truly took root after 1945, when universal suffrage was introduced in most countries. As democracy became fully established in Western Europe, Australia, Canada, and New Zealand,[14] a certain type of capitalism developed not coincidentally: a socially, embedded, and economically (often in a Keynesian form) stabilized and nationally regulated capitalism. However, the general tensions between socioeconomic inequality and the political principle of equality remained unresolved. Nevertheless, their effects were mitigated considerably by regulated labor markets, increased economic welfare, the welfare state, strong labor unions and the activism of class-conscious social democratic or communist (e.g., Italy and France) workers' or center-left parties. Coexistence between (social) capitalism and (social) democracy never functioned better than during this period.

[13]US democracy is, of course, older than that. But even there universal suffrage for women was introduced only in 1920 (in the UK in 1928, in France in 1945). Until the mid-1960s, six southern US states banned African Americans from voting for racist reasons. Only since that period can the "mother country" of democracy be seen as having fully implemented democratic values.

[14]If one takes full suffrage of men and women as the crucial indicator for a complete democracy, then New Zealand (1900) was the first and Australia one of the first democracies, not the USA or UK.

Table 11.1 Democratic drift from KWC to DFC

Partial regime of democracy	Regulated capitalism/Keynesian welfare capitalism (KWC) (1950s–1970s)	Neoliberal financial capitalism (DFC) (1979-today)
Elections	Higher turnout, lower social exclusion	Lower turnout, higher social exclusion
Participation/ association/ representation	Strong labor unions and left-wing parties represented labor and reduced socioeconomic inequalities	Dominance of liberal-conservative parties and doctrines plus weak labor unions support inequalities
Civil rights	Inequalities of gender and lack of minority rights	Movement toward gender equality and more civil rights for minorities; strong political NGOs
Horizontal accountability	Powerful parliaments, few decisions by supranational executives	Weaker parliaments and executives face less parliamentary control
Effective power to govern	Strong executive vis-à-vis markets; political decision-making takes place mainly in democratically legitimate national institutions	Loss of regulating power vis-à-vis markets; shift of political decision-making toward thinly legitimized and controlled supranational governance structures

This coexistence has become gradually more difficult since the late 1970s. The OECD countries have moved closer to the Anglo-Saxon variant of capitalism: they were challenged by the neoliberal policies of deregulation and privatization pushed by Ronald Reagan and Margaret Thatcher. The IMF and the neoliberal concept of the European Single Market (ESM) forced their implementation (Scharpf 2012; Streeck 2013, 2014): tax reforms in favor of companies, capital income, and the rich and labor markets and financial markets deregulated. Even the strongest welfare states of Northern and Western Europe were not able to shield themselves from the neoliberal winds of change. The financialization of capitalist accumulation advanced even in this context and today dominates the world of finance, labor, and trade (Heires and Nölke 2013, p. 252; Heires and Nölke 2014). Table 11.1 summarizes and highlights the democratic drift produced by the transition from Keynesian welfare capitalism (KWC) to deregulated financial capitalism (DFC).

Considering this (very concise) depiction of the development of democracy during the two stages of capitalism since 1945, a deteriorating quality of democracy is to be noted in four out of five partial regimes of embedded democracy. They are not only and not always directly caused by financial capitalism, but financial capitalism plays a relevant role. A closer look, however, suggests two causal explanations:

1. Deregulated financial capitalism led to increasing socioeconomic inequalities. This had a negative effect on elections and political participation, two of the partial regimes of democracy (A, B). Socioeconomic exclusion and inequality largely transformed into political exclusion and inequality. Exclusion and inequality mainly affected the bottom third of social classes.

2. The globalizing transformation of capitalism led to a transnationalization of markets and the partial supranationalization of important decisions on monetary and economic policy. These changes led to a significant loss of parliamentary powers in favor of the executive (partial regime D: horizontal checks on powers), central banks, and the IMF. At the same time, the transnationalization of markets also diminished the effective power of national governments to govern (partial regime E: effective power to govern). This became visible especially during the financial crisis. The losses of the financial sector, forced by "systemic relevance," and the fear of a negative domino effect were "socialized" despite decades of previously reckless and politically supported (through deregulation) profitmaking.

Financial capitalism is harmful for democracy, since it has cracked its social and political "embeddedness." This does not mean that capitalism per se is incompatible with democracy. A sustainable coexistence of capitalism and democracy is best achieved through mutual embedding. The right to private property and functioning markets are vital restrictions on the centralization of political power in democratic regimes. Particularly in conjunction with industrialization, capitalism unleashes demands, protests, and emancipatory movements that can, under favorable conditions, lead to democratization despite diverging capitalist intentions. The history of capitalism and democracy demonstrated this over large periods of the past century.

Since the late 1970s, protest movements have focused more on cultural than on economic issues. These new movements were crucial. However, as social and political protest no longer paid much attention to socioeconomic inequalities, this problem grew in the shadows. The brief, more virtual than real protest of the *Occupy Wall Street* movement cannot be compared with the negotiating power of strong trade unions or labor parties in the 1960s and 1970s. The disembedding of capitalism is challenging democracy's crucial principal of political equality. Representative democracy has not found effective antidotes against the disease of socioeconomic and political inequality. All countermeasures discussed in democratic theory—from referenda to deliberative assemblies, monitoring (Keane 2011), or counter-democracy (Rosanvallon 2008)—may save whales, help control government, and improve certain spheres of local democracy but have little relevance for reregulating markets, restoring social welfare, and halting growing inequality. The cultural turn of progressive democratic politics has forgotten the problem of economic redistribution and now stands empty-handed, without a cure for democracy's most obvious disease: inequality. Is capitalism compatible with democracy? It depends. It depends on the type of capitalism and on the type of democracy. If one insists that democracy is more than the minimalist concept proposed by Joseph Schumpeter and takes the imperative of political equality and Hans Kelsen's dogma of "autonomous norms" seriously, the present form of financialized "disembedded capitalism" poses considerable challenges to democracy. If these challenges are not met with democratic and economic reforms, democracy may slowly transform into oligarchy, formally legitimized by general elections. It is not the crisis of capitalism that challenges democracy but its neoliberal triumph.

References

Bonica, A., McCarty, N., Poole, K. T., & Rosenthal, H. (2013). Why hasn't democracy slowed rising inequality? *Journal of Economic Perspectives, 27*(3), 103–124.
Crouch, C. (2004). *Post-democracy*. Cambridge: Polity Press.
Crouch, C. (2011). *The strange non-death of neo-liberalism*. Cambridge: Polity Press.
Enderlein, H. (2013). Das erste Opfer der Krise ist die Demokratie: Wirtschaftspolitik und ihre Legitimation in der Finanzmarktkrise 2008–2013. *Politische Vierteljahresschrift, 54*, 714–739.
Esping-Andersen, G. (1990). *The three worlds of welfare capitalism*. Cambridge: Polity Press.
Fraenkel, E. (1974[1964]). *Deutschland und die westlichen Demokratien* (6th ed.). Stuttgart: Kohlhammer.
Freedom House. (2010). *Freedom in the world*. Accessed January 22, 2014, from http://www.freedomhouse.org/report/freedom-world/freedom-world-2010#.Uu_OLrS2yF8
Habermas, J. (1975). *Legitimation crisis*. Boston, MA: Beacon Press.
Hacker, J. S., & Pierson, P. (2010). *Winner-take-all politics: How Washington made the rich richer—and turned its back on the middle class*. New York, NY: Simon & Schuster.
Hall, P. A., & Soskice, D. (2001). *Varieties of capitalism. The institutional foundation of comparative advantage*. Oxford: Oxford University Press.
Harvey, D. (2007). *A brief history of neoliberalism*. Oxford: Oxford University Press.
Hayek, F. A. V. (1978). *Law, legislation and liberty*. Chicago, IL: University of Chicago Press.
Heires, M., & Nölke, A. (2013). Finanzialisierung. In J. Wullweber, A. Graf, & M. Behrens (Eds.), *Theorien der Internationalen Politischen Ökonomie* (pp. 253–266). Wiesbaden: Springer VS.
Keane, J. (2011). Monitory democracy? In S. Alonso, J. Keane, & W. Merkel (Eds.), *The future of representative democracy* (pp. 212–235). Cambridge: Cambridge University Press.
Kitschelt, H. (2001). Politische Konfliktlinien in westlichen Demokratien. Ethnisch-kulturelle und wirtschaftliche Verteilungskonflikte. In W. Heitmeyer & D. Loch (Eds.), *Schattenseiten der Globalisierung. Rechtsradikalismus, Rechtspopulismus und separatistischer Regionalismus in westlichen Demokratien* (pp. 418–442). Frankfurt am Main: Suhrkamp.
Kocka, J. (2016). *Capitalism: A short history*. Princeton, NJ: Princeton University Press.
Korpi, W. (1983). *Democratic class struggle*. London: Routledge.
Lash, C., & Urry, J. (1987). *The end of organized capitalism*. Madison: University of Wisconsin Press.
Lehmann, P., Regel, S., & Schlote, S. (2015). Ungleichheit in der politischen Repräsentation. Ist die Unterschicht schlechter repräsentiert? In W. Merkel (Ed.), *Demokratie und Krise. Zum schwierigen Verhältnis von Theorie und Empirie* (pp. 157–180). Wiesbaden: Springer VS.
Lembcke, O. W., Ritzi, C., & Schaal, G. S. (Eds.). (2012). *Zeitgenössische Demokratietheorie, Bd. 1: Normative Demokratietheorien*. Wiesbaden: Springer VS.
Luhmann, N. (1995). *Social systems*. Stanford, CA: Stanford University Press.
Manin, B. (1997). *The principles of representative government*. Cambridge: Cambridge University Press.
Merkel, W. (2004). Embedded and defective democracies. *Democratization, 11*(5), 33–58.
Merkel, W. (2010). *Systemtransformation. Eine Einführung in die Theorie und Empirie der Transformationsforschung* (2nd ed.). Wiesbaden: VS Verlag für Sozialwissenschaften.
Merkel, W. (2016). The challenge of capitalism to democracy. Reply to Colin crouch and Wolfgang Streeck. *Zeitschrift für Vergleichende Politikwissenschaft, 10*(1), 61–80.
Merkel, W., Egle, C., Henkes, C., Ostheim, T., & Petring, A. (2006). *Die Reformfähigkeit der Sozialdemokratie. Herausforderungen und Bilanz der Regierungspolitik in Westeuropa*. Wiesbaden: VS Verlag für Sozialwissenschaften.
Merkel, W., & Petring, A. (2012). Politische Partizipation und demokratische Inklusion. In T. Mörschel & C. Krell (Eds.), *Demokratie in Deutschland. Zustand—Herausforderungen—Perspektiven* (pp. 93–119). VS Verlag für Sozialwissenschaften: Wiesbaden.
Nölke, A., & Heires, M. (2014). Politik der Finanzialisierung. Wiesbaden: Springer VS.

O'Connor, J. (1973). *The fiscal crisis of the state*. London and New York: Routledge.
Offe, C. (1972). *Strukturprobleme des kapitalistischen Staates: Aufsätze zur Politischen Soziologie*. Suhrkamp: Frankfurt am Main.
Offe, C. (1984). *Contradictions of the welfare state*. Cambridge, MA: The MIT Press.
Offe, C. (2003). *Herausforderungen der Demokratie*. Campus: Frankfurt am Main.
Piketty, T. (2014). *Capital in the twenty-first century*. Cambridge, MA: Belknap Press of Harvard University Press.
Polanyi, K. (1944). *The great transformation*. New York, NY: Rinehart.
Przeworski, A. (1986). *Paper stones: A history of electoral socialism*. Chicago, IL: The University of Chicago Press.
Przeworski, A. (2010). *Democracy and the limits of self-government*. Cambridge, MA: Cambridge University Press.
Rosa, H. (2012). *Weltbeziehungen im Zeitalter der Beschleunigung*. Berlin: Suhrkamp.
Rosa, H., & Scheuermann, W. (2009). *High-speed society: Social acceleration, power and modernity*. Pennsylvania, PA: Penn State University Press.
Rosanvallon, P. (2008). *Counter-democracy. Politics in an age of distrust*. Cambridge, MA: Cambridge University Press.
Schäfer, A. (2010). Die Folgen sozialer Ungleichheit für die Demokratie in Westeuropa. *Zeitschrift für Vergleichende Politikwissenschaft, 4*(1), 131–156.
Scharpf, F. W. (2011). *Monetary union, fiscal crisis and the preemption of democracy*. MPIfG Discussion Paper 11/11. Max-Planck-Institut für Gesellschaftsforschung, Köln, July 2011.
Scharpf, F. W. (2012). *Kann man den Euro retten ohne Europa zu zerstören?* Accessed January 20, 2014, from http://www.mpifg.de/people/fs/documents/pdf/Kann_man_den_Euro_retten_2012.pdf
Scheuermann, W. (2004). *Liberal democracy and the social acceleration of time*. Baltimore, MD: Johns Hopkins University Press.
Schmitt, C. (1996[1931]). *Der Hüter der Verfassung* (4th ed.). Berlin: Duncker & Humblot.
Schmitter, P. C. (1974). Still the century of corporatism. *The Review of Politics, 36*, 85–131.
Schmitter, P. C. (1982). Reflections on where the theory of neo-corporatism has gone and where the praxis of neo-corporatism may be going. In G. Lehmbruch & P. C. Schmitter (Eds.), *Patterns of corporatist policy-making* (pp. 259–279). Beverly Hills, CA: Sage.
Simmerl, G. (2012). Europäische Schuldenkrise als Demokratiekrise. Zur diskursiven Interaktion zwischen Politik und Finanzmarkt. *Berliner Debatte Initial, 23*, 108–124.
Soros, G. (1998). *The crisis of global capitalism*. New York, NY: Public Affairs.
Streeck, W. (2009). *Re-forming capitalism. institutional change in the German political economy*. Oxford: Oxford University Press.
Streeck, W. (2013). Vom DM Nationalismus zum Europatriotismus. *Eine Replik auf Jürgen Habermas. Blätter für deutsche und internationale Politik, 9*, 75–92.
Streeck, W. (2014). *Buying time: The delayed crisis of democratic capitalism*. London: Verso.
Walzer, M. (1983). *Spheres of justice: A defense of pluralism and equality*. New York, NY: Basic Books.
Windolf, P. (Ed.). (2005). *Finanzmarkt-Kapitalismus. Analyse zum Wandel von Produktionsregimen*. Wiesbaden: VS Verlag für Sozialwissenschaften.
Winkler, H. A. (Ed.). (1974). *Organisierter Kapitalismus. Voraussetzungen und Anfänge*. Göttingen: Vandenhoek & Ruprecht.
WZB. (2014). *Data collection on elections, parties and governments from 1950–2014*.
Zürn, M. (1998). *Regieren jenseits des Nationalstaates: Globalisierung und Denationalisierung als Chance*. Suhrkamp: Frankfurt am Main.

Chapter 12
Democratic Danger for Democracy? The Precarious Balance Between Security and Freedom

Aiko Wagner and Sascha Kneip

> *There was a 'before 9/11' and there was an 'after 9/11.' After 9/11, the gloves came off. [Quoted from Büsching (2011)]*
> Cofer Black, former director of the CIA Counterterrorist Centers (CTC)

12.1 Introduction

The balance between freedom and security has preoccupied democracy not only since the terrorist attacks in New York and Washington on 11 September 2001. Indeed, it has been a concern of political philosophy at least since the onset of the contractualist age, in other words, for more than 350 years. While Thomas Hobbes had still wanted largely to exchange individual liberty for the security promised by the Leviathan, John Locke, Montesquieu, Alexis de Tocqueville, John Stuart Mill, James Madison, and Benjamin Constant took the view that not so much the upholding of freedom as its restriction required more stringent justification. This way of thinking reached a climax at the end of the eighteenth century in Benjamin Franklin's famous assertion that "Those who would give up essential Liberty, to purchase a little temporary Safety, deserve neither Liberty nor Safety." However, the priority of liberty has never been as undisputed in the history of liberal democracy as Franklin's words would suggest. Not only did such different anti-liberal thinkers as Joseph de Maistre, Jean-Jacques Rousseau, and Carl Schmitt (on the history of anti-liberal thinking see Holmes 1993) oppose the unconditional priority of individual freedom over collective issues and needs (security), the citizens of democratic polities also seem uncommitted to one or other of these perspectives. Empirical studies on public attitudes to these questions show that,

A. Wagner (✉) · S. Kneip
WZB Berlin Social Science Center, Berlin, Germany
e-mail: aiko.wagner@wzb.eu; sascha.kneip@wzb.eu

W. Merkel, S. Kneip (eds.), *Democracy and Crisis*,
https://doi.org/10.1007/978-3-319-72559-8_12

given the choice, in threat scenarios citizens would almost always opt for the curbing of civil liberties (see, e.g., Wagner and Giebler 2009; Pietsch and Fiebig 2011).[1]

Nor is the supposed fundamental trade-off between collective security and individual liberty by any means a new phenomenon in the awareness of democratic societies. Long before the Islamist terror threat scenarios of the 2000s, Western democracies had been menaced by domestic terrorism, violent separatism, and organized crime. And already in the 1970s, 1980s, and still more strongly in the 1990s, their reaction was always the same, general security laws were tightened, new tools for keeping citizens under surveillance were created, and the rights of suspects, accused persons, and convicts were restricted. In brief, individual liberties were curbed to satisfy collective security needs, often with the implicit or explicit consent of the population (see also Grimm 2008, 26).

For both theoretical and empirical democracy research, this development raises a number of important issues. The key question is certainly whether this "democratic reaction" of democracy to new threatening situations—thus the responsive reaction of political elites to the wishes and interests of the population—is really a problem for democracy itself and whether it is indicative of a crisis of modern democratic societies. From the standpoint of the theory of democratic representation, it could be argued that the reactions of political elites to terrorist or criminal threats are not a problem but in essence a democratically responsible and ultimately necessary solution to an objective security problem, which is, moreover, in accordance with the subjective attitudes and wishes of citizens. From this point of view, the security policies of democratic governments demonstrate high responsiveness on the part of democratic systems and far from being symptomatic of a crisis of the democratic regime show that it is working well.

This, however, is only one side of the democratic coin. In the light of the tradition of liberal thinking mentioned above, it can just as convincingly be argued that civil liberties are the conditio sine qua non of liberal democratic governance and that restricting these basic liberties not only violates fundamental human rights but also profoundly harms the functioning of democracy as a whole. In this view, civil liberties are not only intrinsically valuable but also constitutive of political opinion formation and fundamentally important for the functioning and meaningfulness of democratic elections and decision-making processes. From this classical liberal perspective, restricting these rights cannot be justified simply on the grounds that by doing so the political elites are merely reacting to the public and/or published opinion of a population. From a liberal perspective, responsiveness to the detriment of fundamental freedoms is no proof of the quality of democratic

[1]Already Isaiah Berlin considered the preference for individual liberties to be a comparatively modern (elite) phenomenon. "The domination of this ideal has been the exception rather than the rule, even in the recent history of the West. Nor has liberty in this sense often formed a rallying cry for the great masses of mankind" (Berlin 1969, 129).

governance but, on the contrary, points to a serious malfunction of democratic governance and a factual crisis of democracy.[2]

The extent to which the restriction of individual civil rights is indicative of a democratic crisis is thus a contentious theoretical issue. And, beyond intuitive appraisal, it is also empirically far from clear that established democracies have in recent years and decades really massively curtailed civil rights. This chapter therefore addresses these questions from both a theoretical and an empirical point of view.

Four general questions guide our investigation: we first look at whether civil liberties have in fact been restricted in Western democracies in the course of time. In close connection with this, we then examine whether civil rights have been similarly restricted in all the cases under study or whether there are differences between countries. If there is variance, we then investigate how the different reactions to similar threats are to be explained. Fourthly and finally, we discuss the extent to which (possible) restrictions of civil rights actually constitute a crisis of the democratic system involved.

There are four steps to answering these questions. To begin with, the relationship between civil rights and democracy in the framework of embedded democracy is discussed, and the potential of a disturbed functional relationship for generating crisis is analyzed. Then the phenomena to be empirically examined are defined and operationalized, and the selection of cases and study period explained before the findings of the empirical analysis are presented and discussed. We bring the chapter to an end with an interpretation of the results in the light of the general discussion on crisis and a brief conclusion.

12.2 Civil Rights, Embedded Democracy, and the Crisis of Democracy

At first glance, the connection between civil liberties and democracy is by no means obvious. In his major 1958 essay "Two Concepts of Liberty," Isaiah Berlin argues that "negative" freedom, in other words the "freedom from something" as opposed to the "freedom to do or be something," is by no means incompatible with certain varieties of autocracy and does not necessarily presuppose democratic self-government. Democracies, according to Berlin, can withhold numerous liberties from citizens that a "liberal-minded despot" might in principle very well allow his subjects. Logically therefore, negative freedom is at least not necessarily connected

[2]Responsiveness is the degree of agreement between the preference orders and action of elected members of parliament or government and the demands and wishes of the entire electorate or a section of the electorate (see Schmidt 1995, 837). The concept is hence closely associated with the democracy principle (or to be more precise with the representation principle). But this does not mean that high responsiveness per se has to be beneficial for all institutions of democracy and its functioning.

with democratic self-government (Berlin 1969, 129).[3] In its logical import, Berlin's position cannot be fundamentally contradicted. However, it ignores an important question that throws a different light on negative liberties and democracy: the question of the legitimation of individual rights. For, regardless of the strong empirical link between civil liberties and democracy, which Berlin himself expresses, how can individual rights be justified today other than through democratic procedures of self-government? Jürgen Habermas's (2001, 1998, Chap. 10) notion of the "equiprimordiality" of the rule of law and democracy (and of individual liberties and democratic participatory rights) sums it up: positive law can—at least in the post-metaphysical age—now claim legitimacy only if it guarantees equal autonomy for all legal entities (Habermas 1998, 254), which in turn can succeed only through democratic procedures of self-legislation.

The model of democracy underlying this book takes up this idea and supplements it by functionalistic considerations. The embedded democracy model understands democracy as a system of partial regimes that, although autonomous, are interrelated (see the introduction to this volume). Within this model, the partial regime of civil liberties together with the institutional mechanisms for the separation of powers forms the rule of law dimension of embedded democracy (Merkel et al. 2003, 52). In essence, they can be understood as negative individual rights of defense against the state and society. In classical terms, these rights include the freedom of conscience, the right to freedom of expression, the freedom of assembly, and the right to free movement. More specific (and also still more basic) are the rights that have to do with physical integrity, for instance, the right not to be tortured and the right to life (see also the contribution by Tanneberg, Chap. 13), the classical habeas corpus rights (prohibition of detention without judicial warrant of arrest), or the increasingly important right to informational self-determination. The question of what data and what knowledge about its citizens a democratic state governed by the rule of law may collect, store, and if necessary use against them is becoming more and more of a key issue in the field of civil liberties. The principles and rights mentioned are as a rule laid down by the constitution of a country and are the civil rights in John Locke's sense that citizens ideally grant to one another in the course of constitution making and which are protected against interference by the state; they limit the claims to power and the reach of the state and society vis-à-vis the individual. Fundamentally, civil liberties are therefore not at the disposition even of elected (parliamentary)

---

[3]"Freedom in this sense is not, at any rate logically, connected with democracy or self-government. Self-government may, on the whole, provide a better guarantee of the preservation of civil liberties than other régimes, and has been defended as such by libertarians. But there is no necessary connection between individual liberty and democratic rule. The answer to the question 'Who governs me?' is logically distinct from the question 'How far does this government interfere with me?' It is this difference that the great contrast between the two concepts of negative and positive liberty, in the end, consists" (Berlin 1969, 129f.). For Berlin, positive freedom, by contrast, means not to be the "instrument [...] of other men's [. . .] acts of will" (ibid, 131), and to this extent it is much more closely connected with democratic self-government.

majorities or the people. When different principles collide or disputes arise about their interpretation, it is generally the task of the courts to decide on their application.

This shows the close logical and factual connection between civil liberties and their safeguarding by independent courts: if basic rights can be curbed simply by the will of a contingent political majority, its institutionalization is built on sand. If, by contrast, independent courts are entrusted with safeguarding these fundamental civil liberties, this at least ensures as a matter of principle that action by the legislature and the executive can be reviewed with reference to a (written or unwritten) constitution—ultimately against the benchmark of the rights that the citizens have granted each other. The precondition for such judicial review is hence the existence of central rule of law institutions, equality before the law, and equal access to the law for all citizens (see Merkel et al. 2003, 53).

But negative freedoms are not only of intrinsic and constitutional value; overall they are also elementary to the functioning of the democratic system. For example, to talk of the free exercise of the right to political participation makes logical sense only if all associated action is protected against interference by state or societal actors. Political participatory and electoral procedures would make no sense if the state were able simply to curb or completely prevent the free public expression of opinion; the act of voting itself would be seriously restricted if in the run-up to an election the citizens' and parties' right of assembly was curtailed, thus making public political discussion impossible; and the participation of citizens in public discussion (whether oral or written) would be seriously curbed if state authorities were allowed in advance—for example, through simple official registration, through electronic surveillance of private homes, or through the online surveillance of computers—to obtain information about the views, opinions, or attitudes of certain people.[4] In short, without protection for individual liberties under the rule of law, they would not only be threatened in their very substance; the functional logic of democracy would risk serious disruption.

But would such a malfunction already involve a crisis of democracy? It can be argued at least that a theory of representation that sees no symptoms of crisis in the restriction of civil liberties in reaction to the interests and preferences of the population must appear inadequate. Against the background of the embedded democracy model, it is clear that individual civil liberties are not the usual policy issues that under democratic forms of government are legitimately left to political

---

[4]In the words of the German Federal Constitutional Court in their ruling on the national census on the 15 December 1983: "Those who must be unsure if deviant behavior cannot be noticed at any time and persistently stored, used or passed on, will try not to expose themselves by such ways of behavior. Whoever expects that participation in an assembly or a pressure group will be registered by the authorities, causing him future risks, will possibly give up exercising the respective basic rights. This would not only impede the individual development of the personality but also the common good, because self-determination is an elementary precondition for the functioning of a democratic community based on its members' ability to act and participate. It follows that the free development of the personality under the modern conditions of data processing requires the protection of the individual against unlimited collection, storing, use, and passing on of his personal data" (Decision of the German Federal Constitutional Court, BVerfGE 65,1, 43, transl.).

majorities to decide. They must be understood as core constitutive institutional components of democracy whose restriction cannot be at the sole disposition of temporary majorities. From a normative point of view, a discussion about curbing these rights must take account of constitutional law and the functional aspects of democracy and in the event of conflict involve legal actors—generally constitutional courts (see Kneip, Chap. 14).

This is not to assert that every restriction of civil liberties is to be equated with a crisis of democratic governance, especially when such restrictions can be imposed with the approval of the courts. But on the basis of the underlying model of democracy, it could be argued that curbs on freedom of this sort involve at least a loss in the quality of democracy. Such a loss of quality may under certain circumstances seem necessary to all the parties involved (governments, parliaments, parties, courts, citizens) and to be the lesser evil—but a loss of quality it remains. When such a loss turns into a crisis of democracy can at this juncture be described only in abstract terms. In the context under discussion, democracy would be in crisis if fundamental liberties and civil rights were so severely restricted that they are no longer recognizable in substance or if the curtailment caused a fundamental functional disruption of other democratic partial regimes.[5] The "second-order risks" (Huster and Rudolph 2008; Schneckener 2011)—those arising from the reactions of societies to certain crises—would then outweigh the primary risks.

The empirical findings reported in the literature give some cause to suspect that the loss of democratic quality is not trivial. Although there are few transnational, systematic comparative studies, some read like descriptions of decline. For example, Haubrich (2003) lists a broad range of categories under which the bulk of the restrictions of civil liberties in Germany, France, and the UK after 9/11 can be classified. In addition to the right of self-determination over personal data, the right to freedom of expression, the right to free movement, and the competencies of the secret services were affected. Baker (2003) notes similar observations that, with regard to protection from prosecution and protection of privacy from intrusion by the state, the pendulum of freedom is clearly swinging away from the liberal pole. For a number of Western democracies, Busch (2011), too, observes an increase in the power of the executive, blurring boundaries between police, secret services, and the military and growing and less well-controlled exchanges of data between the security authorities of different countries. The extent of secret service surveillance

[5]The systematic denial of civil rights and liberties to large sections of the Afro-American population of the USA until well into the 1960s, for example, reached this roughly defined threshold in both regards. By contrast, the anti-terror measures taken by the Bush administration after 9/11 quite possibly impaired the very substance of civil rights and liberties but caused no fundamental disturbance of the functional logic of American democracy. The contrary is perhaps true for present-day Hungary, where, although the constitutional and legal reforms carried out by the Orbán government do perhaps remain below the threshold, the totality of the measures taken considerably disrupt the functioning of the democratic partial regimes. Without a doubt, all the examples cited involve a loss of democratic quality. Whether they are also cases of "democratic crisis" must first be demonstrated by more precise analysis.

activities by the USA, as well as the UK and other Western countries revealed by former NSA employee Edward Snowden in June 2013, gives a new dimension to what has hitherto been known. The evidently large-scale accessing of the data of American Internet firms, the spying out of worldwide data traffic, and the surveillance of private and official telephone and e-mail communication suggest that suspicions of a distinct international shift from the "rule of law state to the prevention state" (Huster and Rudolph 2008) are more than speculation.

Interestingly enough, this development in security architectures corresponds well with popular preferences. This is at least the conclusion invited by (quasi-) experimental studies in the USA and UK. In a series of investigations, Davis and Silver (2003a, b, 2004) noted that after 9/11 civil liberties competed far less well with governmental promises of security. The extent to which American citizens are willing to exchange freedom for security accordingly depends on their assessment of threats and their confidence in the government. Especially when skepticism toward the executive is strong and when the personal and/or sociotropic sense of threat is low, civil liberties are held to be more important than security interests. Overall, however, 9/11 brought about a marked shift in the willingness of the American population to curb civil liberties in their own country in favor of measures that went under the heading of "war on terrorism."

Similar results are to be found for the UK with regard to popular attitudes toward anti-terror measures (Wagner and Giebler 2009). After the attacks on the London Underground, the British public was much less critical about these measures than they had been. However, another and even stronger factor explaining anti-liberal attitudes is the sense of threat; over and beyond objective threats, the fear of oneself becoming the victim of a terrorist attack clearly increases acceptance for the curtailment of fundamental freedoms without any manifest improvement in security resulting.

Regardless of whether restrictions of liberty culminate in a "crisis" or merely in a "deterioration of quality," this raises a fundamental question for our investigation: What mechanisms and factors can explain how democratic societies react to the threats mentioned? If differences are to be found in how democratic societies react to putative threat scenarios, a plausible theoretical explanation should also be possible for why country A reacts by tightening security laws, while country B does not. In the literature (MacKinnon 2007; Busch 2011), three main factors are repeatedly mentioned: (a) institutional counterweights (federalism, second chambers, constitutional courts), (b) the rule of law and a civil liberties culture, and (c) previous experience with terrorism and "traditions" of anti-terror legislation. As far as institutional counterweights are concerned, it can be argued that where federal structures and constitutional courts are strong, civil liberties will not be so rapidly and not so drastically restricted as in otherwise comparable countries that lack such counterweights. In the UK, for instance, policies curbing freedom can arguably be introduced much more easily—if the executive so will—than, for example, in Germany or the USA. It can also be argued that a high level of rule of law and a civil liberties culture are likely to make it politically more difficult to curtail civil liberties. A dense network of rule of law institutions and effective checks and balances in conjunction with a culture of freedom deeply entrenched in the population should make it "more expensive" for political actors to curb civil liberties, even if the freedom culture of a population is perhaps weaker owing to personal experience of crime or terrorist threats than in less critical times.[6]

A population's culture of freedom includes a pluralistic media system, which ideally discusses, analyses, and questions political processes and policy outcomes, thus processing "policy" and the action of the elites for public discourses. An effective "fourth estate" can help draw the attention of a liberal-minded public to adverse developments and thus in the medium and long term—and beyond electoral opportunities—exercise a monitoring function. It seems likely that the existence of a strong pluralistic media system free of state influence would make it more difficult to restrict civil liberties.

Experience with terrorism, perceived threats, and a tradition of anti-terror legislation would suggest that societies and their political elites are more likely to undertake and accept restrictions on freedom than societies without such a past. The UK, for example, had, even before 9/11, the most comprehensive anti-terror legislation, followed by Spain (MacKinnon 2007). In both cases, it seems likely that experience with domestic terrorism and past legislative reactions would make it easier for political elites to react to new threat situations and scenarios with tougher laws. For the USA, the subjective perception of a terrorist threat situation after 9/11 is likely to have very much facilitated the curtailment of civil liberties. But whether these conclusions can be empirically demonstrated remains to be seen.

Finally, research on the welfare state offers another explanation that can be transferred to the policy area of civil liberties: the partisan theory (Hibbs 1977). In essence, it asserts that differences in the (objective) interests and (subjective) preferences of voters for parties are reflected in the government policy of these parties (Petring 2010, 69; see there for an overview of the status of research). The assumption is then that governments that include liberal parties with an affinity for civil rights will be less likely to restrict civil liberties. Vice versa, governments formed by parties that give less priority to this subject matter will tend to curb civil liberties more strongly.

12.3 Empirical Patterns

As the brief overview of the areas in which the literature posits a loss of quality shows, "civil liberty" is not a clear-cut concept with clearly defined components easily amenable to empirical analysis. Our investigation therefore takes account of

[6]A fundamental break with the "open society" model could, for example, presumably not have been achieved in Norway, even after the terrorist act of the radical right-wing mass murderer Anders Breivik and even if the Norwegian government had sought to do so. But this naturally remains speculation and is mentioned here only to illustrate the basic plausibility of the argument.

all the indicators that can meaningfully be attributed to the concept (see also Skaaning 2008; Møller and Skaaning 2013).

Not only the concept itself is somewhat blurred. Comparative studies also show a certain lack of criteria when it comes to defining the geographical regions in which a decline of democratic quality is suspected. But, at least implicitly, the assertion that democracy could be in crisis with regard to individual civil liberties is always made with reference to the developed democracies of the "West." This empirical study therefore addresses all the "old" OECD democracies. Since the concept of crisis suggests a process—the quality of democracy declining over time—thus presupposing a temporal dimension, empirical investigation has to be not only cross-sectional but also longitudinal, working with time series. A suitable database is therefore the Democracy Barometer (Bühlmann et al. 2013), which contains a large number of indicators that deal with civil liberties from 1990 to 2007 for the 22 countries that belonged to the OECD in 1990.[7] On the basis of these data, the hypotheses developed above can be tested, namely:

H1: There has been a decline in civil liberties since 1990, above all since 2001. The reason is to be expected in the experience with terrorism in the 2000s.

H2: In countries with a more highly developed tradition of protecting civil liberties, they have declined less.

H3: Under governments that adopt a more liberal stance on civil rights, there has been less deterioration in civil liberties.

H4: Open, plural, and independent media hamper excessive curtailment of civil liberties.

H5: In federal countries, the loss of quality is less pronounced.

H6: Strong and independent constitutional courts help to ensure the preservation of civil liberties.

The Democracy Barometer pursues the deductive measurement logic associated with the "embedded democracy" concept. The freely available dataset[8] includes expert assessments and survey data on a number of dimensions and subdimensions. The 22 indicators used—all scaled from 0 to 1—come from the functions "individual liberties," "rule of law," and "public sphere." Specifically, survey data on confidence in the legal system (confjust) and in the fair administration of justice in society (fairjust) are used along with expert assessments of the existence of constitutional provisions banning torture or inhumane treatment (consttort), on freedom of religion (constrel), on freedom of movement (constfreemov), on the fairness of the system of justice (constfair), on constitutional provisions guaranteeing a public trial (pubtrial), on the freedom of assembly and association (constfras and constass), and on freedom of the press and speech (constpress and constspeech).

---

[7]Turkey and Greece are not among the best 30 OECD democracies, so they are not included in the version of the Democracy Barometer used here.

[8]To download and for documentation: http://www.democracybarometer.org/

In addition, the Democracy Barometer contains expert assessments of the de facto provision of rights that can be categorized as civil liberties: the question whether the UN Torture Convention has been ratified (convtort), the extent to which the government effectively restricts the freedom of movement (freemove) and of religion (freerelig), the non-manipulation of the courts (impcourts), the integrity and strength of the legal system as a whole (integrlegal), the actual independence of courts, and the noninterference by government and political parties in the administration of justice (judindepcor and judindepinf). The degree of judges' professionalism (profjudg and proftenure) has also been included, as well as the existence of political terror (politterr) and the practice of torture (torture).[9]

In order to determine the influence of an open, plural media system and federal structures, the variables in the Democracy Barometer that cover these areas have also been included in the analysis.[10] The strength and independence of supreme and constitutional courts, finally, were covered on the basis of Lijphart's coding in four categories (see Lijphart 1999).

The modified partisan hypothesis was tested with the aid of data from the Manifesto Project (Volkens et al. 2013). For each year, the balance was calculated for the categories "freedom and human rights" (201) and "law and order: positive" (605) for the government in office.[11] The result thus reflects the emphasis the government placed on civil liberties as opposed to law-and-order policies in the given year—the very balance this study is addressing.

There are two key questions for the empirical analyses: (1) Has the situation for civil liberties in Western democracies deteriorated over the past two decades? (2) How are the developments in this area of democracy to be explained? We deal with the second question in Sect. 12.4. First we present descriptive findings to test the first two hypotheses.

The course of the various indicators between 1990 and 2007 differs considerably. In the 1990s and 2000s, a certain stability prevailed in many areas of civil liberties, while others experienced ups and downs varying from country to country without discernible (and statistically ascertainable) trends, and in one area there was a positive development. To obtain results that go beyond assessment on the basis of mere face validity, regression analyses[12] were undertaken in which the year variable was used to explain indicator development. In accordance with the postulate that a critical loss of quality took place particularly in the 2000s, the year term is squared. This corresponds to a development that shows no or only weak

[9]Not included were other variables on the protection of physical integrity (see Tanneberg in this volume), on property rights (which in the context of the issues we are discussing are not core civil liberties), as well as variables belonging to explanatory factors.

[10]They are the variables on "freedom of information" and "informational openness" for the media, as well as "degree of federalism" to cover federalism. See Appendix 3 for an overview of variables.

[11]In the case of coalition governments, the parties were weighted in terms of the number of seats held, so that smaller coalition partners were given less weight than larger government parties.

[12]Linear regressions with panel-corrected standard errors were calculated.

deterioration at the beginning of the period under review—in the 1990s—and a stronger decline in quality above all in the 2000s. And some indicators do indeed show increasing deterioration over time (see Appendix 1 for the regression results for the individual variables).

If these results are systematized, they offer three conclusions: first, constitutionally entrenched civil liberties are not affected—no decline is apparent for any of the nine constitutional variables. Where there are changes, they even point to improvement (above all in the 1990s and in only a few countries). This is particularly true for the freedom of assembly and association and for protection of the freedom of religion, independence of the judiciary, and free movement of persons. On the constitutional front, the all-clear can accordingly be given. The deterioration we shall be looking at therefore takes place below the threshold of amendments to constitutional documents. To this positive result must be added a significant increase in the proportion of countries that have ratified the UN Torture Convention. The first conclusion is that a possible crisis would be "only" a crisis of constitutional reality, not of the de jure design of the democratic polity.

Eight indicators show intertemporal variance without a clear structure[13]: there are both ups and downs in some countries as well as weak improvement and slight deterioration in others. In sum, the existence of a democratic crisis can be clearly denied. Neither public access to nor public confidence in the courts and the legal system suffered nor were the independence of judges or their professionalism reduced or the free movement of persons restricted. The all-clear can therefore be given in these areas as well.

However, a number of key civil liberties were in effect markedly curtailed. Four indicators, all based on expert assessments, show significant deterioration over time. The first area affected is the freedom of religion, which was considerably restricted by executive and legislature after the (Islamist) terror attacks in the 2000s. The index value fell by almost half over the period under study (from a mean of 0.95 in 1990 to 0.50 in 2007). This was accompanied by a decline in the strength and integrity of the legal system in many countries. In this regard, the expert assessments of the Democracy Barometer agree with many individual case studies (see, e.g., MacKinnon 2007; Busch 2011), which identify a marked deterioration in the quality of the legal system, in particular in countries like the UK, Spain, and Germany. Overall, this value fell by more than a sixth. To this must be added negative trends in *the Political Terror Scale* (fall of almost a quarter of a point from 0.93 to 0.70) and in the use of torture (also down a quarter of a point). In keeping with the topic of this volume, we shall focus on these indicators. Exploratory factor analysis shows that the similarities in the distribution of these four variables are non-coincidental and that the connections between them can be satisfactorily explained by a single factor. This one-dimensional structure means that a latent variable underlies these four indicators. The resulting factor depicts area of civil

[13]They include the indicators "freemove," "pubtrial," "judindepcor," "judindepinf," "impcourts," "profjudg," "proftenure," and "fairjust."

liberties that deteriorated in the 1990s and 2000s. Figure 12.1 shows the development of this factor in the 22 countries over the period under review.

Variance in development between countries is clear. Whereas factor values in, for example, Denmark, Iceland, or the Netherlands remained surprisingly stable over time, there was a marked negative trend in such countries as Italy, Spain, the UK, and the USA. Inferential statistics confirm the finding: despite only 18 observations within a country, a significant, quadratic, negative trend is apparent for 17 of the 22 countries (78%) (see Appendix 2). This confirms the first part of the first hypothesis: some key civil liberties have been lost or perceptibly restricted. What is more, there was again a marked deterioration after 2001. Whereas in the 1990s there were low values for the civil liberties factor in comparatively few countries, this changes considerably after 2000.

This face validity of this result is also confirmed by statistical models. The decrease in the civil liberties factors between 1990 and 2007 was not linear; it followed a quadratic course—in the 1990s the fall was weaker, in the 2000s stronger.[14] As Fig. 12.2 shows, civil liberties were more strongly restricted in the second half of the period under study, that is to say, in the 2000s. The vertical axis shows the level (calculated in the regression) of civil liberties, the horizontal axis the date. The second hypothesis can be confirmed on the basis of this diagram: the negative development of civil liberties is by no means constant across all countries. The curve varies significantly from country to country.[15] There is therefore no universal trend that holds for all countries. Whereas no significant deterioration in civil liberties took place in the Scandinavian countries, in the Netherlands, and in Luxembourg, the opposite was the case in Spain, France, the USA, and Italy. How this is to be explained in the light of our hypotheses is discussed in the coming section.

Four groups emerge. In the first are countries that in 2007 still had relatively high values which hardly fell over time. Close together with values between 0.7 and 0.4 are the Nordic countries Finland, Denmark, Norway, Sweden, and Iceland, as well as Luxembourg and the Netherlands. In the four countries of the second group, the model already points to a deterioration. With index values between 0.1 and −0.6, this group includes New Zealand, Australia, Canada, and Ireland. The third group is constituted by Japan, Belgium, Austria, Germany, Switzerland, the UK, and Portugal (values between −1.1 and −1.7). In these countries, there is not only a marked drop in the factor value between 1990 and 2007; at the end of the period under study, they were also below the mean of the 22 countries. Finally, the fourth

[14]The likelihood ratio test suggests that a model with squared year term is significantly superior to a model with a linear explanatory variable. A model that contains both terms (year and $year^2$) and thus posits an initial rise and subsequent fall is, by contrast, not superior to the more parsimonious model with only the squared term.

[15]According to the LR test, the random slope multilevel model used, which takes account of the nested data structure, provides a better fit for the data than a single-level model or a model without random slope effect coefficients. In addition, intra-class correlation of the null model shows that cross-country variance is much higher than variance within countries.

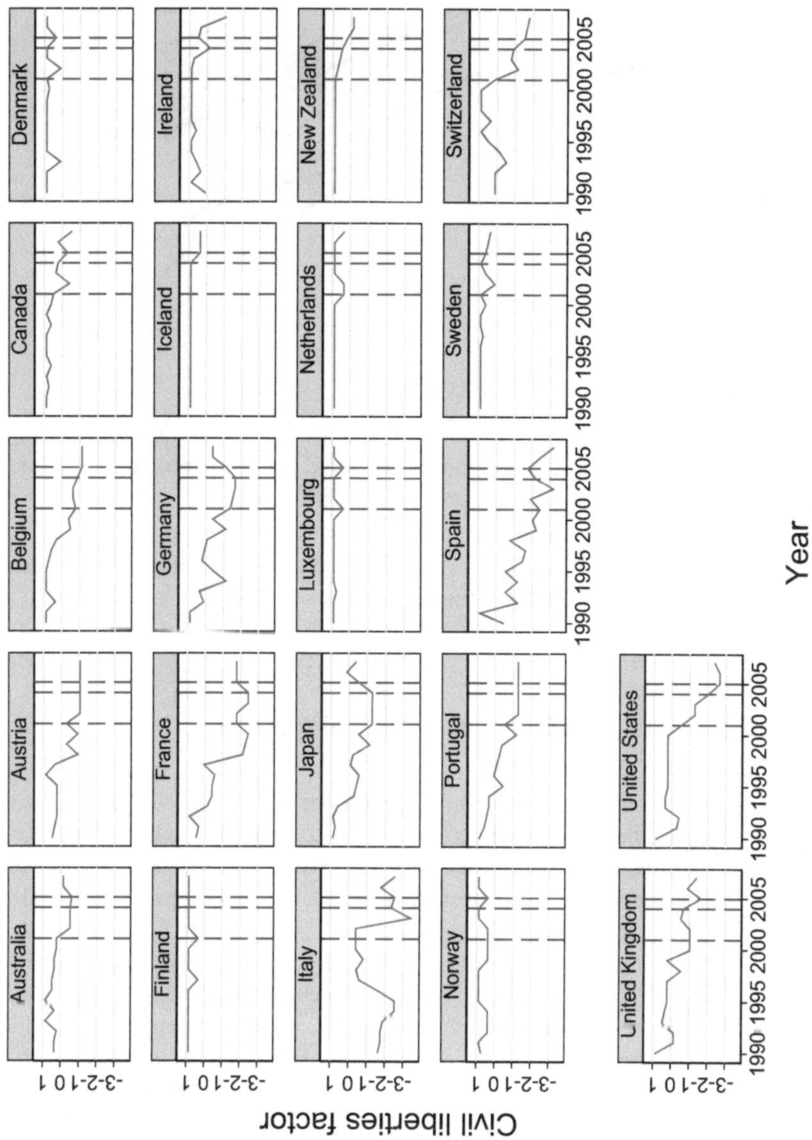

Fig. 12.1 Development of the civil liberties factor in 22 OECD countries between 1990 and 2007. Note: Vertical lines for 2001, 2004, and 2005 mark the date of attacks in the USA, Spain, and the UK. Source: Democracy Barometer

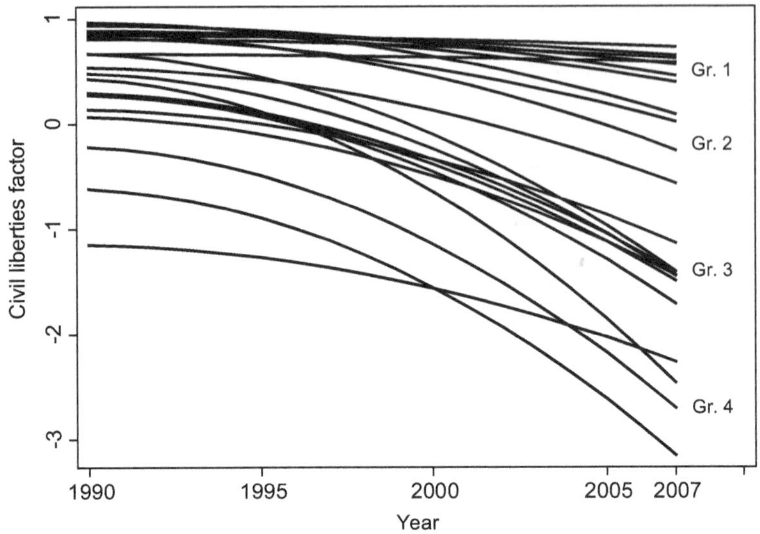

Fig. 12.2 Development of the civil liberties factor, 1990–2007. Note: Results of a random slope multilevel model, x-axis = years, y-axis = civil liberties factor. For the results, see Model 2 in Table 12.1

group comprising Italy, the USA, France, and Spain showed extremely low values and to some extent dramatic deterioration over time.

12.4 Explaining the Differences in Development

What, then, are the causes of this divergent development? On the one hand, it is surprising that, despite the stability of constitutional content, the de facto situation in the different countries often developed very negatively. This can be explained firstly by the fact that constitutional norms, if amenable to interpretation at all, generally offer political actors broad scope for action. Amendment of the constitution is often simply not necessary to introduce or tighten security legislation. On the other hand, political actors from time to time speculate that their action will ultimately be judged constitutional even though this is perhaps uncertain at the time or even a contentious public issue. Whether constitutional courts will in the last resort actually annul supposedly unconstitutional political action is in many cases a moot point and from a political standpoint subject to a great deal of uncertainty. Purposeful circumvention of the constitution is not always punished after the fact, so that politically costly constitutional amendments are often avoided.

As far as differences in constitutional reality are concerned, the literature offers a range of factors to explain the various developments of the past 20 years. Our first hypothesis posits not only a loss of quality in the partial regime "civil liberties" over

Table 12.1 Regression results explaining changes in civil liberties

	Model 0 (Null model)	Model 1 (Year^2)	Model 2 (Year^2–random)	Model 3 (Attack)	Model 4 (Government)	Model 5 (Media)	Model 6 (Federalism)	Model 7 (Rule of law)	Model 8 (Complete)
Year^2		**−0.004*****	**−0.004*****	**−0.004*****	**−0.004*****	**−0.004*****	**−0.004*****	**−0.004*****	**−0.004***
Terrorist attack				−0.569					−0.303
Terrorist. attack × year^2				+0.002					0.001
Liberal cabinet					−0.004				−0.002
Liberal cabinet × year^2					−0.000				−0.000
Free media						**+0.154*****			**+0.130*****
Free media × year^2						**−0.001*****			**−0.001*****
Federalism							**−0.372**		−0.076
Federalism × year^2							**−0.004*****		−0.003
Rule of law								−0.165	−0.012
Rule of law × year^2								**−0.002*****	−0.000
Level in 1990									**1.022*****
Level in 1990 × year^2									**0.003****
Constants	−0.000	**+0.447*****	**+0.447*****	**+0.448*****	**+0.453*****	**+0.481*****	**+0.573*****	**+0.852****	**+0.032**
No. of cases	396	396	396	396	378	396	396	396	378
Log likelihood	−439.61	−358.97	−313.11	−312.86	−276.81	−308.89	−309.56	−309.76	−225.40
BIC	897.17	741.86	662.10	673.57	601.10	665.63	666.97	667.37	557.24

Note: Multilevel model (lower level = years in countries, upper level = countries); freedom of information (FOI), terrorist attacks, and government composition = micro-variables; federalism and strength of constitutional courts = macro-variables; *$p < 0.1$; **$p < 0.05$; ***$p < 0.01$; (significant coefficients are in bold type)

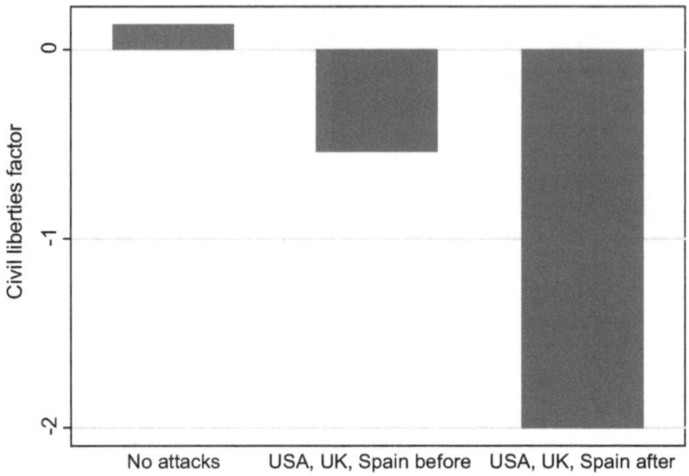

Fig. 12.3 Values for the factor civil liberties for countries spared major terrorist attacks, for the USA, the UK, and Spain before and after the relevant attacks of the 2000s. Source: Own calculations

the period under study but also that this was triggered not least by the bloody terrorist attacks in the Western metropolises—New York, Madrid, and London. This implies that restrictions in this field were mainly introduced in the countries affected after the event (see Fig. 12.3). Figure 12.4 shows that this was the case (without controlling for other factors). In the 19 countries that did not suffer (major) incidents, the level of the civil liberties factor was far higher than in the USA, the UK, and Spain even before the attacks of 2001, 2004, and 2005. In the years following the terrorist incidents, the level fell considerably which can be understood to indicate that this effect was the product of the attacks.

Hypotheses 2 to 6 postulate that curbs on civil liberties should be less drastic in countries with a strong tradition of freedom (and thus with a high base level), under governments with a civil rights/liberal platform, with free media, with federal structures, and with strong constitutional courts. Figure 12.4 confirms the second hypothesis: the higher the liberal base level in 1990 (right-hand side of the figure), the lower was the level of restrictions on liberties (changes close to zero).[16] The Nordic countries along with the Netherlands and Luxembourg are among the states that in 1990 had the highest base level and did not lose it over time. By contrast, where the base level was middling to weak, that is to say, when there had already been restrictions in 1990, the loss of quality is greater. This is particularly pronounced in the cases of Spain and France.

Two runaway results should be mentioned separately. For a low base value, Italy shows moderate deterioration, whereas the "home of the free," the USA, shows severe losses of quality particularly in the 2000s. But even if these special cases are

[16]Confirmation is given by the significant correlation between intercept and slope.

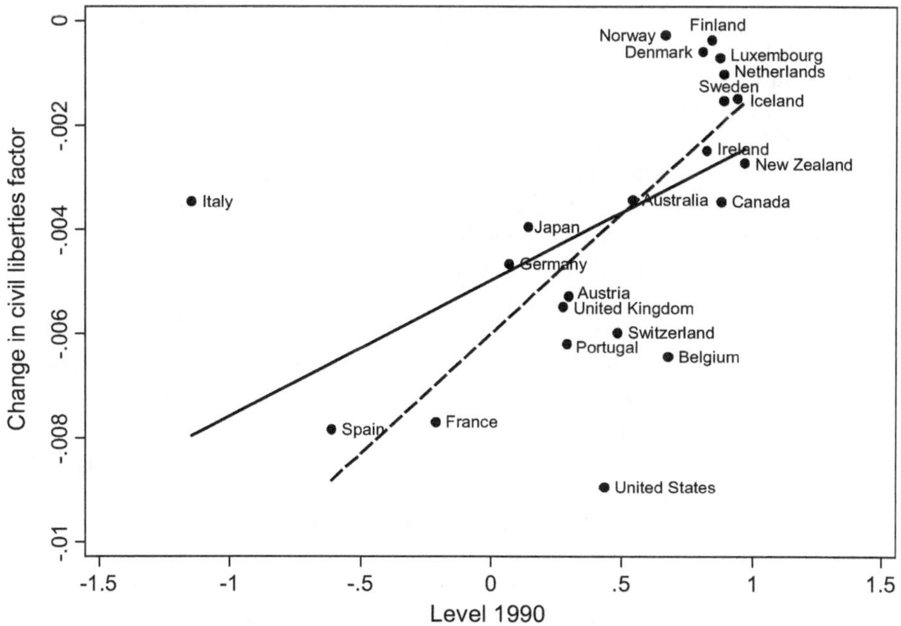

Fig. 12.4 Connection between the level of civil liberties in 1990 and changes up to 2007. Note: Changes in the factor civil liberties independent of the 1990 base level

excluded, the connection fundamentally persists (dashed line). The Scandinavian countries, whose stability has already been noted in describing developments (see Fig. 12.1), have respected individual rights from the outset and over time. Spain, by contrast, is the opposing ideal type: the already comparatively moderate level of civil liberties recorded at the beginning of the 1990s fell strongly in the course of the 1990s and 2000s, which tallies with the Spanish executive's exceeding its powers in fighting terrorism as noted by MacKinnon (2007).

In order to test hypotheses 1 and 3 to 6, multilevel models were estimated (see Table 12.1). The first is the empty or null model without explanatory factors, which is the reference factor. In the second model, the squared year variable was introduced and variation of the intercept; in the third variation of the coefficient (random slope), the rise and fall over time were also allowed. This took into account the variance in the temporal development of civil liberties shown in Figs. 12.2 and 12.4 In each step, the model's goodness of fit increased. In the models that followed, it was attempted to explain this variance on the basis of the explanatory factors presented in the hypotheses. For this purpose, interactions between the squared year variable and the given explanatory variable were modeled. Model 3 introduces experience with terrorism as the first factor. This is the first substantial model to explain the development of the civil liberties factor over time. Although Fig. 12.3 shows an effect of the attacks in the USA, the UK and Spain, it is statistically insignificant (presumably due to the small number of cases: only 11 positive values (six years in the USA, three in Spain, and two in the UK)). Also negative is the finding for the government stance on freedom versus security in the relevant party programs. It clearly made no difference whether party programs were oriented on security or on freedom.

Model 5 introduces an interaction between freedom of the media and the year variable. Here a reliable influence is to be found: the existence of free media systems raises the level of civil liberties by about 0.15 points on the scale. However, in such countries, there is also a somewhat stronger decline than in countries where media systems are restricted, as indicated by the significant negative coefficient of −0.001. However, this is so low that in countries with high free media values, the level of civil liberties in 2007 is still above that in countries with low values for the freedom of the media. Although this negative trend effect is diametrically opposed to our original hypothesis, it is not implausible if one considers the favorable attitude of the population mentioned above to introducing tougher security laws. If the media are seen as a means of communication between political decision-maker elites and citizens and if both sides favor anti-terror measures, a neutral media system needs not lead to more liberal legislation. This would be likely only where democratic public spheres are strongly against anti-terror measures.

Models 6 and 7 introduce, respectively, the macro-variables federalism and strength of constitutional courts, including the given interactions. According to this model, federal states showed a somewhat lower freedom value in 1990. Over time, this difference even grows, as indicated by the significant negative interaction term. In 2007 the difference between federal and unitary states, according to Model 6, amounted to almost half a point on the scale. This is in marked contradiction to the assumption to be found in the literature that federal structures check the curbing of civil liberties. The same holds for countries with strong supreme or constitutional courts: here, too, the decline in civil liberties is stronger rather than weaker. In the coming section, we shall be discussing how this initially surprising result is to be interpreted.

The final Model 8 contains all explanatory factors and additionally the starting value of the civil liberties factor in 1990 (to model the connection of the development over time from the level in the beginning, shown in Fig. 12.4). In this model the macro-variables lose their explanatory value. Only the openness of the media system maintains its effect. The effect of the value in 1990 is significant, though. Countries with stronger civil liberties in 1990 do have higher values in the following years, and civil liberties are strengthened in these countries, which is indicated by the small but significant positive interaction of "level in 1990" and the squared year term. As the reduction of the BIC values indicate, this variable particularly helps to explain the variation in civil liberties in the 1990s and 2000s. Furthermore, we see a reduction in the relevance of the time variable. This implies that parts of the time trend can be attributed to the level of civil liberties in 1990, as Fig. 12.4 already indicated. Higher levels of civil liberties therefore not only translate in higher levels in the 1990s and 2000s, but at the same time significantly hinder the curtailment of civil liberties over time. In those countries that started well, civil liberties have not been cut back.

12.5 Summary, Interpretation, and Conclusion

In sum, it can be said that the assumption widespread in the literature that in recent decades, and particularly after the terrorist attacks of 9/11, civil liberties have been restricted in almost all liberal democracies cannot be confirmed across the board. According to the data of the Democracy Barometer, the civil liberties guaranteed by the constitutional texts of democratic states were not restricted. If changes did occur in this field, they strengthened civil liberties. This is true above all for ratification of the *UN Torture Convention* but also for the freedom of assembly and association, the protection of the freedom of religion, the independence of the courts, and the free movement of persons.

Below the threshold of alterations to constitutional documents, there is no clear development for eight indicators between 1990 and 2007. However, there are four areas in which significant deterioration took place: liberal democracies suffered marked losses in quality in the freedom of religion, the strength and impartiality of the legal system, equality before the law and habeas corpus rights (Political Terror Scale), and the right to physical integrity (torture). Considering that all these rights and principles define nothing less than the basis of democracy under the rule of law, such deterioration is indeed serious. And for these four areas, it proceeded over the entire period under study, but especially after 2001. The terrorist attacks of New York and Washington thus aggravated an already existing trend.

However, the downhill development varies from country to country as much as the base level for countries in 1990 does. Whereas the Nordic countries and the Netherlands maintained their high base level for civil liberties over time, moderate to strong decline took place in the countries of Central and Southern Europe (Germany, Austria, UK, Switzerland, Portugal, as well as Japan and Canada) and very strongly and even dramatically in France, Italy, Spain, and the USA. While in Italy marked deficiencies in the rule of law that had already been apparent at the end of the "first republic" in 1990 worsened under the Berlusconi governments, the partly dramatic losses in freedom in Spain and the USA also appear to be a consequence of the terrorist attacks of the 2000s. Overall it can be said that the countries that set out from a high level of civil liberties suffered lower losses of freedom than those that started from a lower level. This confirms our postulate that liberal rule of law traditions can at least attenuate the decline of individual liberties.

Our hypotheses about liberal party programs of governments, the media system, federalism, and the strength of constitutional courts were not confirmed. Participation in government by liberal parties in a civil rights tradition does not reduce the curbing of civil liberties in times of a dominant security discourse. Open and plural media do not mitigate the increasing restriction of civil liberties but even tend to further it. Liberal media can have an attenuating effect only where the majority of the population is against tougher security laws. But in most "Western" democracies, this is not the case, as the rather moderate reactions by the public sphere to Edward Snowden's revelations confirm. The desire of the population for more protection against crime and terrorism thus tends, also through the conveyance of this desire by the media, to produce curbs on freedom rights rather than the opposite.

The nonsignificant (or even negative) influence of federal structures and strong (constitutional) courts is at first glance and in the light of what the literature has to say surprising. It could be due to a number of things. The first is perhaps a sample problem: empirically it could be that the severest restrictions on civil rights were imposed in countries with federal structures and strong constitutional courts (USA, Spain, Switzerland, Italy). The USA and Spain in particular have had experience with terrorist attacks, which could explain the stronger anti-liberal reactions on the part of politicians and society. By contrast, no attacks took place in countries with unitary structures and without strong courts (Scandinavia, Netherlands). The theoretically plausible mitigating effect of federal and judicial structures could therefore not come to bear in the overall sample. By contrast, in the cases where strong restriction took place, federal veto structures were to some extent ineffectual owing to a lack of institutional powers. Even formally, second chambers in parliament do not in every case handle the relevant legislation; and sometimes they do not differ in political composition from the first chamber, or given the perceived threats, they may share their views on curbing civil liberties. In such cases they cannot play the role of veto actors.

As far as constitutional jurisdiction is concerned, the time lag in proceedings before constitutional courts needs to be taken into consideration. The relevant data cover only the period up to 2007. Much security legislation passed after 2001 may possibly have come before the supreme courts at a much later date, if it all. Another explanation for the lack of comparative influence exerted by constitutional courts may be that strong courts, too, may not necessarily be inclined, when it comes to supposedly existential issues of terrorist threats, to go against decisions of the political authorities shared, moreover, by the population. With their only weak democratic legitimation, courts often hesitate—perhaps rightly—to bring down final decisions on matters of national security for which they cannot ultimately assume democratic responsibility. What is more, in times of war, courts, too, are occasionally seized by "popular panic" (Waldron 2003, 191) and become "more executive-minded than the executive" (Lord Atkin, quoted in ibid; see also Epstein et al. 2005 and Kneip, Chap. 14).

Overall it can be said that our investigation of the development of civil liberties over time does not necessarily reveal a crisis of democracy. Nevertheless, marked losses of quality in certain areas are in evidence that are anything but trivial. The worldwide surveillance practices of American and other secret services that have recently become public cast a further cloud on this situation. At the same time, talk about a crisis of democracy per se appears to have a blind spot: it may focus too strongly on certain obvious "problem cases" (USA, UK, Spain) to the neglect of other countries where democratic politics has kept to its liberal course even under the threat of terrorism. Higher levels of civil liberties in 1990 are obviously connected with fewer (or no) cutbacks in the following years. This is, for example, the case in Scandinavia where the political culture seems to protect liberties from being restricted.

This study could answer the more general question of democratic theory whether and to what extent democratic societies can find a permanent balance between the security needs of the population and constitutionally guaranteed liberal basic rights only in outline and far from satisfactorily. Institutional barriers and mechanisms apparently hinder the restriction of civil liberties only with the support of a freedom-minded political culture. If this culture comes apart, owing, for instance, to (perceived) threat situations, rule of law institutions and actors may succeed in delaying the dismantling of civil liberties, but they cannot prevent it permanently without such liberal backing. Whether the losses of freedom in some democracies of the Western world are permanent or reversible and whether they mutate into a crisis of democracy depend ultimately on the interaction between rule of law institutions, political actors, and the attitudes and values of the democratic societies themselves. The fundamental strength of democratic systems lies not least in their ability to correct adverse developments with its own resources. This should also be the case in the field of civil liberties.

Appendix 1

Regression analyses (with panel-corrected standard errors) of the key variables; explanatory variable: year^2 (1, 1990; $18^2 = 324$, 2007)

Variable	Constitutional provisions banning torture (consttort)	Ratification of the UN torture convention (convtort)	Political terror (politterr)	The use of torture (torture)	Provisions for freedom of religion (constrel)
Year^2	+0.0002	+0.0006**	−0.0007*	−0.0006**	0.0000
Constants	+0.24*	+0.81***	+0.92***	+0.86***	–
No. of cases	396	396	396	396	396
R^2	0.003	0.168	0.230	0.205	–

Variable	Provisions for freedom of movement (constfreemov)	Free practice of religion (freerelig)	Freedom of movement (freemove)	Fairness of the system of justice (constfair)	Public trial (pubtrial)
Year^2	0.0000	+0.0012*	0.0000	0.0000	+0.0002
Constants	–	+0.92***	+0.95	–	+0,42***
No. of cases	396	396	396	396	396
R^2	–	0.118	0.427	–	0.061

Variable	Judiciary independence (judindepcor)	Noninterference by the government in judiciary (judindepinf)	Non-manipulation of the courts (impcourts)	Integrity and strength of the legal system (integrlegal)	Judges' professionalism—degree and experience (profjudg)
Year^2	−0.0001	−0.0003	−0.0004	−0.0005***	0.0000
Constants	+0.99***	+0.76***	+0.77***	+0.97***	–
No. of cases	396	396	396	396	396
R^2	0.059	0.403	0.445	0.377	–

Variable	Judges' professionalism—term of office (proftenure)	Freedom of assembly (constfras)	Freedom of association (constass)	Freedom of speech (constspeech)	Freedom of press (constpress)
Year^2	0.0000	+0.0001	+0.0001	+0.0001	+0.0001
Constants	–	+0.446***	+0.38***	+0.42***	+0.40***
No. of cases	396	396	396	396	396
R^2	–	0.261	0.096	0.238	0.201

Variable	Confidence in the legal system (confjust)	Fairness of transposition of laws (fairjust)
Year^2	−0.0001	−0.0001
Constants	+0.53***	+0.70***
No. of cases		
R^2	0.390	0.381

Note: *$p < 0.05$; **$p < 0.01$; ***$p < 0.001$; original variable names in brackets

Appendix 2

Regression analyses (OLS, countries) pro country, dependent variable, civil liberties; explanatory variable, year^2 [1 (1990) to 324 (2007; = 18^2)]

Variable	Australia	Austria	Belgium	Canada	Denmark
Year^2	−0.003***	−0.005***	−0.007***	−0.004***	0.000
Constants	+0.544***	+0.324**	+0.796***	+0.923***	+0.767***
No. of cases	18	18	18	18	18
R^2	0.575	0.680	0.864	0.697	−0.057

Variable	Finland	France	Germany	Island	Ireland
$Year^2$	0.000	-0.008^{***}	-0.005^{**}	-0.001^{***}	-0.003^{**}
Constants	$+0.799^{***}$	−0.194	+0.039	$+0.946^{***}$	$+0.842^{***}$
No. of cases	18	18	18	18	18
R^2	−0.060	0.507	0.283	0.552	0.234

Variable	Italy	Japan	Luxembourg	Netherlands	New Zealand
$Year^2$	−0.002	-0.004^{**}	−0.000	-0.001^{*}	-0.003^{***}
Constants	-1.406^{***}	+0.099	$+0.846^{***}$	$+0.871^{***}$	$+1.017^{***}$
No. of cases	18	18	18	18	18
R^2	−0.014	0.222	0.001	0.125	0.763

Variable	Norway	Portugal	Spain	Sweden	Switzerland
$Year^2$	+0.000	-0.007^{***}	-0.008^{***}	-0.001^{***}	-0.007^{***}
Constants	$+0.591^{***}$	$+0.344^{**}$	-0.650^{**}	$+0.888^{***}$	$+0.559^{**}$
No. of cases	18	18	18	18	18
R^2	−0.041	0.791	−0.596	0.410	0.541

Variable	Great Britain	USA
$Year^2$	-0.006^{***}	-0.010^{***}
Constants	$+0.304^{*}$	$+0.594^{***}$
No. of cases	18	18
R^2	0.668	0.818

Note: $^{*}p < 0.1$; $^{**}p < 0.05$; $^{***}p < 0.01$

Appendix 3

Overview of variables

Variables	Contents
confjust	Confidence in the legal system: share of survey respondents indicating high confidence/trust
constass	This variable documents the existence of constitutional provisions protecting the freedom of assembly
constfair	Constitutional provisions for fair organization of court system (no exceptional courts and hierarchical judicial system)
constfras	This variable documents the existence of constitutional provisions regarding freedom of association
constfreemov	... measures, weather constitutional provisions guaranteeing freedom of movement exist
constpress	This variable documents the existence of constitutional provisions concerning the freedom of the press
constrel	Existence of constitutional provisions protecting religious freedom
constspeech	This variable documents the existence of constitutional provisions concerning freedom of speech

(continued)

Variables	Contents
consttort	Existence of constitutional provisions banning torture or inhumane treatment
convtort	Ratification of the United Nations convention against torture and other cruel, inhuman or degrading treatment or punishment
efffoi	Effectiveness of Freedom of Information (FOI) laws. FOI is seen as effective if the following conditions are fulfilled: (A) FOI does not only cover the executive and administration (0.5) but also further public authorities (1); (B) official documents are accessible (except for common exemptions such as matters of national security or documents that contain personal information, etc.) (1) but not considerable number of exemptions and/or delay for Cabinet documents (0.5); (C) compliance with FOI is supervised by an independent commission (1) or at least a court review
fairjust	Assessment of the confidence in the fair administration of justice in the society. Measured on a scale ranging from "There is no confidence in the fair administration of justice in the society" (1) to "There is full confidence in the fair administration of justice in the society"
federgeta	Additive variable with two components: federalism and non-bicameralism
freemove	. . . indicates the extent to which governments restrict the freedom of citizens to travel within or leave their own country of birth or the movement of certain groups based on political or religious grounds. It also captures the extent to which there are restrictions on the duration of stay abroad, whether citizens lose their property and other assets if they leave for a very long time, ...
freerelig	... indicates the extent to which the freedom of citizens to exercise and practice their religious beliefs is subject to actual government restrictions. Does the government respect rights including the freedom to publish religious documents in foreign languages? Does religious belief affect membership in a ruling party or a career in government?
impcourts	Global competitiveness report's question: "The legal framework in your country for private businesses to settle disputes and challenge the legality of government actions and/or regulations is inefficient and subject to manipulation (= 1) or is efficient and follows a clear, neutral process (= 7)"
integrlegal	This component is based on the International country risk guide's political risk component I for law and order: "The 'law' subcomponent assesses the strength and impartiality of the legal system." Measured on a scale ranging from 1 to 10
judindepcor	Documents the level of independence in the judiciary, as reported by the annual human rights reports of the department of state
judindepinf	The judiciary in your country is independent and not subject to interference by the government and/or parties to the dispute. Measured on a scale ranging from "strongly disagree" to "strongly agree"
judrev	The extent to which judges (either Supreme court or constitutional court) have the power to review the constitutionality of laws in a given country
legmedia	Legal environment (reversed). "The legal environment category encompasses an examination of both the laws and regulations that could influence media content and the government's inclination to use these laws and legal institutions to restrict the media's ability to operate ..."
politterr	Political terror scale (reversed). The dataset actually provides two scales, one derived from the Amnesty international yearbooks and the other from US State department reports. The two scales were combined here by mutually complementing missing scores

(continued)

Variables	Contents
polmedia	Political environment (reversed). "Under the political environment category, we evaluate the degree of political control over the content of news media . . ."
powjudi	Power of judiciary. Effective possibility to control political decisions
profjudg	Professionalism (law degree, professional experience) is a precondition for appointment of judges to highest courts
proftenure	Professionalism of judges concerning length of tenure. Professionalism is high, if tenure is not restricted, i.e., if it is lifelong
pubtrial	Existence of constitutional provisions guaranteeing a public trial
restricfoi	Restriction of freedom of information/barriers for access to official information
torture	Torture and other cruel, inhumane, or degrading treatment or punishment

Source: Democracy barometer documentation

References

Baker, N. V. (2003). National security versus Civil liberties. *Presidential Studies Quarterly, 33* (3, The Permanent War), 547–567.

Berlin, I. (1969). Two concepts of liberty. In I. Berlin (Ed.), *Four essays on liberty* (pp. 118–172). London: Oxford University Press.

Bühlmann, M., Merkel, W., Müller, L., Giebler, H., Weßels, B., Bochsler, D., Hänni, M., & Bousbah, K. (2013). *Democracy barometer.* Aarau: Zentrum für Demokratie.

Busch, A. (2011). Freiheits- und Bürgerrechte nach 9/11. In T. Jäger (Ed.), *Die Welt nach 9/11. Auswirkungen des Terrorismus auf Staatenwelt und Gesellschaft. ZFAS-Sonderheft 2/2011* (pp. 861–881). VS Verlag für Sozialwissenschaften: Wiesbaden.

Davis, W. D., & Silver, D. B. (2003a, August). Continuity and change in support for civil liberties after 9/11: Results of a panel study. Paper presented at the American political science association annual meeting.

Davis, W. D., & Silver, D. B. (2003b, April). Personal security vs. Civil liberties after 9/11: Some sobering evidence from sober second thoughts. Paper presented at the Midwest political science association annual meeting.

Davis, W. D., & Silver, D. B. (2004). Civil liberties vs. Security: Public opinion in the context of the terrorist attacks on America. *American Journal of Political Science, 48*(1), 28–46.

Epstein, L., Ho, D. E., King, G., & Segal, J. A. (2005). The supreme court during crisis: How war affects only on-war cases. *New York University Law Review, 80*(1), 1–116.

Grimm, D. (2008). Die Freiheit sichern! Ohne starke Bürgerrechte bleibt Sicherheit wertlos. In B. Zypries (Ed.), *Die Renaissance der Rechtspolitik. Zehn Jahre Politik für den sozialen Rechtsstaat* (pp. 25–30). München: Verlag C.H. Beck.

Habermas, J. (1998). *The inclusion of the other: Studies in political theory.* Cambridge, MA: The MIT Press.

Habermas, J. (2001). *Between facts and norms. Contributions to a discourse theory of law and democracy.* Cambridge, MA: The MIT Press.

Haubrich, D. (2003). September 11, Anti-terror laws and civil liberties: Britain, France and Germany compared. *Government and Opposition, 38*(1), 3–28.

Hibbs, D. (1977). Political parties and macroeconomic policy. *American Political Science Review, 71*(4), 1467–1487.

Homels, S. (1993). *The anatomy of antiliberalism.* Cambridge, MA: Harvard University Press.

Huster, S., & Rudolph, K. (Eds.). (2008). *Vom Rechtsstaat zum Präventionsstaat.* Suhrkamp: Frankfurt am Main.

Lijphart, A. (1999). *Patterns of democracy. Government forms and performance in thirty-six countries*. New Haven, CT: Yale University Press.
MacKinnon, A. D. (2007). Counterterrorism and checks and balances: The Spanish and American examples. *New York University Law Review, 82*(2), 602–655.
Merkel, W., Puhle, H.-J., Croissant, A., Eicher, C., & Thiery, P. (2003). *Defekte Demokratie. Band 1: Theorie*. Opladen: Leske + Budrich.
Møller, J., & Skaaning, S. E. (2013). Autocracies, democracies, and the violation of civil liberties. *Democratization, 20*(1), 82–106.
Petring, A. (2010). *Reformen in Wohlfahrtsstaaten*. Wiesbaden: VS Verlag für Sozialwissenschaften.
Pietsch, C., & Fiebig, R. (2011). "Keine besondere Bedrohungslage:" Die Einstellungen der deutschen Bevölkerung zu Maßnahmen der Terrorabwehr. In T. Jäger (Ed.), *Die Welt nach 9/11. Auswirkungen des Terrorismus auf Staaten und Gesellschaft. ZfAS-Sonderheft 2/2011* (pp. 261–284). VS Verlag für Sozialwissenschaften: Wiesbaden.
Schmidt, M. G. (1995). *Wörterbuch zur Politik*. Stuttgart: Kröner.
Schneckener, U. (2011). Zehn Jahre nach 9/11: Zum politischen Umgang mit dem 'Terrorrisiko. *Politische Vierteljahresschrift, 52*(3), 355–372.
Skaaning, S. E. (2008). The civil liberty dataset: Conceptualization and measurement. *Zeitschrift für Vergleichende Politikwissenschaft, 2*(1), 29–51.
Volkens, A., Lehmann, P., Merz, N., Regel, S., & Werner, A. (2013). *The Manifesto data collection. Manifesto project (MRG/CMP/MARPOR)*. Version 2013a. Berlin: WZB Berlin Social Science Center.
Wagner, A., & Giebler, H. (2009). *Counter-terrorist measures, public opinion and party support in Britain. EPOP 2009*. Glasgow: University of Strathclyde.
Waldron, J. (2003). Security and liberty. The image of balance. *The Journal of Political Philosophy, 11*(2), 191–210.

Chapter 13
Why Do Established Democracies Violate Human Rights?

Dag Tanneberg

13.1 Introduction

In October 2001, the US Congress passed the "Uniting and Strengthening America by Providing Appropriate Tools Required to Intercept and Obstruct Terrorism" Act, which was signed into law by then president George W. Bush under the less cumbersome acronym "USA PATRIOT" Act.[1] It authorized a series of measures such as roving wiretapping to be used by federal agencies in the then new "War on Terror." Lesser known but perhaps more important is the joint resolution passed by the Congress on 14 September 2001 under the title "Authorization for Use of Military Force" (AUMF). It gave the president authority "to use all necessary and appropriate force" against those actors found to be either responsible for the September 2001 attacks or future terrorist acts. More than a decade later, both the USA PATRIOT Act and the AUMF resolution have been extended, expanded, and, in the case of the latter, deemed applicable not only to so-called "enemy" combatants but also to US citizens judged to be a threat to national security. The practical relevance of this novel interpretation became apparent in early 2013, when the US government officially acknowledged the killing of four citizens in anti-terrorism operations (Keesing's May 2013b, 52655).

Beyond the "War on Terror" established democracies have repeatedly shown little respect for the physical integrity of their citizens. In Spain, for instance, the Grupos Antiterroristas de Liberación (GAL) was secretly operated by Spanish

[1]This chapter strongly benefited from many critical comments and suggestions by Onawa Promise Lacewell, who also authored parts of an earlier draft. Furthermore, I would like to thank Julian Brückner, Heiko Giebler, Sascha Kneip, Alexander Petring, Aiko Wagner, Annika Werner, Bernhard Weßels, and Wolfgang Merkel who provided invaluable advice.

D. Tanneberg (✉)
Faculty of Economics and Social Sciences, University of Potsdam, Potsdam, Germany
e-mail: dag.tanneberg@uni-potsdam.de

W. Merkel, S. Kneip (eds.), *Democracy and Crisis*,
https://doi.org/10.1007/978-3-319-72559-8_13

government officials with the stated intent of combating ETA terrorism. Among the many human rights violations carried out by the group was a series of kidnappings and assassinations of suspected ETA supporters that occurred between 1983 and 1987. Outside the European context, South Africa is another democratic regime where state repressive tactics such as torture and police brutality are common. The 2011 Amnesty International human rights report red-flagged South Africa because police forces frequently engaged in repressive tactics when dealing with arrested suspects: "Corroborated methods included severe beatings, electric shocks and suffocation torture while the person was shackled or hooded, and death threats" (Amnesty International 2011, p. 4). Hence, the US legislation outlined above is just a striking example of established democracies violating physical integrity rights.

The consequences for the foundations of democracy are grave. Even advocates of a decidedly minimalist conception of democracy assert that "limited government and adherence to some core values about the sanctity of the individual" are essential for democratic self-government (Mainwaring et al. 2001, p. 44). Some scholars even argue that "guaranteeing individual rights under a secure rule of law is one of the minimal conditions for democratic regimes" (Bühlmann et al. 2012a, p. 521). Notwithstanding, democratic governments must refrain from torture, displacement, extrajudicial killings, and political imprisonment if they are to guarantee the free and fair participation of all citizens. Accordingly, human rights violations are irreconcilable with democratic government and directly contradict its normative foundations. Government respect for human rights defines a yardstick against which established democracies measure themselves and must be measured by outside observers. Therefore, consistent disrespect for the sanctity of the individual on the part of high performing democratic regimes would signal a serious democratic malaise: fundamental requisites of democratic self-government would be systematically contradicted by democratic realities.

What causes government human rights violations in established democracies? What temporal and spatial patterns are there, and what institutional remedies prevent encroachments on the sanctity of the individual? In addressing these questions, this paper goes beyond anecdotal evidence. It covers the period from 1995 to 2007 and explores patterns of government human rights practices in 29 established democracies. I argue that physical integrity rights constitute a functional requirement of democratic self-government and apply unconditionally to all citizens. Yet, even democratic governments may resort to violence when facing political threats. Their existence, however, is only necessary for questionable human rights practices by the government. Ultimately, they are triggered by violent opposition tactics. Yet, the executive leeway for violations of physical integrity is constrained by horizontal accountability among the three constitutional powers. More precisely, I hypothesize that peaceful political threats in the form of demonstrations and strikes do not increase physical integrity violations in established democracies, but violent political threats in the form of riots and terrorism do. Yet, the impact of the latter is conditional on the capacity of the judiciary to uphold basic rights against the government, and it is expected to decline as the strength of the judiciary increases. I find partial support for my hypotheses. Violent political threats increase the propensity of democratic governments to engage in repressive behavior systematically, but this relationship is not moderated by the judiciary. In effect, core democratic norms are sacrificed in the name of law and order.

Section 13.2 develops my hypotheses against the backdrop of democratic theory and the literature on state repression, while Sect. 13.3 summarizes design and data of this study. Section 13.4 presents the results, which are discussed and summarized in Sect. 13.5.

13.2 Physical Integrity, Political Threats, and Democracy

In the context of democracy scholarship, physical integrity rights are core components of even minimalist definitions of democracy. So strong is this association that scholars judge conceptions of democracy, which center on elections (e.g., Schumpeter 1942; Downs 1957; Alvarez et al. 1996; Przeworski et al. 2000) as "subminimal" (Mainwaring et al. 2001, p. 38) and inadequate "electoralism" (Karl 1986). However, ultimately normative assumptions on democracy must not be conflated with its analytically rigorous definition (Przeworski 1999, p. 12). Moreover, the assumed connection between democracy and other political phenomena—such as human rights—must not preclude empirical inquiry (Cheibub et al. 2010, p. 73). In other words, although normatively fundamental, the connection between physical integrity rights and democracy cannot be taken for granted. Rather, it is necessary to review, first, why government respect for physical integrity rights is important to democracy; second, why governments engage in questionable human rights practices; and, third, to probe what institutional configurations of democracy can shift state coercion "away from the most lethal techniques" (Davenport 2007b, p. 9).

13.2.1 Why Is Physical Integrity Important to Democracy?

Anchored in the 1948 "Universal Declaration of Human Rights," physical integrity rights constitute "entitlements individuals have in international law to be free from arbitrary physical harm and coercion by their government" and "all its agents" (Cingranelli and Richards 1999, p. 407). Meant to protect life, liberty, and security of person, physical integrity rights are violated whenever government actors engage in torture or other forms of cruel and degrading behavior, kill without due process, make individuals disappear, or imprison them for political reasons. Scholarly concern for physical integrity and human rights gained tremendous momentum in the early 1990s. As a key concern of political order, however, life and security of person have been on the agenda of political philosophy considerably longer.

Ever since Thomas Hobbes published his Leviathan, the responsibility to protect citizens has been advanced as a cornerstone of legitimate state order. In the shadow of the British civil war from 1642 to 1649, Hobbes broke with both the teleological and theological justifications of political order, focusing on the covenant of rational individuals instead (Kersting 2007, p. 212). Hobbes' intention was first and foremost to justify state power as a means to peace. He placed few constraints on the Leviathan and vested it with the unconditional right "to be judge both of the means of peace and defense, and also of the hindrances and disturbances of the same [. . .]" (Hobbes 2010, p. XVIII). Accordingly, Hobbes willingly accepted "inequities" against individual citizens as long as they served the purpose of peace (ibid). He was forcefully rejected by numerous liberal authors. Of these John Locke articulated the most consequential refutation of Hobbes. He argued that states are mandated to protect "lives, liberties and estates," and that states become illegitimate if they unduly interfere with any of these three forms of property (Locke 1988, §123, §§221f.). Whereas Hobbes puts the integrity of the Commonwealth before the sanctity of the individual (Hidalgo 2013, p. 66), Locke takes the opposite position, and he provides the legitimizing credo of modern democracy: political freedom under the secure rule of law.

If we define democracy as the self-government of the sovereign people (Dahl 1989, 175ff.), then political, i.e., collectively binding decisions are only legitimate when they root in the consent of the people. They constitute the ultimate political authority. In this sense, self-government and sovereignty of the people both imply, with reference to Hans Kelsen, that those who are subject to the law must also be able to act as authors of the law (Habermas 2001; Merkel et al. 2003). Therefore, the rights to form and publicly express political preferences are necessary conditions of democracy (Dahl 1971, p. 2).[2] Democratic self-government becomes possible once citizens can participate in government by exercising civil liberties such as the freedoms of speech, assembly, association, and information. Yet, it will be meaningful if and only if there is no threat of retribution by the government for exercising civil liberties (Merkel 2004, 39f.). Ultimately, a meaningful process of democratic self-government crucially depends on the secure protection of the individual from arbitrary harm by the government.

Therein resides the brisance of events such as the Turkish government crackdown on Gezi Park protesters in June 2013, which left four people dead, 8000 injured, and thousands in prison (Keesing's 2013a, 52740). Contrary to the reasoning of the Turkish government, democracies cannot simply adopt a Hobbesian stance and portray their actions as an attempt to maintain public order. Under democratic auspices every single violation of physical integrity rights by the government immediately contradicts the Lockean underpinnings of democratic self-government. Therefore, two questions emerge. What triggers physical integrity violations by democratic governments, and what institutions of democracy can prevent such questionable human rights practices? Both questions will be addressed in the following pages.

---

[2]Note that equality is also widely regarded as a necessary condition (Dahl 1971, p. 2), respectively, "functional requirement" (Merkel et al. 2003, p. 41) of democracy.

13.2.2 Political Threats: When the Gloves Come Off

Scholars widely concur that "when threats are confronted political authorities frequently use repression as a means to control/eliminate them and to establish/extend their tenure" (Davenport 2000, p. 1). Accordingly, violent coercion by the government represents "a particular kind of policy or strategy chosen for dealing with actual or anticipated opposition" (Gurr 1986, p. 45). It has to be understood as a purposeful attempt to either eliminate opposition from the population or to at least hamper its capacity for collective action (Davenport 1995, p. 685). Democracies are no exception. For instance, in 1972 the British army maintained a Military Reaction Force (MRF) in Northern Ireland. A former member of the MRF summarized its purpose as follows: "to draw out the IRA and to minimise their activities [. . .] if they needed shooting, they'd be shot" (Ware 2013). Quoting a more controversial example, when Chicago police forces shot Fred Hampton at point-blank range on 4 December 1969, the Black Panther Party (BPP) not only lost a skilled organizer and political leader with national appeal, Hampton's death also hampered BPP activities in Chicago. In order to understand why political authorities in established democracies engage in physical integrity violations, it is necessary to elaborate on this "Law of Coercive Responsiveness" (Davenport and Inman 2012, p. 622) in the "behavioural dialogue" (Poe et al. 2000, p. 30) of government authorities and political dissidents.

Political groups that government authorities perceive as an "active threat to their continued rule," are a necessary condition for government-sponsored physical integrity violations (Gurr 1986, p. 51). Such groups pose behavioral threats to the government in as much as their members engage in "relatively large-scale actions" that are directed against particular policies or members of the political elite or the government, e.g., anti-government strikes and protests, boycotts, terrorism, and even guerrilla war (Davenport 2000, p. 5). Consequently, the emergence of behavioral threats creates political opportunities which democracies may exploit in order to defend established patterns of social, cultural, or political power by repression (Earl 2011, 262f.). However, whether or not political authorities respond to threats with physical integrity violations is contingent on two major factors. First, what criteria does the government apply to assess the severity of threats? Second, the political-institutional context shapes the expected costs and benefits of physical integrity violations once a threat is identified.

Following Davenport (1995), the contemporary empirical literature on state repression is couched in a multidimensional approach to threat perception. More specifically, it is argued that, with few exceptions, government-sponsored physical integrity violations are inherently nonrandom and depend on the criteria employed to assess threats (Gurr 1986, p. 51). These criteria provide standards by which tolerable political dissent is separated from veritable threats, emphasizing particular attributes of the challenging group such as intensity and scope of demand, (assumed) support among the population and the political elite, the repertoire of challenging behavior, as well as the presence of violence and deviance from cultural norms (Gurr 1986; Davenport 1995; Davenport 1999; Gartner and Regan 1996; Regan and Henderson

2002). For instance, Davenport (2000, p. 3) argues that violent opposition tactics are likely to spark high levels of state repression because such behavior contradicts institutionalized mechanisms of conflict mediation. Ultimately, the more threatening governments perceive political dissent to be, the more likely they are to engage in questionable human rights practices.

But when do governments answer political threats with physical integrity violations? Much of this discussion is dressed in the language of rational choice. Accordingly, at any given level of political threat, the expected benefit of violent coercion is weighed against its costs, its probability of success, and its viable alternatives such as accommodation (Davenport and Inman 2012, p. 621). Formal treatments of this generic decision-making problem borrow predator-prey models from biology (Tsebelis and Sprague 1989; Francisco 1995; Francisco 1996), employ substitution models from microeconomics (Lichbach 1987; Moore 2000), or rely on game theory to analyze the strategic interaction between political dissidents and governments (Pierskalla 2010). Irrespective of the technical nitty-gritty, the common denominator seems to be that accommodative and coercive responses to political threats "are substitutes for the state, and it will move from one toward the other in response to dissident protest behaviour" (Moore 2000, p. 114). While threat perception is necessary for state repression, it is not sufficient. Rather, the decision to actually commit physical integrity violations is triggered by what dissidents do given established limits of acceptable political dissent.[3]

Coming back to democracy, the intensity of political dissent that relies on violent tactics, e.g., riots and terrorism, emerges as a cause of physical integrity violations by democratic governments. Although they may judge peaceful opposition—e.g., demonstrations and strikes—threatening, it does not violate the limits of acceptable political dissent in established democracies. Instead, such dissident behavior represents an exercise in forming and publicly expressing alternative political preferences. To put it in more radical terms, the spirit of democratic self-government roots in the public right to dissent *peacefully* (Arendt 1972). Violent opposition tactics, by contrast, constitute formidable political opportunities for government-sponsored physical integrity violations in established democracies because they disrupt democratic channels of political decision-making and threaten public order. Two hypotheses follow immediately. While even most intense peaceful political opposition should not contribute to physical integrity violations by democratic governments at all, I expect that intense and violent political dissent will increase the level of physical integrity violations in established democracies.

[3]Note that this interpretation boils down to an exclusively reactive take on government-sponsored physical integrity violations. It discards much detail of the behavioral reciprocity between political dissidents and governments. In other words, political dissent might precede as well as follow violent state coercion, implying a certain endogeneity of the research design. However, this analysis ultimately focuses on institutional remedies against government-sponsored physical integrity violations once behavioral threats have been identified. A reactive interpretation suffices for the problem at hand because even an endogenous relationship between political threats and government responses should still be moderated by political institutions.

However, as normative imperatives of democracy, human rights, and the integrity of person are unconditional. In other words, "[t]hat dissidents engage in extremely challenging behavior should not, by definition, override the highly institutionalized system of political and legal protections for citizens' rights existing within a democracy" (Davenport 2007b, p. 67). The question is then whether and how the institutional setup of democracy protects physical integrity rights even in the face of intense violent political dissent.

13.2.3 Does Democracy Serve to Protect?

The literature on state repression offers one clear hypothesis concerning democracy and the sanctity of the individual: "[. . .] [D]emocracy dampens the use of repression. It provides institutions, processes, and norms that are incompatible with political repressive behaviour" (King 2000, p. 221). This "domestic democratic peace" proposition has received robust support in many quantitative applications (Davenport and Inman 2012, p. 622). More specifically, democracy is said to offer citizens numerous channels to signal political grievances, to value peaceful conflict mediation, and to provide mechanisms of control via political competition such that democratic governments are systematically deterred from committing physical integrity violations (Davenport 2007a, 10f.). Therefore, the hypothesis goes on, more democracy equals less physical integrity violations. However, this straightforward thinking is contested, and the competing arguments must prove their value in answering the following question: how does democracy limit government infringements on human rights?

The usual answers emphasize electoral accountability (Bueno de Mesquita et al. 2005; Davenport 2007b). The opportunity to punish governments at the polls "effectively limits their ability to use repression domestically, since citizens could turn out of office those heavy-handed leaders" (Regan and Henderson 2002, p. 121). But this conclusion commonly results from comparing democracies with autocracies (Poe and Tate 1994; Poe et al. 1999; Davenport 1999; King 2000; Keith 2002; Davenport and Armstrong 2004; Armstrong 2009). Such designs probe whether democracies handle the issue of physical integrity differently from autocracies. Yet, it is little surprise that even the most elaborate inquiries judge the electoral accountability of government officials crucial to tame repressive state behavior. By definition, democracy is "a system of governance in which rulers are held accountable for their actions in the public realm by citizens" (Schmitter and Karl 1996, p. 50). Consequently, "open, pluralistic competition for central power positions is the distinguishing difference between democracy and autocracy" (Merkel 2004, p. 38). However, in order to be meaningful, the capability to sanction government behavior by the ballot demands the secure provision of physical integrity rights (Keith 2002, p. 117). Mingling democracies and non-democracies exaggerates the theoretical status of electoral accountability, and alternative theoretical explanations remain underexplored.

Using the concept of "embedded democracy," I argue that horizontal accountability is key to protecting physical integrity rights. Central to "embedded democracy" are five partial regimes, namely, the electoral, political rights, civil rights, effective power to govern, and horizontal accountability regimes (Merkel et al. 2003, 50ff.). Horizontal accountability refers to the "structure of political power" and prescribes a "network of relatively autonomous institutions" to confine elected authorities to "constitutionally defined lawful action" (Merkel 2004, p. 40). It is best described as a system of checks and balances which provides for reciprocal control among executive, legislative, and judicial bodies on an equal footing (Merkel 2010, p. 33). Since democratic election cycles are relatively long, some authors have judged electoral accountability ineffective as a means to punish government violations of physical integrity rights (for references, see Davenport 2007b, p. 24). Horizontal accountability, by contrast, institutes a constant monitoring process among the three constitutional powers. With regard to physical integrity violations, a system of independent courts with the authority to review legislative norms and to survey government activity is decisive. Such courts are able to enforce the rule of law in the sense of a "containment and limitation of the exercise of state power," because they "function as constitutional custodians of the legislature and supervisors of executive conformity to law" (Merkel 2004, 39f.). Horizontal accountability links democracy to physical integrity because it entails an independent judiciary that is able to defend basic human rights against the government.

In effect, deficits in the partial regime of horizontal accountability are responsible for physical integrity violations by the government in established democracies. More precisely, I hypothesize that, given a weak judiciary, even the government of a top-notch democracy is more likely to answer intense and violent political threats with infringements on the sanctity of the individual. In other words, the better the judiciary is able to uphold the rule of law and to defend basic human rights, the less important does the scope of violent political threats become as a cause for human rights violations by the government in established democracies. Using a sample of established democracies, these conditional hypotheses will be tested in the following.

13.3 Design and Data

Summarizing the discussion, I assume that government respect for the integrity of person is necessary for meaningful democratic self-government. Physical integrity rights apply unconditionally to all citizens, and any government-sponsored infringement on the sanctity of the individual contradicts the normative foundation of democracy. Nevertheless, democracies may respond coercively to political threats. The nature of their response depends on the behavior that political dissidents demonstrate. Peaceful dissent in the form of demonstrations and strikes constitutes an exercise of civil liberties, and I hypothesize that it does not lead to physical integrity violations in established democracies. Violent tactics such as riots and terrorism, by contrast, are at odds with the limits of acceptable political dissent, and I hypothesize that they trigger physical integrity violations in established democracies. Yet, horizontal accountability conditions the extent to which democratic governments exploit violent threats for physical integrity violations. More precisely, I hypothesize that the impact of violent dissent on physical integrity violations declines as the capability of the judiciary to defend basic human rights increases. In the following, I describe research design and data used to test these hypotheses.

13.3.1 Design and Sample

In order to test my hypotheses, I run a number of longitudinal multilevel models with varying intercepts and slopes. Multilevel regression has the advantage that it models dependencies in the data directly (Gelman and Hill 2006). Furthermore, such regression models are sensitive to differences in expected levels and temporal dynamics across individuals and groups. These can be addressed by time-varying and time-constant predictors (Hox 2010, 99f.). Moreover, multilevel models with longitudinal data separate temporal from cross-sectional variance. Hence, they are open to two fundamentally different interpretations. On the one hand, they trace temporal developments *within* individual groups and thus link changes in time-dependent predictors to changes in the time-dependent response. On the other hand, they offer insights on differences *between* all groups (ibid, 89).

In less abstract terms, my data clusters repeated measurements of physical integrity violations on the "country-year level" by established democracies on the "group level." Using this data, multilevel regression allows me to trace the contemporaneous effect of political threats on physical integrity violations within individual democracies over time. However, it can also shed light on differences in physical integrity violations between established democracies. Whereas the former, temporal interpretation addresses the question whether established democracies answer increasingly intense political threats with increasing violent coercion over time, the latter, cross-sectional interpretation capitalizes on differences in the average extent of physical integrity violations between established democracies. Finally, multilevel regression makes it possible to condition the impact of time-dependent political threats on the time-constant institutional context, i.e., the capability of the judiciary to defend the rule of law.

The analysis uses the Democracy Barometer blueprint sample. The barometer is an instrument to evaluate the quality of established democracies (Bühlmann et al. 2012a). It offers detailed information on the state of democracy for the period from 1990 to 2007. Attempting to provide an empirically grounded yardstick for the quality of democracy, the Democracy Barometer team sampled 30 countries that have consistently been ranked as full-fledged democracies from 1995 to 2005 (ibid,

527). Accordingly, their blueprint sample represents the entire universe of established democracies (Bühlmann et al. 2012b, p. 132).[4] This claim has two important implications. First, politics in the blueprint countries are firmly based on the principles of democracy. Therefore, infringements on physical integrity rights should not be part and parcel of their governments' behavioral repertoires. Second, the Democracy Barometer team employs the concept of embedded democracy as a "root definition" of democracy (Collier and Levitsky 1997, p. 437), and hence the Barometer data can be used to measure democracy's partial regimes.

Three minor preliminaries remain. First, not all thirty countries can be regarded as having been sovereign democracies over the entire observation period from 1990 to 2007. For instance, the Democracy Barometer treats the Czech Republic as an independent state in 1990 already, but it was part of Czechoslovakia until 1993. Slovenia, however, enters the sample only in 1993 after its independence from former Yugoslavia. Similarly, the South African Apartheid ended only in 1994/1995, signaling South Africa's transition to democracy. In order to minimize the heterogeneity thus introduced into the data, I limit the observation period to the years from 1995 to 2007. Second, information on physical integrity violations in Malta were unavailable for almost the entire observation period. Therefore, I dropped Malta from the sample. The resulting dataset includes 377 observations—13 annual measurements on each of 29 democracies. Finally, when running the analyses, all metric predictors were centered on their sample means as recommended by Hox (2010, 59f.).

13.3.2 Time-Varying Variables

To measure the extent of human rights violations, the physical integrity index from the CIRI Human Rights dataset is used (Cingranelli and Richards 2013). The data provide "standards-based measures of government human rights practices" (Cingranelli et al. 2010, p. 402). Cingranelli and Richards (1999, p. 407) define physical integrity rights as "entitlements individuals have in international law to be free from arbitrary physical harm and coercion by their government" and "all its agents, such as police or paramilitary forces" (Cingranelli and Richards 2008, p. 5). Empirically, this approach captures acts of torture, political imprisonment, extrajudicial killings, and disappearances (ibid). The data are compiled from the annual US State Department Country Reports on Human Rights Practices and the Amnesty International human rights reports using a three-point scale for each type of

[4]The countries are Australia, Austria, Belgium, Canada, Costa Rica, Cyprus, the Czech Republic, Denmark, Finland, France, Germany, Hungary, Iceland, Ireland, Italy, Japan, Luxembourg, Malta, the Netherlands, New Zealand, Norway, Poland, Portugal, Slovenia, South Africa, Spain, Sweden, Switzerland, the UK, and the USA.

violation. The lowest value 0 expresses the frequent and widespread neglect of physical integrity rights, while the value 2 signals that government actors do not at all engage in human rights violations.[5] To compute the physical integrity index, the four items are summed.[6] As my analysis addresses the lack of government respect for individual integrity and security, I recode the original index. In the following, 0 represents the best possible and 8 the worst possible state in physical integrity affairs.

Type and intensity of political threats are measured using event data under the assumption that the more frequently an event occurs, the more intense the threat is. My measurement of the intensity of peaceful dissent is the country-based, year-wise total of demonstrations and strikes. Applying the same strategy, I measure the intensity of violent dissent by the sum of riots and terrorist attacks. Information on demonstrations, strikes, and riots were taken from GDELT, the "Global Database of Events, Language, and Tone" (Leetaru and Schrodt 2013).[7] As my focus is on political threats to democratic governments, the GDELT data were subset such that only events remained, which took place within the territorial jurisdiction of the respective democracy and which either targeted the government or one of its agents.[8] Event counts of terrorist attacks were collected from the "Global Terrorism Database" (GTD), which defines terrorism as "the threatened or actual use of illegal force and violence by a non-state actor to attain a political, economic, religious, or social goal through fear, coercion, or intimidation" (START 2012, p. 6). As this database is deliberately inclusive, I retained only events that fulfil all definitional

[5]Given the importance of the CIRI data, some detail on the coding process is justified. Cingranelli and Richards take only violations into account where *citizens* come to harm by the hands of government agents *within* the internationally recognized borders of the state. This excludes human rights violations such as the events of Abu Ghraib in late 2003. Moreover, each violation is to be treated separately, even if there is only one victim. If, for example, a criminal suspect suffers lethal injuries from police brutality, the incidence will be counted as *both* torture and extrajudicial killing. In order to increase inter-coder reliability, Cingranelli and Richards instruct their coders to rely on numerical thresholds whenever possible. A score of 2 is to be awarded when there are no confirmed incidences, a score of 1 if there is at least one confirmed incident, and a score of 0 if there are at least 50 confirmed incidences of abuse. Finally, Cingranelli and Richards provide their coders with a list of keywords to judge the frequency of physical integrity violations, whenever the information is insufficient to apply the numerical thresholds (see Cingranelli and Richards 2008).

[6]This aggregation strategy is subject to debate (McCormick and Mitchell 1997). Notwithstanding, Cingranelli and Richards (1999) as well as Fariss and Schnakenberg (2013) offer striking empirical evidence on the homogeneity of the index, and aggregation is thus justified.

[7]The following definitions apply: (a) demonstrations ("Dissent collectively, publicly show negative feelings or opinions; rally, gather to protest a policy, action, or actor(s)"), (b) strikes ("Protest by refusing to work or cooperate until certain demands are met, [...]"), (c) riots ("Protest forcefully, in a potentially destructive manner, [...]") (Schrodt 2012, 66ff.).

[8]The set of state actors includes police forces, the government in terms of the executive and governing parties, the military, and the state intelligence agencies (Schrodt 2012, p. 93). Whenever one of these actors was coded as the source of political dissent, the event was excluded from the analysis.

criteria and were not tagged as doubtful by the editors. Since both indicators suffer from extensive skew, I rescaled them using the natural logarithm with a start of 1.

To account for alternative, noninstitutional explanations of physical integrity violation, I control for income inequality, population growth, participation in war, and a linear trend component. Since affluent societies are better able to fulfil the needs of their members, it has long been argued that governments that develop the economy avoid political threats from below (Davenport and Inman 2012, p. 621). However, the mechanism involved remains contested, which is troubling given that most established democracies also rank among the wealthiest countries. With reference to the debate on democratization, I argue that the level of economic development itself does not spark political threats, but the unequal distribution of wealth does (Acemoglu and Robinson 2000, 2006). Therefore, I include Gini data on gross household income as a control (Solt 2013; Teorell et al. 2013). Population pressures have repeatedly been discussed as causes for physical integrity violations (Henderson 1993; Poe and Tate 1994; Poe et al. 1999; Zanger 2000; Keith 2002). According to Henderson (1993), population growth strains national resources, and governments resort to violence as a coping strategy. Hence, using data from Heston et al. (2012), I control for population growth. Finally, Davenport (2007b) shows that democracies engage in domestic repression when facing militarized conflict. Thus, relying on Sarkees and Wayman (2010), I computed an indicator variable, which takes the value of 1 for each year during which an established democracy participated in inter or extra-state war. Table 13.2 in the Appendix summarizes all time-varying variables.

13.3.3 Time-Constant Variables

To contextualize the interplay between political threats and government human rights practices, I calculated the country-based means of the rule of law and electoral competition variables from the Democracy Barometer. In theory both variables range between 0 and 100, but for technical reasons I divided them by 100. In either case higher values denote better quality. Whereas the time-varying indicators above change with each measurement occasion, these latter two variables enter the analysis as time-constant predictors. They explain variations in intercepts across established democracies. Figure 13.1 gives the means of the two variables along with their min-max ranges by country. Together, the rule of law and electoral competition represent the country-based institutional context of the "behavioural dialogue" between democratic governments and political dissidents.

Rule of law measures the strength of the judiciary. The Democracy Barometer equates it with impartial courts, the quality of the legal system, and public confidence in the justice system (Bühlmann et al. 2012a, p. 524). Drawing on a broad range of indicators, this measurement incorporates constitutional provisions, public evaluation of the judiciary, and the professionalization of judicial training. As can be seen from Fig. 13.1, the 30 established democracies cover a broad range of values.

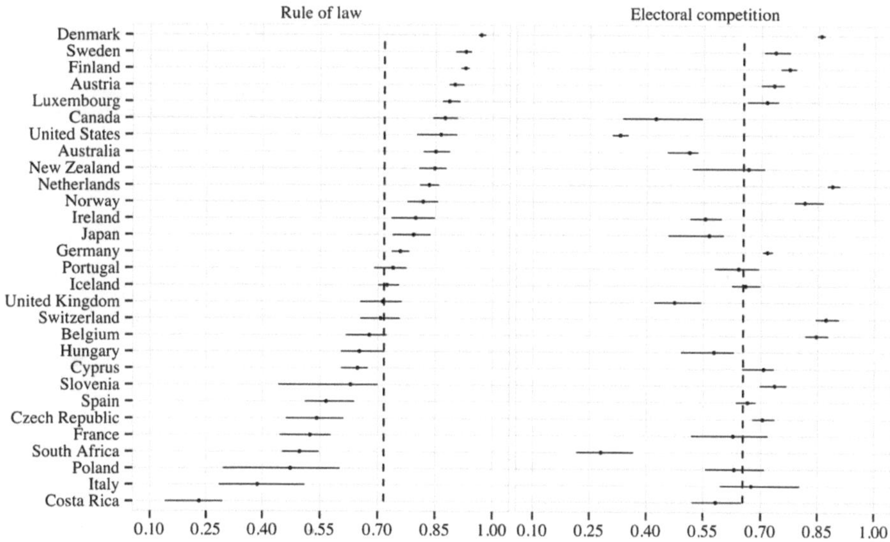

Fig. 13.1 Sample distributions of time-constant variables. Note: Country averages with min-max ranges; dashed lines denote the grand mean. Source: www.democracybarometer.org

Denmark takes the lead with an average value of almost 1, while Costa Rica ranks last with less than 0.25. The grand average is 0.72. To control for electoral accountability, I include electoral competition from the Democracy Barometer. The variable centers on the "[v]ertical control of the government [...] via free, regular, and competitive elections" (ibid). This entails vulnerability and contestability. While the former "corresponds with the uncertainty of the electoral outcome," the latter "refers to the stipulations that electoral competitors have to meet in order to be allowed to enter the political race" (ibid, 524f.). Figure 13.1 also shows that the 30 country averages of electoral competition are not significantly correlated with the corresponding rule of law means ($r_{Pearson} = 0.2$). The Netherlands outperform Denmark with an average close to 0.9, while South Africa now trails the entire sample with about 0.3. The grand mean is 0.65. Taken together, rule of law and electoral competition capture the most important checks on violent government behavior.

13.4 Analyzing Physical Integrity Violations in Established Democracies

Do established democracies respect the right to individual integrity and security? A visual inspection of the data suggests otherwise. Figure 13.2 plots the yearly measurement of the physical integrity index for each established democracy. Darker tiles at the intersection of country and year signal less respect for the sanctity of the

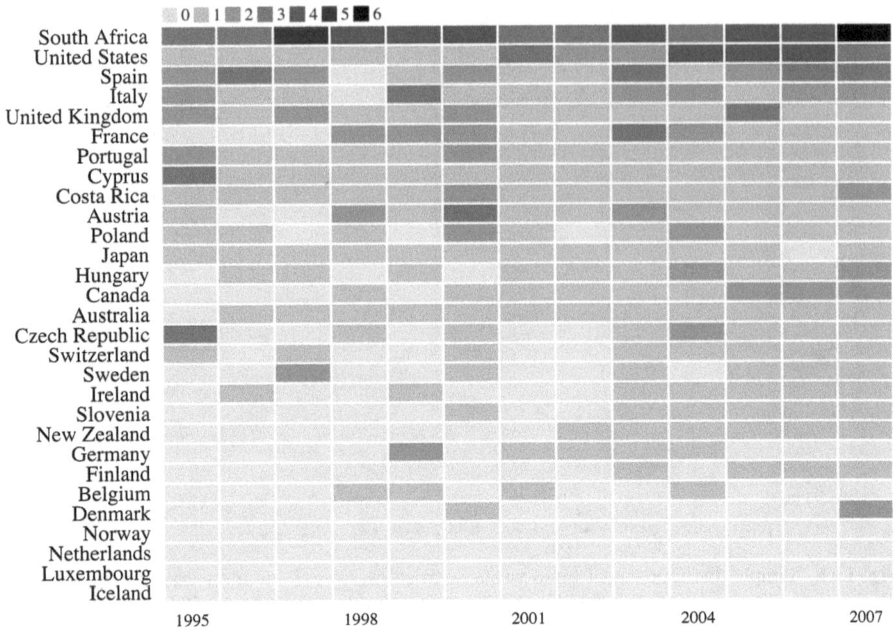

Fig. 13.2 Physical integrity violations in established democracies. Note: Countries ordered by mean level of physical integrity violations. Source: Own calculations

individual by government agents. South African government officials paid the least attention to the sanctity of the individual between 1995 and 2007. In 2007 the South African government even scored 6, indicating widespread torture, extrajudicial killings, displacement, and political imprisonment. This constitutes the poorest record among all established democracies.[9] Notwithstanding, the record of the USA is troubling as well. In 2001 the USA jumps from a score of 1 to a score of 3, and they even rival South African conditions between 2003 and 2006. Only 4 out of 30 established democracies—Norway, Luxembourg, the Netherlands, and Iceland—score 0 over the entire observation period and thus show a completely clean track record. It is clear from Fig. 13.2 that most established democracies at least sometimes engage in questionable human rights practices.

Immediately adjacent to South Africa and the USA is a group of countries that repeatedly engaged in physical integrity violations. This group ranges from Spain to Japan and includes examples such as France in 2003, when the French Ministry of the Interior investigated 611 complaints of police brutality, 87 of which involved serious and 10 lethal injuries (US Department of State, 25 February 2004). A number of democracies in this group never achieved the lowest possible score of 0. Finally, a

[9]South Africa skews the distribution of the dependent variable tremendously. As a precaution against potential problems during the estimation stage I log-transform the index in all subsequent models (see Fox and Weisberg 2011, p. 140).

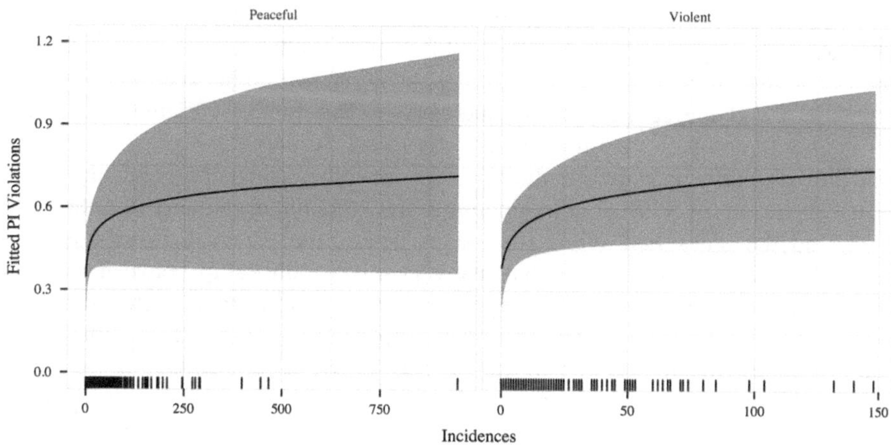

Fig. 13.3 Marginal effects of political threats on physical integrity violations. Source: Own calculations

last group of countries ranges from Canada to Denmark. These democracies mostly started with excellent scores in 1995. However, in many cases their performance visibly deteriorates over time. This tendency is most pronounced in the case of Canada, where, following the "excessive use of force involving taser guns," five men died at the hands of the police in 2005 (Amnesty International 2006, p. 84), one in 2006 (Amnesty International 2007, p. 80), and at least four in 2007 (Amnesty International 2008, p. 87). The remaining members of this group experienced a weaker, but nonetheless, visible decline in the state of physical integrity rights. In sum, government agents in almost all established democracies engaged in physical integrity violations, but there is no evidence for a forceful deterioration across the entire sample.[10]

Figure 13.3 shows that political threats may trigger physical integrity violations in established democracies. The diagram plots the marginal effects of peaceful and

[10]To analyze possible trends, I used variance partition models with varying intercepts and varying slopes on t. I found positive statistically significant trends for the USA, Canada, New Zealand, Slovenia, and France. The most complex of these models reads $y_{it} = \beta_{0u[i]} + \beta_{1u[i]} t_{it} + E_{it}$. Here y_{it} indicates the logged measurement of physical integrity violations in country i at time t, $\beta_{0u[i]}$ is a short-hand notation for the country-varying intercept, and $\beta_{1u[i]}$ denotes the by-country-varying coefficient on the trend indicator t_{it}. Finally, E_{it} denotes the error term. More detail is available from Table 13.3 in the appendix. Moreover, following advice from Rabe-Hesketh and Skrondal (2008, 473ff.) and Gelman and Hill (2006, 243f.), I ran additional cross-classified models. Such models group observations by countries and years simultaneously. They are sensitive to temporal influences that apply to individual observation years and affect all countries jointly. Once I introduced the linear trend, the grouping by observations years became redundant. Thus, my data offer little evidence of temporal influences that stick to particular observation years such as the 9/11 attacks. All models were estimated and inspected using the methods and techniques provided by Wickham (2009), Fox and Weisberg (2011), Bates et al. (2013), Pinheiro et al. (2013), and R Core Team (2013).

violent political threats on the expected level of physical integrity violations. All estimates are based on a multilevel model that includes the full set of time-varying and time-constant controls but not the cross-level interaction between violent political threats and the strength of the judiciary.[11] The control variables were held constant at 0, and thus the fitted values refer to the average established democracy that did not participate in war during 1995. In either panel the solid black line indicates the marginal effect, gray ribbons represent confidence intervals at the 0.95 level, and the black bars along the x-axes denote the observed distributions of political threats. Both plots demonstrate a positive relationship between political threats and the extent of physical integrity violations. For instance, as the number of violent political threats increases from the sample minimum 0 to the sample maximum 148, the average level of physical integrity violations almost doubles from 0.38 to 0.74. Much the same development is estimated for peaceful political threats. However, the effect is weaker, and it takes 950 events to move from 0.34 to 0.72. Moreover, as can be seen from the wide confidence intervals, the impact of peaceful political threats is very uncertain. In fact, only the coefficient on violent political threats reaches statistical significance at the 0.95 level. In short, Fig. 13.3 supports the hypothesis that violent political threats provoke physical integrity violations in established democracies, while peaceful political threats do not.

Moving on to the conditional hypothesis events take an unexpected turn. Earlier I argued that the better the judiciary can defend basic civil liberties against the government, the less important are violent political threats as a cause of human rights violations in established democracies. Figure 13.4 shows the empirical results. It plots the conditional marginal effect that violent political threats have on physical integrity violations by the government at varying levels of rule of law. For the latter, the 5, 25, 50, 75, and 95% quantiles were chosen. They correspond to the levels of rule of law in Poland, Slovenia, Portugal, Australia, and Sweden. All estimates account for the full set of controls and include the cross-level interaction.[12] Control variables were held constant at 0. Consequently, the fitted values show how violent political threats and the rule of law interact in the average established democracy not participating in war during 1995. Remember that rule of law is a time-constant predictor. As such it models country-level differences in the dependent variable.

---

[11]For detailed results, please refer to Table 13.4 in the Appendix.

[12]The fully specified individual level model is:

$y_{it} = \beta_{0i} + \beta_{1i}\, t_{it} + \beta_2\, \text{Threat}_{\text{Peace},it} + \beta_3\, \text{Threat}_{\text{Violent},it} + \beta_4$ Inequality$_{it}$ + β_5 Pop. Growth$_{it}$ + β_6 War$_{it}$ + E_{it},

with varying intercept (β_{0i}) and slope (β_{1i})

$\beta_{0i} = \gamma_{00} + \gamma_{01}$ Rule of Law$_i$ + γ_{02} Electoral Competition$_i$ + u_{0i}

$\beta_{1i} = \gamma_{10} + u_{1i}$,

and cross-level interaction effect

$\beta_3 = \gamma_{30} + \gamma_{31}$ Rule of Law$_i$.

By convention cross-level interactions often include a varying slope for the focal predictor, i.e., β_2 in this case. Since there is little theoretical reason to believe that the effect of violent political threats differs by established democracy and additional testing proved this variance component insignificant, I do not include a varying slope for violent political threats.

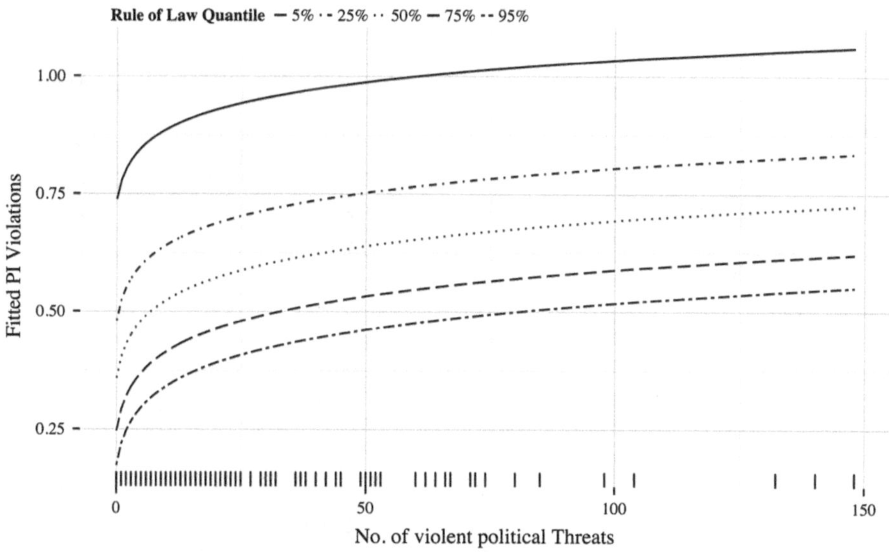

Fig. 13.4 Conditional effect of violent political threats on physical integrity violations

Figure 13.4 shows that if there were no violent political threats at all, then the average level of physical integrity violations would decline as the strength of the judiciary increases. This observation makes intuitive sense, and the corresponding unconditional coefficient is statistically significant at the 0.95 level.[13] Notwithstanding, my conditional hypothesis requires that the *slope* on violent political threats decreases as the level of rule of law increases. This requirement is not met by the data. In fact, all lines in Fig. 13.4 run more or less parallel to one another, and the interaction term itself is not statistically significant. Moreover, as can be seen from a comparison of the AIC and BIC values in Table 13.1, the interaction complicates the model without offering substantive leverage on the data. Consequently, there is scant support for the hypothesis that a strong judiciary confines the government to lawful action in the face of violent political threats.

Finally, Table 13.1 summarizes the fit of the most important multilevel models estimated in course of this analysis. The table entries show how well each model explains the data, and they give reason for concern. Model 1 merely includes an intercept and a linear trend component *t* both of which vary by country. This model constitutes a baseline against which to compare all other estimations. Model 2 introduces political threats into the equation, and Model 3 includes the time-varying controls. Model 4 contextualizes the "behavioural dialogue" between democratic governments and political challengers by the strength of the judiciary, controlling for electoral accountability. Finally, Model 5 introduces the interaction between time-varying, violent political threats and the time-constant strength of the judiciary. In

[13]See column IV of Table 13.4 in the Appendix.

Table 13.1 Model fit statistics

Dep. Variable: $\ln(PI_{it} + 1)$	Model 1	Model 2	Model 3	Model 4	Model 5
Fixed part					
t	✓	✓	✓	✓	✓
Political threats	✗	✓	✓	✓	✓
Time-varying controls	✗	✗	✓	✓	✓
Time-constant controls	✗	✗	✗	✓	✓
Cross-level interaction	✗	✗	✗	✗	✓
Stochastic part					
$\sigma_{Intercept/Country}$	0.34	0.28	0.21	0.15	0.15
$\sigma_{t/Country}$	0.02	0.02	0.02	0.02	0.02
$\sigma_{Residual}$	0.29	0.29	0.28	0.28	0.28
Model fit					
Deviance	233.5	223.2	203.0	185.6	185.5
N	377	377	375	375	375
AIC	243.5	237.2	223.0	209.6	211.5
BIC	263.1	264.8	262.3	256.7	262.5
$ICC_{Country}$	0.59	0.49	0.36	0.21	0.21
Pseudo-R^2		0.17	0.39	0.64	0.64

Notes: ✓ included in the model; ✗ not included in the model. All predictors have been centered on their sample means; t is coded 0 in 1995. For detailed results, see Table 13.4 in the Appendix.

the baseline the intra-class correlation (ICC) for countries is 0.59. In other words, almost 60% of the variance in physical integrity violations can be attributed to differences between established democracies. Adding in more predictors reduces this share to 21%. When comparing Model 4 to the baseline, the complete set of independent variables accounts for an impressive 64% of country-level differences in physical integrity violations. However, not a single model captures time-dependent political dynamics within established democracies. This can be seen from the residual standard deviation $\sigma_{Residual}$, which is constant across all models. The conclusion must be that increasing political threats are not responsible for the contemporaneously decreasing respect that some established democracies pay to the sanctity of the individual. While political threats provide leverage on cross-sectional differences between established democracies, they should not receive causal interpretation.

In sum, between 1995 and 2007 most established democracies committed torture, extrajudicial killings, displacements, or relied on political imprisonment—at least occasionally. In South Africa the situation is worst, but other established democracies demonstrate decreasing respect for individual integrity and security as well, in particular the USA. Nevertheless, there is no evidence for a forceful and widespread deterioration in human rights affairs. Rather, empirical patterns speak to persistent differences between established democracies. These cross-sectional patterns partly root in violent political threats. Democratic governments engage more readily in questionable human rights practices when political dissent is expressed in the form of riots and terrorism. The same is not true for peaceful demonstrations and strikes. More importantly, horizontal accountability does not fence in the "behavioural dialogue" between democratic governments and political opposition. While stronger judiciaries decrease the average level of government human rights violations, they are irrelevant in the face of increasing violent political threats. In other words, terrorism is as harshly dealt with in Costa Rica as in Denmark. Finally, all results tap into between-country differences; they do not readily translate into causality. Nonetheless, my findings are substantively important, because they suggest that the democratic guarantee of physical integrity is conditional on the state of contentious politics.

13.5 Summary

For good reason all normatively substantial conceptions of democracy embrace the integrity of person. It is part and parcel of the normative inventory of democracy. Whereas democratic self-government becomes possible once citizens can participate in government, it will be meaningful if and only if there is no threat of retribution by the state for forming and publicly expressing political preferences. Physical integrity rights apply unconditionally for all citizens, and democratic governments cannot constrain them without violating the normative imperatives of democracy. Consequently, torture, extrajudicial killing, displacement, and political imprisonment by the government are irreconcilable with democratic regimes. Nonetheless, even beyond Abu Ghraib and Guantanamo Bay, examples of established democracies violating basic human rights abound. The US' "War on Terror" provides a striking example of democratic governments failing by their own, constitutional standards. Since consistent disrespect for the sanctity of the individual on the part of top-notch democracies would signal a fundamental democratic malaise, it is imperative to explore what explains such questionable human rights practices in democracies and what institutional remedies established democracies have in stock to prevent them in the future.

More often than not, physical integrity violations are inherently nonrandom and denote a purposeful policy to confront perceived or actual political threats to the political elite, respectively, their policies. However, governments do not exploit all kinds of political threats for questionable human rights practices. Rather, the decision to commit physical integrity violations is conditioned by what political dissidents do given the limits of acceptable political dissent. In the case of established democracies, this translates into the categorical distinction between peaceful and violent political threats. The former are realized in demonstrations and strikes, while riots and terrorism are apt examples of the latter. Given that peaceful political threats constitute an exercise of civil liberties, I hypothesized that they should not trigger physical integrity violations by democratic governments. However, violent political threats contradict democratic mechanisms of conflict mediation and disrupt public order. Therefore, I argued, even established democracies may be tempted to commit more human rights violations as the intensity of violent political threats increases.

At this point the strength of the judiciary comes into play. Much of the literature on state repression theorizes that electoral accountability constitutes the democratic guarantee of physical integrity, because the opportunity to punish governments at the polls "effectively limits their ability to use repression domestically, since citizens could turn out of office those heavy-handed leaders" (Regan and Henderson 2002, p. 121). However, electoral accountability is itself contingent on the meaningfulness of democratic self-government and thus a secure rule of law. Employing the concept of "embedded democracy" I argued that horizontal accountability among the three constitutional powers is logically prior to electoral accountability because it entails a system of independent courts. This system may defend basic human rights against the government even in the face of intense political threats. More precisely, I hypothesized that the stronger the judiciary is, the less important are violent political threats as a predictor of human rights violations by the government in established democracies.

My analysis of 29 established democracies from 1995 to 2007 lent partial support to these hypotheses. During the observation period, most established democracies committed physical integrity violations in the form of torture, extrajudicial killings, displacements, and political imprisonment. Some countries even exhibited a trend toward less respect for the integrity of person, but there was no marked deterioration across all countries in the data. Consistent with my hypotheses, peaceful political threats, i.e., demonstrations and strikes, did not significantly increase the level of physical integrity violations. In contrast, violent political threats in the form of riots and terrorist attacks did demonstrate such an effect. Moreover, the data did not support my reasoning on the interaction between violent political threats and the strength of the judiciary. This non-finding is substantively troubling. It speaks to a conditional validity of core democratic institutions in the face of growing violent political threats. More precisely, my results hinted that even strong judiciaries might not confine governments to lawful action as the frequency of riots and terrorism in established democracies increases. By implication the democratic guarantee of basic human rights depends on the state of contentious politics and may sacrifice in the name of law and order at any time.

These results come with a particular caveat. Albeit firmly nested in the literature on state repression, my analysis proved surprisingly insensitive to temporal patterns in physical integrity violations. This points to severe deficiencies in conventional theories and casts doubt on the strong claim to causality advanced in this literature. Political threats offer potent insights on cross-sectional patterns in government encroachments on individual liberty and security: established democracies that face more violent political threats are systematically less concerned with the integrity of person. Causality, however, requires leverage on the longitudinal dimension of the data. Consequently, my analysis speaks to missing links in the theoretical chain from increasing political threats to increasing human rights violations by democratic governments. One such link could be the categorical difference between state and democratic regime assuming that elected officials may exert only imperfect control over state instruments of organized violence. This may happen intentionally or unintentionally. While the USA PATRIOT Act and the AUMF resolution demonstrate the former, the widely criticized crackdown by the Baden-Württemberg police on Anti-Stuttgart 21 protesters in September 2010 is an instance of the latter. A second plausible link is the responsiveness of elected officials to voter demands. In the shadow of dire political threats, electoral accountability may pervert, and it might reinforce questionable human rights practices by the government in line with citizen demands for law and order. Either mechanism offers promising venues for future research.

In light of the evidence amassed by scholars over the past two decades, there is no denying that political democracy is crucial for taming violent state behavior. Yet, time and again even democracies fail to meet their own normative standards. While established democracies must preach a Lockean ideal of responsible government action, they are nevertheless tempted by the Hobbesian Leviathan when confronting political threats. It would be naïve to expect established democracies never to violate human rights. Still, my analysis speaks a language of systematic reasons and thus established democracies turn out to be more than occasional sinners.

Appendix

Table 13.2 Unstandardized sample distributions of time-varying variables

	Min.	1st Q.	Median	Mean	3rd Q.	Max.	N
Physical integrity	0.00	0.00	1.00	0.89	1.00	6.00	377
ln(peaceful threats + 1)	0.00	1.79	2.64	2.68	3.69	6.86	377
ln(violent threats + 1)	0.00	0.00	1.39	1.48	2.40	5.00	377
Income inequality	34.49	42.01	44.57	45.25	47.25	69.95	375
Pop. growth (%)	−0.29	0.17	0.47	0.64	1.10	2.79	377
War	0.00	0.00	0.00	0.15	0.00	1.00	377
t ($t_{1995} = 0$)	0.00	3.00	6.00	6.00	9.00	12.00	377

Table 13.3 Variance decomposition of logged physical integrity violations, 1995–2007

Dep. variable: $\ln(PI_{it}+1)$	Model 1	Model 2	Model 3
Fixed part			
Constant	0.52 (0.07)	0.36 (0.07)	0.36 (0.07)
t		0.03 (0.00)	0.03 (0.01)
Stochastic part			
$\sigma^2_{Intercept/Country}$	0.12 (0.35)	0.12 (0.35)	0.12 (0.34)
$\sigma^2_{t/Country}$			0.00 (0.02)
$\sigma^2_{Residual}$	0.10 (0.32)	0.09 (0.30)	0.08 (0.28)
Deviance	285.69	244.84	233.48
AIC	291.69	252.84	243.48
BIC	303.48	268.57	263.14
$ICC_{Country}$	0.54	0.57	0.59

Note: Standard errors in parenthesis, 377 repeated measurements nested in 29 countries; t centered on 1995

Table 13.4 The impact of political threats on logged physical integrity violations, 1995–2007

Dep. variable: $\ln(PI_{it}+1)$	Model 1	Model 2	Model 3	Model 4	Model 5
Fixed part					
Intercept	0.36 (0.07)	0.36 (0.05)	0.40 (0.05)	0.39 (0.04)	0.39 (0.04)
ln(peaceful threats + 1)		0.04 (0.03)	0.05 (0.02)	0.03 (0.02)	0.03 (0.02)
ln(violent threats + 1)		0.05 (0.02)	0.05 (0.02)	0.05 (0.02)	0.05 (0.02)
Income inequality			0.02 (0.01)	0.01 (0.00)	0.01 (0.00)
Population growth			0.15 (0.05)	0.08 (0.05)	0.08 (0.05)
War			0.17 (0.07)	0.15 (0.06)	0.15 (0.06)
t	0.03 (0.01)	0.03 (0.01)	0.02 (0.01)	0.02 (0.01)	0.02 (0.01)
Rule of law				−0.71 (0.19)	−0.71 (0.20)
Electoral competition				−0.77 (0.29)	−0.76 (0.29)
ln(Viol. Thr. + 1) * RoL					0.04 (0.10)
Stochastic part					
$\sigma^2_{Intercept/Country}$	0.12 (0.34)	0.08 (0.28)	0.05 (0.21)	0.02 (0.15)	0.02 (0.15)
$\sigma^2_{t/Country}$	0.00 (0.02)	0.00 (0.02)	0.00 (0.02)	0.00 (0.02)	0.00 (0.02)
$\sigma^2_{Residual}$	0.08 (0.28)	0.08 (0.29)	0.08 (0.28)	0.08 (0.28)	0.08 (0.28)
Model fit					
Deviance	285.7	223.2	203.0	185.6	185.5
AIC	243.5	237.2	223.0	209.6	211.5
BIC	263.1	264.8	262.3	256.7	262.5
N	377	377	375	375	375
Countries	29	29	29	29	29

Note: Standard errors in parenthesis, all predictors centered on their sample means, t is coded 0 in 1995

References

Acemoglu, D., & Robinson, J. A. (2000). Democratization or repression? inequality, growth and development. *European Economic Review, 44*, 683–693.

Acemoglu, D., & Robinson, J. A. (2006). *Economic origins of dictatorship and democracy*. Cambridge/New York: Cambridge University Press.

Alvarez, M., Cheibub, J. A., Przeworski, A., & Limongi, F. (1996). Classifying political regimes. *Studies in Comparative International Development, 31*(2), 3–36.

Amnesty International. (2006). *Amnesty International report 2006: The state of the world's human rights*. London: Amnesty International Publications.

Amnesty International. (2007). *Amnesty International report 2007: The state of the world's human rights*. Witney, UK: The Alden Press.

Amnesty International. (2008). *Amnesty International report 2008: The state of the world's human rights*. London: Amnesty International Publications.

Amnesty International. (2011). *Amnesty International report 2011: The state of the world's human rights*. London: Amnesty International Publications.

Arendt, H. (1972). Civil disobedience. In H. Arendt (Ed.), *Crises of the republic* (pp. 49–102). New York, NY: Harcourt Brace Jovanovich.

Armstrong, D. A. (2009). Measuring the democracy-repression nexus. *Electoral Studies, 28*(3), 403–412.

Bates, D., Maechler, M., & Bolker, B. (2013). *lme4: Linear mixed-effects models using s4 classes*. Accessed April 11, 2017, from http://CRAN.R-project.org/package=lme4

Bueno de Mesquita, B., Downs, G. W., & Smith, A. (2005). Thinking inside the box: A closer look at democracy and human rights. *International Studies Quarterly, 49*(3), 439–457.

Bühlmann, M., Merkel, W., Müller, L., & Weßels, B. (2012a). The democracy barometer: A new instrument to measure the quality of democracy and its potential for comparative research. *European Political Science, 11*(4), 519–536.

Bühlmann, M., Merkel, W., Müller, L., Giebler, H., & Weßels, B. (2012b). Demokratiebarometer: Ein neues Instrument zur Messung von Demokratiequalität. *Zeitschrift für Vergleichende Politikwissenschaft, 6*, 115–159.

Cheibub, J. A., Gandhi, J., & Vreeland, J. (2010). Democracy and dictatorship revisited. *Public Choice, 143*(1/2), 67–101.

Cingranelli, D. L., & Richards, D. L. (1999). Measuring the level, pattern, and sequence of government repect for physical integrity rights. *International Studies Quarterly, 43*(2), 407–417.

Cingranelli, D. L., & Richards, D. L. (2008). *The cingranelli-richards (ciri) human rights data project coding manual: Manual version 2008.3.13*. Accessed April 11, 2017, from http://www.humanrightsdata.org/documentation/ciri coding guide.pdf

Cingranelli, D. L., & Richards, D. L. (2013). *The cingranelli-richards (ciri) human rights dataset: Dataset version: 2013.08.01*. Accessed April 11, 2017, from http://www.humanrightsdata.org

Cingranelli, D. L., Richards, D. L., & Cingranelli, D. L. (2010). The Cingranelli and Richards (ciri) human rights data project. *Human Rights Quarterly, 32*(2), 401–424.

Collier, D., & Levitsky, S. (1997). Democracy with adjectives: Conceptual innovation in comparative research. *World Politics, 49*(3), 430–451.

Dahl, R. A. (1971). *Polyarchy: Participation and opposition*. New Haven, CT: Yale University Press.

Dahl, R. A. (1989). *Democracy and its critics*. New Haven, CT: Yale University Press.

Davenport, C. (1995). Multi-dimensional threat perception and state repression: An inquiry into why states apply negative sanctions. *American Journal of Political Science, 39*(3), 683–713.

Davenport, C. (1999). Human rights and the democratic proposition. *Journal of Conflict Resolution, 43*(1), 92–116.

Davenport, C. (2000). Introduction. In C. Davenport (Ed.), *Paths to state repression* (pp. 1–24). Lanham, MD: Rowman & Littlefield.

Davenport, C. (2007a). State repression and political order. *Annual Review of Political Science, 10* (1), 1–23.
Davenport, C. (2007b). *State repression and the domestic democratic peace*. New York, NY: Cambridge University Press.
Davenport, C., & Armstrong, D. A. (2004). Democracy and the violation human rights: A statistical analysis from 1976 to 1996. *American Journal of Political Science, 48*(3), 538–554.
Davenport, C., & Inman, M. (2012). The state of repression research since the 1990s. *Terrorism and Political Violence, 24*(3), 619–634.
Downs, A. (1957). *An economic theory of democracy*. New York, NY: Harper.
Earl, J. (2011). Political repression: Iron fists, velvet gloves, and diffuse control. *Annual Review of Sociology, 37*(1), 261–284.
Fariss, C. J., & Schnakenberg, K. E. (2013). Measuring mutual dependence between state repressive actions. *Journal of Conflict Resolution, 58*(6), 1003–1032. https://doi.org/10.1177/0022002713487314.
Fox, J., & Weisberg, S. (2011). *An R companion to applied regression* (2nd ed.). Beverly Hills, CA & London: Sage.
Francisco, R. A. (1995). The relationship between coercion and protest: An empirical evaluation in three coercive states. *Journal of Conflict Resolution, 39*(2), 263–282.
Francisco, R. A. (1996). Coercion and protest: An empirical test in two democratic states. *American Journal of Political Science, 40*(4), 1179–1204.
Gartner, S., & Regan, P. (1996). Threat and repression: The non-linear relationship between government and opposition violence. *Journal of Peace Research, 33*(3), 273–287.
Gelman, A., & Hill, J. (2006). *Applied regression and multilevel/hierarchical models*. Cambridge/New York: Cambridge University Press.
Gurr, T. R. (1986). The political origins of state violence and terror: A theoretical analysis. In M. Stohl & G. A. Lopez (Eds.), *Government violence and repression* (pp. 45–72). New York, NY: Greenwood Press.
Habermas, J. (2001). *Between facts and norms. Contributions to a discourse theory of law and democracy*. Cambridge, MA: The MIT Press.
Henderson, C. W. (1993). Population pressures and political repression. *Social Science Quarterly, 74*(2), 322–333.
Heston, A., Summers, R., & Aten, B. (2012). *Pwt 7.1: Penn world table version 7.1*. Accessed April 11, 2017, from http://pwt.econ.upenn.edu/php site/pwt index.php
Hidalgo, O. (2013). Der Leviathan zwischen "demokratischer" Zähmung und "totaler" Entgrenzung: Schmitte, Hobbes und der Ausnahmezustand als staatstheoretische Herausforderung. In R. Voigt (Ed.), *Ausnahmezustand, Vol. 57 of Staatsverständnisse* (pp. 58–84). Nomos: Baden-Baden.
Hobbes, T. (2010). *Leviathan, or, The matter, form, & power of a common-wealth ecclesiastical and civil: edited by Ian Shapiro. Rethinking the Western tradition*. New Haven, CT: Yale University Press.
Hox, J. J. (2010). *Multilevel analysis: Techniques and applications* (2nd ed.). London: Routledge.
Karl, T. L. (1986). Imposing Consent? Electoralism vs. Democratization in El Salvador. In P. Drake & E. Silva (Eds.), *Elections and Democratization in Latin America, Vol. 1985, Center for Iberian and Latin American Studies* (pp. 9–36). San Diego, CA: Center for US/Mexican Studies, University of California.
Keesing's. (2013a). Turkey: Anti-government protests. *Keesing's Record of World Events, 59*, 52740.
Keesing's. (2013b). United states: Presidential revision of anti-terrorism strategy. *Keesing's Record of World Events, 59*(5), 52655–52656.
Keith, L. C. (2002). Constitutional provisions for individual human rights (1977–1996): Are they more than mere 'window dressing?'. *Political Research Quarterly, 55*(1), 111–143.
Kersting, W. (2007). Thomas Hobbes, Leviathan (1651). In M. Brocker (Ed.), *Geschichte des politischen Denkens* (pp. 212–225). Frankfurt am Main: Suhrkamp.

King, J. C. (2000). Exploring the ameliorating effects of democracy on political repression: Cross-national evidence. In C. Davenport (Ed.), *Paths to state repression* (pp. 217–239). Lanham, MD: Rowman & Littlefield.

Leetaru, K., & Schrodt, P. (2013). *Gdelt: Global data on events, language, and tone, 1979–2012*. Paper presented at the International studies association annual conference, April 2013, San Diego, CA. Accessed April 11, 2017, from http://gdelt.utdallas.edu/data/documentation/ISA.2013.GDELT.pdf

Lichbach, M. I. (1987). Deterrence or escalation? the puzzle of aggregate studies of repression and dissent. *The Journal of Conflict Resolution, 31*(2), 266–297.

Locke, J. (1988). *Two treatises of government*. Cambridge, MA: Cambridge University Press.

Mainwaring, S., Brinks, D., & Pérez-Linán, A. (2001). Classifying Political Regimes in Latin America, 1945–1999. *Studies in Comparative International Development, 36*(1), 37–65.

McCormick, J., & Mitchell, N. J. (1997). Human rights violations, umbrella concepts, and empirical analysis. *World Politics, 49*(4), 510–525.

Merkel, W. (2004). Embedded and defective democracies. *Democratization, 11*(5), 33–58.

Merkel, W. (2010). *Systemtransformation: Eine Einführung in die Theorie und Empirie der Transformationsforschung*. Wiesbaden: VS Verlag für Sozialwissenschaften.

Merkel, W., Puhle, H.-J., Croissant, A., Eicher, C., & Thiery, P. (2003). *Defekte Demokratien: Bd. 1: Theorie und Probleme*. Wiesbaden: Westdeutscher Verlag.

Moore, W. H. (2000). The repression of dissent: A substitution model of government coercion. *Journal of Conflict Resolution, 44*(1), 107–127.

Pierskalla, J. H. (2010). Protest, deterrence, and escalation: The strategic calculus of government repression. *Journal of Conflict Resolution, 54*(1), 117–145.

Pinheiro, J., Bates, D., DebRoy, S., Sarkar, D., & R Core Team. (2013). nlme: Linear and nonlinear mixed effects models R package version 3.1–108.

Poe, S. C., & Tate, C. N. (1994). Repression of the human right to personal integrity in 1980s: A global analysis. *American Political Science Review, 88*(4), 853–872.

Poe, S. C., Tate, C. N., & Keith, L. C. (1999). Repression of the human right to personal integrity revisited: A global cross-national study covering the years 1976–1993. *International Studies Quarterly, 43*(2), 291–313.

Poe, S. C., Tate, C. N., Keith, L. C., & Lanier, D. (2000). Domestic threats: The abuse of personal integrity. In C. Davenport (Ed.), *Paths to state repression* (pp. 27–70). Lanham, MD: Rowman & Littlefield.

Przeworski, A. (1999). Minimalist conception of democracy: A defense. In I. Shapiro & C. Hacker-Cordón (Eds.), *Democracy's value* (pp. 23–55). Cambridge: Cambridge University Press.

Przeworski, A., Alvarez, M., Cheibub, J. A., & Limongi, F. (2000). *Democracy and development: Material well-being in the world, 1950–1990*. Cambridge/New York: Cambridge University Press.

R Core Team. (2013). *R: A language and environment for statistical computing*. Accessed April 11, 2017, from http://www.R-project.org/

Rabe-Hesketh, S., & Skrondal, A. (2008). *Multilevel and longitudinal modeling using STATA* (2nd ed.). College Station, TX: Stata Press Publication.

Regan, P. M., & Henderson, E. A. (2002). Democracy, threats and political repression in developing countries: Are democracies internally less violent? *Third World Quarterly, 23*(1), 119–136.

Sarkees, M. R., & Wayman, F. W. (2010). *Resort to war: A data guide to inter-state, extra-state, intra-state, and non-state wars, 1816–2007*. Washington, DC: CQ Press.

Schmitter, P. C., & Karl, T. L. (1996). What democracy is ... and is not. In L. Diamond & M. F. Plattner (Eds.), *The global resurgence of democracy* (pp. 49–62). Baltimore, MD: Johns Hopkins University Press.

Schrodt, P. A. (2012). *Cameo: Conflict and mediation event observations event and actor codebook: Event data project*. State College, PA: Department of Political Science, Pennsylvania State University, Pond Laboratory.

Schumpeter, J. A. (1942). *Capitalism, socialism, and democracy*. New York, NY: Harper.

Solt, F. (2013). *The standardized world income inequality database*. Accessed April 11, 2017, from http://hdl.handle.net/1902.1/11992

START. (2012). *Global terrorism database: gtd 91to11 1012dist'*. Accessed April 11, 2017, from http://www.start.umd.edu/gtd

Teorell, J., Charron, N., Dahlberg, S., Holmberg, S., Rothstein, B., Sundin, P., & Svensson, R. (2013). *The quality of government dataset: Version 15may13*. Accessed April 11, 2017, from http://www.qog.pol.gu.se

Tsebelis, G., & Sprague, J. (1989). Coercion and revolution: Variations on a predator-prey model. *Mathematical and Computer Modeling, 12*(4–5), 547–559.

U.S. Department of State (2004, February 25). *Country reports on human rights practices: France*. Accessed April 11, 2017, from http://www.state.gov/j/drl/rls/hrrpt/2003/27837.htm

Ware, J. (2013). *Undercover soldiers 'killed unarmed civilians in Belfast'*. Accessed April 11, 2017, from http://www.bbc.co.uk/news/uk-24987465

Wickham, H. (2009). *ggplot2: Elegant graphics for data analysis*. New York, NY: Springer. Accessed April 11, 2017, from http://had.co.nz/ggplot2/book

Zanger, S. C. (2000). A global analysis of the effect of political regime changes on life integrity violations, 1977–93. *Journal of Peace Research, 37*(2), 213–233.

Chapter 14
Constitutional Courts in Democracy: Inducing or Preventing Crisis?

Sascha Kneip

14.1 Introduction

In recent decades, constitutional courts have developed into powerful players in democratic politics (see, e.g., Waltman and Holland 1988; Vallinder 1995; Stone Sweet 2000; Epstein et al. 2001; Guarnieri and Pederzoli 2002; Ginsburg 2003; Koopmans 2003; Sandler and Schoenbrod 2003; Epstein and Knight 2004; Scheppele 2005; Horowitz 2006; Romeu 2006). The "triumphant progress" of constitutional jurisdiction in the second half of the twentieth century makes this period an age not only of democratization but also of the constitutionalization of politics (Elster and Slagstad 1993; Henkin 1994; Bellamy 1996; Alexander 1998; Hilbink 2008). Whereas in 1920 constitutional jurisdiction was established in only a handful of countries, nowadays there is hardly a democracy to be found without a constitutional court of one sort or another. In almost all democracies, there are either supreme courts, which in addition to their normal activities are entrusted with interpreting the constitution and settling constitutional disputes ("diffuse" or "American model" of constitutional jurisdiction), or specialized constitutional courts, which pronounce exclusively on constitutional matters and procedures ("specialized" or "European model" of constitutional jurisdiction; for an overview of court types in the member states of the European Union, see Kneip 2008). Three contemporary OECD democracies, the United Kingdom, the Netherlands, and Switzerland, have expressly denied their supreme courts any formal powers as constitutional courts to review parliamentary legislation (judicial review in the narrower sense of the term), but in a somewhat diluted form, these courts also exercise constitutional jurisdiction. In 2009, for example, the United Kingdom, the

S. Kneip (✉)
WZB Berlin Social Science Center, Berlin, Germany
e-mail: sascha.kneip@wzb.eu

W. Merkel, S. Kneip (eds.), *Democracy and Crisis*,
https://doi.org/10.1007/978-3-319-72559-8_14

"mother of parliamentary sovereignty," institutionalized a supreme court, which, despite the lack of judicial review powers, can examine the compatibility of acts of the executive with the law and unwritten constitutional principles and sanction any breach. In the United Kingdom, too, the informal self-commitment of politics to fundamental rights and standards is gradually giving way to formal commitment through institutionalized procedures under the rule of law. The Human Rights Act passed in 2000 has laid the foundation for a system of constitutional review, whose impact is only gradually becoming apparent (see Kavanagh 2009).[1] In brief, constitutional courts and the judicial review of legislative and/or executive acts by such courts are now an integral element in the lives of established democracies. Today the subjection of politics to constitutions and basic rights is just as much part of how modern democracies see themselves as the safeguarding of basic rights by constitutional courts.

However, the empirical fact of their existence is no guarantee for the normative or factual acceptance of constitutional jurisdiction. Neither political actors nor scholars necessarily share the view that constitutional courts are indispensable for democracies. On the contrary, in both normative and empirical democracy research, skepticism has now and then been expressed about the status, function, and role of constitutional courts. Whereas normative democratic theory and legal theory take a fundamentally critical view of legal restraints on democratic procedures (e.g., Maus 1992, 2004, 2005; Waldron 1999, 2006), empirical research occasionally suspects that constitutional courts—democratically too weak, because only indirectly legitimated—intervene too much in political affairs (see, e.g., Landfried 1984, 1985, 1994; Höffe 1999; Schneider 1999; Scholz 1999; Tushnet 1999, 2008; Sandler and Schoenbrod 2003; Hirschl 2007). This assessment is mostly backed by assertions that constitutional courts are "veto players" or "opponents" in the political game (Alivizatos 1995; Magaloni and Sánchez 2001; Volcansek 2001; Tsebelis 2002; Wagschal 2006), that they are driving forces behind the "judicialization" of politics (e.g., Landfried 1984, 1994; Vallinder 1994, 1995; Tate and Vallinder 1995; Stone Sweet 1999, 2000; Shapiro and Stone Sweet 2002), and that from a normative point of view, their activities are detrimental or harmful to democracy.[2]

[1]The incorporation of the European Convention for the Protection of Human Rights and Fundamental Freedoms into English law gives all courts in the United Kingdom the right to measure acts of the executive by the yardstick of the basic and human rights under the ECHR and, where necessary, to sanction any violation. However, this does not involve annulling acts of the parliament. What is more, the United Kingdom, like the Netherlands and Switzerland, is integrated into a multi-level, European constitutional (court) system and has submitted itself to the authority of the European Court of Justice (ECJ) and/or the European Court of Human Rights (ECHR). The idea that democratic governance in these countries is not safeguarded by rule-of-law institutions has long since been belied by legal reality.

[2]Such appraisal is based firstly on analysis of the formal power and institutionalized influence of constitutional courts on democratic politics (see also Lijphart 1999) and secondly on specific consideration of the sometimes far-reaching judicial review powers and activities of constitutional courts in modern democracy.

If we take these postulates a step further, we could argue that constitutional court action is evidence of a crisis of modern democracy. At least according to critics of modern constitutionalism, this crisis is signaled by the fact that the weal and woe of democratic politics are no longer decided by democratically legitimated actors; more and more often, the final decision for the democratic polity is made by a sort of judicial "council of elders." The "real" democratic authorities—the people, parliament, or the executive—have retained too little scope for action, and "governing with judges" (Stone Sweet 2000) is claimed to be becoming "governing by judges." To put it in a nutshell, participatory democracy has long since been replaced by judicial expertocracy.

Now there is certainly no doubting that constitutional court action limits the scope of political action. Not infrequently, court rulings curtail the decision-making powers of political actors, and the prospect of judicial review influences political thinking even before decisions are made. However, whether this strong position of constitutional jurisdiction—if it can be empirically demonstrated—is good or bad for a given democracy or is even symptomatic of crisis has yet to be shown. Whether constitutional jurisdiction is beneficial or detrimental to democratic governance and whether it is a cause or symptom of, or even a solution to, democratic crises remain to be seen; this is the question the present chapter addresses.[3]

We begin by asking how the relationship between democracy, crisis, and constitutional jurisdiction is to be theoretically formulated. We then empirically examine whether in recent decades constitutional courts have indeed become stronger, more independent, and above all more disposed to intervene. Finally, we reunite theoretical/normative and empirical aspects and discuss what influence constitutional court action has on the quality of established democracies. Two general, interrelated questions are particularly interesting: Are constitutional courts really increasingly exceeding their powers within the system of the horizontal separation of powers? And do such courts sufficiently protect key areas and partial regimes of democracy? This is discussed in depth with the focus on civil liberties before a brief conclusion brings the chapter to a close.

14.2 Democracy, Constitutional Jurisdiction, and the Crisis of Democracy

Whether constitutional courts are seen as key and legitimate actors in democracy depends primarily on the choice of the model of democracy. If by democracy we understand exclusively the production of generally binding decisions by majority vote, as Robert Dahl (1971, 1989, 2000) and John Hart Ely (1980) tend to do, such a model naturally leaves little scope for far-reaching legitimate action by rule-of-law

[3]Sections of this chapter are based on Kneip (2009, 2011, 2013) and take the arguments developed there a step further.

actors. Although constitutional courts can then be entrusted with overseeing the operation of democratic (majoritarian) procedures themselves or of arbitrating in jurisdictional conflicts, their task in democracy is essentially limited to these two functions. The model of embedded democracy underlying this volume (see Chap. 1) goes far beyond this primarily procedural understanding of democracy. It treats civil liberties and rights as a key, constitutive element of democracy, even beyond their function in the democratic process; civil rights are thus of intrinsic value. On the other hand, embedded democracy sees horizontal accountability as performing an important role in democracy that goes beyond Dahl's polyarchy model; indeed, checks and balances and the rule of law constitute a key partial regime of democracy without which democracy cannot work (see Merkel et al. 2003; on the fundamental differences between the proceduralist and the constitutionalist approaches, see Becker 2001 and Kneip 2006).

These two additions to Dahl's liberal democracy model imply a functional extension of constitutional jurisdiction. This model sees constitutional courts as being no longer responsible solely for the functioning of the democratic process in the narrower sense; in interaction with the other relevant actors but vested with the power of final decision, they bear responsibility for the quality and functioning of *all* partial regimes of democracy (electoral regime, political participation rights, civil liberties, horizontal accountability, effective power to govern). Ideally, a constitutional court hence watches over the interplay between the partial regimes of democracy, authoritatively resolves potential conflicts in accordance with the constitution, thus ensuring that the basic rights and institutional rules that define democracy are respected. In effect, this expresses the particular logic of liberal democratic institutions: the protection of key rights and procedures is entrusted not to political authorities alone but also to an external arbitrator that is not part of the political game (see, e.g., Holmes 1993).

The peculiar charm of a functionalist approach is that, in the democratic constitutional state, the function of constitutional jurisdiction can be seen as drawing the line between the political and judicial scopes for action (on functions in general and with reference to the Federal Constitutional Court, see Grimm 1977; Moreira Cardoso da Costa 1988; Brohm 2001; Kranenpohl 2004). Ideally, a constitutional court should ensure "that the other institutions of the state behave as they ought to under the constitution," as Dieter Grimm has aptly put it (Grimm 1977, 87). In other words, it should ensure that all democratic actors actually fulfill the functions allotted to them. Grimm continues that constitutional court action does not curtail the power of politics but imposes only a "loss of the power to violate the constitution with impunity" (ibid.). But when do political actors infringe the constitution? Whenever a constitutional court says that they have done so?

This conclusion may well be empirically correct,[4] but it is unsatisfactory in theoretical terms. It is of course conceivable in principle that a constitutional court

[4]"We are under a Constitution, but the Constitution is what the judges say it is," as the 11th chief justice of the US Supreme Court, Charles Evan Hughes (1930–1941) put it tersely and aptly.

oversteps its remit and interferes illegitimately everywhere as a final authority neither elected by the citizens nor accountable to them. But how are the limits of constitutional jurisdiction to be determined if the courts can themselves define and set them at any time? The only approach that can ultimately help is to consider the tasks of constitutional jurisdiction in terms of the *functions of democracy* (see Kneip 2006). Democratic functionalism examines if and under what circumstances constitutional jurisdiction fulfils functions that the intrinsic functional logic of political institutions prevents political actors from performing. This could occur mainly in two situations: in settling conflicts of competence between institutions of the state and above all in protecting basic rights and fundamental constitutional principles.[5]

Even though the question of when a concrete political decision or action affects rights, including basic rights, and when constitutional courts are authorized to intervene remain a controversial one,[6] such courts are the venue for settling disputes about the application of key rights and procedures. This consideration of constitutional jurisdiction from the perspective of democratic functions allows a first conclusion: if it is the task of constitutional courts to perform specific functions for democracy, it cannot be claimed across the board that judicial self-restraint would be good for democratic governance. On the contrary, such self-restraint can have a markedly negative impact on democracy if it means that unconstitutional legislation or action is not sanctioned.[7]

From a functionalist point of view, a crisis of democracy can thus arise for two reasons: firstly because constitutional courts overstep their own functional boundaries to make final decisions that in democracies should be made by authorities with better legitimation to do so—the people, parliaments, governments and secondly constitutional courts do not fulfill their function satisfactorily and do not sanction unconstitutional infringements of rights and procedures by (majoritarian) political actors. In the first case, democratic procedures would operate only pro forma because the democratic link between citizen preferences, party and parliamentary

[5]Conflicts of competence between two or more actors should obviously be decided by a third, independent, and neutral party, since the majority position would otherwise always prevail ("arbitration function" of constitutional jurisdiction). But for reasons of legal logic, decisions on the application and reach of basic rights cannot be left to contingent political majorities as well. If basic rights were in principle at the free disposition of a political majority, their status of *basic* rights would be forfeit. This is not to argue that political majorities cannot respect or guarantee basic rights. But the purpose of legally entrenched basic rights is to bind the lawmaker; the legislature should not be able to repeal or amend the law pertaining to basic rights by a simple majority (on the collision between basic rights and the democracy principle, see also Alexy 2010, 416–417).

[6]Precise determination can be provided only empirically and with the aid of fundamental democratic principles and concrete constitutional norms. An attempt at operationalization is to be found in Kneip (2009).

[7]This also shows why the call for judicial restraint contributes nothing to analytical clarity and in effect misses the point: judicial restraint is not a question of the right judicial role model but a legal or democratic functional requirement (see also Grimm 1976).

functions, and governmental activities would no longer exist or would be ineffective. In the terminology of embedded democracy, this would mean that the functions of the core regimes democratic elections, political participation rights, and effective power to govern would suffer fundamental damage. In the second case, a crisis of democracy would consist in the absence of opposition to and sanctioning of substantial violations of rights and procedures by political actors. A pillar of democracy would come to harm precisely because the constitutional court does *not* intervene. In principle, all the partial regimes of embedded democracy could be affected, but in the first place the electoral regime, political participation rights, and civil liberties are concerned. Common to both cases is that the system of horizontal accountability is dissolved unilaterally to the advantage of one authority. In the first case, the constitutional court establishes illegitimate supremacy over the other two powers; in the second, mutual constraints are unilaterally abandoned to the advantage of political authorities—in actual fact mostly the executive.

In sum, we can conclude from this cursory discussion of democratic theory that both action and inaction by constitutional courts can influence the quality of democratic governance—for the better or the worse. Typically, four categories of constitutional court action relevant to the quality of democracy and democratic crises can be identified (detailed treatment in Kneip 2006, 2009, 80–88): functional intervention and nonintervention (positive effect) and dysfunctional intervention and nonintervention (negative effect).

When, however, do these scenarios not only express improvement or deterioration in the quality of democracy but also signal a crisis of democracy? We can address this question only in abstract terms here. A loss of quality in this context would lead to a crisis of democratic governance if, first, the democratic links between citizens, parties, parliaments, and governments were to suffer enduring and structural harm and constitutional courts were to make all essential decisions in their place. Second, we would have to speak of a crisis of democracy if key rights and procedures were curtailed by a democratic majority—without the constitutional court intervening—to such an extent that their substance, their regulatory purpose, is no longer apparent. In both cases, the interplay between the partial regimes of democracy would be so strongly disturbed that we would be justified to speak of a crisis of democracy.[8]

[8]In principle, constitutional courts are always in danger of inducing or preventing crises in both regards. First, it is characteristic of the modern constitutional state that nearly all aspects of society are subject to legal regulation and thus also to judicial review by constitutional courts. The fact that courts can in principle concern themselves with every conceivable facet of societal and political life increases the risk of them overstepping their functional bounds. The danger is particularly great when such cases have to be decided on the basis of open constitutional provisions. On the other hand, constitutional courts are not in a position to review executive or legislative acts on their own initiative. Contraventions of fundamental rights and principles can be sanctioned only if authorized parties actually bring such matters before the court. Constitutional courts will therefore, for structural reasons alone, be able to examine only a fraction of complaints about violations of the law and if necessary sanction such violations.

However, there is empirical evidence to date neither that constitutional courts, particularly institutionally strong ones, do actually intervene frequently in political governance nor that basic rights are in fact adequately protected through intervention by constitutional courts. Whether, for example, the curtailment or restriction of civil liberties can be effectively prevented by constitutional courts is a largely unanswered question (see also Wagner and Kneip, Chap. 12). The section to come takes a closer look at these issues.

14.3 Constitutional Jurisdiction in Democracy: Power Resources and Actual Activities

Two questions about the link between constitutional court action and the quality of democracy, as well as the development of democratic crises, are particularly relevant: first, whether constitutional courts do in fact intervene in politics more often than in the past, thus disturbing the balance of power between the democratic branches of government. This is closely associated with the question of whether the institutional power of the courts has actually grown over time or not. Second, whether in substance courts adequately perform their democratic function and task—whether they sufficiently safeguard basic rights and procedures even in the face of political resistance. A look at countries where the institutions of constitutional jurisdiction are strong will help us answer the first of these questions. It is at least likely that institutionally strong courts will run into the danger of disturbing the balance of power (Sect. 14.3.1). The second question is best tackled from the perspective of basic rights themselves. This requires a closer examination of the activities of constitutional courts in the field of civil liberties (Sect. 14.3.2).

14.3.1 Strength, Independence, and Intervention Behavior of Constitutional Courts over Time

Constitutional courts are important players in the democratic process only if they have sufficient institutional power resources, institutional strength, and independence. Empirical research on constitutional courts generally measures the strength of a court in terms of its formal powers and the openness of access to it (see, e.g., Ginsburg 2003, 34ff.; Hönnige 2007, 101ff.; Kneip 2009, 158ff.). The important formal powers include decision-making competence in concrete and abstract judicial review proceedings, in proceedings on constitutional complaints, and on horizontal and vertical conflicts of competence. Powers in the field of objective protection of the constitution include, for example, jurisdiction on the prohibition of parties, on electoral matters, and on removal from office or the power to measure supranational norms and international law against the national constitution (for an overview, see the comparative study by Brünneck 1992). In this regard, empirical variance among constitutional courts is comparatively low. Many of the constitutional courts set up over the past 20–30 years in Eastern Europe, Latin America, Asia, and also Africa have very similar jurisdictional structures, differing little from such institutions in the Western OECD world, which differ only slightly from one another in the powers vested in them (see also Kneip 2013). However, there are still relatively marked differences between constitutional courts on the American model and those on the European model following Kelsen (classical: Kelsen 1942).[9] The American model of constitutional court generally knows no form of abstract judicial review and sometimes *no erga omnes* jurisdiction, i.e., although rulings on constitutional matters apply for the parties to the case, they do not apply in general for all comparable cases. Although decisions set precedent, they do not automatically apply to other cases. Even if the court rules that a given provision is unconstitutional, this does not necessarily entail its formal annulment. Another important difference between the two models is that, in the American model, all courts in principle have powers of judicial review at the successive levels of appeal, whereas in the European model, judicial review is reserved exclusively to the constitutional court. This also explains the conceptual distinction between diffuse and specialized constitutional court models.

Open access to the court—the second important criterion for the strength of a constitutional court—is usually measured in terms of the number of actors vested with the right of action (e.g., executive, legislature, federal levels, individual citizens, normal courts, ombudspersons, political parties, professional associations, etc.) in conjunction with factual barriers to taking action. There are major differences between courts from country to country in this regard. And there are fundamental differences between the American and European models. The former gives regular access to the court only via the normal, successive stages of appeal; parties in interest therefore have to work their way up to the supreme court through the system. By contrast, specialized constitutional courts can, under certain circumstances, grant some parties direct access.

Whereas in almost all cases the executive has the right of action before the specialized constitutional court, the obstacles for the legislature are much greater. If the right of action is vested in the legislature as a collective institution at all—this is generally the case only for specialized constitutional courts that also exercise abstract judicial review[10]—the quorum is usually between 10% and one third of the elected members of parliament. Whether federal executives and legislatures, parties and associations, ombudspersons, and normal courts are also entitled to take action before the constitutional court also differs widely from country to country.

---

[9]If not explicitly stated, the term "constitutional courts" always refers to both types.

[10]Moreover, specialized constitutional courts do not always grant the legislature (or legislative minorities) the right of action. Particularly in cases where the constitutionality of laws is reviewed only incidentally (and not in the context of a concrete legal dispute), the legislature often has no look in. This is the case in Italy.

However, most important for the openness of access to the court (and thus for the factual efficacy of a constitutional court) is that citizens have the right to take action in the form of constitutional complaints. This considerable enlarges the circle of parties with access to the court and the range of matters that can be heard by a constitutional court. The direct constitutional complaint (including the constitutional complaint against court decisions) is not known in the American model, and not all specialized constitutional courts have the authority to hear constitutional complaints.[11]

However, formal and institutional power are not factual powers. Formal powers have to be "actualized" through action. Another factor is decisive in this regard: empirical legitimacy. Only if a court has sufficient backing in the population and among political elites will it be in a position to implement its decisions—for the enforcement of which it needs the aid of other actors—even against resistance. It is empirical legitimacy—or as David Easton puts it (1965): diffuse and specific support—that turns the potential power of a court into factual power. Such empirical support for constitutional courts varies very strongly from country to country (see also Gibson et al. 1998). The courts that traditionally enjoy a high level of approval include the German Federal Constitutional Court, the Supreme Court of the United States,[12] the Supreme Court of Canada, and, among younger institutions, the Polish Constitutional Tribunal.

Over longer periods of time, these courts record rates of approval among the population of between 60 and 70%, giving them far more empirical support for their work than is received by political actors in their countries (governments, parliaments, parties). The supreme courts of the Scandinavian countries and the *Hoge Raad* of the Netherlands have also traditionally enjoyed high approval rates (see Gibson et al. 1998) but are far less active than the courts mentioned above.

What is the situation with the institutional independence of the courts? This can be measured in terms of the inclusiveness of procedures for selecting judges, the rules pertaining to terms of office, reelection and removal, and the insulation of judges from political pressure. The more inclusive selection procedures are and the more in line with consensus democracy, the more independent the elected or appointed judges will be, ceteris paribus, since under these circumstances no political authority would be able unilaterally to place "its" partisans in a supreme

[11]In Europe, for instance, only the courts in Belgium, Germany, Estonia, Slovakia, Slovenia, Spain, and the Czech Republic hear constitutional complaints lodged by citizens. Although Austria and Poland have generally institutionalized constitutional complaints, they have not introduced constitutional complaints against court decisions. Although the popular or collective action is allowed in Hungary, it cannot be brought directly against infringements of basic rights but only against the underlying law, which the constitutional court may meanwhile no longer be able to review.

[12]In recent years, however, the American Supreme Court has suffered a considerable loss of reputation. See the Gallup data under http://www.gallup.com/poll/4732/supreme-court.aspx. Accessed: 30 November 2012. They show that approval for the work of the Supreme Court fell from 62% in 2000 to 46% in the late summer of 2012.

court. But the empirical institutional variance in this field is considerable. Selection methods range from purely professional procedures under which the judiciary appoints judges more or less independently to representative and cooperative and even sequential procedures, which decide to varying degrees on the independence of selected candidates. Differing quorums for selecting judges (from simple majority to supermajority) also contribute to the empirical differentiation of procedures.[13]

The potential independence of judges increases, secondly, with their length of tenure. Long or even life tenure where removal from office or reelection is excluded considerably increases the independence of a court and its judges. Life tenure is to be found in the American constitutional court model; in the European model of specialized constitutional courts, tenure for judges ranges—at least in Europe—from 9 to 12 years. Unlike in the United States, life tenure comes to an end on reaching retirement age, generally set at between 65 and 70.

Of great importance for the independence of a court from an institutional point of view is its insulation against political pressure over and beyond the possibility of judges being removed from office. It is furthermore important whether a court has the formal status of an organ of the constitution, whether it is subsumed under a government department or can act independently, whether it has a budget of its own under its own control, and whether it can be politically disciplined through financial and employment incentives and sanctions. These at first glance merely technical arrangements are also important for the factual independence of a court; empirically such arrangements can differ widely.

If we look at the institutional strength, empirical legitimacy, and independence of constitutional courts in the "old" OECD world, four courts stand out under all headings and which the literature counts among the institutionally strongest, most independent, and most active courts in established democracies: the German Federal Constitutional Court, the Austrian Constitutional Court, the Supreme Court of the United States, and the Supreme Court of Canada (see the assessments, differing in detail, offered by Cooter and Ginsburg 1996; Lijphart 1999, 225ff.; Alivizatos 1995; Tsebelis 2000, 225ff.). Table 14.1 shows the key structural characteristics of these four courts, which we shall be looking at in greater detail.

It is striking that the courts in the United States, Canada, Austria, and Germany, which are seen as being particularly strong, differ structurally quite markedly in

[13]The cooperative and sequential appointment procedures in the United States, for example, under which the Senate has to confirm by a simple majority a candidate proposed by the President, mean that, where the Senate and the administration are in the hands of the same party, candidates are likely to share the political and ideological views of the institutions appointing them. This is less likely where there is a party difference between the two. The representative selection procedure in Germany, which requires a supermajority (two-thirds in the Bundestag and Bundesrat), by contrast, ensures that, regardless of current political majorities, candidates are more neutral. This is at least so in principle; in fact, however, both catch-all parties CDU-CSU and SPD make use of their right of veto only in exceptional cases. Judges with stronger ideological leanings are, by contrast, to be expected where representative procedures do not require qualified majorities, where, in other words, different political institutions can appoint judges autonomously (state president, government) or by simple majority (parliament).

Table 14.1 Comparative structures of strong constitutional courts

	United States	Canada	Austria	Germany
Start of operation	1790	1875/1982[a]	1946	1951
Type of court	Diffuse	Diffuse	Specialized	Specialized
Constitutional Complaint	No	No	Yes (not against court decisions)	Yes
Abstract judicial review	No	No (but "reference question"[b])	Yes	Yes
Concrete judicial review	Yes	Yes	Yes	Yes
Number of judges	9	9	14	16
Tenure	Life	Life, retirement age 75	Life, retirement age 70	12 years, retirement age 68
Recruitment of judges	Appointment by the president after approval by the Senate with simple majority	De jure: Appointment by the governor-general on recommendation of the Crown Council; De facto: Prime minister	Appointment by the federal president after nomination by the Federal Government (president and vice-president plus six other judges), National Council (3), and Federal Council (3)	Election by the Bundestag and the Bundesrat (eight judges each by a two third majority)

[a]The Constitutional Act of 1982, which, among other things, implemented the Canadian Charter of Rights and Freedoms, considerably expanded the functions of the Supreme Court of Canada and the scope of judicial review (see, e.g., Kelly 1999)
[b]The Canadian Federal Government can seek a legally non-binding decision of the Supreme Court on the constitutionality of legislation or action. Although a decision in response to a "reference question" is not formally binding, in effect it has binding force

formal powers and the formal independence of judges. Whereas formal powers of the specialized courts in Austria and Germany have greater institutional diversity, the Supreme Court of Canada is formally the least independent. The Democracy Barometer data (see Table 14.2) also show marked differences in the strength and independence of the courts under study.

The Democracy Barometer shows variance over time only in political influence on courts in the given country. 2001 appears to be the starting point for deterioration in all four cases, varying in intensity and duration. At first glance, this deterioration can plausibly have to do with the debate on the post-9/11 restriction of rule-of-law guarantees, but this is no more than an assumption at this point. Moreover, it should be remembered that the Democracy Barometer measures influence on the legal system as a whole and not necessarily on supreme courts. Caution is also called for

Table 14.2 Independence and strength of courts (or legal systems[a]) according to the Democracy Barometer, 1990–2007

	United States	Canada	Austria	Germany
Independence of the judiciary in general	High	High	High	High
Independence from political influence	Medium to high until 2001, since slight decline	High until 2001, since marked decline	High, marked decline 2001–2005	High, slight decline 2001–2005
Strength of judicial review	High	Medium	High	High
Effective strength of review of political decisions	Medium	High	Low	High

[a]For the two independent variables, the Democracy Barometer takes the legal system as a whole into consideration and for the strength of judicial review the given supreme or constitutional court. But it can be assumed that the four courts under study have as much factual independence as the court systems as a whole.
Source: Democracy Barometer indicators JUDINDEPCOR, JUDINDEPINF, JUDREV, POWJUDI

in assessing the effective strength of judicial review of political decisions by the Austrian court. At the latest since the early 1990s, the Austrian Constitutional Court has been becoming much more active than the Democracy Barometer data would suggest. The court has long since abandoned the restraint it had exercised in the Kelsian tradition toward the legislative branch; its active performance in relation to political institutions is not adequately reflected by the Democracy Barometer data (see Barfuß 1989; Korinek 2000, and below).

Have these structural differences had an impact on the degree of activity by the courts under study? How strongly and frequently do they actually intervene in democratic processes? Two things are of particular interest: the caseload and the actual intervention frequency.

There are interesting differences and commonalities between the four courts with regard to caseload (see Fig. 14.1). While the Supreme Court of Canada received between 500 and 600 cases a year, the three other courts received several thousand each. On average, the Austrian Constitutional Court received some 3200 cases every year,[14] the German Federal Constitutional Court about 5300, and the Supreme Court of the United States no less than 7400 on average between 1990 and 2011. If the population of the different countries (Austria, 8 million; Canada, 34 million; Germany, 89 million; and the United States, 313 million; status 2011) is taken into account, the number of cases received by the Austrian Constitutional Court is particularly high. In relation to the number of potential parties with locus

[14]Subtracted from these figures are parallel proceedings in the same matter. The increase in the number of proceedings after 2009 is due, among other things, to the fact that since 2008 the Austrian court has been the final court of appeal for asylum cases. The marked increase in 1995/1996 is due largely to asylum cases.

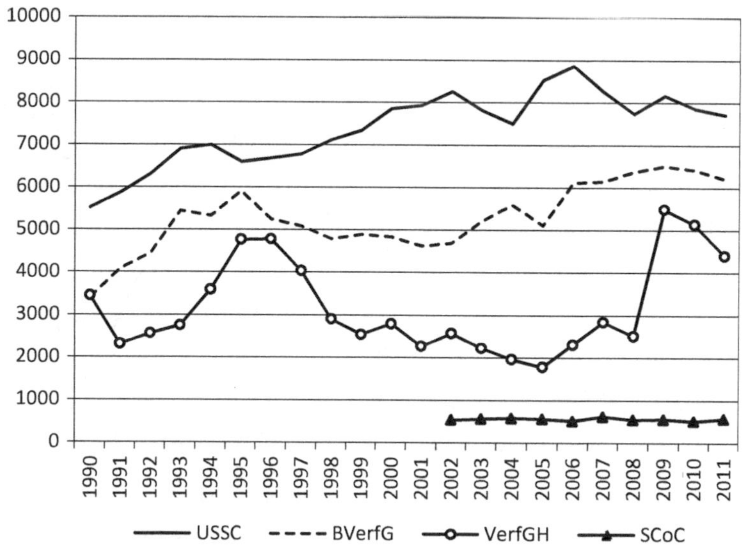

Fig. 14.1 Annual number of incoming cases (caseload), 1990–2011. Note: USSC, US Supreme Court (United States); BVerfG, Federal Constitutional Court (Germany); VerfGH, Austrian Constitutional Court (Austria); SCOC, Supreme Court of Canada (Canada)

standi, the figure for Austria is much higher than for the others, even if asylum cases are subtracted after 2008. If we consider that the Supreme Court of the United States and the Supreme Court of Canada act not only as constitutional courts in the narrower sense of the term but are also courts of appeal for "normal" cases under civil and criminal laws, it is clear that the two specialized constitutional courts of Germany and Austria are much more involved in specific constitutional questions than the other two courts.

The number of incoming cases also conceals the fact that supreme courts on the diffuse model actually rule on no more than 80–120 cases each year. The free selection of cases procedure practiced by the Supreme Court of the United States means that only about 1% of those reaching the court are actually heard and adjudicated. The specialized courts in Germany and Austria may not freely select the cases they hear; in principle they have to rule on the merits of every single case. The large proportion of rejections, particularly in constitutional complaint proceedings, show, however, that the two courts have found a practicable way to reduce the number of proceedings, especially as cases are frequently rejected on formal rather than substantive grounds. Finally, the number of major senate decisions made by the Federal Constitutional Court, for instance, does not much exceed that of adjudications by the Supreme Court of the United States.

Have constitutional courts thus dealt with more and more cases in the course of time and accordingly intervened more and more strongly in democratic politics? This is clearly not the case for the Supreme Court of Canada nor for the Austrian Constitutional Court. At first glance, the number of cases in Germany and the

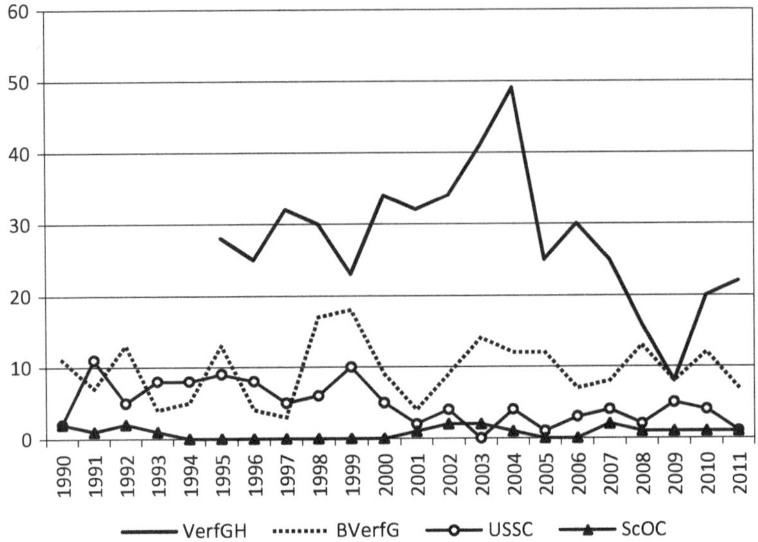

Fig. 14.2 Annulment of laws [Annulments at all three levels (federal, state, and local)] by constitutional courts (1990–2011). Note: VerfGH, Austrian Constitutional Court (Austria); BVerfG, Federal Constitutional Court (Germany); USSC, US Supreme Court (United States); SCOC, Supreme Court of Canada (Canada)

United States points to such a trend; but if the number of cases actually adjudicated is considered, this impression is deceptive.

Nevertheless, because of the high general number of proceedings, these last three courts potentially deal with a greater number of important issues and could thus exercise greater influence on politics and society. The question is therefore what the courts actually do when they accept cases and adjudicate them. How often do they actually intervene in "politics?" Probably the most potent indicator is the frequency with which parliamentary legislation is annulled (see Fig. 14.2).[15]

Here, too, the courts under study differ considerably. While the Supreme Court of Canada found only one to two laws unconstitutional each year, the Austrian Constitutional Court is far more active. Until 2007, it was regularly annulling more than 20 laws a year, at its peak almost 50. The German Federal Constitutional Court and the Supreme Court of the United States have been far more hesitant. Up to the turn of the millennium, the US Supreme Court found fault with an average of about seven laws per year, but since 2000, this figure has fallen to just under three per

[15]Judicial review is the strongest, but certainly not the only way in which constitutional courts can intervene in politics. Reviewing acts of the executive or settling conflicts of competence between democratic institutions can have just as great an impact on politics. As far as the impact that constitutional courts have on society is concerned, it can be assumed that, for instance, judicial review of administrative acts (including court decisions) has much greater influence on the lives of citizens in democracies than the review of acts of parliament.

year. The Federal Constitutional Court, by contrast, has an annual annulment record over the entire period under study of about 9.5 laws. It is far more active than the American court but cannot compete with its Austrian counterpart.

However, the informational value of this comparison should be treated with caution. On the one hand, courts on the diffuse model do not need to annul a legal provision themselves if a lower court has already done so, and the supreme court dismisses the action to reverse this decision (and thus confirms annulment by the lower court). In the specialized model, which reserves the right of annulment to the constitutional court, the court must itself act if it considers legislation to be unconstitutional. The figures for the two models of court can therefore be compared only to a limited extent. On the other hand, the ratio of annulled to confirmed laws qualifies the seemingly high level of annulment by the two specialized constitutional courts. The annulment balance reflects court activity more realistically in that, given the number of confirmations, it also includes the absolute figure of incoming cases in the analysis. Figure 14.3 shows this for the two specialized courts.

Up to 2005, the average annual annulment balance for the Federal Constitutional Court was positive, but after that date, it becomes markedly negative.[16] In other words, until the mid-2000s, the court confirmed more laws than it annulled. Since then, the trend has reversed; since 2003 the annulment balance has been negative. The Austrian Constitutional Court exhibits a contrary trend but at a much higher (more negative) overall level. Only since 2008 has the annulment balance been positive for the Austrian court.

What does all this mean for the questions raised above? Have constitutional courts become the real decision-making centers in liberal democracy? The four institutionally strong constitutional courts under study—with the exception of the Supreme Court of Canada—have become important players in the democratic process alone through the increasing numbers of cases with which they deal. In the course of time, the importance of the two European specialized constitutional courts within their democratic systems has considerable increased. The growing number of cases of all sorts with which the courts deal is, however, not necessarily reflected in the number of laws annulled. The annulment rate either remains at a low (Canada) or moderate (Germany) level or even falls over time (the United States and, with reservations, Austria, albeit from a high base level). It can therefore, thirdly, not be claimed that the courts under study have fostered the judicialization of politics in the course of time by assuming more and more decision-making power and increasingly appropriating the role of the formal lawmaker. At least on the basis of the figures on incoming cases and annulments, no fundamental malfunction of checks and balances can be diagnosed. The courts have remained important actors

[16] From 1951 to 1990, it was positive.

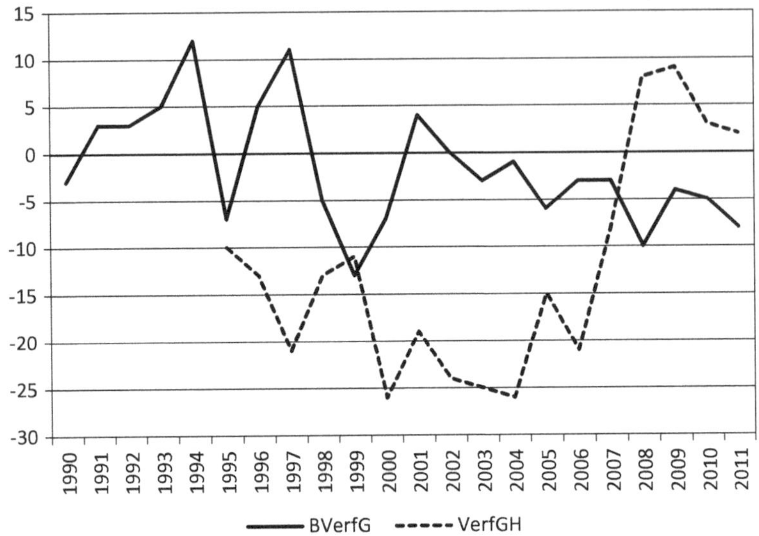

Fig. 14.3 Annulment balance of the BVerfG and VerfGH compared (1990–2011). Note: BVerfG, Federal Constitutional Court (Germany); VerfGH, Austrian Constitutional Court (Austria)

in their democracies; however, they are far from establishing a monopoly on decision-making that would justify claims that democracy is in crisis.[17]

However, the question of constitutional courts exceeding their powers or of disturbance of the horizontal separation of powers is only one crisis scenario for rule-of-law democracies. We have argued that another possible scenario is that constitutional courts could fail adequately to protect fundamental rights and procedures and would thus fail to fulfill their function in democracy. We turn to this question in the following section.

14.3.2 Constitutional Court Action in the Field of Civil Liberties

The embedded democracy model sees the protection and defense of fundamental rights and liberties—under certain circumstances even against democratic majorities—as a key task of constitutional courts. A crisis of democracy can hence be induced not only by constitutional courts systematically exceeding their powers (which the courts under study in this chapter largely do not do) but also by such courts failing to perform their key function of satisfactorily protecting the core

[17]But the figures provide no information about whether the most important societal issues are nevertheless decided by constitutional courts. Only qualitative analysis of the courts' concrete decision output can tell us this. This is beyond the scope of this chapter, but for Germany, see Kneip (2009).

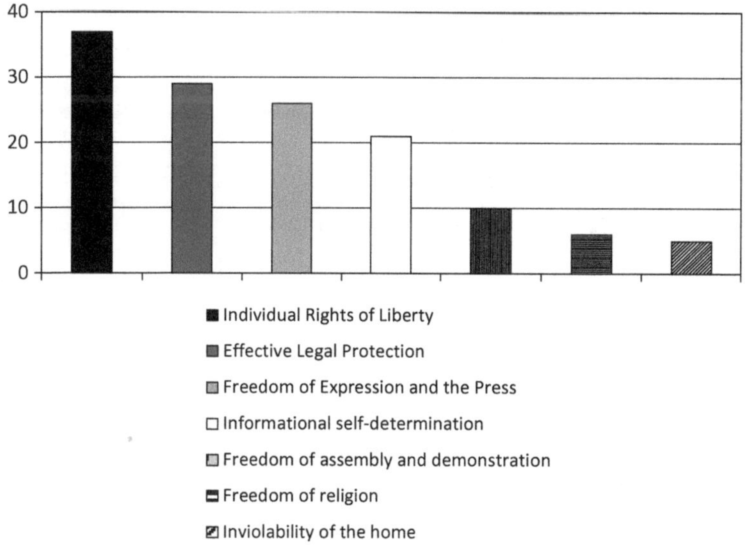

Fig. 14.4 Judgments of the Federal Constitutional Court on civil liberties by subject matter (1990–2012). Source: Author's own figure

elements of democracy against harm. There have been frequent complaints in recent decades that the democratic lawmaker has excessively restricted civil liberties in the face of perceived criminal and terrorist threats (see, e.g., Busch 2011; Chaps. 12 and 13 in this book). However, this would bring lasting damage to or even cause a crisis of democracy only if these restrictions were not at the same time reviewed and where necessary sanctioned by vigilant constitutional courts. The empirical question is therefore whether and to what extent constitutional courts review these potential restrictions of liberty and where appropriate declare them to be unconstitutional. We shall take the example of the German Federal Constitutional Court.

To begin with, it is interesting to see what types of cases the Federal Constitutional Court has dealt with in the field of civil liberties. Figure 14.4 analyzes all 108 rulings in this field[18] between 1990 and 2012 in terms of subject matter. The Federal Constitutional Court dealt most frequently with individual rights of liberty, followed by effective legal protection, the freedom of expression and the press, and informational self-determination (including the privacy of correspondence, posts, and telecommunications) ["G-10 Basic Rights"]. The court heard far fewer cases concerned with the freedom of assembly and demonstration, freedom of religion, and the inviolability of the home.

These categories cover many of the major subjects of dispute about freedom in the reunited federal republic: in the field of individual rights of liberty, for instance,

[18]The data covers only orders and judgments published in the official law reports of the Federal Constitutional Court. Judgments that cover a number of subjects were counted more than once.

disputes about life imprisonment, abortion, private *Cannabis* consumption, preventive detention, the European arrest warrant, and about the Aviation Security Act—on which perhaps the most important judgment in the context of anti-terrorist measures after 9/11 was pronounced; in the field of effective legal protection disputes about the right to be heard in the event of deprivation of liberty, the seizure of personal property and electronic resources by investigating authorities, the general judicial review of administrative action, and the development of the code of criminal procedure; in the field of the freedom of expression, the press, and art such as famous issues as defamation of symbols of the state (flag, national anthem), the disparagement of politicians, the indexing of literature (Josefine Mutzenbacher, Esra), defamation of the Bundeswehr ("born murderers," "soldiers are murderers"), the glorification of National Socialism, and the legality of police searches of media premises (Cicero); and in the field of informational self-determination/G 10, we find proceedings on the surveillance powers of the Federal Intelligence Service (BND), on interception circuits, on the surveillance of journalists' mobile telephones, the use of GPS tracking in criminal prosecution, on the surveillance powers of the Customs Criminal Investigation Office, on police telecommunications surveillance, on genetic fingerprinting, on preventive dragnet surveillance, on automatic access to primary account data, on online searches, on data retention, on the seizure of e-mails at Internet providers, and on the automatic evaluation of IP addresses.

Numerically less significant topics were also addressed in proceedings and judgments of great importance for society. Under the category freedom of assembly and demonstration, for example, many of the major proceedings on demonstrations are included ("runway west," definition of coercion, sit-ins), on the protection of assembly for (right-wing) extremists, or on the conditions for the official prohibition of assembly. Important proceedings addressing the freedom of religion included cases on the prohibition of crucifixes in Bavarian classrooms, of headscarves in the public service, of ritual slaughter or on the legal recognition of religious communities. In relation to Article 13 of the Basic Law (inviolability of the home), decisions were concerned mostly with search orders of the criminal prosecution authorities and, above all, with acoustic surveillance of the home.

Without exaggeration, it can be said that these 108 proceedings addressed key questions relating to freedom, ruling on the factual application and content of civil liberties in the Federal Republic. That the highest German court dealt with these issues does not, however, tell us what impact its rulings have actually had—whether in effect they have served to expand liberties or to restrict them. This requires classification of decisions in terms of the two categories.[19] Figure 14.5 shows that

[19] In terms of their effect, the 108 decisions under study were categorized as enlarging freedom (liberal) or restricting freedom (conservative). A decision was considered to enlarge freedom if it removed restrictions imposed on liberty by legislation, by other courts, or the executive, or which confirmed enlarged freedoms introduced by these institutions. A decision was classified as restricting freedom if it removed an enlargement of freedom introduced by legislation, other courts, or the executive or confirmed such restrictions. This classification is based on the

the decisions of the Federal Constitutional Court have tended to be liberal and have thus favored freedom. The impact of some 77% of the court's decisions can be classified as liberal or rather liberal and 23% as conservative or rather conservative.[20]

Decisions that tended to restrict freedom were pronounced in three main fields:[21] first, the right of assembly and demonstration, where the Federal Constitutional Court has tended to adopt a conservative stance, especially when criminal conduct was involved (e.g., sit-ins or coercion in the course of demonstrations); second, parts of criminal law itself (e.g., the extradition of offenders to other countries, incest between siblings, and the glorification of National Socialism, or preventive detention); and third, police measures to avert danger (surveillance of journalists' mobile telephones, GPS tracking in criminal prosecution, undercover police investigations, seizure of e-mails). Particularly with regard to averting dangers, the court sought, despite (or perhaps even precisely because of) its generally liberal stance in this field,[22] to give investigating authorities a certain amount of leeway in concrete cases and to interpret proportionality generously.

Almost all restrictive decisions confirmed corresponding laws, decisions, or acts of others. In other words, restrictive effects arise mainly through the nonintervention of the court. In only a single case, the second abortion ruling of 1993, did the court intervene against planned freedom-enlarging legislation. Vice versa, the freedom-enlarging decisions of the Federal Constitutional Court show that the court has generally moved against restrictive laws, decisions, or acts and that it has accordingly intervened actively. We have already mentioned the liberal rulings in the field of averting imminent danger and criminal prosecution (see note 22); in other fields, too, innumerable proceedings can be cited that strengthened the freedom of expression and the right to demonstrate, that interpreted the freedom of religion in liberal terms, made legal protection more effective, and consolidated individual liberties. Overall it can therefore be said that—with few, albeit sometimes major exceptions—the court has lastingly strengthened civil liberties.

What does this mean for the question whether democracy is in crisis? Three things are to be noted: first, in the field of civil liberties, the Federal Constitutional Court has actually made liberal, freedom-enhancing decisions and effectively monitored and sanctioned attempted restrictions of liberty by legislature, courts,

---

established classification of the Supreme Court Database (http://scdb.wustl.edu/, accessed 05.09.2017).

[20]Three decisions could not be clearly categorized and were therefore not included in the analysis.

[21]Decisions enlarging freedom are to be found in all categories.

[22]Among other things, the Federal Constitutional Court found fault with the Act on the Suppression of Crime, the unreserved storage of genetic fingerprints, police searches in the event of imminent danger, the seizure of lawyers' computer files, acoustic surveillance of the home, the European arrest warrant, police telecommunications surveillance, the Aviation Security Act, preventive dragnet surveillance, automatic primary account data access, online searches, automatic recording of vehicle registration numbers, data retention, and the automatic evaluation of IP addresses.

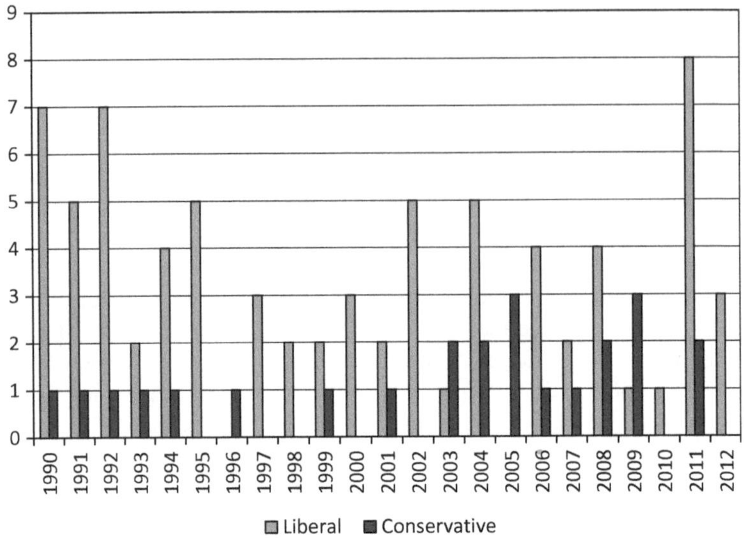

Fig. 14.5 Liberal and conservative tendencies in Federal Constitutional Court decisions on civil liberties (1990–2012). Source: Author's own figure

and executive. Second, it has thus effectively prevented other democratic institutions from inflicting harm on democracy and ensured the functioning of the freedom dimension of German democracy. It effectively controlled the tightening of security laws after 9/11 and by its intervention has secured and enhanced freedom. Third and finally, it can be said that the Federal Constitutional Court has successfully fulfilled its function in democracy to protect the civil liberties of citizens. It has shown itself to be a true custodian of liberal democracy under the rule of law and has averted harm from aspects of the constitutional state before German democracy was threatened by any serious crisis.

14.4 Conclusion

A crisis of democracy induced by constitutional courts can in principle take two forms. The first, as we have argued, can be that a constitutional court systematically oversteps the powers assigned to it, establishes itself as the ultimate decision-making authority in democracy, and thus seriously infringes the democratic separation of powers. A crisis of this sort thus manifests itself in excessive action by the constitutional court, so that the court can be said to set off the crisis itself. This is to be distinguished from a second form of crisis. Characteristic of this type is that constitutional courts take no action in the face of serious damage to democracy caused by other actors, thus failing adequately to fulfill their democratic function of protecting core areas of democracy against harm. In this second form of crisis, the constitutional court falls short of its institutional possibilities and of the normative expectations made of it. Theoretically, both forms of crisis can seriously disrupt the functioning of modern democracy and trigger or aggravate a trend toward crisis.

Empirically, however, or at least in the cases under study, constitutional courts are far from inducing crises of either sort. Although the four constitutional courts identified in the literature as particularly strong, those of the United States, Canada, Austria, and Germany, have an institutionally strong and independent position in their respective political systems and can—to go by the absolute figures on cases dealt with—indeed be described as active players in the political game, they show no general trend toward judicialization over time or toward higher rates of annulment of legislation. However, the high annulment rates of the Austrian Constitutional Court and the increasing annulment balance of the German Federal Constitutional Court are striking. Nevertheless, the two courts are far from becoming the real decision-making centers of their democracies and usurping the place of the legislature. Thus, no systematic disruption of the democratic system of horizontal accountability is in evidence.

Furthermore, the example of the Federal Constitutional Court shows that constitutional courts can also effectively prevent the second crisis scenario from materializing, namely, harm caused to the key partial regimes of democracy by other democratically legitimated actors. With respect to civil liberties, the German Federal Constitutional Court has successfully intervened when freedom has been threatened with restriction by legislative, judicial, or executive action. The qualitative loss of freedom in the fields of individual rights of liberty, effective legal protection, freedom of expression and the press, and informational self-determination was thus effectively controlled and sanctioned, thus preventing harm to a key partial regime of German democracy.

This reviewing activity of the Federal Constitutional Court directs attention once again to the assessment of constitutional court intervention in general. It makes it impressively clear that it is not primarily the number of interventions by a constitutional court that decides the quality of the interplay between the constitutional court and democracy but above all its quality. Countries with strong constitutional courts willing to intervene are in no danger of having to accept losses in the quality of their democracy as long as the courts are aware of the function entrusted to them under democracy. Such constitutional courts cause no crisis of democracy; on the contrary, they are the most important allies of democratically demanding governance.

References

Alexander, L. (Ed.). (1998). *Constitutionalism. Philosophical Foundations*. Cambridge: Cambridge University Press.

Alexy, R. (2010). *A theory of constitutional rights*. Oxford: Oxford University Press.

Alivizatos, N. C. (1995). Judges as Veto Players. In H. Döring (Ed.), *Parliaments and majority rule in Western Europe* (pp. 566–589). Frankfurt am Main & New York: Campus & St. Martin's Press.
Barfuß, W. (1989). Neue Entwicklungen in der Rechtsprechung des Verfassungsgerichtshofs. *Österreichische Juristen-Zeitung, 44*(22), 673–681.
Becker, M. (2001). Grundrechte versus Volkssouveränität. Zur Achillesverse des demokratischen Prozeduralismus. In M. Becker, H.-J. Lauth, & G. Pickel (Eds.), *Rechtsstaat und Demokratie* (pp. 45–68). Opladen: Westdeutscher Verlag.
Bellamy, R. (Ed.). (1996). *Constitutionalism, democracy and sovereignty: American and European Perspectives*. Aldershot: Avebury.
Brohm, W. (2001). Die Funktion des BVerfG—Oligarchie in der Demokratie? *Neue Juristische Wochenschrift, 54*(1), 1–10.
Brünneck, A.v. (1992). *Verfassungsgerichtsbarkeit in den westlichen Demokratien*. Baden-Baden: Nomos.
Busch, A. (2011). Freiheits- und Bürgerrechte nach 9/11. In T. Jäger (Ed.), *Die Welt nach 9/11. Auswirkungen des Terrorismus auf Staatenwelt und Gesellschaft. ZFAS-Sonderheft 2/2011* (pp. 861–881). VS Verlag für Sozialwissenschaften: Wiesbaden.
Cooter, R. D., & Ginsburg, T. (1996). Comparative judicial discretion: An empirical test of economic models. *International Review of Law and Economics, 16*(3), 295–313.
Dahl, R. A. (1971). *Polyarchy. Participation and opposition*. New Haven, CT: Yale University Press.
Dahl, R. A. (1989). *Democracy and its critics*. New Haven, CT: Yale University Press.
Dahl, R. A. (2000). *On democracy*. New Haven, CT: Yale University Press.
Easton, D. (1965). *A systems analysis of political life*. New York, NY: John Wiley and Sons.
Elster, J., & Slagstad, R. (Eds.). (1993). *Constitutionalism and democracy*. Cambridge: Cambridge University Press.
Ely, J. H. (1980). *Democracy and distrust*. Cambridge, MA: Harvard University Press.
Epstein, L., & Knight, J. (2004). Courts and judges. In A. Sarat (Ed.), *The Blackwell Companion to Law and Society* (pp. 170–194). Oxford: Blackwell Publishing.
Epstein, L., Knight, J., & Shvetsova, O. (2001). The Role of Constitutional Courts in the establishment and maintenance of democratic systems of government. *Law & Society Review, 35*(1), 117–163.
Gibson, J. L., Caldeira, G. A., & Baird, V. A. (1998). On the legitimacy of National High Courts. *American Political Science Review, 92*(2), 343–358.
Ginsburg, T. (2003). *Judicial review in new democracies. Constitutional Courts in Asian cases*. Cambridge: Cambridge University Press.
Grimm, D. (1976). Verfassungsgerichtsbarkeit im demokratischen System. *Juristenzeitung, 31* (22), 697–703.
Grimm, D. (1977). Verfassungsgerichtsbarkeit—Funktion und Funktionsgrenzen im demokratischen Staat. In W. Hoffmann-Riem (Ed.), *Sozialwissenschaften im Studium des Rechts. Band 2* (pp. 83–108). München: Verlag C.H. Beck.
Guarnieri, C., & Pederzoli, P. (2002). *The power of Judges. A comparative study of Courts and democracy*. Oxford: Oxford University Press.
Henkin, L. (1994). A new birth of constitutionalism: Genetic influences and genetic defects. In M. Rosenfeld (Ed.), *Constitutionalism, identity, difference, and legitimacy* (pp. 39–53). Durham, NC: Duke University Press.
Hilbink, L. (2008). Assessing the new constitutionalism. *Comparative Politics, 40*(2), 227–245.
Hirschl, R. (2007). *Towards juristocracy. The origins and consequences of the new constitutionalism*. Cambridge, MA: Harvard University Press.
Höffe, O. (1999). Wieviel Politik ist dem Verfassungsgericht erlaubt? *Der Staat, 38*(2), 171–193.
Holmes, S. (1993). Precommitment and the paradox of democracy. In J. Elster & R. Slagstad (Eds.), *Constitutionalism and democracy* (pp. 195–240). Cambridge: Cambridge University Press.

Hönnige, C. (2007). *Verfassungsgericht, Regierung und Opposition. Eine vergleichende Analyse eines Spannungsdreiecks*. Wiesbaden: VS Verlag für Sozialwissenschaften.

Horowitz, D. L. (2006). Constitutional Courts: A primer for decision makers. *Journal of Democracy, 17*(4), 125–137.

Kavanagh, A. (2009). *Constitutional review under the UK Human Rights Act*. Cambridge: Cambridge University Press.

Kelly, J. B. (1999). The charter of rights and freedoms and the rebalancing of liberal constitutionalism in Canada, 1982–1997. *Osgoode Hall Law Journal, 37*(3), 625–695.

Kelsen, H. (1942). Judicial review of legislation: A comparative study of the Austrian and the American Constitution. *Journal of Politics, 4*(2), 183–200.

Kneip, S. (2006). Demokratieimmanente Grenzen der Verfassungsgerichtsbarkeit. In M. Becker & R. Zimmerling (Eds.), *Politik und Recht. PVS-Sonderheft 36/2006* (pp. 259–281). VS Verlag für Sozialwissenschaften: Wiesbaden.

Kneip, S. (2008). Verfassungsgerichtsbarkeit im Vergleich. In O. W. Gabriel & S. Kropp (Eds.), *Die EU-Staaten im Vergleich* (pp. 631–655). Wiesbaden: VS Verlag für Sozialwissenschaften.

Kneip, S. (2009). *Verfassungsgerichte als demokratische Akteure. Der Beitrag des Bundesverfassungsgerichts zur Qualität der bundesdeutschen Demokratie*. Baden-Baden: Nomos.

Kneip, S. (2011). Gegenspieler, Vetospieler oder was? Demokratiefunktionales Agieren des Bundesverfassungsgerichts 1051–2005. *Politische Vierteljahresschrift, 52*(2), 220–247.

Kneip, S. (2013). Rolle und Einfluss des Bundesverfassungsgerichts in international vergleichender Perspektive. *Zeitschrift für Politik, 60*(1), 72–89.

Koopmans, T. (2003). *Courts and political Institutions. A comparative view*. Cambridge: Cambridge University Press.

Korinek, K. (2000). *Grundrechte und Verfassungsgerichtsbarkeit*. Wien: Springer.

Kranenpohl, U. (2004). Funktionen des Bundesverfassungsgerichts. Eine politikwissenschaftliche Analyse. *Aus Politik und Zeitgeschichte, B50-51*, 39–46.

Landfried, C. (1984). *Bundesverfassungsgericht und Gesetzgeber. Wirkungen der Verfassungsrechtsprechung auf parlamentarische Willensbildung und soziale Realität*. Baden-Baden: Nomos.

Landfried, C. (1985). The impact of the German Federal Constitutional Court on politics and policy output. *Government and Opposition, 20*(4), 522–541.

Landfried, C. (1994). The judicialization of politics in Germany. *International Political Science Review, 15*(2), 113–124.

Lijphart, A. (1999). *Patterns of democracy. Government forms and performance in thirty-six countries*. New Haven, CT: Yale University Press.

Magaloni, B., & Sánchez, A. (2001). Empowering Courts as Constitutional Veto Players: Presidential Delegation and the New Mexican Supreme Court. Paper presented at the Annual Meeting of the American Political Science Association. San Francisco, September 2001.

Maus, I. (1992). *Zur Aufklärung der Demokratietheorie. Rechts- und demokratietheoretische Überlegungen im Anschluß an Kant*. Frankfurt am Main: Suhrkamp.

Maus, I. (2004). Vom Rechtsstaat zum Verfassungsstaat. Zur Kritik juridischer Demokratieverhinderung. *Blätter für deutsche und internationale Politik, 49*, 835–850.

Maus, I. (2005). Zur Ideengeschichte der Gewaltenteilung und der Funktionsweise der Justiz. In T. Hitzel-Cassagnes & T. Schmidt (Eds.), *Demokratie in Europa und europäische Demokratien. Festschrift für Heidrun Abromeit* (pp. 224–262). VS Verlag für Sozialwissenschaften: Wiesbaden.

Merkel, W., Puhle, H.-J., Croissant, A., Eicher, C., & Thiery, P. (2003). *Defekte Demokratie. Band 1: Theorie*. Opladen: Leske + Budrich.

Moreira Cardoso da Costa, J. M. (1988). Die Verfassungsrechtsprechung im Rahmen der staatlichen Funktionen. Arten, Inhalt und Wirkungen der Entscheidungen über die Verfassungsmäßigkeit von Rechtsnormen. Generalbericht. *Europäische Grundrechte-Zeitschrift, 15*, 236–248.

Romeu, F. R. (2006). The establishment of Constitutional Courts: A study of 128 democratic constitutions. *Review of Law and Economics, 2*(1), 104–135.
Sandler, R., & Schoenbrod, D. (2003). *Democracy by Decree: What happens when courts run government*. New Haven, CT: Yale University Press.
Scheppele, K. L. (2005). Democracy by judiciary. Or, why courts can be more democratic than parliaments. In A. Czarnota, M. Krygier, & W. Sadurski (Eds.), *Rethinking the rule of law after communism* (pp. 25–60). Budapest: Central European University Press.
Schneider, H.-P. (1999). Acht an der Macht! Das Bundesverfassungsgericht als "Reparaturbetrieb" des Parlamentarismus? *Neue Juristische Wochenschrift, 52*(18), 1303–1305.
Scholz, R. (1999). Das Bundesverfassungsgericht: Hüter der Verfassung oder Ersatzgesetzgeber? *Aus Politik und Zeitgeschichte, B16*, 3–8.
Shapiro, M., & Stone Sweet, A. (2002). *On law, politics, and judicialization*. Oxford: Oxford University Press.
Stone Sweet, A. (1999). Judicialization and the construction of governance. *Comparative Political Studies, 32*(2), 147–184.
Stone Sweet, A. (2000). *Governing with judges. Constitutional politics in Europe*. Oxford: Oxford University Press.
Tate, C. N., & Vallinder, T. (Eds.). (1995). *The global expansion of judicial power*. New York, NY: New York University Press.
Tsebelis, G. (2000). Veto players and institutional analysis. *Governance: An International Journal of Policy and Administration, 13*(4), 441–474.
Tsebelis, G. (2002). *Veto players. How political institutions work*. Princeton, NJ: Princeton University Press.
Tushnet, M. (1999). *Taking the constitution away from the courts*. Princeton, NJ: Princeton University Press.
Tushnet, M. (2008). *Weak courts, strong rights. Judicial review and social welfare rights in comparative constitutional law*. Princeton, NJ: Princeton University Press.
Vallinder, T. (1994). The judicialization of politics—A World-wide Phenomenon: Introduction. *International Political Science Review, 15*(2), 91–99.
Vallinder, T. (1995). When the courts go marching in. In C. N. Tate & T. Vallinder (Eds.), *The global expansion of judicial power* (pp. 13–26). New York, NY: New York University Press.
Volcansek, M. L. (2001). Constitutional courts as veto players: Divorce and decrees in Italy. *European Journal of Political Research, 39*, 347–372.
Wagschal, U. (2006). Verfassungsgerichte als Vetospieler in der Steuerpolitik. In M. Becker & R. Zimmerling (Eds.), *Politik und Recht. PVS-Sonderheft 36/2006* (pp. 559–584). VS Verlag für Sozialwissenschaften: Wiesbaden.
Waldron, J. (1999). *Law and disagreement*. Oxford: Clarendon Press.
Waldron, J. (2006). The core of the case against judicial review. *Yale Law Journal, 115*(6), 1346–1406.
Waltman, J. L., & Holland, K. M. (Eds.). (1988). *The political role of law courts in modern democracies*. New York, NY: St. Martin's Press.

Chapter 15
Conclusion: Is the Crisis of Democracy an Invention?

Wolfgang Merkel

Crisis cannot be a permanent state of affairs. It is not in semantic the logic of the concept. This can also be said for the so-called latent crisis. Moreover, a reference model is required if the notion is to be of use for analytical purposes. It can set a normative ideal or define a normal state as standard for comparison. A "golden" or even simply "normal" age of democracy has at times been identified when the practice of democracy met the demands made of it. For Colin Crouch (2004, 7), the "democratic moment" for the United States and Scandinavia was shortly after the Second World War, for Europe the 1950s and 1960s. In the German debate, the late 1960s and early 1970s are not infrequently cited.[1] A particular aspect of democracy is usually implied or explicitly referred to. Colin Crouch stresses the corporatively organized countervailing power of labor as opposed to structurally privileged capital. Such a procedure is theoretically one-sided and empirically anecdotal, even if some specific aspects such as the unresolved challenges of globalization are appropriate. But the logical conclusion that a crisis of the entire, now post-democratic system is to be deduced from a partial crisis of democracy is neither theoretically acceptable nor empirically plausible.[2] More exacting and productive for the systematic analysis of crisis are concepts that define the properties of democracy and relate them to one another normatively and functionally. Only by ascertaining the key identifying

[1] It is not uninteresting that political theory enjoyed a boom in the analysis of crises and in the critical diagnosis of prevailing conditions during the few years following the actual democratic phase in the Federal Republic (Willy Brandt: "Dare more democracy;" see, e.g., Jänicke 1972; Offe 1972; Habermas 1975).

[2] In the introduction to this volume, I pointed out that neither Afro-American "semi-citizens" in six Southern States of the defective US democracy nor women or ethnic and sexual minorities can share the idealizing view of the then democratic world.

W. Merkel (✉)
Department of Democracy and Democratization, WZB Berlin Social Science Center, Berlin, Germany

Humboldt-Universität zu Berlin, Berlin, Germany
e-mail: wolfgang.merkel@wzb.eu

W. Merkel, S. Kneip (eds.), *Democracy and Crisis*,
https://doi.org/10.1007/978-3-319-72559-8_15

elements of the democratic system and investigating their interdependence can light be cast on democracy as such, on the democratic whole, on the system. The trajectory of developments exacerbating or mitigating crises from one partial regime of democracy to the next then becomes apparent and empirically accessible to informed interpretation. At the same time, however, criteria[3] have to be set for deviation from the reference state of democracy. Empirically determining and theoretically explaining the threshold that separates democracy in its normal state from democracy in crisis is one of the issues crisis theory has yet to resolve, an issue perhaps never to be completely elucidated in theoretical, abstract terms. At least in retrospect, it is easier in the case of acute crises—at any rate when democracies actually collapse as they did in the 1920s and 1930s in Europe or in the 1960s in Latin America. For if a regime collapses, a crisis is likely to have preceded the event. In all other crisis scenarios, such diagnosis is much more difficult. This is particularly true of the "latent" crisis.[4]

Our analyses focus on the world of developed OECD democracies. With the exception of Greece[5] (1967–1973), no such democracy has ever collapsed since 1950. We can at least see no indication of an immediate threat of collapse in these countries that was warded off. This can also be said for the "test case" Greece after 2008, a country that, since the outbreak of the financial and euro crisis, has suffered welfare losses the like of which would have led to acute regime crises and even to the collapse of democracy during the interwar years. In Greece, by contrast, even this profound socioeconomic crisis did not call the democratic system into question. This points to the fact that the national and international capacity of established democratic systems to process crises politically and administratively, as well as their legitimacy reserves are now greater than Habermas and Offe had still theoretically posited in the early 1970s. In our analyses we have therefore insisted on the hypothetical assumption of a "latent" crisis as predicated in the post-democracy literature. The concept of "embedded democracy" has served as reference model (Merkel 2004). With a mid-range frame of reference, we have sought to avoid the normative under- and overestimation typical of minimalist and maximalist concepts of democracy.

Against this theoretical and conceptual backdrop, our book takes an empirical approach. The studies are original and not simply a compilation of crisis analyses by others. Being committed to the concept of embedded democracy, we have divided our tasks. The studies mostly concentrate on separate partial regimes of this embedded democracy without losing sight of the most important aspects of

---

[3]This does not mean only quantitative measurement. But if a state x is to be distinguished from a state y of democracy over time, some idea is necessary about how this difference can be appropriately investigated and expressed.

[4]A "latent" crisis is to be distinguished from a "permanent" crisis (which is a logical contradiction). Latent crises are simmering crises which can drag on for long periods and do not arouse expectations of collapse (see the introduction).

[5]In this context, socioeconomic and sociocultural developments in the Greece of the 1960s qualify the country at best as a borderline case of a developed democratic society.

interdependence between abutting regimes. This concluding chapter seeks to overcome analytical deconstruction, bringing the parts together in a general review.

One of the greatest challenges facing current democracies is the erosion of the principle of political equality. The socioeconomic inequality that has been growing for over three decades in the societies of the OECD world has continuously translated into political inequality. In recent decades, voter turnout has declined moderately in Western Europe and dramatically in Eastern Europe. It is mainly lower-class voters who stay away from the ballot box. Bernhard Weßels shows, however, that socioeconomic inequality finds expression not solely in the disproportionately low turnout among voters from the lower strata of society. The survey data on 47 democracies on which he draws show far less knowledge among the lower income and education strata about their own political preferences and how these preferences are reflected in the programs and policies of political parties. This is in marked contrast to the situation among better educated people, who not only vote more frequently but also know very well which party best represents their personal political preferences. Every uncast vote and "every less well informed electoral choice reduces the probability that the outcome of elections will reflect preferences in such a way that interests can be effectively represented" (Weßels, Chap. 3).

From a comparative perspective, the situation can be summed up as follows: the greater socioeconomic differences are and the concomitant inequality in cognitive resources among citizens, the greater political inequality will be. The greater political inequality is, the more seriously the fundamental democratic principle of political equality will have been contravened. At least from this point of view, the egalitarian societies of Scandinavia provide better conditions for equal democratic elections than the unequal societies of Anglo-Saxon capitalism. The equal voting rights granted by formal equality before the law is therefore a necessary but not a sufficient condition for democratic elections to attain their full democratic significance. Social liberalism from John Stuart Mill to Ralf Dahrendorf had always been aware of this, but the reduced forms of neoliberalism in the late twentieth century had suppressed it or rejected it as crypto-socialist. We argue that the democratization of democracy requires socioeconomic inequality and inequalities in educational resources to be reduced in a manner compatible with the principles of freedom and of socially accepted and meritocratically legitimated inequality. All things being equal, the less socioeconomic inequality there is, the better the quality of democracy will be.

There are preconditions for such a suggestive equation. One is the pluralistic assumption that free competition in democratic party systems also produces programmatic alternatives, representing different socioeconomic and sociocultural interests. If this assumption is unfounded, elections lose much of their democratic meaning. Even the unequal distribution of educational resources would become largely irrelevant at the ballot box: inequality between social strata in the distribution of knowledge, which also determines inequality in accurately choosing the right representatives, would then be unimportant if as a result party programs offered no alternatives. That this is increasingly the case is a widespread topos in the critical debate on democracy and parties. Drawing on the manifesto data, Andrea Volkens and Nicolas Merz have therefore examined and interpreted no fewer than 2103 party programs from 21 OECD countries for the period 1951–2011. This far-reaching empirical study focuses on four particularly important aspects of representative democracy: the differentiation of programmatic positions, public awareness of these positions, the clarity of program statements, and the "heterogeneity of priorities," in other words, the degree of difference between alternative programs. Three political dimensions were examined: socioeconomic, sociocultural, and center-periphery. The findings give only a qualified all-clear for representative democracy. In the period under study, the clarity of party positions and thus public awareness of these positions increased. In sociocultural matters and the conflict between center and periphery, clarity was constant, differentiation exists, and the degree of difference between party programs did not decrease. That is the good news for party democracy. But an important political dimension supplies the bad news. In economic policy and extended socioeconomic matters, the pluralistic spectrum offered by the range of party programs narrowed. But if citizens can no longer choose between economic and sociopolitical alternatives, they may well vote, but in one of the most important policy areas, they no longer have a choice.

In extremis, this is the case with the debtor countries in Southern Europe, where Rubén Ruiz-Rufino and Sonia Alonso speak of "democracy without choice" during the financial and Eurozone crisis (see Chap. 9). Here, not only the citizens but also their respective governments had no free choice to choose between policy alternatives due to the provisions—some would even say: the curtailments—of the so-called Troika. If we switch from the democratic demand side to the programmatic supply side, harmonization of economic and social policy programs suggests that this is a reaction on the part of big (governing) parties to the loss of political options in a globalized economy in general and to neoliberal competition policy within the European Union in particular (see also Streeck 2014).

A decline in voter turnout, social difficulties within the electorate, the reduced ability of educationally disadvantaged voters to choose in keeping with their preferences, and the narrower spectrum of social and economic alternatives offered by parties do indeed point to deterioration in conventional participation and representation. Formal equality in political rights translates worse into actual equality in participation, measured against the initial concept of embedded democracy and over recent decades. These shifts have tended to be gradual rather than dramatic. They do not yet justify the post-democratic thesis that the key legitimation pattern of representative democracy has been undermined. But they do raise the question of whether the losses of legitimation described can be compensated for by non-electoral possibilities to participate (della Porta 2013; Kneip and Merkel 2017). However, the optimism of many researchers of social movements and theoreticians of deliberative democracy calls for skepticism. Elections do not translate the political principle of equality into democracy perfectly and sometimes not sufficiently, as Weßels and Lehman et al. have shown in their chapters. Nevertheless, democratic elections are the most egalitarian form of participation because they require the least in the way of individual resources. To this extent we agree with Adam Przeworski when he argues that, "[. . .] in the end elections are the most egalitarian political mechanism we have and can have. Too often the calls for increased participation privilege those who have more resources to participate" (Przeworski 2010, 169). Furthermore, it is not the established democracies of the old West, let alone those of Eastern Europe, that have been noted in recent decades for innovative forms of participation. For some years now, such reform has concentrated in the new democracies of Latin America. "There are simply no analogs of similar scale and depth in North America, Europe, Asia or Africa," as Archon Fung (2011, 868) writes.

It is interesting to note that the participatory reforms in some Latin American countries have managed in particular to involve the lower strata of society in political participation and decision-making (de Sousa Santos 1998; Avritzer 1999; Pogrebinschi and Samuels 2014). In Europe, let alone North America, this is certainly not to be expected directly; it is more likely that the middle classes, who have a great deal of voice, will benefit from the reforms to overrun new bastions of participation. Although this is not to be seen a priori as a bad thing, it would increase the overrepresentation of the upper middle classes and contribute little to integrating the politically passive lower classes in the res publica. Moreover, in Europe and Japan, unlike in South or North America, strong parties can be expected to resist such developments. They see extended forms of participation not primarily as a welcome broadening of democratic involvement but as competition. This is apparent, for example, in direct-democratic referendums, which parties influence in far greater measure than the proponents of direct democracy are willing to admit (Merkel and Ritzi 2017). However, if one takes a less hostile view of parties, the closer meshing of representative organizations with direct-democratic procedures can be judged positive because their different legitimation patterns do not simply have to replace one another but can prove complementary.

Although the embedded democracy model indicates a preference for representative democracy procedures, the concept is both functionally and normatively open to direct-democratic complementation. Direct democracy, if not deployed primarily as a substitute for representative procedures, can help revitalize democracy and improve its quality. Nevertheless, we assume that it is not the displacement of parties but their democratic quality and efficiency that is decisive in determining the legitimation capacity of democracy. This is true for both input and output. For, unlike referendums, for instance, parliamentary democracy does not pursue an exclusive zero-sum logic, which excludes the losers in a ballot from any further say in deciding policy content. What is more, large parties ensure a certain continuity and rationality in politics, which referendums with their contingent majorities can never be expected to provide.[6]

The quality of representative democracy thus continues to depend strongly on the behavior and development of big parties. But one of the common assumptions of party research is that big (catch-all) parties have had their day. Heiko Giebler, Onawa Lacewell, Sven Regel, and Annika Werner have examined this assumption more systematically than has hitherto been attempted. Their analysis shows in

[6]This is different only where, as in Switzerland, referendums are embedded in a strongly consensual representative democracy and where parties are the most important actors in referendums.

exemplary manner that scrupulous comparative analysis often uncovers the ambivalence of a development and does not simply confirm unilinear trends pointing to post-democratic decline or giving a "nothing new" all clear. Although their data, too, show lower voting scores for large parties, they interpret this rather as a democratizing development in the pluralistic party spectrum. Moreover, the authors show that fears that the differentiation of party systems is accompanied by greater instability in (coalition) governments cannot be empirically confirmed at the aggregate level of 15 countries over the period 1960–2010.

Second, they contradict Kirchheimer's widespread but rarely systematically tested hypothesis that big parties have transformed themselves into catch-all parties. The authors distinguish three types of big party: the mass party, the programmatic party, and the catch-all party. The mass-integration party, which combines a large membership with a high proportion of voters, is a phenomenon of the twentieth century, of the industrial modern age. It is now an anachronistic relict even not to be found any longer in once statist-corporatist countries. However, in most countries mass-integration parties have not developed into catch-all parties. The only current exception is Denmark. Most big parties present themselves to the voter today in the form of programmatic parties. Although programmatic parties are not entrenched in society through their membership in the same way as mass parties, they are not so diffuse and without contour as catch-all parties in their programmatic substance. However, they are no longer as good at mobilizing voters as mass parties had been. Although they are better than catch-all parties in the accuracy with which they represent the interests of their voters, they are less good at this than mass-integration parties. As far as mobilization, representation, and government stability are concerned, programmatic parties are thus the democratic "average pupils" among the three types of big party. The message of the authors is clear, "Overall, we are nevertheless dealing primarily with a change in party systems and party types and not with a crisis of democracy triggered by the decline of political parties" (Giebler et al., Chap. 7).

The existence of programmatic parties is a necessary but far from sufficient condition for responsive behavior on the part of political parties. Only if parties respond in their programs to the ideas, wishes, and demands of voters can we speak of a "responsive party model" (Schattschneider 1942; Thomassen and Schmitt 1997). How responsive party programs are cannot be better illustrated than by their reaction to the issue of socioeconomic inequality, which has steadily increased over the past three decades. In order to test responsiveness to this important democratic and social problem, Alexander Petring has compared surveys from the *International Social Survey Programme* (ISSP) of citizens in 22 developed democracies with the development of party programs in the same countries. For the period from 1987 to 2009, the analysis reveals ideas among citizens about inequality and redistribution that vary widely within and between countries. There are also clear differences between the programs of various parties. However, across all countries and the entire period under study, no stable connection is apparent between changes in attitude and changes in program. In this regard, there are accordingly limits to responsiveness. The fact that examples of isolated responsive program behavior are to be observed in all countries does nothing to change this. But these examples do not suffice to establish a stable trend. It appears that the given competitive situation in national party systems strongly distorts any such trend. "The propensity for responsiveness seems to be greater if a party's own voters appear to be moving in the direction of the opposing political camp" (Petring, Chap. 8).

Party responsiveness that can be shown in the development of party programs is therefore very limited. But responsive party behavior can be detected not only in shifts in party programs. A more comprehensive understanding of democratic responsiveness also requires an analysis of policy: account needs to be taken of the political decisions (output) and results (outcomes) of the parties in government. This is still lacking. However, the growing inequality in income and wealth over the past three decades points to the lack of any effective policy for redistribution to the advantage of the lower classes. This is a fatal rationality trap for representative democracy. Parties do not have to be responsive toward lower-class citizens who stay away from the ballot box because they are relatively unlikely to gain the support of these difficult to mobilize voters without having to accept major losses in the middle-class electorate. The absence of a clear redistribution policy in party programs is in so far attributable to the rational behavior of parties' intent on maximizing voter support. Center-left parties, too, clearly fear losing more voters in the center than are to be gained on the left. But for democratic politics that seeks to take account of the varying interests of the entire demos in pursuit of the common good, responsive behavior always has to be complemented and at times moderated by responsible action. Over the past three decades, parties have shown little responsibility in the inequality issue toward social cohesion in their societies.

If the two democratic imperatives of responsive and responsible action are to be implemented, representative democracy requires the right representatives. It would not be enough if in its parliamentary totality it were to responsively represent only the people who have actually gone to the polls. This would automatically mean that the interests of the middle and upper classes, who take part in elections more frequently than the lower classes, would always be better represented in parliament. Two-thirds participation would result in two-thirds representation,[7] to the neglect of the bottom third that is already economically and socially disadvantaged. Pola Lehman, Sven Regel, and Sara Schlote have examined this thesis of stratum-specific representation. What is at issue is not a "descriptive" representation of the society and groups (proportional representation of classes, groups, and genders in parliament) but a representation of the interests, values, attitudes, and hence of the preferences of the citizens ("substantial" representation). The analysis shows that membership of a given stratum of society determines individual political preferences only to a certain degree. The heterogeneity of preferences within a social stratum is greater than this simplistic social determinism suggests. "Nevertheless," the authors write, "the analysis has shown that the lower classes are worse represented than the middle and upper classes in all the cases under study" (Lehman et al., Chap. 6). However, there are considerable differences between countries. They are to some extent greater than between classes. The more frequent abstentionism of the lower classes can only partly explain their worse representation.

[7]This would mean that, in the USA, for example, more than 50% of the demos regularly have no representation in Congress. The same is true of Poland.

There is good reason to assume that the interests of the middle and upper classes simply appear to be more compatible with the constraints that deregulated markets, investors, and cosmopolitanism place on democratic politics in an age of globalization.

The studies on participation and representation that are concerned primarily with the electoral regime and with political rights and participation opportunities have revealed no dramatic deterioration of democratic quality in any aspect over the past three decades that would justify the theses of post-democracy, façade democracy, or an acute crisis of democracy. However, erosion is noted everywhere, erosion that has become particularly conspicuous in recent years, such as the creeping political exclusion of lower social strata, but also differences that have always distinguished democracies "on the ground" from their ideal state. Participation and representation are important democratic dimensions that concern input and sections of internal decision-making procedures. But they tell us nothing about the extent to which input translates into output, i.e., material decisions. For even if participation and representation fully meet the democratic ideal of political equality—which, as we have shown, they do not—we would still have no answer to the questions "Who governs?" and "How do they govern?" The key question for democratic theory is whether elected governments in the age of globalization actual govern or whether the perceived economic, social, and legal restrictions have become so narrow that fundamental decisions are made or influenced over the heads of democratically legitimated actors. Another question is whether democratically elected governments also govern democratically and respect and protect fundamental rights such as the civil liberties of the governed even if they are up against challenges from other collective goods such as collective security in the face of terrorist threats.

One of the fundamental principles of representative democracy is that those who are affected by political decisions have to be able to consider themselves to be the authors of these decisions. Hans Kelsen (1925, 320) called this the democratic principle of "autonomy" as opposed to the "heteronomy" prevailing in autocratic systems, where those who make the rules and those governed by them are not identical. If this principle is extended to binding decisions under democratic government—with or without rules sanctioned by parliament—the question is whether the elected representatives in parliament and government are really the people who decide on monetary, financial, social, and competition policy. One of the assertions made about crisis in the post-democracy debate from Crouch to Streeck is that the key economic decisions in times of globalization and Europeanization are increasingly made not by governments but by banks, pension and hedge funds, major investors, and supranational financial institutions in deregulated financial markets. If this is the case, even perfect participation patterns would have little significance in policy-making and come to nothing in a democratic void.

Lea Heyne addresses exactly that question of governance in times of globalization at a high level of aggregation. She investigates how globalization affects the quality of democracy in the 30 best democracies. She draws on the KOF Globalization Index developed in Zurich (Dreher 2006) and the database of the Democracy Barometer (democracybarometer.org) developed in Zurich (NCCR) and Berlin (WZB). The results are interesting, revealing differing trends. Although globalization generally influences the measured quality of established democracies, it is far from having the negative effect we would expect on the basis of theoretical considerations by Crouch and Streeck and Kelsen's autonomy principle. The effects of globalization differ in the political, social, and economic dimensions. The author notes that political and social globalization has a positive impact on democracy but economic globalization a negative one. Heyne attributes the positive effects mainly to the increased attainment of rights for minorities and the growing equality for the two genders. International norms, institutions, watchdogs of global civil society (Keane 2011, "monitory democracy"), and the intensifying transnational communication on human rights appear to exert considerable pressure on societies lagging behind in civil rights, pressure that democratic systems can escape only at the risk of global "blaming and shaming." The negative impact of globalization, by contrast, is indicated by the deteriorating values for the "control principle" of democracy. In this field, the loss of power by political institutions to the deregulated markets has an impact, as does the loss in the legislature's capacity to control the executive.

Data on globalization and the quality of democracy are constructions and analytical approximations of reality. Data do not tell the whole story. They are tied to indicators, which for measuring purposes reduce complicated states of affairs on the basis of theory. To this extent, indicators are constructs and always no more than approximations of reality. This has to be kept in mind in a volume based above all on quantitative studies. Wolfgang Merkel accordingly addresses the fundamental question of compatibility of capitalism and democracy over and beyond statistical regression analysis. The two systems follow different logics: the unequal distribution of property rights confronts the ineluctable principle of equal political rights in democracy; in capitalism transactions pursue the individual objective of profit maximization, while democracy is ideally committed to the common good. In democracies, political power is legitimated by universal elections; in capitalism, power and influence are tied to disposition over property; in democracy decisions are the outcome of discourses, votes, and majorities; in capitalism small minorities really decide.[8] But these antonymous principles are not all there is to the relationship between capitalism and democracy. There is also common ground: both spheres are based on competition, and legal constraints preserve both systems from self-destructive forces. Furthermore, the private power of property owners and the governmental power of the people are mutually restrictive. The coexistence of capitalism and democracy succeeds best if a balance of power, mutual constraints, and interdependence can be established politically.

Since 1950 there have been two periods of two different kinds of coexistence. The phase of embedded capitalism submitted to national and welfare-state regulation and the disembedded capitalism period of neoliberal deregulation. The first marked the postwar period until well into the 1970s, and the second has dominated the capitalist world since the 1980s.[9] The author leaves no doubt that capitalism "embedded" in or

[8]We do not deny that the majority of consumers have some power of discretion as well. Nevertheless, their power can only be "collectivized" and "organized" under rare circumstances. The real market power rests with the minority of investors.

[9]Of course, there have also been varieties of capitalism at every stage. However, it is typical of the two phases mentioned that the given other types of capitalism tended to become a dominant paradigm, albeit with a certain range of variants in reality.

"coordinated" by the (welfare) state—as Hall and Soskice (2001) put it—with its containment of socioeconomic inequality, the limitation of private power, and the balance between market and state was and remains more compatible with the principles of democracy than the neoliberal variant of Anglo-Saxon capitalism. The latter permits greater socioeconomic and thus political inequality, leaving key fields of monetary, financial, commercial, and employment policy to private actors and deregulated markets. The structural changes that have taken place since the 1970s with the accelerating rise of a globalized and deregulated financial capitalism have fractured the social and political embeddedness of capitalism. The tension between capitalism and democracy has intensified. Despite the considerable differences between Scandinavian and continental European capitalism on the one hand and Anglo-Saxon capitalism on the other, the democratic decisions on deregulation[10] made in the 1980s and 1990s have put democracy under pressure in all three worlds of capitalism. Effective democratic "antidotes" to growing inequality and the capability of big banks and big investors to pressurize parliament, government, and the taxpayer have yet to be found.

Democracy had to abandon certain positions in the confrontation with the economic sphere. The opposite is the case in the field of gender and minorities policy. This can be said for almost all established democracies. But is not such reinforcement of individual and group rights to be observed in all fields of civil rights? Or, in the political conflict between collective security and individual civil rights, has rule-of-law democracy abandoned legal positions to the detriment of these rights? These questions concern human and basic rights such as the right to physical integrity, public information rights, the freedom of opinion, and protection of the privacy of personal communication. The three studies by Kneip, Tanneberg, and Wagner address this problem area.

Aiko Wagner and Sascha Kneip investigate whether established democracies have succumbed to the temptation to abandon individual civil rights in the interests of supposedly greater collective security. They look beyond the singular evidence that, for example, the leading democratic power of the West, the United States, has imprisoned or executed citizens of its own or of other countries without trial on suspicion of terrorism, has maintained torture centers outside the United States, and is intent on intercepting the communications of anyone who could potentially harm the national interest: enemies, friends, politicians, citizens, and business people—a very particular form of globalization. In their systematic study, the two authors examined 22 countries over the period from 1990 to 2007 on the basis of 12 civil rights indicators. For eight of these indicators, no clear trend is apparent over the study period. There was neither deterioration nor improvement. In four fields, however, the data reveal a clear negative trend: freedom of religion, the strength and impartiality of the legal system, equality before the law, and habeas corpus rights. All four domains belong to the rule-of-law core of every democracy.

[10]This is not to deny that Anglo-Saxon capitalist countries, headed by the USA, have pushed these decisions with particular determination.

The negative trend did not set in only after 9/11 but became more visible after the terrorist attacks in New York and Washington. Not all countries have contributed to this development. Once again, it was the Scandinavian countries and the Netherlands that showed a high base level of protection for civil rights not only in the 1990s: they maintained these high standards throughout the period under study. They are followed by the model democracies in New Zealand, Australia, Canada, and Ireland. In these countries, minor violations of civil rights were found. Then come Belgium, Austria, Germany, Switzerland, the United Kingdom, and Portugal. The data reveal marked deterioration in this group. They are already below the mean of the 22 states under study. Italy, France, Spain, and the United States form a group of their own. They show evidence of "dramatic deterioration over time" (Kneip and Wagner Chap. 12). Especially in Spain and the United States, terrorist attacks were the occasion for drastic restrictions on the fundamental defensive rights of citizens. Any claims that federalism, the media, and strong constitutional jurisdiction curb the dismantling of civil liberties could not be confirmed. They appear to have had no influence on developments. The authors detect a negative trend in the influence of the media on the protection of civil rights, especially where the majority of the population and the political elites adopt a positive stance toward more drastic security legislation. Both in the media and in the political elites, responsiveness to market and electorate triumphed over responsibility toward civil rights as fundamental preconditions for democracy.

The more detailed analysis by Dag Tanneberg confirms these findings. Tanneberg asks whether democracies strictly respect the fundamental human right to physical integrity or whether under certain circumstances they come to violate it. In his sample of 29 states (1995–2007), only four countries did not violate this right: Iceland, Luxembourg, Norway, and the Netherlands. Not inconsiderable violations took place in South Africa, the United States, Spain, and Italy. However, the author finds on average no trend toward deterioration of the human rights situation over time in the countries under study. It was not vertical accountability to the electorate that held executives back from breaches of human rights such as extrajudicial killings, abductions, and torture. If there was an institutional brake on violations by the state, it was a strong and independent justice.

In the second half of the twentieth century, democratic theory and empirical studies often took a skeptical view of constitutional courts, especially when endowed with far-reaching powers of judicial review. From a democratic theory perspective, superior legitimation is ascribed to parliament as the elected representative of the demos. If constitutional courts with their meager democratic legitimation trump the institution that represents the people, it is claimed, this runs counter to the idea of popular sovereignty in representative democracy. The logic of this argument cannot be denied. Sascha Kneip, a specialist in constitutional jurisdiction, looks at the question of whether constitutional courts strengthen or weaken democracy from a functional point of view. He sees two ways in which constitutional courts can have an adverse effect on democracy. They either overstretch their powers and ignore the virtues of judicial self-restraint, thus judicializing politics, or they make too little use of their prerogatives to protect the constitution, basic rights, and democracy from attack by state authorities. Considering the examples of the United States, Canada, Germany, and Austria which, in comparison to other countries, are considered to have strong constitutional jurisdiction, Kneip shows that neither a tendency toward the judicialization of politics nor passivity harmful to democracy can be detected. This is particularly the case in the field of judicial review. Nevertheless, if we take a sober look at results, it should be noted that the strong Supreme Court of the United States has been unable to put a stop to flagrant violations of human rights by the American administration such as the extrajudicial killings and torture perpetrated by American agents. That these acts took place outside the territory of the United States may well be of constitutional relevance, but it also shows that the United States in its double character of democracy and superpower challenged by terrorism exhibits less sensitivity to the rule of law than democracies with no imperial pretensions. Overall, Kneip draws a cautiously positive conclusion: strong constitutional courts tend to strengthen the rule-of-law foundations of democracy rather than undermine the representative idea of popular sovereignty. This can be said not least of the Federal Constitutional Court in Germany.

15.1 Conclusion: Erosion, No Crisis

If we pass in review the empirical studies on the question of a general crisis of democracy, what does all this mean? Unlike in the social surveys and quality indices of experts, almost all individual analyses revealed erosions in all five partial regimes of embedded democracy. A general pattern emerges: formal rights, rules, and procedures generally remain intact, but the chances of participation and actual participation and representation have changed. This is not an instance of "trendless fluctuations" as Pippa Norris (2011) argues; taken together, the deteriorations constitute a trend. Gains for democracy, like progress in gender equality and eliminating the discrimination of ethnic and sexual minorities, are doubtlessly significant. Cultural sensitivity has increased in mature democracies. At the same time, however, indifference to serious socioeconomic inequalities in wealth, income, and life chances has grown. But rapid translation into political inequality seriously contravenes the democratic principle of equality. The disadvantaged lower strata of society do hardly anything to make their voice heard and heard effectively against this development. This clearly distinguishes the last quarter of the twentieth century from the preceding three quarters. Social democratic parties have to some extent taken their distance from their core clientele (Merkel et al. 2008). The new social movements represent ecological, cultural, and cosmopolitan interests. Their activists come from the middle classes. Organizations like the trade unions, by contrast, have lost much influence. Moreover, representing skilled workers and the (lower) middle classes, they no longer stand for the lower classes. The latter are not excluded but simply forgotten. Their reaction is to exit without this having any consequences. Their exit from political participation proceeds silently. What is dwindling in democracies is loyalty, not loyalty to the idea of democracy but to its institutional core. Active support for the institutions of representative democracy has declined. Although "critical citizens" (Norris 1999, 2011) from the middle classes are just that, critical, they are less interested in socioeconomic equality and thus in political equality. If they are young and organized in social movements, they are more concerned, if we think specifically of Germany, with railway stations, power-line routing, clean air, climate change, nuclear power, tax increases, the political class, or "big government." The remedy is often sought in referendums, deliberative civic forums, direct codetermination in infrastructure projects, or civil society in general. Much is simulative; we see the contours of a mostly very selfish and narcissistic "simulative democracy" (Blühdorn 2013) apparent in the protest culture of the middle classes.

No all-clear can be given on the globalization front. Power and the arenas of decision-making have shifted away from the nation-state to globalized markets and supranational political regimes. The former operate in the individual pursuit of profit, and the latter have so far not been democratized to any considerable degree. "Governance beyond the nation-state" (Zürn 1998) has not been followed by the democratization of this governance. This will be even more crucial in an enlarged European Union. Shifts in competence from the national to the European level may well be legitimized at times by greater problem-solving capability, but it has been at the cost of losses in democracy (Scharpf 2011; Streeck 2014). The democratic deficit of the EU—complained about for decades—has tended to grow despite complaints. This has been shown not least by the euro crisis. Blühdorn's concept of simulative democracy describes the democratic façades of the European Union much more accurately than it does the state of democracy in individual countries to which it was originally applied. This is demonstrated not least by elections to the European Parliament and by this institution itself. The citizens know little about it, hold it in low esteem, feel themselves to be hardly represented by it, and consequently stay away from the polls. Many of the few who do turn out do not vote for "their" European Parliament but want to teach their national governments a lesson: simulation instead of participation, representation, and responsibility. After more than three decades of direct elections, the European Parliament has still failed to meet expectations as the bearer of democratic hopes. Growing powers have been met by lower turnout at each succeeding election. It is thus a misinterpretation to simply brand the German Federal Constitutional Court's reluctance to transfer powers to the European level "conservative." From a democratic theory point of view, it is rather to be seen as progressive, since it slows down or prevents the ill-considered surrender of national, democratically better controlled powers to the less democratic European Union, especially if it does so explicitly in the interests of democracy.

In the introduction we distinguished between challenges and crises. Whether challenges become crises depends on the action of the relevant agents. Citizens' action groups, protests, and social movements are the one side. The other is the action of political elites in key political organizations and institutions. Although crises are processes "in which the structure of a system is called into question" (Offe 1972, 198), challenges to democracy transform into systemic crises only if they also produce actors who have the resources and strategic capabilities to confront the important power elites of the old system. Actors in this category can be powerful movements, strong anti-system parties, or the military. Such actors are hardly to be found in the OECD democracies. Right-wing populist parties such as those in Switzerland, Austria, Scandinavia, or even France are problematic from a democratic point of view, but they have neither the force nor the programmatic will to destroy democracy. They fill a representation gap along the conflict line between cosmopolitan liberalism and national communitarianism that is not filled by the established parties. As Marcus Spittler has shown in his contribution to this volume, right-wing populist parties address especially left-authoritarian voters who are otherwise unrepresented by the mainstream parties. Populist parties can have a stabilizing function to play in the established representative democracies of the OECD world: they parry the emergence of the "median voter" nurtured by the logic of competition, lending greater, pluralistic differentiation to party competition (Mouffe 2005). With regard to the effects on democratic quality, our results show that the presence of right-wing populists in the party system leads to enhanced participation of the electorate but likewise also to a reduced quality of public discourses and individual liberties. Although basic democratic norms and procedures are not deeply affected by populist parties, there is a real danger for democracies becoming less liberal. This does not constitute a crisis of democracy as long as populist parties are encircled and checked by a majority of democratic parties and citizens and as long as the populists stick to the rules of the game. If this is no longer the case, however, a minor threat to democracy could possibly evolve into a major crisis as it can be observed in Poland and Hungary.

In the introduction we outlined three scenarios for political elites and citizens in the face of the wide range of challenges to democracy (socioeconomic inequality, decline of catch-all parties, the deregulation and globalization of markets, and the protection of fundamental civil liberties): failure, muddling through, and reform. How appropriate the pattern of action chosen is will help decide whether challenges condense into latent or manifest crisis. It should be remembered that political action in established democracies does not take place in a deinstitutionalized vacuum. The contrary is the case. Institutions act as restricting and enabling opportunity structures for political actors. The restrictions they impose are relatively severe. The institutional procedural bounds for reforming the core institutions of representative democracy are narrow. This gives the advantage to piecemeal engineering over grand designs for new democratic institutions. Although surveys tell us that the core institutions of representative democracy have been losing support, major institutional alternatives are not available. This can also be said of the deliberative forums favored by some democracy scholars, which can usually cover only small political domains. For the mass of political decisions to be made at the national level, such reform proposals are not very relevant. The irrelevance and lack of popular legitimacy of other institutions largely immunizes the core institutions of representative democracy against further crisis-driven erosion. If there is an institutional alternative that meets with the approval of large sections of the population, it is the referendum. But referendums must be so institutionalized that they play a crucial role in the decision-making process of policy production. Only in Switzerland is this so. Even two to three national referendums per year are likely to be more symbolic, democratizations rather than constituting a major shift of political decision-making from representative to direct democracy.[11] The existing institutions of representative democracy have created an institutional path dependency that make fundamental changes improbable where the dysfunctionalities in these institutions are limited, as most of our studies have shown to be the case, and the expected gains for democracy are either small or are supported by too few actors. Despite all institutional constraints, there is still political scope for action that can be exploited in different ways. What, then, does political action contribute toward accelerating or decelerating the advent of a crisis of democracy?

Failure: The financial elites, banks, and speculation funds failed in the financial crisis of 2008 and the euro crisis that followed. The political elites spurred this failure by deregulating the financial markets in the developed capitalist world. A specific contribution was also made by governments in Greece, Ireland, Iceland, Cyprus, Italy, and, in somewhat weaker form, in Spain and Portugal: corruption, cronyism, the waste of public funds, and above all the inability to collect taxes effectively and justly were the marks of state failure. The stubborn intervention by the EU Troika exacerbated the crisis through dogmatic austerity dictates. Despite one-sided burden sharing at the expense of the taxpayers, international crisis management held firm in the last resort: guarantees from the European Central Bank and the donor countries prevented the worst. National democracies suffered damage to their sovereignty. But not even in Greece did democracy come to the brink of collapse. The supranational coordination capacity of the community of democracies, the actions taken by the European Central Bank, and the internal resilience of individual national democracies prevented escalation into a system-threatening crisis, such as had occurred in 1929. Protracted failure by individual states was compensated by successful international collective action. However, acute economic crisis had been averted at the cost of democratic legitimation losses for both recipient and donor countries.

The established democracies of the West are largely safe from abrupt democratic collapse. The successful coordination of monetary and financial policy across national borders in the face of crisis bears witness to a learning process in capitalist democracies since the 1920s and 1930s. However, such economic crisis management has had a price for democracy: the influence of parliament has weakened, executives dominate, and sometimes it is even central banks that set the political agenda.

But the governing elites and those who vote for them are to be accused of failure above all in the question of growing economic and social inequality. The parliaments and governments of the developed democratic world have been either unwilling or unable to stop the growth in inequality or to prevent its translation into political inequality. This challenge to democracy has thus transformed into a creeping crisis. The class-forming force of disembedded democratic capitalism has

[11]Over and beyond this, we consider the democratization potential of referendums to be not only limited but also fraught with unintended, undemocratic side effects (Merkel and Ritzi 2017).

harmed the principle of political equality. Politics has not prevented it. This applies more strongly in Anglo-Saxon and Southern European democracies than in the countries of Northern and Western Europe, but it happened everywhere.

However, the cases of Hungary and Poland signal that crises of democracy can emerge beyond economic crises or even in times of (relative) economic prosperity. Strong illiberal and nationalist forces have emerged in Hungary and Poland as a backlash against a supposedly too far-reaching European integration and multiculturalization. They have already damaged the liberal dimension of democracy in the name of popular majorities.

Muddling through: On the three functional levels of democracy—participation, representation, and governance—we have diagnosed erosion, albeit with considerable differences between countries. But the consequence has not been strong growth in "voice" but rather the subdued "exit" of the disadvantaged lower classes. If protest by oppositional groups or social movements had really grown as strongly as social movement scholars sometimes suggest, established institutions and political elites would have reacted more conspicuously, if only in the rational pursuit of their own interest in preserving their power and influence. They have tended rather to muddle through with minor internal party reforms, acceptance of the diminished importance of parliament, and modest improvements in participative decision-making at the local level. Minority rights and the social and political position of women have been strengthened. However, the decrease in cultural and gender discrimination coincides with growing socioeconomic inequality. To call this a crisis of democracy per se would be to perpetuate the diffuse usage of a concept whose omnipresence has already left the analytical boundaries inordinately vague. However, there have been winners and losers in democratic developments in recent decades. The winners are the cosmopolitan upper and middle classes; the losers are the lower classes. Sections of the middle classes may well have suffered slight socioeconomic losses (United States, Southern Europe), but, particularly in Western Europe, they have been descriptive and generally overrepresented from a substantial point of view. The political elites in their rational calculations have conceded only minor socioeconomic reforms. The signals from the electoral arena gave no clear incentive for thoroughgoing democratic reforms. The key political institutions and organizations, parties, parliament, and government experienced an internal shift of power and a remarkable loss of trust among the citizens. But this did not lead to drastic losses of legitimation among the citizens, which could have induced these elites to undertake far-reaching reforms. Muddling through was for them the most rational strategy.

Reform: Nowhere are far-reaching democratic reforms in evidence that could have halted the crumbling of participative assent to the political polity or which could even adapt democracy to meet the greater demands of critical citizens. The political elites wait and see; civil society intervenes but without having a grand design for a renewed democracy. It has notably no recipe for tackling the two main challenges, the erosion of political equality and the shift of political decision-making competence to the technocratic and only scarcely democratic supranational sphere; indeed, it has not even proved particularly sensitive to these challenges. It shows that "voice" and "exit" do not exert enough pressure to induce fundamental reforms.

The typical answer to challenges to democracy has thus been to "wait and see," to make minor reforms, to muddle through, and to provide institutional continuity. This is not overwhelming. But it is obviously in accordance with the broad intentions of the majority of the demos. Where this is not the case, the consequence is not collective protest but individual withdrawal into an unpolitical private sphere. This also explains the strong sympathy among citizens for "expertocratic impartiality" in lieu of the clash of opinions between parties. To a certain extent, this is also to be seen in democratic theory. Pluralistic conflicts are not addressed (or no longer), nor are partisan solutions declaimed; nonpartisan reason and deliberative rationality unburdened by interests are preferred (see, e.g., Habermas 1985; Fishkin 1991; Dryzek 2000). Philip Pettit (2005, 53) calls this "depoliticizing democracy." Rosanvallon (2011, 100) even lauds this rational "impartiality" as one of the "[...] constituent elements of democratic order." Michelsen and Walter (2013) rightly call this the path to "unpolitical democracy." Ernesto Laclau and Chantal Mouffe (2001) lament the loss of the political. But it is astonishing that beyond Laclau and Mouffe or Michelsen and Walter, theoreticians with left-wing sympathies have no eye for the oligarchical and exclusive patterns of deliberative democracy. But they would also not deny that such procedures can be no substitute for supra-regional parties, national parliaments, and elected governments. Nowhere is it evident what could replace the key institutions (parliament) and legitimation patterns (universal elections) either in the theory or in the practice of democracy.

Is democracy in crisis? Throughout the book, we clarified that there can be no precise answer on solid empirical grounds to this very general question. Finland, Denmark, Sweden, and even Germany are not in crisis. Brazil certainly is; but Greece is not, despite having been confronted with a deep economic crisis. Democracy was never at the verge of collapse, despite the deep economic crises in Greece, Portugal, and Spain. There is a great deal of variation in the quality and stability of advanced democracies, even if we restrict the sample of countries to the traditional OECD countries.

There is also great variation across the different spheres or partial regimes of democracy. However, if it comes to political equality in participation and representation, the quality of most OECD democracies has declined. We have called this phenomenon of the participatory (self-)exclusion of the lower strata "two-thirds democracy." Undoubtedly, this is the most serious of the broken promises of democracy. Looking at "the power to govern" of the democratically authorized elites in parliament and government, we observed a further loss of political sovereignty caused by the increased autonomy of deregulated markets or supranational regimes from democratic control. But the moderate decline of democratic substance in these two partial regimes does not justify speaking of a crisis of democracy in general. Moreover, if we look at the spheres of civil rights, gender equality, cultural rights, and gay and lesbian rights on the one hand and the more effective monitoring of political organizations, institutions, and elites by civil society watchdogs on the other, most of the OECD democracies are much better off than they were in the 1950s, 1960s, or 1970s. There is no general crisis of democracy but nonsimultaneous developments across different partial regimes and countries that have strengthened and weakened the quality and stability of advanced democracies. We do not claim like Fukuyama the "end of history." Democracy has not become the only game in town globally. Rather, there are different worlds of democracy. While the well-established democracies have remained rather stable, including those of the early "third wave of democratization" in Southern Europe, many of the younger democracies such as in Eastern Europe, the Middle East, Latin America, or Africa have either failed to consolidate like in Russia and Turkey or have deconsolidated like in Poland and Hungary. Neither the general crisis of democracy claimed by some theoreticians of democracy nor the final historical triumph of it holds when we refrain from sweeping theoretical or historical claims and dig deeper into systematic comparative analyses. This is the overall message of the book.

References

Avritzer, L. (1999). Teoria democrática, esfera pública e participação local. *Sociologias, 7*(2), 18–47.

Blühdorn, I. (2013). *Simulative Demokratie. Neue Politik nach der postdemokratischen Wende.* Berlin: Suhrkamp.

Crouch, C. (2004). *Post-democracy.* Cambridge: Polity Press.

Della Porta, D. (2013). *Can democracy be saved?* Cambridge: Polity Press.

Dreher, A. (2006). Does globalization affect growth? Evidence from a new Index of Globalization. *Applied Economics, 38*(10), 1091–1110.

Dryzek, J. (2000). *Deliberative democracy and beyond.* Oxford: Oxford University Press.

Fishkin, J. (1991). *Democracy and deliberation. new directions for democratic reform.* New Haven, CT: Yale University Press.

Fung, A. (2011). Reinventing democracy in Latin America. *Perspectives on Politics, 9*(4), 857–871.

Habermas, J. (1975). *Legitimation crisis.* Boston, MA: Beacon Press.

Habermas, J. (1985). *The theory of communicative action* (Vol. 2). Boston, MA: Beacon Press.

Hall, P. A., & Soskice, D. (2001). *Varieties of capitalism: The institutional foundations of comparative advantage.* Oxford: Oxford University Press.

Jänicke, M. (1972). Krisenbegriff und Krisenforschung. In M. Jänicke (Ed.), *Herrschaft und Krise* (pp. 10–26). Opladen: UTB-Westdeutscher Verlag.

Keane, J. (2011). Monitory democracy? In S. Alonso, J. Keane, & W. Merkel (Eds.), *The future of representative democracy* (pp. 212–235). Cambridge: Cambridge University Press.

Kelsen, H. (1925). *Allgemeine Staatslehre. Enzyklopädie der Rechts- und Staatswissenschaften* (Vol. 23). Berlin: Springer-Verlag.

Kneip, S., & Merkel, W. (2017). *The idea of democratic legitimacy* (WZB Discussion Paper). Berlin: WZB (forthcoming).

Laclau, E., & Mouffe, C. (2001). *Hegemony and socialist strategy. Towards a radical democratic politics* (2nd ed.). London: Verso.

Merkel, W. (2004). Embedded and defective democracies. *Democratization, 11*(5), 33–58.

Merkel, W., Petring, A., Henkes, C., & Egle, C. (2008). *Social democracy in power. The capacity to reform.* London/New York: Routledge.

Merkel, W., & Ritzi, C. (Eds.). (2017). *Die Legitimität direkter Demokratie. Wie demokratisch sind Volksabstimmungen?* Wiesbaden: Springer VS.

Michelsen, D., & Walter, F. (2013). *Unpolitische Demokratie. Zur Krise der Repräsentation.* Berlin: Suhrkamp.

Mouffe, C. (2005). *The return of the political.* London: Verso.

Norris, P. (1999). *Critical citizens. Global support for democratic governance.* Oxford: Oxford University Press.

Norris, P. (2011). *Democratic deficit: Critical citizens revisited*. Cambridge: Cambridge University Press.
Offe, C. (1972). *Strukturprobleme des kapitalistischen Staates: Aufsätze zur Politischen Soziologie*. Frankfurt am Main: Suhrkamp.
Pettit, P. (2005). Depoliticizing democracy. *Ratio Juris, 17*(1), 52–65.
Pogrebinschi, T., & Samuels, D. (2014). The impact of participatory democracy. Evidence from Brazil's National Public Policy Conferences. *Comparative Politics, 46*(3), 313–332.
Przeworski, A. (2010). *Democracy and the limits of self-government*. Cambridge: Cambridge University Press.
Rosanvallon, P. (2011). *Democratic legitimacy: Impartiality, reflexivity, proximity*. Princeton, NJ: Princeton University Press.
Santos, B. d. S. (1998). Participatory budgeting in Porto Alegre: Toward a redistributive democracy. *Politics & Society, 26*(4), 461–510.
Scharpf, F.W. (2011). *Monetary Union, fiscal crisis and the preemption of democracy*. MPIfG Discussion Paper 11/11. Max-Planck-Institut für Gesellschaftsforschung, Cologne, July 2011.
Schattschneider, E. E. (1942). *Party Government*. New York, NY: Rinehart.
Streeck, W. (2014). *Buying time: The delayed crisis of democratic capitalism*. London: Verso.
Thomassen, J., & Schmitt, H. (1997). Policy representation. *European Journal of Political Research, 32*(2), 165–184.
Zürn, M. (1998). *Regieren jenseits des Nationalstaates*. Frankfurt am Main: Suhrkamp.

Index

W. Merkel, S. Kneip (eds.), *Democracy and Crisis*,
https://doi.org/10.1007/978-3-319-72559-8